The Philosophy of Film

Introductory Text and Readings

Edited by Thomas E. Wartenberg and
Angela Curran

Blackwell
Publishing

BLACKWELL PUBLISHING
350 Main Street, Malden, MA 02148-5020, USA
108 Cowley Road, Oxford OX4 1JF, UK
550 Swanston Street, Carlton, Victoria 3053, Australia

First published 2005 by Blackwell Publishing Ltd

Library of Congress Cataloging-in-Publication Data

The philosophy of film : introductory text and readings / Edited by Thomas E.
Wartenberg and Angela Curran.
    p. cm.
  Includes bibliographical references and index.
  ISBN 1–4051–1441–X (alk. paper) — ISBN 1–4051–1442–8 (pbk. : alk. paper)
  1. Motion pictures—Philosophy. I. Wartenberg, Thomas E. II. Curran, Angela.

  PN1995.P4993 2005
  791.43′01—dc22

                                    2004022204

A catalogue record for this title is available from the British Library.

Set in 11/13pt Perpetua
by Graphicraft Limited, Hong Kong
Printed and bound in the United Kingdom
by TJ International, Padstow, Cornwall

The publisher's policy is to use permanent paper from mills that operate a sustainable forestry
policy, and which has been manufactured from pulp processed using acid-free and elementary
chlorine-free practices. Furthermore, the publisher ensures that the text paper and cover
board used have met acceptable environmental accreditation standards.

For further information on
Blackwell Publishing, visit our website:
www.blackwellpublishing.com

Contents

Part VI: Can Films Be Socially Critical?   209

Part VII: What Can We Learn From Films?   247

Acknowledgments

We could not have completed this book without the generous assistance and advice from a number of people. We thank Richard Allen, Berys Gaut, Noël Carroll, Cynthia Freeland, Carl Plantinga, Steven Schneider, Daniel Shaw, Murray Smith, and George Wilson for their helpful suggestions for articles to include. At Mount Holyoke College, Anna May Dion, Hannah Hauser, Kathryn M. Lindeman, and Ekaterina Vavova provided indispensable manuscript support. We are grateful for a faculty development grant from Franklin and Marshall College that enabled us to enlist the assistance of Evan Gumz, whom we thank for his outstanding work in creating the film illustrations for this book. Nirit Simon at Blackwell Publishing provided valuable manuscript assistance in getting the book through the final stages of production. We also thank the students in our philosophy of film classes, whose perceptive responses gave us essential feedback on which essays to include in the volume and who have confirmed our sense that this is an important topic for undergraduate philosophy courses.

Most of all we owe a special thanks to Jeffrey Dean, a fellow cineaste and our wonderful editor at Blackwell. He did not give up on the book or us, even when we all were in doubt that the project would see the light of day. His confidence and encouragement enabled us to press on and make the book a reality.

Tom dedicates this book to Alan Schiffmann, whose example of intellectual and critical engagement has been an ongoing source of inspiration to him. Angela dedicates the book in memory of her parents, Lucille O'Brien Curran and John Vincent Curran, for all the years of their love and support.

The editor and publisher gratefully acknowledge the permission granted to reproduce the copyright material in this book:

Text Acknowledgments

1 Noël Carroll, "Prospects for Film Theory: A Personal Assessment," © 1996 from David Bordwell and Noël Carroll (eds.), *Post-Theory: Reconstruction Film Studies* (Madison, WI:

University of Wisconsin Press, 1996), pp. 37–41, 56–68. Reprinted by permission of The University of Wisconsin Press.

2   Malcolm Turvey, "Can Scientific Models of Theorizing Help Film Theory?" This is a revised version of an article originally published in *The Journal of Moving Image Studies* 1: 1 (2001). Reprinted by permission.

3   Gilles Deleuze, "Philosophy of Film as the Creation of Concepts." "Having an Idea in Cinema" (trans. Eleanor Kaufman), from Eleanor Kaufman and Kevin Jon Heller (eds.), *Mappings in Politics, Philosophy, and Culture* (Minneapolis and London: University of Minnesota Press, 1998), pp. 14–16. "Cinema and the Philosophy of Film," from Gilles Deleuze (trans. Hugh Tomlinson and Robert Galeta), *Cinema 2: The Time Image* (Minneapolis: University of Minnesota Press, 1989), pp. 270–1, 276–8, 280. Both extracts reprinted by permission of the University of Minnesota Press and Athlone/Continuum London.

4   Hugo Münsterberg, "Defining the Photoplay," © 2002 from Allan Langdale (ed.), *Hugo Münsterberg on Film* (New York and London: Routledge, 2002), pp. 128–38. Reproduced by permission of Routledge/Taylor & Francis Books, Inc.

5   Rudolf Arnheim, "The Artistry of Silent Film," from Rudolf Arnheim, *Film as Art* (Berkeley: University of California Press, 1957), pp. 199–205, 207–15, 224–30. © 1957, 1985 by Rudolf Arnheim. Reprinted by permission of the University of California Press.

6   André Bazin "Cinematic Realism," from André Bazin (trans. Hugh Gray), *What is Cinema?* (Berkeley: University of California Press, 1967), pp. 12–28, 33–7, 39–40. © 1967 by The Regents of the University of California. Reprinted by permission of the University of California Press and Les éditions du cerf.

7   Kendall L. Walton, "Film, Photography, and Transparency," from "Transparent Pictures," in *Critical Inquiry* 11 (December 1984), pp. 250–4, 262–5, 273. Reprinted by permission of the University of Chicago Press.

9   François Truffaut, "La Politique des Auteurs," originally "A Certain Tendency of the French Cinema," in *Cahiers du Cinéma in English*, vol. 1 (1966), pp. 31–41. © 1966 by Cahiers du Cinéma. Reprinted by permission.

10 Andrew Sarris, "*Auteur* Theory and Film Evaluation," from *Film Culture* 27 (Winter 1962/63), pp. 1–8.

11 Pauline Kael, "The Idea of Film Criticism," from *I Lost It at the Movies* (Boston: Little, Brown, and Company, 1965), pp. 295–304, 306–14, 318–19.

12 Stephen Heath, "Against Authorship," from *Screen* 14: 3 (autumn 1973), pp. 86–91. Reprinted by permission.

13 Deborah Parker and Mark Parker, "DVDs and the Director's Intentions," originally published as "Directors and DVD Commentary: The Specifics of Intention," in *Journal of Aesthetics and Art Criticism* 62: 1, pp. 13–21. Reprinted by permission of Blackwell Publishing.

14 Gregory Currie, "Narrative Desire," from Carl Plantinga and Greg M. Smith (eds.), *Passionate Views: Film, Cognition, and Emotion* (Baltimore and London: Johns Hopkins University Press, 1999), pp. 183–9, 197–9, 278–9 (notes). © 1999 by Carl Plantinga and Greg M. Smith. Reprinted by permission of Johns Hopkins University Press.

15 Carl Plantinga, "Spectator Emotion and Ideological Film Criticism," originally published as "Notes on Spectator Emotion and Ideological Film Criticism," in Richard Allen and Murray Smith (eds.), *Film Theory and Philosophy* (Oxford: Clarendon Press, 1997), pp. 372–83, 385–93. Reprinted by permission of Oxford University Press.

16   Murray Smith, "Engaging Characters," from Murray Smith, *Engaging Characters: Fiction, Emotion and the Cinema* (Oxford: Clarendon Press, 1995), pp. 73–5, 81–95, 108 (notes), 254 (notes). Reprinted by permission of Oxford University Press.

17   Noël Carroll, "The Paradox of Horror," © 1990 from Noël Carroll, *The Philosophy of Horror: or Paradoxes of the Heart* (New York and London: Routledge, 1990), pp. 160–1, 179, 181–90. Reproduced by permission of Routledge/Taylor and Francis Books, Inc.

18   David Bordwell, "Principles of Film Narration," © 1996 from David Bordwell, *Narration in the Fiction Film* (Madison: University of Wisconsin Press: 1985), pp. 49–53, 61–2. Reprinted by permission of the University of Wisconsin Press.

19   Seymour Chatman, "The Cinematic Narrator," from Seymour Chatman, *Coming to Terms: The Rhetoric of Narrative in Fiction and Film* (Ithaca: Cornell University Press, 1990), pp. 90–6, 124–5, 127, 130–7. © 1990 by Cornell University. Reprinted by permission of the publisher, Cornell University Press.

20   George M. Wilson, "Narration as Showing," from *"Le Grand Imagier Steps Out,"* pp. 298–303, 305–11, 314–16. Reprinted by permission of the University of Arkansas Press and the author.

21   Michael Ryan and Douglas Kellner, "The Politics of Representation," from *Camera Politica: The Politics and Ideology of Contemporary Hollywood Film* (Bloomington and Indianapolis: Indiana University Press, 1988), pp. 266–75, 279–80, 282–7, 291–2, 295. Reproduced by permission of Indiana University Press.

22   Thomas E. Wartenberg, "But Would You Want Your Daughter To Marry One? Politics and Race in *Guess Who's Coming to Dinner*," from *Unlikely Couples: Movie Romance as Social Criticism* (Boulder, CO: Westview Press, 1999), pp. 111–30. Reprinted by permission.

24   Stanley Cavell, "Knowledge as Transgression: *It Happened One Night*," from Stanley Cavell, *Pursuits of Happiness: The Hollywood Comedy of Remarriage* (Cambridge, MA and London: Harvard University Press, 1981), pp. 80–5, 91–3, 100–1, 103–4, 107–9. Originally published as Stanley Cavell, "Knowledge as Transgression: Mostly a Reading of It Happened One Night," *Daedalus* 109: 2 (Spring, 1980), pp. 147–76. © 1980 by the American Academy of Arts and Sciences.

25   Cynthia A. Freeland, "Realist Horror," © 1995 from Cynthia A. Freeland and Thomas E. Wartenberg, *Philosophy of Film* (New York: Routledge, 1995), pp. 126–42. Reproduced by permission of Routledge/Taylor & Francis Books, Inc.

26   Thomas E. Wartenberg, "Philosophy Screened: Experiencing *The Matrix*" from *Midwest Studies in Philosophy* 27: 1 (August 2003), pp. 139–52. Reprinted by permission of Blackwell Publishing.

27   Joseph H. Kupfer, "Virtue and Happiness in *Groundhog Day*," from *Visions of Virtue in Popular Film* (Boulder, CO: Westview Press, 1999), pp. 35–55, 58. Reprinted by permission.

Illustrations

1   "The director turning the camera on the audience who is watching his film," from *Man With A Movie Camera* (*Chelovek s kinoapparatom*) (director: Dziga Vertov, 1929; produced by the Soviet Union (no studio listed)).

2   "Parisians in a traffic jam as they flee the city on the weekend," from *Week End* (director: Jean-Luc Godard, 1968; producer: Grove Press, sub-titled).

3 "The use of close-up shots is a distinguishing feature of film as an artistic medium," from *Birth of a Nation* (director and producer: D. W. Griffith, 1915).

4 "Sherlock, Jr. (Buster Keaton) aspires to be a detective," from *Sherlock, Jr.* (director: Roscoe "Fatty" Arbuckle, Buster Keaton, 1924; producer: Buster Keaton).

5 "A deep focus shot of Charles Foster Kane (Orson Welles) playing in the background while his parents make plans to send him East," from *Citizen Kane* (director: Orson Welles, 1941; producer: Mercury Productions).

6 "Cary Grant," from *Notorious* (director: Alfred Hitchcock, 1941; producer: RKO Radio).

7 "Hitler rallying the troops," from *Triumph of the Will* (director and producer: Leni Riefenstahl, 1934).

8 "Jean Renoir (pictured here) sometimes acted in the films he directed," from *Rules of the Game (Règle du jeu)* (director: Jean Renoir, 1939; producer: Nouvelle édition française).

9 "The Dance of Death," from *Seventh Seal (Det Sjunde inseglet)* (director: Ingmar Bergman, 1957; producer: Svensk Filmindustri).

10 "Rick (Humphrey Bogart) and Ilse (Ingrid Bergman) driving in Paris," from *Casablanca* (director: Michael Curtiz, 1942; producer: Warner Brothers).

11 "The Blind Flower Girl and the Tramp," from *City Lights* (director: Charles Chaplin, 1931; producer: Charles Chaplin Productions).

12 "Louis Bernard (Daniel Gélin) reveals the details of an assassination plot to Ben McKenna (James Stewart)," from *The Man Who Knew Too Much* (director: Alfred Hitchcock, 1956; producer: Paramount).

13 "L. B. Jeffries (James Stewart) spies on his neighbors and becomes convinced one of them has committed murder," from *Rear Window* (director: Alfred Hitchcock, 1954; producer: Paramount).

14 "Jonathan Cooper (Richard Todd) questions his lover, Charlotte Inwood (Marlene Dietrich), concerning the circumstances surrounding her husband's death," from *Stage Fright* (director: Alfred Hitchcock, 1950; producer: Warner Brothers).

15 "Joe Morton as the alien 'brother' who crash-lands on earth and lands in New York City," from *Brother From Another Planet* (director: John Sayles, 1984; producer: Anarchist convention films).

16 "Dr John Prentice (Sidney Poitier) discusses his desire to marry Joanna Drayton (Katharine Houghton) with Joanna and her father, Matt Drayton (Spencer Tracy)," from *Guess Who's Coming to Dinner* (director: Stanley Kramer, 1967; producer: Columbia).

17 "Stella (Barbara Stanwyck) embarrasses her daughter, Laurel (Anne Shirley)," from *Stella Dallas* (director: King Vidor, 1929; producer: Samuel Goldwyn).

18 "Ellie (Claudette Colbert) and Peter (Clark Gable) on either side of the blanket, a.k.a. 'The Wall of Jericho', in the motel room," from *It Happened One Night* (director: Frank Capra, 1934; producer: Columbia).

19 "Murder as Style? Another victim of sociopath Hannibal Lecter (Anthony Hopkins)," from *Silence of the Lambs* (director: Jonathan Demme, 1991; producer: Orion).

20 "Neo (Keanu Reeves) realizes the illusion of the Matrix with the help of Morpheus (Laurence Fishburne)," from *The Matrix* (directors: Andy and Larry Wachowski, 1999; producer: Silver Pictures).

21   "A changed Phil Connors (Bill Murray) buys a homeless man (Les Podewell) a meal," from
     Groundhog Day (director: Harold Ramis, 1993).

Every effort has been made to trace copyright holders and to obtain their permission for the use of copyright material. The publisher apologizes for any errors or omissions in the above list and would be grateful if notified of any corrections that should be incorporated in future reprints or editions of this book.

General Introduction

Imagine Hildy Johnson (Rosalind Russell), the beautiful reporter and ex-wife of the fast-talking editor of the *Chicago Morning Post*, Walter Burns (Cary Grant), in Howard Hawks's 1940 film, *His Girl Friday*, on the phone: "Hold the presses, Walter! Philosophers have discovered film!" Fanciful as this scenario may be, it conveys an important truth: over the past two decades philosophers have turned their attention to film in an unprecedented manner. Whereas when the two of us were students philosophers seldom showed films in their classes, today's students in an introductory philosophy class frequently find themselves confronted with a popular film, such as the Wachowski Brothers' 1999 instant classic *The Matrix*, and are asked whether it is possible that they themselves are trapped in the virtual reality of the film's title. Film and philosophy now intersect on a daily basis in college and university classrooms across the country and even the world.

Although students' increasing familiarity with visual culture is a partial explanation of this phenomenon, a perhaps more important factor is philosophers' genuine acknowledgment of film as a subject for philosophic reflection. It has been a long time coming. Hugo Münsterberg's 1916 book, *The Photoplay*, was one of the first academic studies of the new art form, but prior to 1985 a book on the philosophy of film was a rarity; today, they are being published with increasing frequency. Indeed, there has been a vast influx of philosophical writing on film. Not only have numerous books on film been published by philosophers, but there is also now a journal, *Film and Philosophy*, dedicated to publishing scholarly articles in the field. The philosophy of film has become a thriving academic sub-discipline.

The goal of this anthology is to acquaint undergraduate students in both philosophy and film departments with the issues and controversies that constitute the philosophy of film. We have brought together a wide range of essays by philosophers, film theorists, and even film critics that reflect the variety of approaches taken to the philosophy of film. The seven questions that we use to group these readings reflect the most basic issues that philosophers have raised about film as an artistic and cultural medium.

Part I includes essays that ask whether it is necessary to develop a *theory* of film and, if so, what such a theory might look like. The issue here involves understanding what a philosopher does in reflection on a specific subject matter, such as film.

Part II brings together essays that attempt to specify exactly the nature of film. Settling this ontological question is generally seen by philosophers as a necessary prerequisite to being able to decide the other philosophic issues raised in this text. The question of whether films have authors raises the issue of whether the immense technological apparatus necessary to produce a contemporary film renders the traditional concept of authorship inapplicable to films. This is the question raised in Part III.

Ever since Plato banished artists from his ideal state because their works appealed to the emotions rather than to reason, philosophers have been suspicious of art. The essays in Part IV take up the question of our emotional involvement with film, less concerned to condemn it than to understand it.

We are all familiar with voice-over narrators who give us information about a film not transmitted by the images or dialogue. The essays in Part V raise the more general question of whether we need to think of all films – even those without an explicit narrator – as in fact having narrators. In exploring this question, philosophers make explicit the rhetorical structure of film, which often escapes viewers' notice.

Can films raise deep criticisms of the societies they depict or is there something about film as a medium that condemns it to supporting existing structures? This issue is addressed in Part VI by philosophers who want to explore the relationship between film and society.

Finally, Part VII asks what is perhaps the quintessential philosophical question about film: can we learn from films? The essays here ponder how film can be a vehicle for philosophical enlightenment.

Given the thematic structure of this text, in the remainder of this introduction we will provide a brief historical overview of how the philosophy of film has developed into a thriving brand of academic philosophy. These remarks will serve to provide a broader context for understanding the various issues raised in this volume.

The *classic* period of the philosophy of film dates from 1916 – the year of publication of Münsterberg's ground-breaking study – to around 1971 – the year in which Stanley Cavell published *The World Viewed: Reflections on the Ontology of Film*. The fundamental concern of these philosophers and theorists was the question of what made film the unique art form that it is. In attempting to answer this question, they connected to a tradition in philosophical aesthetics going back to Aristotle that attempted to specify the unique nature of each art form. These theorists had a second goal in mind besides that of clarifying the nature of film, namely to render respectable the study of film itself. Because film was – and still remains – a popular art form, its serious study aroused suspicion, especially in academia. In attempting to secure artistic status for film, philosophers of this classic period also sought to gain acceptance for film as a suitable object of academic and other serious study.

The classic period came to an end as a result of the successful academization of the study of film in film studies programs. It is as if, with their task done, classical theorists were now rendered obsolete. Their victory was therefore a Pyrrhic one, for in place of their approach to film as an art form, a new sub-discipline arose that claimed a monopoly on theorizing about film, dubbing itself "film theory" and presenting itself as the successor to early, less systematic ways of reflecting on film and films.

Film theory embodied a very specific approach to the study of film, one that put forward a global account of film as a cultural form. Armed with a mixture of Althusserian Marxism and Lacanian psychoanalysis, film theorists attempted to show that the institution of film fulfilled the political agenda of constituting its viewers as passive, receptive subjects. Although this paradigm achieved great prominence, it gradually became clear that there were serious intellectual problems with it. First, pressure from feminists, theorists of color, and queer theorists exploded the idea that there was a single "subject position" into which films attempted to place people. Second, partly through the influence of the newly developed field of cultural studies, it became clear that the film theory paradigm conceived of viewers too passively, as mere receptacles for dominant views with no critical capacities of their own.

Although these cracks in film theory's hegemony revealed internal stresses in its approach to film, the real death blow was delivered by a new generation of philosophers of film. What these philosophers have in common is a belief that film theory distorted both the nature of viewers' experience of films and the content of the films themselves. The herald of the new movement was Noël Carroll, who attempted to show that the emperor of film theory had no clothes. Less polemical but no less insightful were contributions from many philosophers and film scholars – including many of the contributors to this volume – who showed that certain basic assumptions made by film theory lacked warrant.

An important area of agreement among this diverse group of philosophers of film was that the model of film viewing that film theory embraced was fundamentally mistaken. Instead of seeing the film viewer as completely constituted by the twin processes of interpellation (Althusser) and ideal projection (Lacan), the broad consensus of philosophers of film and their fellow travelers from the discipline of film studies was that film viewers should be treated as conscious subjects capable of interpretive and critical appropriations of the films they watched. At the same time, they were suspicious of the grand generalizations made about film, favoring a more local and dispersed theory.

This very general consensus conceals the incredible diversity of approaches taken and methods employed by contemporary philosophers of film in analyzing film. One approach favors the development of detailed "readings" of individual films. Although many philosophers employ this approach because they believe that films can convey important philosophic truths, others are interested in showing the complex narrative structure that underlies many apparently simple films. The essays in Parts VI and VII of this book illustrate examples of this approach.

Another contemporary philosophic orientation to film focuses almost exclusively on theoretical issues. Philosophers working in this vein seek to develop accounts of film considered as a branch of the philosophy of art. Traditionally, philosophers of art have sought to answer some very general questions about specific art forms. These contemporary philosophers of film take up questions from their classic forebears but employ novel strategies to produce new answers. Paramount here is the use of cognitive science to shed light on viewers' experience of watching films.

We will end our introduction with a few pragmatic suggestions about using this anthology. Each Part has a general introduction that establishes the context for the individual readings. In addition, there is a set of study questions designed to assist in both understanding and assessing the philosophical claims made in each essay. Finally, at the end of the volume there is a list of suggestions for further reading to help guide the reader to additional sources that go into the various topics covered in this text in more detail.

We find the philosophy of film to be an endlessly fascinating area of study. We hope this anthology will help you become acquainted with this field in a way that stimulates your appetite for looking at and reflecting upon one of the great art forms of our contemporary world.

Part I

Do We Need Film Theory?

Introduction

As a lover of film, you might think you know enough about movies without needing to analyze basic concepts that are implicit in your experience of film. Yet if you were to see a film that violated all your expectations of what film is, you would need to think about the basic question, "What makes this a film?" Take, for example, *Week End* (1967), French New Wave director Jean-Luc Godard's film about middle-class life *circa* 1968. The plot of this film is hard to follow, the editing is unconventional, the music often disrupts your concentration of what you see on screen, and the film includes a ten-minute scene – which seems to last for an eternity – that depicts an immense traffic jam as Parisians flee from the city for a weekend holiday. After seeing *Week End*, you might well need to figure out just what makes this a film. Film theory – the study of the basic concepts that are inherent in the experience and making of film – would help you address your puzzle.

Film critic Roger Ebert has been quoted as saying, "Film theory has nothing to do with film."[1] Ebert's comment was directed against what he sees as a pernicious tendency in contemporary film theoretic circles to use "occult and arcane" language that is hard to follow and seems to have nothing to do with the experience of film. This criticism raises the questions of what exactly film theory is, how it is related to our experience of film, and what is to be gained by doing it.

The three chapters in this Part – two by philosophers and one by a film studies scholar – address these issues. The first two essays – by Noël Carroll and Malcolm Turvey – debate the nature of film theory and its resemblance to scientific models of theorizing about the natural world. Chapter 3, by French philosopher Gilles Deleuze, examines more specifically the relationship between the cinema and philosophy and why this pairing of disciplines makes for a fruitful partnership.

Philosopher of film Noël Carroll targets for critical discussion what he sees as a pernicious trend in the discipline of film theory over the last 20 years or more. This is a certain way of approaching theorizing about film, which he calls film Theory, with a capital "T." When practitioners engage in film Theory, they think of creating a grand, unified set of answers to "just about every legitimate question you might have about film." The application of Freudian psychoanalysis to the cinema – a prominent strand in contemporary film studies – is one such grand Theory, according to Carroll. Here, psychoanalytic film theorists seek to use psychoanalysis to explain a wide variety of issues relating to film, including the pleasure that viewers take in *all* genres of film, in terms of pre-existing psychological patterns at work in an idealized spectator.

Carroll argues that the methodology adopted by grand theorists inhibits productive theorizing about film. For one thing, there is no reason to think that the questions film scholars pose should be answerable in terms of a monolithic theory, such as psycho-analysis. Instead this question might be more fruitfully approached through a variety of disciplinary frameworks, including economics, anthropology, and narrative theory. For another, the questions that grand Theory investigates are posed at a very general level of abstraction. Yet inquiry into film, like other areas of knowledge, takes place at a certain historical time and place, and so must pose questions that are context-specific and historically sensitive. Carroll concedes that it is possible to work up to asking larger-scale questions as film theorizing proceeds, but before reaching that point we must first constrain ourselves to asking and answering "middle-range" questions related to film.

Carroll appeals to what he calls a "post-positivist" model of scientific theorizing to explain how film theory should proceed. Film theory is most likely to advance to the truth when it engages in dialectical competition with other theories addressing the same question, and appeals to sound standards of evidence and reasoning. Carroll concludes his essay by showing how this approach to film theory can help us decide between the answers presented by psychoanalytic film theory versus those offered by cognitivism, a theoretical orientation in film studies pioneered by Carroll and David Bordwell that seeks to describe the actual cognitive processes viewers undergo as they watch movies.

In chapter 2, Malcolm Turvey, a professor of film studies, takes issue with Carroll's suggestion that doing film theory can be analogized to models of scientific theorizing. Turvey argues that film studies, as a discipline in the humanities, has a subject matter that is distinct from the phenomena examined in the natural sciences. He develops this idea to call into question the idea that theory-building in the physical sciences gives an appropriate model for *all* the kinds of questions that film theorists tackle.

Scientific theorizing aims to discover natural laws of which we have no prior know-ledge, Turvey says. Typically, scientific laws are formulated through a process of induction – generalizing from observed instances – or deductively, through proposing universal hypotheses and deducing observable consequences that will either confirm or disconfirm the postulated laws. As such, the laws of natural science are falsifiable claims about physical phenomena we can discern through our senses. But Turvey argues that film theorists seldom test their theoretical claims, such as "Cinema is montage," against any empirical "data." This is surprising if film theorists seek answers that are like the laws governing natural phenomena.

Turvey argues that the fundamental task of film theory is not theory building accord-ing to the natural sciences; rather, it is about clarifying the practices and concepts that human beings already engage in and know. Most of us already know how to recognize a film in the genre of comedy, for example, yet we do not have available a general account of what comedy is, or even what is a sight gag. Or we are familiar with the distinction between fiction and non-fiction films, but we could not give a clear explanation of why any given film falls into one or other of these genres.

When we experience film, we grasp and apply *norms* that are internal to the practice of cinema – e.g. the distinction between fiction and non-fiction films. These norms fundamentally constitute our filmic practices, in much the way that the linguistic practice of speaking and writing English is constituted or governed by the norms or rules of English grammar. The task of film theory is not therefore, in general, to discover laws that hold about phenomena that exist independently of human knowledge of them: it is to clarify the concepts and norms we already grasp in our practice of film viewing and making. Turvey concludes that this consideration shows that, generally speaking, the scientific model of theorizing is inapplicable for understanding film theory.

French philosopher Gilles Deleuze adopts an entirely different approach to the issue of the relationship between film and theory or, more specifically, film and philosophy. He rejects the idea that the role of philosophy in relation to cinema is to interpret or clarify the concepts implicit in our experience or making of movies. Further, philosophy does not, and should not, "reflect" on the philosophical themes implicit in cinema. The creator of cinema does not need the help of philosophers in order to understand the deeper significance of film. Deleuze says that filmmakers are themselves perfectly capable of reflecting on the meaning and significance of their films, including their philosophical significance.

What then is there left for the philosopher to do? Deleuze argues that the essence of philosophy as a practice is the creation of concepts. The ancient Greek philosopher, Plato, for example, introduces the concepts of "Forms" – ideal, abstract objects that serve as the reference of predicate expressions ("is beautiful," "is just") and are set over against the changing world of sensible things. Plato thought that our words could be understood only with the help of a suitable paradigm. The paradigm for our words "justice" and "beauty" cannot be found in the physical world, the world known by the senses. So we must supply the missing paradigm and posit the existence of ideal Forms that we have encountered in a previous lifetime as disembodied souls. Plato's development of the concept of Forms is an example of what Deleuze takes the mission of philosophy to be: to create new concepts that help open up new possibilities for thinking about the world and our place in it. But what then is the role of the philosopher of film? It is, according to Deleuze, to explain how film itself gives rise to perceptual experiences that can alter our modes of thinking about movement and time.

Deleuze argues that what is distinctive about cinema is that it enables us to reflect on time and movement as a whole: this is because cinema allows us to imagine movement and time *itself*. Our normal perceptual experience is one in which we experience a series of successive "percepts" or sensations, such as my perceptions of the blackness and softness of my cat, for example, which my mind unites and then experiences as unified wholes. Put otherwise, our everyday experience is of unified things *in* time; it is not of time itself. Yet Deleuze argues that modern cinema, in particular the filmic practices embodied by European directors such as Jean-Luc Godard or Jean-Marie Straub and Danièle Huillet, alter our modes of perception. The devices of modern cinema as practiced by what Deleuze regards as cinema's best directors enable us to perceive time itself.

Films employing these techniques give rise to what Deleuze calls the "time-image." This is achieved through the use of editing practices that make illogical cuts and juxtapositions. For example, in Godard's *Week End*, mentioned above, there is frequently a separation and discrepancy between sound and image — e.g., images with a disturbing background noise that disrupts the unity of the image we are seeing. This way of breaking up what we see on screen is a perceptive force that challenges our concept of time and thereby gives rise to reflection on the flow of time itself.

The pairing of philosophy and cinema, therefore, is a productive one, according to Deleuze's theory, but not for the reasons that many philosophers typically think. Cinema is a form of art that has the power to affect and challenge our usual modes of experience by presenting new ways of experiencing movement and time. The philosophy of film, in turn, provides conceptual analysis of these new modes of perception.

The readings in Part I present several divergent views on what film theory is, why we should do it, and on the relation between philosophy and film. But no matter which view you decide on as being most compelling, we hope that you will find that the essays open up a whole new way of looking at film and your experience of it.

Study Questions

1. What is the difference between doing film theory and doing film "Theory," with a capital "T," according to Carroll? Why does Carroll think that the methodology of film "Theory" stands in the way of productive theorizing about film?
2. What is the "dialectical" approach to film theorizing that Carroll defends? Why does Carroll think it is useful to compare this dialectical approach to film theory with models of scientific theorizing?
3. How does Carroll think we should decide between cognitivism and psychoanalytic film theory as theories of film?
4. In what way does film theory concern what human beings already know and do, according to Turvey? What are some examples he uses to illustrate this idea?
5. Why does Turvey argue that Carroll's scientific model of film theorizing is not suited to the subject matter of film?
6. Turvey assumes that the goal of scientific theory is to grasp phenomena that lie outside the realm of human experience and knowledge. Film theory, on the other hand, Turvey argues, grasps concepts that are already previously understood or apprehended, albeit in a pre-theoretical form. Do you agree with Turvey's description of the distinction between science and film?
7. What is the characteristic activity of philosophical "theory," according to Deleuze?
8. Deleuze sees science, philosophy, and cinema as human practices that are essentially *creative* in one way or another. Do you agree with the similarities that Deleuze draws between these three disciplines?

9. Why does modern cinema, in its best form, present a challenge to our concepts? Have you seen a film that might illustrate the point Deleuze is getting at?
10. In what way can philosophy create new modes of thought by responding to the power of cinema to affect our concept of time?
11. Do you think that the practice of film should be judged based on what its "best" practitioners can achieve with it? What criteria of good film do you find implicit in Deleuze's discussion?

NOTE

1 As quoted in an interview with David Weddle in the *Los Angeles Times*, July 13, 2003.

1 ■ "The director turning the camera on the audience who is watching his film," from *Man With A Movie Camera*.

Prospects for Film Theory:
A Personal Assessment

Noël Carroll

Introduction: The Theory Is Dead, Long Live Theory

The rapid expansion of the film studies institution over the last two decades in the United States was undoubtedly abetted, in one way or another, by something called film theory, or, as its acolytes are apt to say, simply Theory – a classy continental number, centrally composed of elements of Louis Althusser, Jacques Lacan, and Roland Barthes, often with optional features derived, often incongruously, from Michel Foucault, Julia Kristeva, Pierre Bourdieu, Gilles Deleuze, and (*maybe* sometimes) Jacques Derrida, along with contributions from French cinéphiles like Christian Metz, Raymond Bellour, and Jean-Louis Baudry, although generally filtered, albeit with a difference, through exegetes like Stephen Heath, Kaja Silverman, and Teresa de Lauretis.

Universities regarded film studies programs as an economic boon, likely to spur demand and, in this context, Theory, so called, played an economic role in legitimating the formation of film programs. For what went by the name of Theory was surely abstruse enough to convince an uninformed administrator or a hesitant trustee that film studies was at least as complex intellectually as string theory, DNA, or hypotheses about massive parallel processing.

Whether it was necessary to enfranchise film studies in this way is an open question. Perhaps (as I tend to think) market forces alone would have sufficed to establish the institution. But, in any case, Theory appears to have played the ideological-institutional role of enfranchiser, even if the role was ultimately an epiphenomenal one. Furthermore, the expectation of gold in "them thar hills" also encouraged too many university presses to invest in film publications, especially when the arcane peregrinations of Theory facilitated their rationalization of their relaxation of their traditional role as academic gatekeepers. Hence film studies has been flooded with repetitive decoctions of the Theory in search of the same market in much the same way that consumers are confronted with so many marginally differentiated shampoos.

Interestingly, now that film studies seems ensconced in American universities – with TV studies and cultural studies queuing up behind it for legitimation – Theory looks to be on the wane. Certainly people like myself would like to imagine that this is a result of the recognition that the Theory has been soundly refuted, though even I would have to concede that more accurate explanations may be that Theory has outlived its academic utility or that it has merely run out of gas (that is, exhausted itself). But, in any case, however the demise of Theory came about, as it continues to petrify, it becomes appropriate to speculate about whether theorizing – in a small "t," not-a-proper-name sort of way – is possible. For even if Theory is dead, one wonders whether theorizing about film has a future.

Given these circumstances, it is the aim of this essay to explore the prospects for film theory. In order to approach this subject, I shall begin by sketching [. . .] what I take to be major obstacles to film theorizing at present, many of which are legacies of the Theory alluded to above. It is my conviction that as long as these obstacles continue to grip the imaginations of scholars, fruitful theorizing about film will be unlikely.

I will also attempt, in a more abbreviated way, to provide a minimal characterization of what I take to be the most useful framework that we might employ for film theorizing today. Lastly, I will look at the consequences of adopting that framework for assessing one of the leading debates (or, maybe, one of the *only* debates) among contemporary film theorists, namely: the rivalry between psychoanalytic film theory and cognitive theory. [. . .]

Impediments to Film Theorizing

1. Monolithic conceptions of film theory. The history of film theorizing, it seems to me, has been dominated by a conception of what a film theory should be in terms of the model of a unified body of ideas with certain core propositions from which conclusions about concrete cases follow in various ways, once certain empirical possibilities are considered. Metaphorically, we might call such a construal of film theory foundationalist. It is my contention that such monolithic conceptions of film theory stand in the way of productive theorizing about film, which theorizing might be best construed in terms of producing film theories rather than Film Theory.

Film theory, as most frequently practiced heretofore, has been singular; a film theory was generally conceived to be a rather comprehensive instrument that was supposed to answer virtually every legitimate question you might have about film. This view naturally contrasts with a view of our arena of inquiry as plural, that is, a view that commends thinking in terms of film theor*ies* rather than in terms of film theor*y*. That is, rather than theorizing about every element of film style in light of a set of limited theoretical presuppositions – for example, about the purported commitment of the medium to a realism or about its inevitable ideological destiny to suture – one might proceed by constructing local theories – for example, of film suspense, of film metaphor, of camera movement, or narrative comprehension, and even of the rhetoric of ideology – without expecting that these small-scale theories can be collected and unified under an overarching set of presuppositions about either the nature or function of cinema.

[. . .]

This view of film theorizing conflicts sharply with certain of the most traditional preconceptions of film theory. What is often called classical film theory not only conceptualizes the activity as Film Theory, but as *Film* Theory – that is, as committed to medium specificity in such a way that whatever counts as theorizing about film must be connected to features of the medium that are thought to be uniquely or essentially cinematic. Film theory must pertain to what is distinctly cinematic, otherwise it shall not count as film theory but as something else, like narrative theory.

Admittedly, narrow, essentialist views of film theory of this sort are infrequently voiced nowadays. However, where they remain influential, as they do in the work of the psychoanalytic film theorist Christian Metz and in the conception of photography of Roland Barthes and his cinematic followers, they are impediments to film theory and need to be dismantled dialectically.

Of course, the greatest problem with essentialist film theory is that it gives every indication of being false. But at the very least, another problem with essentialist film theory is that it blinkers the theoretical imagination by limiting what questions are the correct ones to ask about cinema. Yet, especially since cinematic essentialism seems philosophically dispensable, there appears to be scant reason to abide its restrictions.

Instead of thinking of film theory as a unified, single theory, it might be better to think of it as a field of activity, perhaps like sociological theory, where many different projects – theories of homelessness in America, of generic social cohesion, of class conflict in India, of the resurgence of religious fundamentalism worldwide – of different levels of generality and abstraction coexist without being subsumed under a single general theory. Similarly, film theorizing today should proceed at varying levels of generality and abstraction.

Even if some day, film theorizing might be organized into a general theory (which seems unlikely to me), nevertheless we are hardly in a position to frame such a theory now, since we know so little at this time. And, in any event, the only way that we shall come to know more is by developing small-scale theories about virtually every imaginable aspect of film.

Film theorizing, as I have argued elsewhere, should be piecemeal. But it should also be diversified. Insofar as theorists approach film from many different angles, from different levels of abstraction and generality, they will have to avail themselves of multidisciplinary frameworks. Some questions about film may send the researcher toward economics, while others require a look into perceptual psychology. In other instances, sociology, political science, anthropology, communications theory, linguistics, artificial intelligence, biology, or narrative theory may provide the initial research tools which the film theorist requires in order to begin to evolve theories of this or that aspect of film.

[. . .]

What makes something film theory is that it is a general answer to a general question that we have about some phenomenon which we think, pretheoretically, falls into the bailiwick of film. Such inquiry is theoretical because it is general, and it is film theory because it pertains to filmic practice. Furthermore, since we can ask so many different kinds of general questions about film, there is no common feature that all of our answers should be expected to share. Some theoretical questions about film – for example, about cinematic perception – may have answers that primarily advert to cinematic forms and structures, whereas other different answers to different questions might refer to economic forces. That is, some theories may be formal, while others may be social. Our collection of film theories may very well comprise a mixed bag. There simply is no reason to think that every film theory will have something to tell us about the same subject – such as the way in which each and every aspect of film figures in the oppression or emancipation of the film viewer.

[. . .]

A Framework for Film Theorizing

I have just indicated my conviction that criticism is integral to film theory. In this, I am not claiming film theory is distinctive, but that, like most other forms of theoretical inquiry, it proceeds dialectically. Theories are framed in specific historical contexts of research for the purpose of answering certain questions, and the relative strengths of theories are assayed by comparing the answers they afford to the answers proposed by alternative theories. This conception of theory evaluation is pragmatic because: (1) it compares actual, existing rival answers to the questions at hand (rather than every logically conceivable answer); and (2) because it focuses on solutions to contextually motivated theoretical problems (rather than searching for answers to any conceivable question one might have about cinema).

[. . .]

Speaking as a self-appointed reformer, I wish to emphasize the need for film theorizing to become more conscious of its dialectical responsibilities. Where film theory blurs into film criticism, there is the ever-present danger that theoretical premises will be taken as given – as effectively inoculated from criticism – and, once so assumed, then used to generate "interesting" interpretations. My concern is that more attention be focused on these premises, that they be subjected to intense theoretical criticism, and that alternative answers to the questions these theories address be developed and analyzed through dialectical comparison with each other.

[. . .]

Theory building builds on previous histories of theorizing as well as upon data (which may be theory-laden). Present theories are formulated in the context of past theories. Apprised of the shortcomings in past theories, through processes of continued scrutiny and criticism, present theories try to find more satisfactory answers to the questions that drive theoretical activity. Sometimes advances involve incremental improvements within existing paradigms; sometimes new paradigms are required to accommodate the lacunae made evident by the anomalies that beset previous theorizing. Sometimes the driving theoretical questions need to be redefined; sometimes they need to be broken down into more manageable questions; sometimes these questions need to be recast radically. And all this requires a free and open discursive context, one in which criticism is not the exception, but the rule.

Methodologically, as I have already indicated, I believe that in the present context piecemeal theorizing is the way to go. In many cases, this means breaking down some of the presiding questions of the Theory into more manageable questions, for example, about the comprehension of point-of-view editing, instead of global questions about something vaguely called suture. As compelling answers are developed to small-scale, delimited questions, we may be in a position to think about whether these answers can be unified in a more comprehensive theoretical framework.

The considerations here on behalf of piecemeal theorizing are practical, not philosophical. For it is my hunch that we do not yet know enough to begin to evolve a unified theory, or even the questions that might lead to a unified theory. So, for the duration, let us concentrate on more manageable, small-scale theorizing. Perhaps one day we will be in a position to frame a unified or comprehensive theory of film. I have no argument to show that this is not possible. But whether our theories are large-scale or piecemeal, the process of theorizing will always have a dialectical component.

By emphasizing the dialectical dimension of theorizing, one concedes that it is historical. For debates will be relative to the disputants involved and the situated questions that perplex them. Thus, film theorizing under the auspices of the dialectical model does not pretend to the discovery of Absolute Truth. The theoretical answers it advances are shaped in response to the existing questions it answers and refines and to the perspectives and theoretical interests that are inscribed in those questions. Moreover, insofar as a dialectical conception of film theorizing admits that theorizing evolves over time, the dialectical film theorist must be aware that his or her theories may be open to revision as the debate matures. [. . .]

Nevertheless, in conceding the historicity and revisability of theories, I have not given up truth as a regulative ideal for film theorizing. For the fact that theorizing has a history does not compromise the possibility of discovering what is the case, since that history may involve, among other things, the successive elimination of error. Furthermore, the fact that we are constantly revising our theories in the light of continued criticism and new evidence does not preclude the possibility that our theories are getting closer and closer to the truth. [. . .] Moreover, there is no persuasive reason to concede that we cannot also craft film theories in the here and now that are approximately true.

The dialectical conception of film theory that I am advocating is consistent with trends in the postpositivist philosophy of science. It respects the Kuhnian, antipositivist emphasis on the importance of historical and social contexts for inquiry. It is also not positivist in that it conceives of the process of theoretical argumentation as situated as a debate between existing rivals, rather than as a debate between every conceivable theory, before a court of fully rational participants, endowed with full information.

[. . .]

I am presuming that what can be claimed for science may be claimed eventually for film theory. This does not mean that I think that film theory is a science, or that it can be or should be transformed into one, though I do think that there may be certain questions of film theory – perhaps concerning perception – that may be pursued scientifically. Rather, I invoke discussions about scientific methodology in proselytizing for a dialectical conception of film theory, not because I believe film theory is a natural science, but only because the philosophy of science provides us with some of our best models for understanding theoretical inquiry.

Undoubtedly, some will dismiss my suggestions on the grounds that I am confusing film theory with natural science. Let me say now that this is a misinterpretation. What I am saying is: let us take advantage of the insights derived from reflection on the scientific enterprise in order to think about what the structure of our own practice might be. We should not attempt to slavishly imitate any of the natural sciences. We need to be alert to the special features of our own field of inquiry, and to modify our methods appropriately. And yet we may still derive some useful hints about the process of inquiry by listening to sophisticated discussions about science.

[. . .]

Nowadays, humanists, including film scholars, express misgivings about science because they claim that it parades its findings as if they were infallible. This is merely a variation on the argument from Absolute Truth. [. . .] The argument begins by noting, as I have, that scientific theories are historically situated and revisable. Hence, again for reasons I have already produced, scientific theories cannot pretend to Absolute Truth. Therefore, they are arbitrary. In effect, we are presented with a disjunctive syllogism: either scientific theories are absolutely true or they are arbitrary. They are not absolutely true; so they are arbitrary. And if they are arbitrary, why should they or the methodologies that yield them be privileged?

But as is always the case with such arguments, the conclusion depends on canvassing all the viable alternatives. And in this instance, it is easy to see that there are overlooked options. One is what is called *fallibilism*, which I would contend provides a much better framework for comprehending scientific practice than the allegation that it aspires to infallibility.

The fallibilist agrees that he or she may have to revise his or her theories in light of future evidence or in response to the implications of later theoretical developments, because the fallibilist realizes that theories are at best well-justified and that a well-justified theory may turn out to be false. There is no claim to Absolute Truth here. But that does not entail that the theories in question are arbitrary. For we are not open to revising our theories in any which way, but only in virtue of the best available, transcultural standards of justification, that is, ones that have a reliable track record.

The fallibilist does not believe that we can revise all our theories and methods at once. He or she accepts the possibility that any subset thereof might be revised in the appropriate circumstances, and even that all our theories might be revised, but only ad seriatim. Theories and methods are revisable. They do not yield Absolute Truth. But they are not arbitrary either. For they are only revisable in accordance with practices that, though themselves incrementally revisable, have a reliable record for tracking the truth. The truth, here, where we do secure it, is approximate truth, in the garden variety sense of the term, not Absolute Truth. But if we can conceive of science in such a way that detaches it from pretensions to Absolute Truth, then taking note of its failure to deliver Absolute Truth should not dispose us to dismiss it as arbitrary.

[. . .]

I have spent so much time sparring with contemporary academic skepticism about science for two reasons: first, because in the current context of debate, any proposal, like mine, that a framework for aesthetic theorizing might profit from thinking about scientific theorizing is apt to elicit an intemperate rejoinder on the basis of one or more of the considerations I have just attempted to undercut; and second, because it is frequently alleged that cognitivism [. . .] is an attempt to turn film theory into science, and, therefore, cognitivism can be "refuted" handily by the preceding skeptical arguments about the integrity of science. But I contend that these arguments refute nothing. [. . .]

Many of these arguments begin, as I do, with an acknowledgment of the insights of postpositivist philosophy of science. However, where many humanists and film scholars often take those insights to imply the arbitrariness of science, I try to exploit them in favor of a view of science as a dialectical, incremental process for securing approximate truths through practices of, among other things, error elimination and criticism. Furthermore, this very broad conception of inquiry may be fruitful to our thinking about film theory. In order to test its usefulness and to descend from the preceding perhaps unduly rarefied stratosphere of abstraction, I shall apply this conception of the dialectical framework for film theory to a contemporary question, namely, the issue of cognitivism.

Cognitivism versus Psychoanalysis

Psychoanalysis, conjoined with Marxism and later blended with various other radical, political perspectives, has dominated film theorizing for two decades. In the eighties, an approach to film theorizing, labeled cognitivism, began to take shape as an alternative to psychoanalysis. Cognitivism is not a unified theory. Its name derives from its tendency to look for alternative answers to many of the questions addressed by or raised by psychoanalytic film theories, especially with respect to film reception, in terms of cognitive and rational processes rather than irrational or unconscious ones. This might involve explicit reference to cognitive and perceptual psychology or to Anglo-American-style linguistics rather than to psychoanalysis. Or the hypotheses might be more homemade.

[. . .]

Cognitivism is not a unified theory, not only because the theoretical domains cognitivists explore differ, but because cognitivist film theorists, like cognitive psychologists, may disagree about which proposals – of the competing cognitivist proposals – best suit the data. So, once cognitivists stop arguing with psychoanalysts, they will have to argue with each other. And this is why it is a mistake to imagine that cognitivism is a single, unified theory. It is a stance.

However, it is a stance that has increasingly come to define itself as an alternative to psychoanalysis in film studies. It advances its hypotheses, as diverse and as discordant as they may be, by claiming to characterize or to explain phenomena better than extant psychoanalytic theories. Cognitivists have increasingly come to conceptualize their project dialectically. Cognitivists take their task to be a matter of answering certain questions about film, especially about film reception and comprehension, most of which questions have already been asked or at least acknowledged by psychoanalytic film theorists. But cognitivists claim that they do a better job answering those questions than psychoanalytic film theorists have.

[. . .]

[. . .] Theories compel assent, at least provisionally, by demonstrating that they provide certain explanatory advantages and solutions to certain anomalies lacking in their opposing number.

This view of theory should not surprise psychoanalytic film theorists. For they should recall the way in which Freud argues for his own theory of dreams. Prior to Freud, dream research regarded dreams as purely somatic phenomena, the reaction of a mental organ veritably sunk in the state of sleep in response to environmental stimuli which partially activate it. By examining the content of certain dreams, Freud showed that this theory was not comprehensive – it did not cover a great many facts presented by the data – and that it was unable to provide any functional-biological account of why we dream. [. . .]

Freud's own theory not only supplied the wherewithal to account for the anomalies ignored by previous dream research but was also able to identify a candidate for the function of dream, namely, that it was the guardian of sleep. It has been the burden of subsequent researchers to see how well Freud's theory squares with the data and to develop alternative hypotheses to accommodate the anomalies in the data that erupt from the collision between the evidence and Freud's famous generalizations, such as the hypothesis of wish fulfillment.

Staging the debate between psychoanalytic film theory is too elaborate a task. [. . .] One reason for this is that, since cognitivism often proposes piecemeal theories, a thorough confrontation would require facing off each cognitivist theory – of narrative comprehension, of cinematic perception, of the horror film, of melodrama, of film music, and so on – with its psychoanalytic counterparts, where there are counterparts. [. . .] Nevertheless, it is still possible to offer some overarching comments about the rivalry between cognitivism and psychoanalysis. [. . .]

[. . .]

Psychoanalysis [. . .] kicks in [when] there is an apparent breakdown in the normal functioning of our cognitive-perceptual processing, our capacities for rational calcula-tion and decision making, our conative and emotional behavior, our motor capabilities, and so on, which breakdowns cannot be explained either organically or in virtue of the structural features of the processes in question.

If I cannot walk because I have lost my legs in a car accident, there is no call for psychoanalysis. But if I am biologically sound, and no rational motive can be supplied for my inaction, psychoanalysis is appropriate. If I am angry when I am mugged, ceteris paribus, that is a rational response, where psychoanalysis is out of place. But if I consistently explode whenever a teacher asks me a question, we think about psychoanalysis. [. . .] In short, there is a conceptual constraint on psychoanalysis; it is restricted to dealing with phenomena that cannot be explained by other means.

Moreover, this has interesting consequences for the debate between cognitivist and psychoanalytic film theories. Namely, wherever a plausible cognitivist theory can be secured, the burden of proof is shifted to the psychoanalytic theorist. For a plausible cognitivist theory precludes the necessity for psychoanalysis. The mere plausibility of a cognitivist theory gives it a special advantage over psychoanalytic theories of the same phenomenon.

It is not generally the case that the mere plausibility of one scientific theory excludes a respectable, competing theory from the field. But insofar as psychoanalysis is defined as just what explains what otherwise has no *plausible* explanation, psychoanalytic explanation starts with a disadvantage where plausible cognitivist theories are available.

Contemporary film theorists, like Judith Mayne in her recent book *Cinema and Spectatorship*, tag cognitivist theorists with the complaint that they simply bracket the psychoanalytic approach, as if willfully. What such criticism fails to comprehend is that where we have a convincing cognitivist account, there is no point whatsoever in looking any further for a psychoanalytic account. It is not the case that psychoanalysis is being unfairly or inexplicably bracketed. It is being *retired*, unless and until good reasons can be advanced to suppose otherwise.

Psychoanalytic theories face a special burden of proof when confronting cognitivist theories. For a psychoanalytic theory to reenter the debate, it must be demonstrated that there is something about the data of which given cognitivist (or organic) explanations can give no adequate account, and which, as well, cannot be explained by some other cognitive theory, which remainder is susceptible to psychoanalytic theory *alone*. I have no argument to prove conclusively that no psychoanalytic theory will ever be able to cross this hurdle. But, at the same time, I think it is also fair to say that psychoanalytic film theorists behave as though they are unaware of this obstacle and, in any event, they have failed to meet it *even once* in their skirmishes with cognitivists.

Because of this special burden of proof, the possibility of pluralistic coexistence between cognitivism and psychoanalysis is never a foregone conclusion. Confronted by cognitivist hypotheses about the perception of the cinematic image, the psychoanalytic critic must show that there is something about the phenomena that is alien to cognitivist theorizing. That is why it is not enough for psychoanalytic theorists, like Richard Wollheim and Richard Allen, to merely tell a coherent, psychoanalytic story about pictorial perception; they must also establish that there is something about the data that cognitivists are unable to countenance before they, the psychoanalysts, postulate the operation of *unconscious* psychic mechanisms like projection. For if their cognitivist competitors can frame a coherent, comprehensive account of the data without resorting to unconscious mechanisms, postulating unconscious ones is a nonstarter.

Dialectical arguments are primarily matters of shifting the burden of proof between rival theories that are grappling with roughly the same questions. Quite frequently (most frequently?) it is difficult to find a completely decisive refutation of rival theories. That is one reason why we must fall back on the laborious processes of removing the burden of proof from ourselves and redistributing it amongst our competitors. The preceding argument has not shown that psychoanalytic theories of film will never be admissible. At best, what it may show is that the burden of proof is now with the psychoanalysts. Perhaps they will rise to the occasion.

However, if I am correct in maintaining that psychoanalytic film theorists have not yet even recognized that they have this burden of proof, then that indicates that, at present, the ball belongs to the cognitivists. Psychoanalytic film theory may succeed in countering this argument dialectically, but unless it does, the continued elaboration of the psychoanalytic paradigm, conducted in isolation from cognitivist challenges, represents an evasion of film theory, not a contribution to it.

[. . .]

Concluding Remarks

[. . .]

The prospects for film theory hinge on critical debate. In the best of circumstances, the participants of that discussion will include cognitivists, psychoanalysts, and unaligned scholars. In my view, over the last two decades, film studies has squandered what may turn out to have been a once-in-a-lifetime opportunity by effectively stifling debate between Theory and alternative paradigms. Whether film theory has a genuine future depends on its becoming truly dialectical.

2

Can Scientific Models of Theorizing Help Film Theory?

Malcolm Turvey

And we may not advance any kind of theory. There must not be anything hypothetical in our considerations. . . . The problems are solved, not by giving new information, but by arranging what we have always known. . . . Since everything lies open to view there is nothing to explain. For what is hidden . . . is of no interest to us.

Ludwig Wittgenstein, *Philosophical Investigations* §109, §126

Over the last forty years, the prestige of *theory* as a method or form of explanation has grown exponentially within humanistic disciplines. When scholars of literature and the arts want to know what something is or to explain something – a genre, for example, or narrative – they are now apt to claim that a theory is needed. Film studies is no exception.[1] Film theory has existed almost since the cinema's invention in the 1890s. However, it has proliferated since the 1960s, when film scholars began following the lead of Claude Lévi-Strauss, Roland Barthes, and others in France who adapted and applied the "structural" theory of language to a number of cultural forms in the hope of explaining all types of representation, not just language, by the same underlying structure. This theoretical paradigm, known as semiology or semiotics ("the science of signs"), was quickly extended to the cinema, as were a number of others in the years following, including psychoanalysis, a variety of linguistic and philosophical theories, and cognitivism. While these paradigms vary considerably, their application is premised on the same assumption: that traditional humanistic methods – understanding the intentions of filmmakers, interpreting the meanings of their films, identifying the formal and stylistic conventions they are employing and the innovations, if any, they are introducing – are insufficient if not misguided in the absence of theoretical explanations.[2]

Indeed, the prestige of theory has been so great that few within the humanities have stopped to ask whether theory is an appropriate method for explaining humanistic subject matter. Things are different elsewhere. In the social sciences, history, philosophy, and the natural sciences, there has been a wide variety of debates since the eighteenth century about whether there is something unique to humanistic subject matter requiring forms of explanation different from those, such as theory, that are used to explain the natural universe.[3] These debates continue to this day, for example in the argument between the prominent biologists Edward O. Wilson and Stephen Jay Gould over the degree of "consilience" that is possible between the humanities and natural sciences.[4] But among scholars of literature and the arts, such debate has been sorely lacking.

Part of the problem is that the term "theory" is notoriously vague, and scholars of literature and the arts rarely clarify what they mean by it. One salutary exception is philosopher and film scholar Noël Carroll, who has recently recommended that we turn to the philosophy of science in order to better understand what theory is. As he puts it, "the philosophy of science provides us with some of our best models for understanding theoretical inquiry."[5] According to contemporary "post-positivist" philosophy, a natural scientific theory consists of one or more hypotheses formulated through robust dialectical criticism of rivals.

> Theory building builds on previous histories of theorizing as well as upon data (which may be theory-laden). Present theories are formulated in the context of past theories. Appraised of the shortcomings in past theories, through processes of continued scrutiny and criticism, present theories try to find more satisfactory answers to the questions that drive theoretical activity. (p. 57)

Through rigorous dialectical criticism of competitors – exposing logical flaws in their arguments, revealing new empirical data they cannot account for, postulating superior explanations of the existing evidence – better and better theories of the natural universe are proposed, and science makes progress. However, this means that any natural scientific theory is fallible, at best nothing more than an approximation of the truth. It, too, will be revised and even rejected in the future, just as it revised or rejected previous theories.

This post-positivist model of theory now more or less dominates mainstream philosophy of science. Unlike positivist models, it admits that natural scientific theorizing has an historical dimension, but resists the relativism that a few philosophers have argued is the consequence of this historical dimension. For as Carroll points out:

> The fact that theorizing has a history does not compromise the possibility of discovering what is the case, since that history may involve, among other things, the successive elimination of error. Furthermore, the fact that we are constantly revising our theories in the light of continued criticism and new evidence does not preclude the possibility that our theories are getting closer and closer to the truth. (p. 58)

Certainly, this post-positivist model seems to be a good explanation for why natural scientific theorizing has been so successful in explaining and predicting the natural world. But should we employ it in film studies?

Carroll seems to think so. Although he is careful to state that "We should not attempt to slavishly imitate any of the natural sciences," and that "We need to be alert to the special features of our own field of inquiry," he expresses the hope that "what can be claimed for science may be claimed eventually for film theory" (p. 59). What I take him to mean here is something like the following: while film studies is certainly not a natural science, it has a good chance of achieving the explanatory successes of the natural sciences if it employs their model of theory, if, in other words, film theories consist of fallible hypotheses formulated through robust dialectical criticism of rivals.

Employing this post-positivist model of theory in film studies is a noble goal, and Carroll recommends it with the best of intentions. For it is undoubtedly the case that rigorous dialectical criticism is essential for progress in any pursuit of knowledge, and, as Carroll and others have shown, "sustained, detailed, intertheoretical debate and criticism is rare in the history of film theory" (p. 57). Furthermore, it is perfectly reasonable to turn to the natural sciences to find methods and forms of explanation, considering their enormous explanatory successes and prestige.

However, the natural sciences do not have a monopoly on dialectical criticism – it can be a feature of any rational form of inquiry, whether scientific or not, if participants are willing. And while the post-positivist model of theory recommended by Carroll may help film scholars to explain some things about the cinema, I think we need to examine carefully whether it – or indeed any model of theory – can help us explain everything about it. This is because, as Carroll himself points out, the subject matter of humanistic disciplines such as cinema studies possesses features of its own that set it apart from the phenomena studied by the natural sciences. But what Carroll does not take into consideration is the possibility that, because of these features, the methods employed by the natural sciences – including the model of theory he recommends – may be *logically* inappropriate for explaining much humanistic subject matter.

My suggestion is that before we adopt Carroll's proposal wholesale, we need something like the philosophy of the humanities called for by the philosopher G. H. von Wright, a propaedeutic philosophy that will clarify precisely which methods are logically appropriate for explaining humanistic subject matter, and which are not.[6] Once we have such a philosophy, we will understand better what type of things theory can help us explain, and what type theory may be of no help in explaining. Obviously, such a philosophy is beyond the scope of this paper. Here, I will simply point to one feature of the cinema that is a good candidate for distinguishing it from the phenomena studied by the natural sciences, a feature it shares with humanistic subject matter in general and that any, more general, philosophy of the humanities would have to take into consideration. I will then argue that this feature rules out, on logical grounds, theory as a method of explanation.

I

It is easy to understand why the natural sciences attempt to find out about natural phenomena using the post-positivist model of theory. For the natural sciences typically aim to discover the explanatory principles governing the nature and behavior of natural phenomena, principles which are usually invisible to normal, everyday observation. Because such explanatory principles are *hidden*, we have to undertake research to find out about them, and theoretical claims about them are necessarily hypothetical and fallible, at best approximating the truth. Such claims are accepted only while they provide better explanations than rivals, and they are open to being revised or rejected. A classic example is Isaac Newton's theory of gravity. Newton's theory was revolutionary in its day because nothing about our ordinary experience of the world shows that the same force is responsible for keeping the earth in orbit around the sun and for causing an apple to fall from a tree. And while this theory enjoyed enormous success up until the end of the nineteenth century because it accurately predicts the motion of objects such as planets and apples in most contexts, twentieth-century physics, using empirical evidence unavailable to Newton, has demonstrated that it is much less accurate at the sub-atomic level and at speeds approaching the speed of light, thereby giving rise to rival theories – quantum mechanics and general relativity – that better explain the new evidence.

In recommending the post-positivist model of theory to film scholars, Carroll assumes that the explanatory principles governing cinema, which film scholars aim to discover, resemble the explanatory principles governing natural phenomena in at least one way: we have to find out about them using the same post-positivist model of theory. This in turn assumes that, like the explanatory principles governing natural phenomena, the explanatory principles governing cinema are *hidden*, unknown to us prior to research, and that the only way we can find out about them is through proposing theories in the form of fallible hypotheses that, at best, approximate the truth.

But if we look at the history of film theory, one of the most obvious things we notice is that film theorists rarely if ever treat their claims about cinema as fallible hypotheses about explanatory principles we have no knowledge of prior to research. For they hardly ever undertake systematic empirical investigations into them. Although they sometimes draw on empirical research from the human and natural sciences, they do not themselves collect and analyze data. When Eisenstein, for instance, argues that the essence of cinema is editing, or Metz claims that the cinema is like "the Imaginary" in Jacques Lacan's psychoanalytical theory, neither of them offers much beyond brief, anecdotal evidence to support their assertions.

Carroll would probably argue that this is because these particular film theorists are insufficiently scientific. But if we look at more recent film theories putatively formulated in a more scientific spirit, we find a similar absence of systematic empirical research. Consider David Bordwell's Constructivist cognitivist theory of film comprehension proposed in *Narration in the Fiction Film*. In this theory, Bordwell makes some major claims about the cinema and human beings. For example, he argues that "the organism [by which he means a human being] enjoys creating unity" in order to support his claim that the spectator of a fiction film attempts to mentally construct a coherent story out of the perceptual cues the film provides.[7] However, Bordwell does not undertake any investigation into what real spectators actually enjoy doing when they view a film. Similarly, in his book *Engaging Characters*, the film theorist Murray Smith proposes a theory of our engagement with characters in cinematic fictions by developing the concepts of "recognition, alignment, and allegiance."[8] However, again, Smith does not undertake any research into real spectators and the way they actually feel about fictional characters. Although Bordwell and Smith both draw on research in the human and natural sciences in order to formulate their theories, just as Eisenstein and Metz did, neither of them seems to think it is necessary to undertake systematic empirical investigations themselves.

Why is this? Why is there a lack of systematic empirical research in film theory if the explanatory principles governing the cinema are like the explanatory principles governing natural phenomena? The latter are hidden, and the only way we can find out about them is through research. While much natural scientific theorizing is at least initially speculative, typically due to the absence of empirical evidence or the means to obtain it, natural scientific theories are only ever accepted if the data eventually confirms them (or fails to falsify them). The reason that Newton's theory of gravity, for example, was widely accepted until the end of the nineteenth century is because empirical investigation shows that it repeatedly predicts the motion of a wide range of objects in a wide range of contexts with a high degree of accuracy. If the explanatory principles governing cinema are also hidden, unknown to us prior to research, how is it that theories about them ever convince anyone they are plausible in the absence of the sort of systematic empirical investigations we find in the natural sciences? Considering the influence of Metz's and Bordwell's theories, why is it that so many of us so readily assent to them, and so quickly?

One reason, I suggest, is because unlike theories of the natural universe, film theories concern *what human beings already know and do*, and this points to a major difference between natural phenomena and the cinema. The explanatory principles governing natural phenomena, such as gravity, are not known to human beings prior to research. In the case of the cinema, however, human beings already know a good deal prior to research. This is because the cinema is a human creation, and it is embedded in human practices and institutions that most of us engage with regularly. For example, most of us know what a romantic comedy film is, and how to respond to one appropriately, without doing any research into romantic comedy. Although the average person may not be able to list all of the conventions that define a romantic comedy, most of us nevertheless know romantic comedies when we see them, and have no problem responding to them in appropriate ways.

This is one reason, I suggest, why film theories command assent in the absence of sustained empirical investigation.[9] We already have a good idea of what they are talking about, and the most powerful and plausible ones seem, at least in part, to clarify what we already know and do. When someone like Metz, for example, compares the cinema to phenomena such as dreams, daydreams, and fantasies, some of us are tempted to agree with him because we think – "Ah yes, he's right. Some films are like dreams, the experience of cinema is sometimes fantasy-like," and so on. Or when Bordwell claims that we try and construct a coherent story when watching a fiction film, some of us might concur because we think – "Yes, that's true. When I watch a film, I do make inferences, try and fill in missing information, anticipate and form hypotheses," and so on.

When we look at theoretical explanations of the nature and behavior of natural phenomena, however, we immediately see a difference. For with such explanations, the question of whether or not they clarify something we already know and do does not play any role in whether we accept them or not. For example, the claim that the "ventromedial prefrontal region" of the "frontal lobe" of the human brain controls normal decision-making, and that damage to this region – as in the famous case of Phineas Gage – impairs our ability to plan for the future, is not something we accept because it clarifies something we already know and do.[10] Rather, we accept it because systematic empirical research shows that it is the most plausible hypothesis. When this area of the brain is damaged either by accident or in controlled experiments, we find that it causes an impairment of normal decision-making. Because the causal connection between the ventromedial prefrontal region and normal decision-making is, like gravity, hidden from normal, everyday observation, for all we knew prior to empirical research it could have been the area of the brain known as Broca's area that controls normal decision-making. This is simply another way of saying, along with Hume, that "For all we know a priori, anything may be the cause of anything."

Is this an important difference, and does it tell us anything about the logical appropriateness of the method of theory for explaining humanistic subject matter?

Carroll might agree that we know more about a humanistic phenomenon such as the cinema than we do about natural phenomena, and that this knowledge plays a role in our acceptance or rejection of film theories that it does not play with theories of the natural universe. But he might characterize this knowledge as empirical data, and argue that we simply have more empirical data about the cinema because of our regular engagement with it. Because it is a humanistic phenomenon, he might say, it stands to reason that we know more about it pre-theoretically than we do about natural phenomena, because we invented it. But this does not mean, he might continue, that we need to stop improving upon our pre-theoretical knowledge of the cinema by theorizing.

However, I think the fact that we know more about the cinema shows that it is fundamentally different from natural phenomena. This is because we *need* to know more about the cinema in order to be able to engage with it, while the same is not true of natural phenomena. For example, when we make the decision to watch a film at the local multiplex, we can do so without any knowledge of the fallible hypothesis that it is the ventromedial prefrontal region of the frontal lobe of our brains, as opposed to Broca's area, that enables us to make such a decision. We simply use our decision-making capacity. Similarly, when we watch the film we have decided upon, we can use our eyes perfectly well without any fallible, hypothetical knowledge of the explanatory principles governing their nature and behavior. We simply rely on the fact that they work. But we cannot watch the same film if we do not already know (as opposed to having a fallible hypothesis about) what a film is; what the difference between fiction and non-fiction is; what a cut as opposed to a dissolve means; what the differences between horror, comedy, and other genres are; if we have not been taught the appropriate ways to respond intellectually and emotionally to cinematic fictions and the roles they play in our culture; if we do not know the customs, conventions, and a whole host of other *norms* that govern films and film viewing; as well as much else that film scholars are interested in. If these things were equivalent to the explanatory principles governing natural phenomena, then knowledge of them would be as unnecessary to us in order to be able to engage with cinema as is knowledge of the principles that govern the nature and behavior of our eyes.

Philosophers such as von Wright and Charles Taylor tend to draw this distinction in the following way: while natural phenomena are what they are *independently* of knowledge of the explanatory principles that govern them, a humanistic phenomenon such as the cinema is *constituted*, at least in part, by human norms and human beings who know and use these norms. The cinema would not be what it is if there were not human beings who know these norms, while natural phenomena are what they are independently of whether human beings know anything about the explanatory principles that govern them.[11]

The philosopher Ludwig Wittgenstein clarified this difference by using games as an analogy for humanistic phenomena. When we learn to play tennis, for example, we master various concepts, customs, and conventions and the patterns of behavior they inform.[12] We learn what a serve is, what a return of serve is, what a lob is, what "out" means, that we should not shout at our opponent during a match, what emotions we should feel and when, and so on and so forth. In order to play tennis, we have to master these various types of norms. Tennis, however, is also *shaped* by the natural universe. If gravity was six times weaker than it actually is, for example, tennis would be a very different game. Tennis balls (among other things) would behave very differently. However, we do not need to know anything about gravity or any of the other explanatory principles governing the nature and behavior of tennis balls in order to be able to play tennis, and gravity is the way that it is independently of whether we know anything about it. Knowledge of it is *external* to playing tennis. Gravity does not constitute tennis, although it shapes it. When we play tennis, we simply rely on the fact that tennis balls will act in a certain way when hit with a certain amount of force in a certain direction. That's why tennis could be played before gravity and its laws were discovered by Newton. Knowledge of the variety of norms of tennis, however, is *internal* – they do constitute it. Without knowledge of them, we would not be able to play tennis. Indeed, there would be no such thing as tennis.

Similarly, our ability to understand and respond appropriately to a film is dependent, at least in part, on our knowledge of a whole host of norms that are internal to our engagement with cinema, such as the distinction between fiction and non-fiction. Certainly, like tennis, the cinema is shaped in profound ways by the natural universe – think, for example, how different the cinema would be if our eyes were able to perceive each individual frame of a film, or if our vision was triocular instead of binocular. But knowledge of the explanatory principles governing the nature and behavior of our eyes is external to our practice of engaging with cinema. We do not need any knowledge of the way our eyes work, least of all a *theory*, in order to watch a film.

II

If this distinction between external and internal is valid, then it means that at least some of the questions we ask about the cinema are likely to be about the internal norms that constitute it, such as the distinction between fiction and non-fiction, or the conventions that define romantic comedy. And if this is the case, then the post-positivist model of theory recommended by Carroll is not a logically appropriate method for answering such questions. For this method is used in the natural sciences to make discoveries about hidden explanatory principles, such as gravity, that we have no knowledge of prior to research. But the various norms that constitute cinema are ones *we already know and use*. Hence, we do not need to propose fallible hypotheses in order to find out about them, *because we already know and use them*. Instead, in order to answer questions about them, we need to *clarify* what we already know and do, the concepts, customs, and conventions we already do have and use, rather than finding out new information about something we have no prior knowledge of. Answering questions of this kind, I would suggest, is akin to clarifying the variety of grammatical rules that govern our everyday use of language. For we follow grammatical rules all the time when we speak or write, such as the rules that govern the position of adjectives before nouns. But we are typically not able to notice these rules until they are clarified for us by grammarians.

It is also akin, as the philosopher Oswald Hanfling has pointed out, to the type of knowledge aesthetics seeks. Not all forms of rational inquiry, Hanfling has reminded us, involve finding out new information about something we have no prior knowledge of, aesthetics being the classic example.[13] Typically, gaining aesthetic knowledge about a work of art consists of having our attention drawn to features of that work that lie in clear view before our eyes, but that we have not noticed or paid attention to, or paid the right kind of attention to. A good example is the playful patterning of space in Yasujiro Ozu's films that Bordwell has illuminated so well, something that lies in clear view before any viewer of an Ozu film, but that is not necessarily noticeable to that viewer until pointed out to him or her.[14] Similarly, I am suggesting, answers to questions about the internal norms that constitute cinema (or any other type of humanistic phenomenon for that matter) consist of drawing our attention to the various concepts, customs, and conventions we already know and use when engaging with cinema, norms that – like grammatical rules – in one sense lie in plain view before our eyes because we use them everyday, but that we are typically not able to notice until they have been clarified for us.

Several caveats are in order. First, nothing I have argued means that the post-positivist model of theory recommended by Carroll is of no help to film scholars. For as I have already acknowledged, cinema, like any humanistic phenomenon, is shaped in profound ways by the natural universe. Consider the following example of a cinematic norm: those stylistic conventions, such as staging the most important information in the center of the frame, or using motion or light to draw the viewer's attention to information in part of the frame, that occur in filmmaking practices from a wide variety of nations, cultures, and periods. The fact that these conventions are universally used by filmmakers probably has a lot to do with universal features of human perception that are, in part, innate. If a film scholar wanted to go beyond acknowledging the way these perceptual features shape these stylistic conventions to explaining their nature and behavior, he or she would be well advised to employ the best method available for explaining natural phenomena, which for most is the post-positivist model of theory recommended by Carroll.

However, it should be pointed out that all that such theorizing can do is explain the natural constraints on the use of stylistic conventions, not why a specific group of filmmakers actually uses, or does not use, these conventions in a specific situation. To understand the latter, the film scholar has to undertake a traditional humanistic investigation into the *intentions* of the group of filmmakers – into the specific historical context in which they are using these conventions, how they understand their use, and the reasons they have for using the stylistic conventions that they do. Such a humanistic investigation has no place, of course, in the natural sciences – there are no *reasons* for the blind movements of matter in space to be investigated. As P. M. S. Hacker puts it:

> The behavior of man has to be *understood*, and sometimes *interpreted*, in a sense in which the behavior of inanimate nature and much of animal behavior do not. . . . A man raises his hand and moves it back and forth: the movement can be described and explained physiologically and neurophysiologically. But such hand movements may be an act of greeting, or warning or beckoning. It may be signaling that a run [in cricket] has been scored, it may be part of the activity of conducting an orchestra, or part of an explanation of what "waving" means – and doubtless many other things too. Making a mark on a piece of paper can be described physically and neurophysiologically, but whether making a mark on a piece of paper is writing one's name or something else, and whether the writing of one's name is signing a letter, a cheque, a contract, or a will, inserting a name in a book one owns or dedicating to a friend a book one has written, all these and much else too requires reference to the endless rules, conventions, and institutions of social life, which are not reducible to anything sub-normative, and are products of social life at particular historical times.[15]

Nor does what I have argued rule out employing other natural scientific methods. A good example is the use of statistical analysis in film history.[16] Just as statistical analysis is used in order to make generalizations about tennis – the percentage of first serves in, speed of service, number of unforced errors, and so on – so too it has been used by Barry Salt, Bordwell, and others to make generalizations about cinema, such as the average length of shots during certain periods in certain group styles. However, while the method of statistical analysis may enable many important generalizations about cinema, as it does in the study of history, economics, and society, such generalizations are not akin to the explanatory principles discovered by natural scientific theorizing. For, once again, in order to understand the generalities about cinema revealed by statistics, such as the average length of shots, further humanistic investigation is required into the *intentions* behind their use – the specific historical conditions under which specific shot lengths are used, the ways in which filmmakers understand their use, and their reasons for using them. Again, such an investigation has no place in the natural sciences – there are no intentions behind gravity (unless you believe in a divinely ordered cosmos).

The distinction between the methods of clarification and theory also means that, in principle at least, our answers to questions about the cinema's internal norms are not fallible and do not need improving upon in the future. They are measured instead by how well they make sense of the norms they seek to clarify. For unlike the explanatory principles governing natural phenomena, the norms that govern the cinema or a game such as tennis are visible. If they were not, we would not be able to learn about them or use them. If, for example, the distinction between fiction and non-fiction – like the causal connection between the "ventromedial prefrontal region" of the "frontal lobe" of the human brain and normal decision-making – was hidden from us and was therefore something we needed to make fallible hypotheses about in order to find out about, we would not be able to use it in the first place. We would not currently know how to distinguish between fiction and non-fiction in practice. Potentially, therefore, we can clarify once and for all the distinction that we currently operate with between fiction and non-fiction, because it will consist of a clarification of something we already know and use.

Of course, the distinction between fiction and non-fiction may change over time in subtle and not so subtle ways, just like any conceptual distinction, thereby necessitating that we clarify it anew. But new clarifications are not *better* than their predecessors. Rather, they are clarifications of *different* conceptual distinctions, of practices in which the distinction between fiction and non-fiction is drawn differently. Similarly, the game of tennis may have new rules added to it, and any overview of the rules of tennis would have to be revised to take these new rules into consideration. But such an overview would not be better than its predecessors. Rather, it would be an overview of a different game – a new, modified tennis.

None of what I have argued here is enough, probably, to change the mind of somebody committed to theoretical explanations of literature and the arts. Theory enjoys too much prestige in the humanities, and too many academic careers and institutions are now dependent on it to do that. Furthermore, traditional humanistic methods, including the method I have recommended in this paper – clarifying what lies open to view but that is not necessarily noticeable until pointed out – have been widely denigrated. Since the 1960s, humanistic scholars have increasingly felt that such methods are inadequate if not misguided without theoretical explanations. Although they have typically failed to formulate their theories with the dialectical rigor of natural scientific theories, they have, like the natural scientific theorist, attempted to use theory to reveal a variety of hidden explanatory principles putatively governing literature and the arts – the unconscious desires and drives motivating all human behavior postulated by psychoanalysis; the infinite deferral of meaning within all forms of meaning postulated by Deconstruction; the inference from incomplete perceptual cues underlying all comprehension postulated by constructive cognitive psychology, and so on. If I am correct in this paper, then in as much as these theories purport to make discoveries about the internal, normative dimension of cinema, they are misguided. For, to repeat, the internal norms that constitute cinema (or any other humanistic phenomenon) must, by definition, be ones we already know and use. They cannot be hidden, awaiting discovery by a theory.

To possibly change the minds of contemporary scholars about theory, the fully fledged philosophy of the humanities called for by von Wright is necessary, one that will flesh out in more detail the interrelated distinctions between internal and external, and the methods of clarification and theory, that I have labored to illuminate here, and that might point to other features of humanistic subject matter that require other methods and forms of explanation different from the natural sciences. But even if these distinctions are shown ultimately to be spurious, it is, I believe, crucial that we examine carefully whether there are such distinctions to be made. For without doing so, we cannot know whether the method favored over the last forty years in disciplines that study literature and the arts is a logically appropriate one for explaining humanistic subject matter. If we undertake such an examination, we may find that, at least in answering some questions about literature and the arts, theory is of no help to us at all.

NOTES

An earlier version of this paper was presented at the Society for Cinema Studies conference in 1999 at a panel I chaired, titled "Cinema Studies after Cognitivism: Science in the Humanities." Another version was published in the on-line journal *The Journal of Moving Image Studies* 1, no. 1 (2001) (<http://www.uca.edu/org/ccsmi/journal/issue1_table_contents.htm>)

1 For anecdotal evidence, see David Weddle, "Lights, Camera, Action. Marxism, Semiotics, Narratology. Film School Isn't What It Used To Be, One Father Discovers," *Los Angeles Times*, 13 July 2003. I thank Federico Windhausen for alerting me to this article.

2 As David Bordwell has argued, film theorists on the whole have simply used theories to generate premises for interpreting films. In other words, the traditional humanistic method of interpretation has remained in place, but disguised as theory. See Bordwell, *Making Meaning: Inference and Rhetoric in the Interpretation of Cinema* (Cambridge, Mass.: Harvard University Press, 1989), pp. 4–6.

3 For an overview of these debates, see P. M. S. Hacker, "Wittgenstein and the Autonomy of Humanistic Understanding," in *Wittgenstein, Theory and the Arts*, ed. Richard Allen and Malcolm Turvey (London: Routledge, 2001).

4 Edward O. Wilson, *Consilience: The Unity of Knowledge* (New York: Alfred A. Knopf, Inc., 1988); Stephen Jay Gould, *The Hedgehog, The Fox, and the Magister's Pox: Mending the Gap between Science and the Humanities* (New York: Harmony Books, 2003).

5 Noël Carroll, "Prospects for Film Theory: A Personal Assessment," in *Post-Theory: Reconstructing Film Studies*, ed. Carroll and David Bordwell (Madison: University of Wisconsin Press, 1996), p. 59. [See also this volume, ch. 1.] Hereafter cited in the text.

6 G. H. von Wright, "Humanism and the Humanities," in *The Tree of Knowledge and Other Essays* (Leiden: E. J. Brill, 1993), p. 164. Richard Allen and I make this argument in more detail in the introduction to our anthology, *Wittgenstein, Theory and the Arts*.

7 David Bordwell, *Narration in the Fiction Film* (Madison: University of Wisconsin Press, 1985), p. 39.

8 Murray Smith, *Engaging Characters: Fiction, Emotion, and the Cinema* (Oxford: Clarendon Press, 1995).

9 There are, of course, other reasons that film theories, like theories in general, are accepted in the absence of sustained empirical research. For example, theories are often appealing because they reduce a wide variety of phenomena to an easily comprehensible, single concept – for instance "unconscious desire" in the case of Freudian psychoanalysis, "inference from incomplete perceptual data" in the case of constructivist cognitive psychology. Wittgenstein, borrowing from Goethe, called such concepts *Urphanomen* in order to diagnose their appeal. See Jacques Bouveresse, *Wittgenstein Reads Freud: The Myth of the Unconscious* (Princeton, N.J.: Princeton University Press, 1995), pp. 49–50.

10 I am borrowing this example from Antonio R. Damasio, *Descartes' Error: Emotion, Reason, and the Human Brain* (New York: Avon Books, 1994), chapter 2.

11 Charles Taylor elucidates this distinction in a number of works, including "Cognitive Psychology," in his *Philosophical Papers*, vol. 1 (Cambridge: Cambridge University Press, 1985), pp. 187–91.

12 The following discussion is indebted to P. M. S. Hacker, *Insight and Illusion: Themes in the Philosophy of Wittgenstein* (Oxford: Oxford University Press, 1972; revised 1986), pp. 185–93.

13 Oswald Hanfling, "Wittgenstein on Language, Art and Humanity," in *Wittgenstein, Theory and the Arts*, pp. 89–90.

14 David Bordwell, *Ozu and the Poetics of Cinema* (Princeton, N.J.: Princeton University Press, 1988).

15 P. M. S. Hacker, "Wittgenstein and the Autonomy of Humanistic Understanding," p. 68.

16 I am indebted to Murray Smith for this example.

3

Philosophy of Film as the Creation of Concepts

Gilles Deleuze

Having an Idea in Cinema

I, too, would like to pose some questions. Pose them to you and to myself. They would be in this vein: What exactly do you, who do cinema, do? And for me: What exactly do I do when I do, or hope to do, philosophy?

I could pose the question otherwise: What is having an idea in cinema? If one does or wants to do cinema, what does having an idea mean? What happens when one says: "Wait, I have an idea"? For, on the one hand, everyone clearly knows that having an idea is an event that rarely takes place; it is a sort of celebration, very uncommon. And then, on the other hand, having an idea is not a general thing. One

2 ■ "Parisians in a traffic jam as they flee the city on the weekend," from *Week End*.

does not have an idea in general. An idea – like the one who has the idea – is already dedicated to this or that domain. It is sometimes an idea in painting, sometimes an idea in fiction, sometimes an idea in philosophy, sometimes an idea in science. And it is certainly not the same thing that can have all that. Ideas must be treated as potentials that are already engaged in this or that mode of expression and inseparable from it, so much so that I cannot say that I have an idea in general. According to the techniques that I know, I can have an idea in a given domain, an idea in cinema or rather an idea in philosophy.

What is having an idea in something?

So I begin again with the principle that I do philosophy and that you do cinema. Given this, it would be too easy to say that since philosophy is prepared to reflect on anything at all, why wouldn't it reflect on cinema? This is ridiculous. Philosophy is not made for reflecting on anything at all. In treating philosophy as a power of "reflecting on," much would seem to be accorded to it when in fact everything is taken from it. This is because no one needs philosophy for reflecting. Only filmmakers or cinema critics, or even those who like cinema, can effectively reflect on cinema. These people have no need of philosophy in order to reflect on cinema. The idea that mathematicians would need philosophy to reflect on mathematics is comical. If philosophy had to serve as a means of reflecting on something, it would have no reason to exist. If philosophy exists, it is because it has its own content.

What is the content of philosophy?

It is very simple: philosophy is a discipline that is just as creative and inventive as any other discipline, and it entails creating or even inventing concepts. And concepts do not exist ready-made in the sky waiting for a philosopher to seize them. Concepts must be made. To be sure, they are not made just like that. It's not that one just says one day, "Look, I'm going to invent such and such a concept," no more than a painter says one day, "Look, I'm going to make a painting like this," or a filmmaker, "Look, I'm going to make such and such a film!" There must be a necessity, as much in philosophy as elsewhere, for if not there is nothing at all. A creator is not a being who works for pleasure. A creator does only what he or she absolutely needs to do. The fact remains that this necessity – which, if it exists, is a very complex thing – makes a philosopher (and here, I at least know what the concerns of the philosopher are) propose to invent, to create, concepts and not to concern himself or herself with reflecting, even on cinema.

I say that I do philosophy, which is to say that I try to invent concepts. What if I say, to you who do cinema: What do you do?

What you invent are not concepts – which are not your concern – but blocks of movements/duration. If one puts together a block of movements/duration, perhaps one does cinema. It is not a matter of invoking a story or of contesting one. Everything has a story. Philosophy tells stories as well. Stories with concepts. Cinema tells stories with blocks of movements/duration. Painting invents entirely different types of blocks. These are neither blocks of concepts nor blocks of movements/duration, but blocks of lines/colors. Music invents other types of blocks, equally specific. Beside all this, science is no less creative. I don't really see oppositions between the sciences and the arts.

If I ask a scientist what he or she does, the answer is that the scientist also invents. He or she does not discover – discovery exists, but it is not what defines scientific activity as such – but rather creates just as much as an artist. It is not complicated: a scientist is someone who invents or creates functions. And the scientist is the only one. A scientist as such has nothing to do with concepts. On the one hand, it is precisely – and fortunately – for this that there is philosophy. On the other hand, there is one thing that only a scientist knows how to do: invent and create functions. What is a function? There is a function as soon as at least two wholes are put into fixed correspondence. The fundamental notion of science – and not just of late but for a long time – is the notion of the whole. A whole has nothing to do with a concept. As soon as you put wholes into fixed correlation, you obtain functions and can say, "I do science."

If anyone can speak to anyone else – if a filmmaker can speak to a scientist, if a scientist can have something to say to a philosopher and vice versa – it is according to and by function of each one's creative activity. It is not that talk of creation took place – creation, to the contrary, is something very solitary – but it is in the name of my creation that I have something to say to someone. If I lined up all these disciplines that are defined by their creative activity, I would say that there is a limit common to all of them. The limit common to all these series of inventions – inventions of functions, inventions of blocks of movements/duration, inventions of concepts – is space-time. If all the disciplines communicate together, it is on the level of that which never emerges for itself, but which is, as it were, *engaged* in every creative discipline, and this is the constitution of space-times.

An example of a cinematographic idea is the famous sight-sound dissociation in the relatively recent cinema of Hans-Jürgen Syberberg, the Straubs, and Marguerite Duras, to take the best-known cases. What is common to these, and in what sense is this disjunction of the visual and the auditory a properly cinematic idea? Why could this not take place in theater? Or at least if this happened in theater, if the theater found the means, then one can say without exception that the theater borrowed it from cinema. There is nothing necessarily wrong with this, but the operation of disjunction between sight and sound, between the visual and the auditory, is just the sort of cinematographic idea that would respond to the question. What, for example, is having an idea in cinema?

[. . .]

Cinema and the Philosophy of Film

We can now summarize the constitution of this time-image in modern cinema, and the new signs that it implies or initiates. There are many possible transformations, almost imperceptible passages, and also combinations between the movement-image and the time-image. It cannot be said that one is more important than the other, whether more beautiful or more profound. All that can be said is that the movement-image does not give us a time-image. Nevertheless, it does give us many things in connection with it. On one hand, the movement-image constitutes time in its empirical form, the course of time: a successive present in an extrinsic relation of before and after, so that the past is a former present, and the future a present to come. Inadequate reflection would lead us to conclude from this that the cinematographic image is necessarily in the present. But this ready-made idea, disastrous for any understanding of cinema, is less the fault of the movement-image than of an over-hasty reflection. For, on the other hand, the movement-image gives rise to an image *of* time which is distinguished from it by excess or default, over or under the present as empirical progression: in this case, time is no longer measured by movement, but is itself the number or measure of movement (metaphysical representation). This number in turn has two aspects, which we saw in the first volume: it is the minimum unity of time as interval of movement or the totality of time as maximum of movement in the universe. The subtle and the sublime. But, from either aspect, time is distinguished in this way from movement only as indirect representation. Time as progression derives from the movement-image or from successive shots. But time as unity or as totality depends on montage which still relates it back to movement or to the succession of shots. This is why the movement-image is fundamentally linked to an indirect representation of time, and does not give us a direct presentation of it, that is, does not give us a time-image. The only direct presentation, then, appears in music. But in modern cinema, by contrast, the time-image is no longer empirical, nor metaphysical; it is "transcendental" in the sense that Kant gives this word: time is out of joint and presents itself in the pure state. The time-image does not imply the absence of movement (even though it often includes its increased scarcity) but it implies the reversal of the subordination; it is no longer time which is subordinate to movement; it is movement which subordinates itself to time. It is no longer time which derives from movement, from its norm and its corrected aberrations; it is movement as *false movement*, as aberrant movement which now depends on time. The time-image has become direct, just as time has discovered new aspects, as movement has become aberrant in essence and not by accident, as montage has taken on a new sense, and as a so-called modern cinema has been constituted post-war. However close its relations with classical cinema, modern cinema asks the question: what are the new forces at work in the image, and the new signs invading the screen?

[. . .]

The so-called classical image had to be considered on two axes. These two axes were the co-ordinates of the brain: on the one hand, the images were linked or extended according to laws of association, of continuity, resemblance, contrast, or opposition; on the other hand, associated images were internalized in a whole as concept (integration), which was in turn continually externalized in associable or extendable images (differentiation). This is why the whole remained open and changing, at the same time as a set of images was always taken from a larger set. This was the double aspect of the movement-image, defining the out-of-field. [. . .]

The modern image initiates the reign of "incommensurables" or irrational cuts: this is to say that the cut no longer forms part of one or the other image, of one or the other sequence that it separates and divides. It is on this condition that the succession or sequence becomes a series, in the sense that we have just analyzed. The interval is set free, the interstice becomes irreducible and stands on its own. The first consequence is that the images are no longer linked by rational cuts, but are relinked on to irrational cuts. We gave Godard's series as an example, but they can be found everywhere, notably in Resnais (the moment around which everything turns and repasses in *Je t'aime je t'aime*, is a typical irrational cut). By relinkage must be understood, not a second linkage which would come and add itself on, but a mode of original and specific linkage, or rather a specific connection between de-linked images. There are no longer grounds for talking about a real or possible extension capable of constituting an external world: we have ceased to believe in it, and the image is cut off from the external world. But the internalization or integration of self-awareness in a whole has no less disappeared: the relinkage takes place through parcelling, whether it is a matter of the construction of series in Godard, or of the transformations of sheets in Resnais (relinked parcellings). This is why thought, as power which has not always existed, is born from an outside more distant than any external world, and, as power which does not yet exist, confronts an inside, an unthinkable or unthought, deeper than any internal world. In the second place, there is no longer any movement of internalization or externalization, integration or differentiation, but a confrontation of an outside and an inside independent of distance, this thought outside itself and this un-thought within thought. This is the unsummonable in Welles, the undecidable in Resnais, the inexplicable in the Straubs, the impossible in Marguerite Duras, the irrational in Syberberg. The brain has lost its Euclidean co-ordinates, and now emits other signs. The direct time-image effectively has as noosigns the irrational cut between non-linked (but always relinked) images, and the absolute contact between non-totalizable, asymmetrical outside and inside. We move with ease from one to the other, because the outside and the inside are the two sides of the limit as irrational cut, and because the latter, no longer forming part of any sequence, itself appears as an autonomous outside which necessarily provides itself with an inside.

What Is the Nature
of Film?

Introduction

One of the first tasks that a philosopher concerned with a specific discipline faces is that of defining the object of her study. Part II brings together readings in which philosophers of film attempt to specify exactly what film is.

When the question of the nature of film was first raised by theorists of film, it was intertwined with a related issue that was not always kept distinct from it. Because of its origins in such disreputable places as peep shows and vaudeville – early films were screened in such venues – film was often denied the status of an art form. As a result, early theorists who proffered definitions of film did so as part of a larger strategy of assuring film its rightful place alongside the other, more traditional arts.

Hugo Münsterberg was a professor of philosophy at Harvard University when he published his path-breaking study, *The Photoplay*, in 1916. Münsterberg was particularly worried that film would not be treated as an art form in its own right but only as a means of disseminating theatrical dramas to a wider audience. For this reason, his account presents a variety of different features of film as an artistic medium that distinguish it from the theater. What particularly interests Münsterberg are the formal devices that films use to tell their narratives – such relatively straightforward techniques as the close-up and editing. As he points out, the use of these devices distinguishes film from the theater, although the latter can attempt to mimic film's narrative techniques. It is these innovative structures, Münsterberg claims, that account for film being its own unique art form.

What is particularly relevant to contemporary discussions of film is Münsterberg's account of how viewers understand these technical devices. He analyzes each of them as an objectification of a specific mental function, so that viewers are already familiar with them prior to encountering films. To choose just one example: a close-up is for Münsterberg just a visual analogue of the act of paying attention to one feature of our experience. As such, viewers can nearly automatically understand its role in a film.

This claim marks Münsterberg as a precursor to recent cognitive philosophers of film who also see people's ability to understand film as based on the use of cognitive capacities acquired in the course of normal life.

Rudolph Arnheim, the famous psychologist of art, emigrated to the United States from Germany to avoid persecution by the Nazis. Our selection comes from his book, *Film as Art*, originally published in German in 1933. Arnheim is writing shortly after the birth of the "talkie." Alan Crosland's 1927 film, *The Jazz Singer*, starring Al Jolson, brought sound to the movies for the first time, at least in the form of a simultaneous soundtrack that allowed audiences to hear actors speaking and singing at the same time as they watched them perform. In reflecting on this technological achievement, Arnheim takes a surprising stand. He argues that the introduction of the simultaneous soundtrack into films marks an artistic disaster. The reason for this, Arnheim argues, is that the mixing of image and sound that constitutes the talkie lacks the unity necessary for significant forms of art. In making this assertion, he relies on Gotthold Ephraim Lessing's view, made in *Laocoon: An Essay on the Limits of Painting and Poetry* (1766), that arts that stick to a single medium are superior to those that attempt to mix them.

André Bazin, arguably the most influential theorist of film, was not an academic but a journalist and general advocate for film. Among other achievements, he co-founded the journal *Cahiers du Cinéma*, the journal that ushered in the French New Wave. The impact of his thinking on filmmakers and film theorists has been enormous. Bazin's central contention is that film, because of its basis in photography, is an inherently realistic medium. He saw photography as making a revolutionary impact on painting, for a photograph could present the actual world to its viewers in a way that no painting could. Because they also depicted motion, films could attain an even higher degree of realism than photographs. For this reason, Bazin championed film as achieving the age-old dream of presenting a world whose realism could rival that of the real one.

On the basis of this ontological thesis about the nature of the cinema, Bazin is an advocate for the style of filmmaking that he also calls *realism*. Because stylistic realism eschews editing and allows the viewer to focus undisturbed on the scene that is filmed, Bazin sees it as more closely in touch with the medium's nature than *montage*, the style that emphasizes editing. In supporting this claim, Bazin equivocates between realism as an ontological fact about film and as a specific film style. Nonetheless, his rejection of the sound–silent dichotomy as central to film history is an important insight.

Kendall L. Walton, professor of philosophy at the University of Michigan, is one of the most influential contemporary philosophers of art. Walton wants to defend realism as an ontological feature of film and photography, but he is critical of Bazin's inconsistencies and overstatements. He therefore attempts to give a clear and precise statement of what realism is. For Walton, film and photography are *transparent* artistic media. What this means is that the objects depicted in a film or photograph are not merely representations, as is the case in a painting. As Walton puts it, we actually *see* the objects that are there in a photograph, such as his great-grandfather, and not merely an artistic representation of them. He offers a number of fascinating considerations in support of his view that it is worth focusing on in detail.

Walton's defense of realism as an ontological feature of film has sparked a great deal of controversy. Many philosophers of film have attacked his claims, though not all reject the attempt to support a realistic understanding of film. Whatever you may think of his contribution, it has advanced the discussion of realism among contemporary philosophers of film.

As you have been thinking about film as an artistic medium, you may naturally have been focusing on the fiction film. However, there are many other traditions of filmmaking besides that of the fiction film, including documentaries and art films. One of the features that many theorists have used to distinguish non-fiction from fiction films is the former's concern for truth, for accurately representing the world as it is. In his selection, written specially for this volume, Trevor Ponech denies the assertion that non-fictional cinematic works are inherently realist, i.e., that their aim is to convey information or convince their audiences of the truth of certain beliefs. To the contrary, he asserts that many works of this type are primarily works of art that should be judged not by their truthfulness but by their artistic achievement. Even though Ponech argues that non-fiction films should be judged in this way, he argues that their epistemic virtues can contribute to their value as works of art. For this reason, he praises Errol Morris's *The Thin Blue Line* (1988) while criticizing Leni Riefenstahl's *Triumph of the Will* (1934).

Ponech's discussion rounds out our consideration of the nature of film. By drawing our attention to traditions other than that of the mainstream fiction film, Ponech reminds us to be inclusive in our ruminations about film's nature.

Study Questions

1. Münsterberg argues that film involves the objectification of specific mental processes. What are the mental processes that he discusses and what film technique does he see as objectifying them?
2. Münsterberg contends that film is a distinct art form from the theater. What is the basis for this claim? Do you agree with it? Why or why not?
3. Arnheim believes that the silent film is more artistically worthwhile than the sound film. What is the basis for this claim? Do you see any merit in it?
4. In opposition to Arnheim, Bazin argues that the distinction between silent and sound films does not represent a fundamental distinction in the history of filmmaking. What is his reason for making this assertion? How does he back it up? Do you agree with Bazin or Arnheim on this point? Why or why not?
5. Explain the distinction between realism as an ontological characteristic of film and as a film style. Bazin supports both. Do you? Why or why not?
6. Walton likens cameras to other optical devices like telescopes. Why does he do so? Do you accept his claims about cameras?
7. Bazin and Walton think that there is something automatic about photography. Why is this important to their respective arguments? Do you agree with them? Why or why not?

8. What is Ponech's definition of non-fiction? How does he criticize Grierson's theory?
9. Why does Ponech think that *The Thin Blue Line* is a great work of art? Why is he critical of *Triumph of the Will*? Do you agree with his view of the relationship between the films' worldviews and their artistic success?
10. Based on your readings, do you think it is important to give a definition of film? What problems might there be in developing an adequate one?

4

Defining the Photoplay

Hugo Münsterberg

We have now reached the point at which we can knot together all our threads, the psychological and the aesthetic ones. If we do so, we come to the true thesis of this whole book. Our aesthetic discussion showed us that it is the aim of art to isolate a significant part of our experience in such a way that it is separate from our practical life and is in complete agreement within itself. Our aesthetic satisfaction results from this inner agreement and harmony, but, in order that we may feel such agreement of the parts, we must enter with our own impulses into the will of every element, into the meaning of every line and color and form, every word and tone and note. Only if everything is full of such inner movement can we really enjoy the harmonious cooperation of the parts. The means of the various arts, we saw, are the forms and methods by which this aim is fulfilled. They must be different for every material. Moreover, the same material may allow very different methods of isolation and elimination of the insignificant and reinforcement of that which contributes to the harmony. If we ask now what are the characteristic means by which the photoplay succeeds in overcoming reality, in isolating a significant dramatic story, and in presenting it so that we enter into it and yet keep it away from our practical life and enjoy the harmony of the parts, we must remember all the results to which our psychological discussion in the first part of the book has led us.

We recognized there that the photoplay, incomparable in this respect with the drama, gave us a view of dramatic events which was completely shaped by the inner movements of the mind. To be sure, the events in the photoplay happen in the real space with its depth. But the spectator feels that they are not presented in the three dimensions of the outer world, that they are flat pictures which only the mind molds into plastic things. Again, the events are seen in continuous movement, and yet the pictures break up the movement into a rapid succession of instantaneous impressions. We do not see the objective reality, but a product of our own mind which binds the pictures together. But much stronger differences came to light when we turned to the processes of attention, of memory, of imagination, of suggestion, of division of interest, and of emotion. The attention turns to detailed points in the outer world and ignores everything else; the photoplay is doing exactly this when, in the close-up, a detail is enlarged and everything else disappears. Memory breaks into present events by bringing up pictures of the past; the photoplay is doing this by its frequent cut-backs when pictures of events long past flit between those of the present. The imagination anticipates the future or overcomes reality by fancies and dreams, the photoplay is doing all this more richly than any chance imagination would succeed in doing. But chiefly, through our division of interest, our mind is drawn hither and thither. We think of events which run parallel in different places. The photoplay can show in inter-twined scenes everything which our mind embraces. Events in three or four or five regions of the world can be woven together into one complex action. Finally, we saw that every shade of feeling and emotion which fills the spectator's mind can mold the scenes in the photoplay until they appear the embodiment of our feelings. In every one of these aspects, the photoplay succeeds in doing what the drama of the theater does not attempt.

If this is the outcome of aesthetic analysis on the one side, of psychological research on the other, we need only combine the results of both into a unified principle: *the photoplay tells us the human story by overcoming the forms of the outer world, namely, space, time, and causality, and by adjusting the events to the forms of the inner world, namely, attention, memory, imagination, and emotion.*

We shall gain our orientation most directly if once more, under this point of view, we compare the photoplay with the performance on the theater stage. We shall not enter into a discussion of the character of the regular theater and its drama. We take this for granted. Everybody knows that highest art form which the Greeks created and which, from Greece, has spread over Asia, Europe, and America. In tragedy and in comedy from ancient times to Ibsen, Rostand, Hauptmann, and Shaw, we recognize one common purpose and one common form for which no further commentary is needed. How does the photoplay differ from a theater performance? We insisted that every work of art must be somehow separated from our sphere of practical interests. The theater is no exception. The structure of the theater itself, the framelike form of the stage, the difference of light between stage and house, the stage setting and costuming, all inhibit in the audience the possibility of taking the action on the stage to be real life. Stage managers have sometimes tried the experiment of reducing those differences, for instance, keeping the audience also in a fully lighted hall, and they always had to discover how much the dramatic effect was reduced because the feeling of distance from reality was weakened. The photoplay and the theater in this respect are evidently alike. The screen, too, suggests from the very start the complete unreality of the events.

But each further step leads us to remarkable differences between the stage play and the film play. In every respect, the film play is further away from the physical reality than the drama, and in every respect, this greater distance from the physical world brings it nearer to the mental world. The stage shows us living men. It is not the real Romeo and not the real Juliet, and yet the actor and the actress have the ringing voices of true people, breathe like them, have living colors like them, and fill physical space like them. What is left in the photoplay? The voice has been stilled: the photoplay is a dumb show. Yet we must not forget that this alone is a step away from reality which has often been taken in the midst of the dramatic world. Whoever knows the history of the theater is aware of the tremendous role which the pantomime has played in the development of mankind. From the old half-religious pantomimic and suggestive dances out of which the beginnings of the real drama grew to the fully religious pantomimes of medieval ages, and further on, to many silent mimic elements in modern performances, we find a continuity of conventions which make the pantomime almost the real background of all dramatic development. [. . .]

3 ■ "The use of close-up shots is a distinguishing feature of film as an artistic medium," from *Birth of a Nation*.

Moreover, the student of a modern pantomime cannot overlook a characteristic difference between the speechless performance on the stage and that of the actors of a photoplay. The expression of the inner states, the whole system of gestures, is decidedly different, and here we might say that the photoplay stands nearer to life than the pantomime. Of course, the photoplayer must somewhat exaggerate the natural expression. The whole rhythm and intensity of his gestures must be more marked than it would be with actors who accompany their movements by spoken words and who express the meaning of their thoughts and feelings by the content of what they say. Nevertheless, the photoplayer uses the regular channels of mental discharge. He acts simply as a very emotional person might act. But the actor who plays in a pantomime cannot be satisfied with that. He is expected to add something which is entirely unnatural, namely a kind of artificial demonstration of his emotions. He must not only behave like an angry man, but he must behave like a man who is consciously interested in his anger and wants to demonstrate it to others. He exhibits his emotions for the spectators. He really acts theatrically for the benefit of the bystanders. If he did not try to do so, his means of conveying a rich story and a real conflict of human passions would be too meager. The photoplayer, with the rapid changes of scenes, has other possibilities of conveying his intentions. He must not yield to the temptation to play a pantomime on the screen, or he will seriously injure the artistic quality of the reel.

The really decisive distance from bodily reality, however, is created by the substitution of the actor's picture for the actor himself. Lights and shades replace the manifoldness of color effects and mere perspective must furnish the suggestion of depth. We traced it when we discussed the psychology of kinematoscopic perception. But we must not put the emphasis on the wrong point. The natural tendency might be to lay the chief stress on the fact that those people in the photoplay do not stand before us in flesh and blood. The essential point is rather that we are conscious of the flatness of the picture. If we were to see the actors of the stage in a mirror, it would also be a reflected image which we perceive. We should not really have the actors themselves in our straight line of vision; and yet this image would appear to us equivalent to the actors themselves, because it would contain all the depth of the real stage. The film picture is such a reflected rendering of the actors. The process which leads from the living men to the screen is more complex than a mere reflection in a mirror, but, in spite of the complexity in the transmission, we do, after all, see the real actor in the picture. The photograph is absolutely different from those pictures which a clever draughtsman has sketched. In the photoplay we see the actors themselves, and the decisive factor which makes the impression different from seeing real men is not that we see the living persons through the medium of photographic reproduction, but that this reproduction shows them in a flat form. The bodily space has been eliminated. We said once before that stereoscopic arrangements could reproduce somewhat this plastic form also. Yet this would seriously interfere with the character of the photoplay. We need there this overcoming of the depth, we want to have it as a picture only and yet as a picture which strongly suggests to us the actual depth of the real world. We want to keep the interest in the plastic world and want to be aware of the depth in which the persons move, but our direct object of perception must be without the depth. That idea of space which forces on us most strongly the idea of heaviness, solidity and substantiality must be replaced by the light flitting immateriality.

But the photoplay sacrifices not only the space values of the real theater; it disregards no less its order of time. The theater presents its plot in the time order of reality. It may interrupt the continuous flow of time without neglecting the conditions of the dramatic art. There may be twenty years between the third and the fourth act, inasmuch as the dramatic writer must select those elements spread over space and time which are significant for the development of his story. But he is bound by the fundamental principle of real time, that it can move only forward and not backward. Whatever the theater shows us now must come later in the story than that which it showed us in any previous moment. The strict classical demand for complete unity of time does not fit every drama, but a drama would give up its mission if it told us in the third act something which happened before the second act. Of course, there may be a play within a play, and the players on the stage which is set on the stage may play events of old Roman history before the king of France. But this is an enclosure of the past in the present, which corresponds exactly to the actual order of events. The photoplay, on the other hand, does not and must not respect this temporal structure of the physical universe. At any point the photoplay interrupts the series and brings us back to the past. We studied this unique feature of the film art when we spoke of the psychology of memory and imagination. With the full freedom of our fancy, with the whole mobility of our association of ideas, pictures of the past flit through the scenes of the present. Time is left behind. Man becomes boy; today is interwoven with the day before yesterday. The freedom of the mind has triumphed over the unalterable law of the outer world.

[. . .]

But the theater is bound not only by space and time. Whatever it shows is controlled by the same laws of causality which govern nature. This involves a complete continuity of the physical events: no cause without following effect, no effect without preceding cause. This whole natural course is left behind in the play on the screen. The deviation from reality begins with that resolution of the continuous movement which we studied in our psychological discussions. We saw that the impression of movement results from an activity of the mind which binds the separate pictures together. What we actually see is a composite; it is like the movement of a fountain in which every jet is resolved into numberless drops. We feel the play of those drops in their sparkling haste as one continuous stream of water and, yet, are conscious of the myriads of drops, each one separate from the others. This fountainlike spray of pictures has completely overcome the causal world.

In an entirely different form, this triumph over causality appears in the interruption of the events by pictures which belong to another series. We find this whenever the scene suddenly changes. The processes are not carried to their natural consequences. A movement is started, but, before the cause brings its results, another scene has taken its place. What this new scene brings may be an effect for which we saw no causes. But not only the processes are interrupted. The intertwining of the scenes which we have traced in detail is itself such a contrast to causality. It is as if different objects could fill the same space at the same time. It is as if the resistance of the material world had disappeared, and the substances could penetrate one another. In the interlacing of our ideas, we experience this superiority to all physical laws. The theater would not have even the technical means to give us such impressions, but if it had, it would have no right to make use of them, as it would destroy the basis on which the drama is built. We have only another case of the same type in those series of pictures which aim to force a suggestion on our mind. We have spoken of them. A certain effect is prepared by a chain of causes, and yet when the causal result is to appear, the film is cut off. We have the causes without the effect. The villain thrusts with his dagger – but a miracle has snatched away his victim.

While the moving pictures are lifted above the world of space and time and causality and are freed from its bounds, they are certainly not without law. We said before that the freedom with which the pictures replace one another is to a large degree comparable to the sparkling and streaming of the musical tones. The yielding to the play of the mental energies, to the attention and emotion, which is felt in the film pictures, is still more complete in the musical melodies and harmonies in which the tones themselves are merely the expressions of the ideas and feelings and will impulses of the mind. Their harmonies and disharmonies, their fusing and blending, is not controlled by any outer necessity, but by the inner agreement and disagreement of our free impulses. And yet, in this world of musical freedom, everything is completely controlled by aesthetic necessities. No sphere of practical life stands under such rigid rules as the realm of the composer. However bold the musical genius may be, he cannot emancipate himself from the iron rule that his work must show complete unity in itself. All the separate prescriptions which the musical student has to learn are ultimately only the con-sequences of this central demand which music, the freest of the arts, shares with all the others. In the case of the film, too, the freedom from the physical forms of space, time, and causality does not mean any liberation from this aesthetic bondage either. On the contrary, just as music is surrounded by more technical rules than literature, the photoplay must be held together by the aesthetic demands still more firmly than is the drama. The arts which are subordinated to the conditions of space, time, and causality find a certain firmness of structure in these material forms which contain an element of outer connectedness. But where these forms are given up and where the freedom of mental play replaces their outer necessity, everything would fall asunder if the aesthetic unity were disregarded.

This unity is, first of all, the unity of action. The demand for it is the same which we know from the drama. The temptation to neglect it is nowhere greater than in the photoplay where outside matter can so easily be introduced or independent interests developed. It is certainly true for the photoplay, as for every work of art, that nothing has the right to existence in its midst which is not internally needed for the unfolding of the unified action. Wherever two plots are given to us, we receive less by far than if we had only one plot. We leave the sphere of valuable art entirely when a unified action is ruined by mixing it with declamation and propaganda which is not organically interwoven with the action itself. It may be still fresh in memory what an aesthetically intolerable helter-skelter performance was offered to the public in *The Battlecry of Peace*. Nothing can be more injurious to the aesthetic cultivation of the people than such performances, which hold the attention of the spectators by ambitious detail and yet destroy their aesthetic sensibility by a complete disregard of the fundamental principle of art, the demand for unity. But we recognized also that this unity involves complete isolation. We annihilate beauty when we link the artistic creation with practical interests and transform the spectator into a selfishly interested bystander. The scenic background of the play is not presented in order that we decide whether we want to spend our next vacation there. The interior decoration of the rooms is not exhibited as a display for a department store. The men and women who carry out the action of the plot must not be people whom we may meet tomorrow on the street. All the threads of the play must be knotted together in the play itself, and none should be connected with our outside interests. A good photoplay must be isolated and complete in itself like a beautiful melody. It is not an advertisement for the newest fashions.

This unity of action involves unity of characters. It has too often been maintained by those who theorize on the photoplay that the development of character is the special task of the drama, while the photoplay, which lacks words, must be satisfied with types. Probably this is only a reflection of the crude state which most photoplays of today have not outgrown. Internally, there is no reason why the means of the photoplay should not allow a rather subtle depicting of complex character. But the chief demand is that the characters remain consistent, that the action be developed according to inner necessity and that the characters themselves be in harmony with the central idea of the plot. However, as soon as we insist on unity, we have no right to think only of the action which gives the content of the play. We cannot make light of the form. As in music, the melody and rhythms belong together; as in painting, not every color combination suits every subject; and as in poetry, not every stanza would agree with every idea, so the photoplay must bring action and pictorial expression into perfect harmony. But this demand repeats itself in every single picture. We take it for granted that the painter balances perfectly the forms in his painting, groups them so that an internal symmetry can be felt and that the lines and curves and colors blend into a unity. Every single picture of the sixteen thousand which are shown to us in one reel ought to be treated with this respect of the pictorial artist for the unity of the forms.

The photoplay shows us a significant conflict of human actions in moving pictures which, freed from the physical forms of space, time, and causality, are adjusted to the free play of our mental experiences and which reach complete isolation from the practical world through the perfect unity of plot and pictorial appearance.

5

The Artistry of Silent Film

Rudolf Arnheim

The following inquiry was suggested by a feeling of uneasiness that every talking film arouses in the author and that is not appeased by increased acquaintance with the new medium. It is a feeling that something is not right there: that we are dealing with productions which because of intrinsic contradictions of principle are incapable of true existence. Apparently the uneasiness is due to the spectator's attention being torn in two directions. In their attempts to attract the audience, two media are fighting each other instead of capturing it by united effort. Since the two media are striving to express the same matter in a twofold way, a disconcerting coincidence of two voices results, each of which is prevented by the other from telling more than half of what it would like to tell.

[. . .]

For this purpose I set out to investigate the conditions under which, quite in general, works of art can be based upon more than one medium – such as the spoken word, the image in motion, the musical sound – and what the range, nature, and value of such works might be. The result of this necessarily sketchy exploration was then applied to the talking film.

The theater successfully combines image and speech.　The two elements whose rivalry the motion picture cannot reconcile are, of course, image and speech. It is a surprising rivalry, if we remember that in daily life talk rarely keeps us from seeing, or seeing from listening. But as soon as we sit in front of the movie screen we notice such disturbances. Probably we react differently because we are not used to finding in the image of the real world the kind of formal precision that in the work of art presents – by means of the sensory data – the subject and its qualities in a clear-cut, expressive way. Normally we gather from the world that surrounds us little more than vague hints, sufficient for practical orientation. Physical reality shapes and assembles things and events only in approximation of the pure, authentic "ideas" that are at the bottom of the empirical world. The imprecision of a color, the discord in a composition of lines do not necessarily interfere with our perception when we are observing for practical purposes only; and the literary impurity of a sentence may not prevent us from understanding its meaning. Therefore, when in everyday life an unbalanced combination of visual and auditory elements fails to produce discomfort, we need not be surprised either. In the realm of art, on the contrary, the unsure expression of an object, the inconsistency of a movement, a badly put phrase will impair at once the effect, the meaning, the beauty conveyed by the work. This is why a combination of media that has no unity will appear intolerable.

[. . .]

Parallelism of complete and segregated representations. The enrichment and unity that may result in art from the cooperation of several media are not identical with the fusion of all sorts of sense perception that is typical for our way of experiencing the "real" world. Because in art the diversity of the various perceptual media requires separations among them – separations that only a higher unity can overcome.

Obviously it would be senseless and inconceivable to try to fuse visual and auditory elements artistically in the same way in which one sentence is tied to the next, one motion to the other. For instance, the unity that exists in real life between the body and the voice of a person would be valid in a work of art only if there existed between the two components a kinship much more intrinsic than their belonging together biologically. The artist conceives and forms his image of the world through directly perceivable sensory qualities, such as colors, shapes, sounds, movements. The expressive features of these percepts serve to interpret the meaning and character of the subject. The essence of the subject must be manifest in what can be observed directly. On this (lower) level of the sensory phenomena, however, an artistic connection of visual and auditory phenomena is not possible. (One cannot put a sound in a painting!) Such a connection can be made only at a second, higher level, namely, at the level of the so-called expressive qualities. A dark red wine can have the same expression as the dark sound of a violoncello, but no formal connection can be established between the red and the sound as purely perceptual phenomena. At the second level, then, a compounding of elements that derive from disparate sensory realms becomes possible artistically.

Such compounding, however, must respect the segregations established at the lower level. It presupposes, in fact, that in each of the sensory areas concerned a closed and complete structure has been formed on that lower plane – a structure that in its own way and by itself must present the total subject of the work of art. When at the second level the purely material barrier disappears, the elements deriving from the different areas (for instance, the visual and the auditory) must nevertheless preserve the groupings and segregations established at the primary level. On the other hand, they may take advantage of the way they resemble each other or contrast with each other as far as expression is concerned and thus create interrelationships. For instance, all the movements of a group of dancers remain unified among one another and, together, segregated from the accompanying music. Within the musical structure also all sounds are interconnected. But the similarity of the expression conveyed by the patterns of the two sensory areas makes it possible to combine them in one unitary work of art. For example, a certain gesture of one of the dancers may resemble a corresponding musical phrase with regard to expression and meaning . . . just as the gesture of an actor may correspond to the meaning of the sentence he is uttering.

The combination of several means of expression in a work of art provides us with a formal device whose particular virtue lies in that at the second structural level a relationship is established among patterns that are complete, closed, and strictly segregated at the lower or primary level. In addition to the two levels I have mentioned there may be others, higher ones – in fact, there almost always are – but they are less important. One of them concerns the characteristics of the objects represented in the work of art inasmuch as they belong to our real physical world, for example, the practical, material connections between the human body and the human voice. This level is closer to everyday life and the relations created at it are, therefore, more obvious to our common sense. But the kind of connection established at this level between patterns from different perceptual areas is not sufficient to make them homogeneous, fusable, or exchangeable. Their disparity at the primary level is in the way. For what happens at the primary level is binding for the entire work. [. . .]

[. . .]

The conditions for the combination of artistic media. Artistic media combine, I asserted before, as separate and complete structural forms. The theme to be expressed by a song, for instance, is given in the words of the text and again, in another manner, in the sounds of the music. Both elements conform to each other in such a way as to create the unity of the whole, but their separateness remains evident, nevertheless. Their combination resembles a successful marriage, where similarity and adaptation make for unity but where the personality of the two partners remains intact, nevertheless. It does *not* resemble the child that springs from such a marriage, in whom both components are inseparably mixed.

Similarly, in a theatrical performance the visible action and the dialogue must each present the total subject. If there is a gap in one of the two components it cannot be made up by the other. It is the duty of the director to interpret the content of the dialogue for the eyes of the audience through color, shape, and motion, through the appearance and gestures of the actors, through the spatial organization of the setting and the way the bodies move within this space. The visual performance cannot be interrupted, except if the gap serves as a delimiting interval, that is, a caesura, which does not break up the action but is a part of it. The visible action must never be permitted to become inexpressive or empty for the benefit of the dialogue because even the most substantial lines of speech could not make up for such a deficiency: they could not mend a visual gap. In the same way, an interruption of the dialogue can only take the form of an interval; it cannot be justified as a temporary shift from audible to visible action. There can be, of course, a contrapuntal opposition of a rest in the pantomime against a simultaneous exchange of heated retorts in the dialogue, or of a moment of silence against a significant piece of pantomimic action – but only in the sense in which the harmonic play of a piece of music is enriched by the frequent exits and entrances of the various voices or instruments.

The dialogue must be complete. Enough has been said to make it clear that there is little justification for a current fad on the part of some "highbrow" film directors who have the action carried almost entirely by the visual performance on the screen and only here and there add a touch of dialogue to the dramatic development. Such a procedure evidently does not create a parallelism between two complete components, namely, a very dense visual part and a very "porous" auditory one: instead the dialogue is fragmentary; it consists of pieces that are separated by unbridgeable interruptions. The expressed intention of these directors is to have speech emerge, in certain highspots, as a kind of condensation of the visual image. The distinction of the media is entirely neglected, and as a result scraps of speech pop up with a ludicrous surprise effect, out of empty auditory space, in which they float without anchor. The defect cannot be eliminated by filling the stretches of silence with appropriate noises or music; for the example of the song has taught us already that even within the realm of auditory art, music and speech can be combined only when a parallelism between two complete and segregated components – a poem and a melody – is provided. If the dialogue were not dispersed in pieces but collected in large complexes, each of which were a closed and continuous structure, one could at least refer to the great example of Beethoven's *Ninth Symphony*, and the later similar attempt by Mahler, in which at the climax of the composition the instrumental music is completed by human voices so that from that moment on the work proceeds on a broader, more monumental base. However, in the talking film even that device would not help because there still would remain the obstacle of the difference in visual style between the silent scenes and those completed with dialogue.

The practical experience of what goes on in the movie theater would demonstrate to everybody that a true fusion of word and image is impossible if the image on the screen were ever shut off so that the dialogue could try to "take over." The visual action is always complete – at least technically, although not artistically. The complete visual action accompanied by occasional dialogue represents a partial parallelism, not a fusion. The fragmentary nature of the dialogue is the fundamental defect. [. . .]

[. . .]

In comparison, the approach of the more modest craftsmen who work in the studios at the service of the film industry is artistically saner. By their daily contact with their medium they have attained some intuitive understanding of its intrinsic requirements, and for that reason – at least partly – they tend toward the "100 per cent dialogue" film. In these productions, speech accompanies the film throughout its length, more or less without gaps, and in that way fulfills one of the elementary conditions for the compounding of media, namely, parallelism. In the average film of that kind one notices, in addition, an ever more radical curtailment of the means of visual expression as they were developed during the period of the silent movies. This tendency also derives, as I am going to show, from the aesthetic conditions created by the talking film. Even so, the disequilibrium between image and speech is not avoided by this procedure nor does it create artistically valid sound films. Instead, the studio practice moves toward the traditional style of the theater without being ready to renounce the novel charms of the moving picture.

In any case, complete dialogue would be the basic premise for any use of speech in film – an artistically complete and closed word pattern. We need to inquire now whether or not this condition can be met by a technique that would be different in principle from that of the theater.

4 ■ "Sherlock, Jr. (Buster Keaton) aspires to be a detective," from the silent film *Sherlock, Jr.*

Can image and word be combined in a manner different from that of the theater? The specialty of such a new art form might be based on some fundamental difference between theater action and film action, as far as the visual part of the performance is concerned. Commonly it is taken for granted that such a difference does exist and is demonstrated by actual practice. And yet there is no fundamental reason why the distinguishing traits of the film image should be denied to the theater. Unquestionably, the theater as an art form would remain essentially what it is if the flesh-and-blood actor were replaced with his photographic image: the theater performances on television prove it. The theater also could substitute black-and-white for natural color – and, of course, monochrome is no essential characteristic of the movies anyway. The displacement of the entire picture, as produced by traveling shots in film, has recently been obtained also in the theater through rotating stages and similar devices – more modestly, to be sure, but matters of degree count little for distinctions in principle. The modern theater has also used actual film projections, for instance, as backdrops. Granted that in its present form the theater cannot change the distance or the angle of view, nor can it leap from place to place as the film does by means of montage. But here again we merely need to think of television in order to realize that what is technically impossible for the theater as we know it today may be familiar tomorrow.

In this connection we might as well realize that film is art, yes, but not an entirely new and isolated art. The art of the moving image is distinct from that of the static image, as we have it in painting or sculpture. However, it comprises not only the film but also dance and pantomime; and the question is at least debatable whether or not the properties that film derives from the technique of mechanical registration are weightier than the others it shares with dance, pantomime, and therefore also with the theater. One thing seems certain: if one tries to ignore the properties that the film shares with other media – as has been done *ad majorem gloriam* of the movies – one cannot hope correctly to evaluate the art of the film. The art of the moving image is as old as the other arts, it is as old as humanity itself, and the motion picture is but its most recent manifestation. What is more, I would venture to predict that the film will be able to reach the heights of the other arts only when it frees itself from the bonds of photographic reproduction and becomes a pure work of man, namely, as animated cartoon or painting.

There is, then, no difference in principle between the visual action of the theater and the moving image of the film. Therefore, the experiences made with the "enriched image" in the theater can be directly applied to the talking film. What are these experiences? They show that attempts at "enrichment" have quickly turned out to be deviations from serious stage art. When the designer indulges in dazzling contrivances and the director crowds the stage with action, the visual performance distracts from the words of the playwright rather than interprets them.

Of course, this contention presupposes that the stage performance has the purpose of providing the dialogue with its due position in the foreground while leaving to the image only a secondary, supporting function. We need now to explore the possibility of other artistic forms that might do without this presupposition.

The simpler the wording of the dialogue, the less likely the audience will be kept from following the dramatic conversation attentively. Now a work of dramatic literature, just as any other work of art, can assume any degree of density – from the intricate and heavy thought of a Shakespeare, who presents our receptive powers with almost insoluble tasks even when there is nothing visual at all to distract us from the recital (as, for example, in radio performances), to the loosest lines of plainest concreteness. The simpler forms of dialogue – which might not be less valuable literarily – could receive a richer visual presentation without suffering from it. Perhaps the history of literature offers few examples of such simple dialogue, but conceivably this could change if the playwright got used to the idea of seeing his works completed by a richer stage action. In fact, perhaps the writer himself might undertake the task of working in both media, that is, of creating by himself the twofold total work. Let us assume this happened and the scales tipped gradually in favor of the visual action: we should then arrive first at works in which the audible and the visible were in balance, and finally at others in which the picture predominated whereas the dialogue would accept a secondary function, similar to that reserved nowadays for the pantomimic action on the theater stage.

Would productions of this latter kind belong to a new and autochthonous species of art? Could a mere quantitative shift of the components give birth to a new art form? The performance of a large group of dancers may be accompanied by nothing but one flute or, conversely, the solo of one dancer may be accompanied by a whole symphony orchestra . . . are we dealing with different art forms? There would be no particular hurry in deciding whether we were faced with a mere variety of theater art or rather with a special form all of its own – if only the indicated shift of elements would give us new ways of representing our life, new ways of saying things for which so far there is no tongue. All depends now on deciding whether or not the procedure that we have drawn up in theory is capable of life in practice.

[. . .]

Possible advantages of the film dialogue.   We have now worked out some fundamental concepts, which can be useful in judging the talking film. From what I have said it follows that, first of all, there should be a dominant medium. This part would fall to the moving image since predominance of the word would lead to the theater. The question is, then, whether the art of the animated image, which has been developed as the silent film, could use the kind of libretto through which the opera provides a skeleton of the dramatic action.

First of all, we must repeat here that by means of the opera libretto (as well as its predecessors in church music, etc.) music conquered a vast new realm, namely, that of dramatic music or the musical drama. In the case of the film, the dialogue does not give access to a new type of work. At best, it enlarges what exists. We have to remember that in silent film the dialogue, as given in the titles, was not at all the foundation and starting point of the work, from which the pictures were developed. They were a mere expedient added secondarily and for the purpose of explanation to works conceived and realized in images. Perhaps the spoken dialogue may not be able to fulfill even this humble function. What is useful for the opera, may be harmful for the film.

Will an artist, that is, a person guided by a sure sensitivity for the medium he employs, ever feel impelled to "set" a dialogue "to pictures" instead of creating in pictures? Since pictures are what attract him, he might be tempted by speech as a technical device that would sharpen the meaning of his scenes, save him the tortuous detours necessary to explain the plot, and open up a larger field of subjects. Now, in fact, dialogue makes possible an extensive development of the external action, and particularly also the internal action. No fairly complicated event or state of mind can be conveyed by pictures alone. Therefore, the addition of spoken dialogue has made storytelling easier. In this sense, film dialogue has been defined by some critics as a device for saving time, space, and ingenuity – a saving that would reserve the available limited length of the film and the creative energy of the maker for the truly relevant content of the work. It remains to be seen, however, whether there is, in the movies, any justification for the kind of involved plot that we find in the novel and the play.

We can easily understand why the large movie audience has applauded the introduction of the spoken word. What the audience wants is to take part in exciting events as fully as possible. The best way of achieving this is, in a certain sense, the mixture of visual action and dialogue: external events are shown concretely to the eye, and at the same time the thoughts, intentions, and emotions of the characters are communicated through words in the directest and most natural way. Moreover the felt presence of the events is enormously enhanced by the sound of voices and other noises. The audience will object only when the dialogue is cut down so much that it does not explain the action or when, on the contrary, there is too little outer action, and all the talking becomes tiresome. In a crude way, these objections to the talking film are the same as those of the connoisseur.

Dialogue narrows the world of the film. The example of the opera seemed to justify and recommend the use of dialogue. But not without caution can we compare the art of sound and the art of pictures in their relation to the spoken word. One of the main characteristics of dramatic dialogue is that it limits the action to the human performer. This suits music perfectly since, as we said, the opera was created precisely in order to represent human beings in dramatic action musically. The image, of course, does not need dialogue to present man, but in the visual world the human kind does not enjoy the leading role it has on the stage. Granted that in certain paintings human figures hold the foreground gigantically; but just as often painting shows man as a part of his environment, which gives meaning to him and to which he gives meaning. Man appears as a part of the Creation, from which he can be isolated only artificially. The moving picture was from the beginning more concerned with the world animated by man than with man set off against his world. Therefore, to be limited by dialogue to the performances of the human figure was bound to seem intolerable.

The presentation of man's natural setting had been one of the achievements that justified the existence of the movies next to the theater. Naturally, the silent film also had often shown the actor in close-ups. But more importantly, it had created a union of silent man and silent things as well as of the (audible) person close-by and the (inaudible) one at a far distance. In the universal silence of the image, the fragments of a broken vase could "talk" exactly the way a character talked to his neighbor, and a person approaching on a road and visible on the horizon as a mere dot "talked" as someone acting in close-up. This homogeneity, which is completely foreign to the theater but familiar to painting, is destroyed by the talking film: it endows the actor with speech, and since only he can have it, all other things are pushed into the background.

Now there is a limit to the visual expression that can be drawn from the human figure, particularly if the picture has to accompany dialogue. Pure pantomime knows of three ways to overcome this limitation. It can give up the portraying of plots and instead present the "absolute" movement of the body, that is, dance. Here the human body becomes an instrument for melodic and harmonic forms, which are superior to mere pantomime, as music is superior to a (hypothetical) art of natural noises. Secondly, pantomime can adopt the solution of the silent film, namely, become a part of the richer universe in motion. And finally, it can become subservient to dramatic speech – as it does in the theater. But to the pantomime of the talking film all three of these solutions are inaccessible: it cannot become dance because dance does not need speech and perhaps does not even tolerate it; it cannot submerge in the huge *orbis pictus* of the silent film because of its tie to the human figure; and it cannot become the servant of speech without giving up its own self.

The dialogue paralyzes visual action. Not only does speech limit the motion picture to an art of dramatic portraiture, it also interferes with the expression of the image. The better the silent film, the more strictly it used to avoid showing people in the act of talking, important though talking is in real life. The actors expressed themselves by posture and facial expression. Additional meaning came from the way the figure was shown within the framework of the picture, by lighting, and particularly by the total context of sequence and plot. The visual counterpart of speech, that is, the monotonous motions of the mouth, yields little and, in fact, can only hamper the expressive movement of the body. The motions of the mouth convincingly demonstrate that the activity of talking compels the actor into visually monotonous, meaningless, and often ludicrous behavior.

It is obvious that speech cannot be attached to the immobile image (painting, photography); but it is equally ill-suited for the silent film, whose means of expression resemble those of painting. It was precisely the absence of speech that made the silent film develop a style of its own, capable of condensing the dramatic situation. To separate or to find each other, to win or to give in, to be friends or enemies – all such themes were neatly presented by a few simple attitudes, such as a raising of the head or of an arm, or the bowing of one person to another. This had led to a most cinegenic species of tale, which was full of simple happenings and which, with the coming of the talking film, was replaced by a theater-type play, poor in external action but well developed psychologically. This meant replacing the visually fruitful image of man in action with the sterile one of the man who talks.

As far as the opera is concerned, there is no objection to the dialogue centering the action around the human character; nor is there any to the visual paralysis of the actor. What the opera wants is, we said, the musical expression of man in action. It has little use for the expressive virtues of the animated image on the stage, which remains secondary, complementary, explicatory. The opera director does not hesitate to stop the stage action in favor of long arias. This gives the dialogue plenty of time, and in fact too much time: phrases have to be stretched and repeated to comply with the music. So that what hurts the film does not hurt the opera.

If after discussing the theoretical difficulties that lie in the way of the talking film we look around to see whether in practice the motion-picture production has worked out satisfactory solutions, we find our diagnosis confirmed. The average talking film today endeavors to combine visually poor scenes full of dialogue with the completely different traditional style of rich, silent action. In comparison with the epoch of the silent film there is also an impressive decline of artistic excellence, in the average films as well as in the peak productions – a trend that cannot be due entirely to the ever increasing industrialization.

It may seem surprising that mankind should produce in large number works based on a principle that represents such a radical artistic impoverishment if compared with the available purer forms. But is such a contradiction really surprising at a time at which in other respects, too, so many people live a life of unreality and fail to attain the true nature of man and its fitting manifestations? If the opposite happened in the movies, would not such a pleasant inconsistency be even more surprising?

There is comfort, however, in the fact that hybrid forms are quite unstable. They tend to change from their own unreality into purer forms, even though this may mean a return to the past. Beyond our blundering there are inherent forces that, in the long run, overcome error and incompleteness and direct human action toward the purity of goodness and truth.

6

Cinematic Realism

André Bazin

The quarrel over realism in art stems from a misunderstanding, from a confusion between the aesthetic and the psychological; between true realism, the need that is to give significant expression to the world both concretely and its essence, and the pseudorealism of a deception aimed at fooling the eye (or for that matter the mind); a pseudorealism content in other words with illusory appearances. That is why medieval art never passed through this crisis; simultaneously vividly realistic and highly spiritual, it knew nothing of the drama that came to light as a consequence of technical developments. Perspective was the original sin of Western painting.

It was redeemed from sin by Niepce and Lumière. In achieving the aims of baroque art, photography has freed the plastic arts from their obsession with likeness. Painting was forced, as it turned out, to offer us illusion and this illusion was reckoned sufficient unto art. Photography and the cinema on the other hand are discoveries that satisfy, once and for all and in its very essence, our obsession with realism.

No matter how skillful the painter, his work was always in fee to an inescapable subjectivity. The fact that a human hand intervened cast a shadow of doubt over the image. Again, the essential factor in the transition from the baroque to photography is not the perfecting of a physical process (photography will long remain the inferior of painting in the reproduction of color); rather does it lie in a psychological fact, to wit, in completely satisfying our appetite for illusion by a mechanical reproduction in the making of which man plays no part. The solution is not to be found in the result achieved but in the way of achieving it.[1]

[. . .]

Originality in photography as distinct from originality in painting lies in the essentially objective character of photography. [Bazin here makes a point of the fact that the lens, the basis of photography, is in French called the "objectif," a nuance that is lost in English. – Tr.] For the first time, between the originating object and its reproduction there intervenes only the instrumentality of a nonliving agent. For the first time an image of the world is formed automatically, without the creative intervention of man. The personality of the photographer enters into the proceedings only in his selection of the object to be photographed and by way of the purpose he has in mind. Although the final result may reflect something of his personality, this does not play the same role as is played by that of the painter. All the arts are based on the presence of man, only photography derives an advantage from his absence. Photography affects us like a phenomenon in nature, like a flower or a snowflake whose vegetable or earthly origins are an inseparable part of their beauty.

This production by automatic means has radically affected our psychology of the image. The objective nature of photography confers on it a quality of credibility absent from all other picture-making. In spite of any objections our critical spirit may offer, we are forced to accept as real the existence of the object reproduced, actually *re-presented*, set before us, that is to say, in time and space. Photography enjoys a certain advantage in virtue of this transference of reality from the thing to its reproduction.

A very faithful drawing may actually tell us more about the model but despite the promptings of our critical intelligence it will never have the irrational power of the photograph to bear away our faith.

Besides, painting is, after all, an inferior way of making likenesses, an *ersatz* of the processes of reproduction. Only a photographic lens can give us the kind of image of the object that is capable of satisfying the deep need man has to substitute for it something more than a mere approximation, a kind of decal or transfer. The photographic image is the object itself, the object freed from the conditions of time and space that govern it. No matter how fuzzy, distorted, or discolored, no matter how lacking in documentary value the image may be, it shares, by virtue of the very process of its becoming, the being of the model of which it is the reproduction; it *is* the model.

Hence the charm of family albums. Those grey or sepia shadows, phantomlike and almost undecipherable, are no longer traditional family portraits but rather the disturbing presence of lives halted at a set moment in their duration, freed from their destiny; not, however, by the prestige of art but by the power of an impassive mechanical process: for photography does not create eternity, as art does, it embalms time, rescuing it simply from its proper corruption.

Viewed in this perspective, the cinema is objectivity in time. The film is no longer content to preserve the object, enshrouded as it were in an instant, as the bodies of insects are preserved intact, out of the distant past, in amber. The film delivers baroque art from its convulsive catalepsy. Now, for the first time, the image of things is likewise the image of their duration, change mummified as it were. Those categories of *resemblance* which determine the species *photographic* image likewise, then, determine the character of its aesthetic as distinct from that of painting.

[. . .]

Photography can even surpass art in creative power. The aesthetic world of the painter is of a different kind from that of the world about him. Its boundaries enclose a substantially and essentially different microcosm. The photograph as such and the object in itself share a common being, after the fashion of a fingerprint. Wherefore, photography actually contributes something to the order of natural creation instead of providing a substitute for it. The surrealists had an inkling of this when they looked to the photographic plate to provide them with their monstrosities and for this reason: the surrealist does not consider his aesthetic purpose and the mechanical effect of the image on our imaginations as things apart. For him, the logical distinction between what is imaginary and what is real tends to disappear. Every image is to be seen as an object and every object as an image. Hence photography ranks high in the order of surrealist creativity because it produces an image that is a reality of nature, namely, an hallucination that is also a fact. The fact that surrealist painting combines tricks of visual deception with meticulous attention to detail substantiates this.

So, photography is clearly the most important event in the history of plastic arts. Simultaneously a liberation and a fulfillment, it has freed Western painting, once and for all, from its obsession with realism and allowed it to recover its aesthetic autonomy. Impressionist realism, offering science as an alibi, is at the opposite extreme from eye-deceiving trickery. Only when form ceases to have any imitative value can it be swallowed up in color. So, when form, in the person of Cézanne, once more regains possession of the canvas there is no longer any question of the illusions of the geometry of perspective. The painting, being confronted in the mechanically produced image with a competitor able to reach out beyond baroque resemblance to the very identity of the model, was compelled into the category of object. Henceforth Pascal's condemnation of painting is itself rendered vain since the photograph allows us on the one hand to admire in reproduction something that our eyes alone could not have taught us to love, and on the other, to admire the painting as a thing in itself whose relation to something in nature has ceased to be the justification for its existence.

On the other hand, of course, cinema is also a language.

[. . .] The cinema is an idealistic phenomenon. The concept men had of it existed so to speak fully armed in their minds, as if in some platonic heaven, and what strikes us most of all is the obstinate resistance of matter to ideas rather than of any help offered by techniques to the imagination of the researchers.

[. . .] Any account of the cinema that was drawn merely from the technical inventions that made it possible would be a poor one indeed. On the contrary, an approximate and complicated visualization of an idea invariably precedes the industrial discovery which alone can open the way to its practical use. Thus if it is evident to us today that the cinema even at its most elementary stage needed a transparent, flexible, and resistant base and a dry sensitive emulsion capable of receiving an image instantly – everything else being a matter of setting in order a mechanism far less complicated than an eighteenth-century clock – it is clear that all the definitive stages of the invention of the cinema had been reached before the requisite conditions had been fulfilled. In 1877 and 1880, Muybridge, thanks to the imaginative generosity of a horse-lover, managed to construct a large complex device which enabled him to make from the image of a galloping horse the first series of cinematographic pictures. However to get this result he had to be satisfied with wet collodion on a glass plate, that is to say, with just one of the three necessary elements – namely instantaneity, dry emulsion, flexible base. After the discovery of gelatino-bromide of silver but before the appearance on the market of the first celluloid reels, Marey had made a genuine camera which used glass plates. Even after the appearance of celluloid strips Lumière tried to use paper film.

Once more let us consider here only the final and complete form of the photographic cinema. The synthesis of simple movements studied scientifically by Plateau had no need to wait upon the industrial and economic developments of the nineteenth century. [. . .] Nothing had stood in the way, from antiquity, of the manufacture of a phenakistoscope or a zootrope. It is true that here the labors of that genuine savant Plateau were at the origin of the many inventions that made the popular use of his discovery possible. But while, with the photographic cinema, we have cause for some astonishment that the discovery somehow precedes the technical conditions necessary to its existence, we must here explain, on the other hand, how it was that the invention took so long to emerge, since all the prerequisites had been assembled and the persistence of the image on the retina had been known for a long time. [. . .]

I emphasize the fact that this historical coincidence can apparently in no way be explained on grounds of scientific, economic, or industrial evolution. The photographic cinema could just as well have grafted itself onto a phenakistoscope foreseen as long ago as the sixteenth century. The delay in the invention of the latter is as disturbing a phenomenon as the existence of the precursors of the former.

But if we examine their work more closely, the direction of their research is manifest in the instruments themselves, and, even more undeniably, in their writings and commentaries we see that these precursors were indeed more like prophets. Hurrying past the various stopping places, the very first of which materially speaking should have halted them, it was at the very height and summit that most of them were aiming. In their imaginations they saw the cinema as a total and complete representation of reality; they saw in a trice the reconstruction of a perfect illusion of the outside world in sound, color, and relief.

[. . .]

The guiding myth, then, inspiring the invention of cinema, is the accomplishment of that which dominated in a more or less vague fashion all the techniques of the mechanical reproduction of reality in the nineteenth century, from photography to the phonograph, namely an integral realism, a recreation of the world in its own image, an image unburdened by the freedom of interpretation of the artist or the irreversibility of time. If cinema in its cradle lacked all the attributes of the cinema to come, it was with reluctance and because its fairy guardians were unable to provide them however much they would have liked to.

If the origins of an art reveal something of its nature, then one may legitimately consider the silent and the sound film as stages of a technical development that little by little made a reality out of the original "myth." It is understandable from this point of view that it would be absurd to take the silent film as a state of primal perfection which has gradually been forsaken by the realism of sound and color. The primacy of the image is both historically and technically accidental. The nostalgia that some still feel for the silent screen does not go far enough back into the childhood of the seventh art. The real primitives of the cinema, existing only in the imaginations of a few men of the nineteenth century, are in complete imitation of nature. Every new development added to the cinema must, paradoxically, take it nearer and nearer to its origins. In short, cinema has not yet been invented!

It would be a reversal then of the concrete order of causality, at least psychologically, to place the scientific discoveries or the industrial techniques that have loomed so large in its development at the source of the cinema's invention. Those who had the least confidence in the future of the cinema were precisely the two industrialists Edison and Lumière. Edison was satisfied with just his kinetoscope and if Lumière judiciously refused to sell his patent to Méliès it was undoubtedly because he hoped to make a large profit out of it for himself, but only as a plaything of which the public would soon tire. As for the real savants such as Marey, they were only of indirect assistance to the cinema. They had a specific purpose in mind and were satisfied when they had accomplished it. The fanatics, the madmen, the disinterested pioneers, capable, as was Bernard Palissy, of burning their furniture for a few seconds of shaky images, are neither industrialists nor savants, just men obsessed by their own imaginings. The cinema was born from the converging of these various obsessions, that is to say, out of a myth, the myth of total cinema. This likewise adequately explains the delay of Plateau in applying the optical principle of the persistence of the image on the retina, as also the continuous progress of the syntheses of movement as compared with the state of photographic techniques. The fact is that each alike was dominated by the imagination of the century. Undoubtedly there are other examples in the history of techniques and inventions of the convergence of research, but one must distinguish between those which come as a result precisely of scientific evolution and industrial or military requirements and those which quite clearly precede them. Thus, the myth of Icarus had to wait on the internal combustion engine before descending from the platonic heavens. But it had dwelt in the soul of everyman since he first thought about birds. To some extent, one could say the same thing about the myth of cinema, but its forerunners prior to the nineteenth century have only a remote connection with the myth which we share today and which has prompted the appearance of the mechanical arts that characterize today's world.

By 1928 the silent film had reached its artistic peak. The despair of its elite as they witnessed the dismantling of this ideal city, while it may not have been justified, is at least understandable. As they followed their chosen aesthetic path it seemed to them that the cinema had developed into an art most perfectly accommodated to the "exquisite embarrassment" of silence and that the realism that sound would bring could only mean a surrender to chaos.

In point of fact, now that sound has given proof that it came not to destroy but to fulfill the Old Testament of the cinema, we may most properly ask if the technical revolution created by the sound track was in any sense an aesthetic revolution. In other words, did the years from 1928 to 1930 actually witness the birth of a new cinema? Certainly, as regards editing, history does not actually show as wide a breach as might be expected between the silent and the sound film. On the contrary there is discernible evidence of a close relationship between certain directors of 1925 and 1935 and especially of the 1940s through the 1950s. Compare for example Erich von Stroheim and Jean Renoir or Orson Welles, or again Carl Theodore Dreyer and Robert Bresson. These more or less clear-cut affinities demonstrate first of all that the gap separating the

1920s and the 1930s can be bridged, and secondly that certain cinematic values actually carry over from the silent to the sound film and, above all, that it is less a matter of setting silence over against sound than of contrasting certain families of styles, certain basically different concepts of cinematographic expression.

Aware as I am that the limitations imposed on this study restrict me to a simplified and to that extent enfeebled presentation of my argument, and holding it to be less an objective statement than a working hypothesis, I will distinguish, in the cinema between 1920 and 1940, between two broad and opposing trends: those directors who put their faith in the image and those who put their faith in reality. By "image" I here mean, very broadly speaking, everything that the representation on the screen adds to the object there represented. This is a complex inheritance but it can be reduced essentially to two categories: those that relate to the plastics of the image and those that relate to the resources of montage, which, after all, is simply the ordering of images in time.

Under the heading "plastics" must be included the style of the sets, of the make-up, and, up to a point, even of the performance, to which we naturally add the lighting and, finally, the framing of the shot which gives us its composition. As regards montage, derived initially as we all know from the masterpieces of Griffith, we have the statement of Malraux in his *Psychologie du cinéma* that it was montage that gave birth to film as an art, setting it apart from mere animated photography, in short, creating a language.

The use of montage can be "invisible" and this was generally the case in the prewar classics of the American screen. Scenes were broken down just for one purpose, namely, to analyze an episode according to the material or dramatic logic of the scene. It is this logic which conceals the fact of the analysis, the mind of the spectator quite naturally accepting the viewpoints of the director which are justified by the geography of the action or the shifting emphasis of dramatic interest.

But the neutral quality of this "invisible" editing fails to make use of the full potential of montage. On the other hand these potentialities are clearly evident from the three processes generally known as parallel montage, accelerated montage, montage by attraction. In creating parallel montage, Griffith succeeded in conveying a sense of the simultaneity of two actions taking place at a geographical distance by means of alternating shots from each. In *La Roue* Abel Gance created the illusion of the steadily increasing speed of a locomotive without actually using any images of speed (indeed the wheel could have been turning on one spot) simply by a multiplicity of shots of ever-decreasing length.

Finally there is "montage by attraction," the creation of S. M. Eisenstein, and not so easily described as the others, but which may be roughly defined as the reenforcing of the meaning of one image by association with another image not necessarily part of the same episode – for example the fireworks display in *The General Line* following the image of the bull. In this extreme form, montage by attraction was rarely used even by its creator but one may consider as very near to it in principle the more commonly used ellipsis, comparison, or metaphor, examples of which are the throwing of stockings onto a chair at the foot of a bed, or the milk overflowing in H. G. Clouzot's

Quai des orfèvres. There are of course a variety of possible combinations of these three processes.

Whatever these may be, one can say that they share that trait in common which constitutes the very definition of montage, namely, the creation of a sense or meaning not objectively contained in the images themselves but derived exclusively from their juxtaposition. The well-known experiment of Kuleshov with the shot of Mozhukhin in which a smile was seen to change its significance according to the image that preceded it, sums up perfectly the properties of montage.

Montage as used by Kuleshov, Eisenstein, or Gance did not show us the event; it alluded to it. Undoubtedly they derived at least the greater part of the constituent elements from the reality they were describing but the final significance of the film was found to reside in the ordering of these elements much more than in their objective content. The substance of the narrative, whatever the realism of the individual image, is born essentially from these relationships — Mozhukhin plus dead child equal pity — that is to say an abstract result, none of the concrete elements of which are to be found in the premises; maidens plus appletrees in bloom equal hope. The combinations are infinite. But the only thing they have in common is the fact that they suggest an idea by means of a metaphor or by an association of ideas. Thus between the scenario properly so-called, the ultimate object of the recital, and the image pure and simple, there is a relay station, a sort of aesthetic "transformer." The meaning is not in the image, it is in the shadow of the image projected by montage onto the field of consciousness of the spectator.

Let us sum up. Through the contents of the image and the resources of montage, the cinema has at its disposal a whole arsenal of means whereby to impose its interpretation of an event on the spectator. By the end of the silent film we can consider this arsenal to have been full. On the one side the Soviet cinema carried to its ultimate consequences the theory and practice of montage while the German school did every kind of violence to the plastics of the image by way of sets and lighting. Other cinemas count too besides the Russian and German, but whether in France or Sweden or the United States, it does not appear that the language of cinema was at a loss for ways of saying what it wanted to say.

If the art of cinema consists in everything that plastics and montage can add to a given reality, the silent film was an art on its own. Sound could only play at best a subordinate and supplementary role: a counterpoint to the visual image. But this possible enhancement — at best only a minor one — is likely not to weigh much in comparison with the additional bargain-rate reality introduced at the same time by sound.

Thus far we have put forward the view that expressionism of montage and image constitute the essence of cinema. And it is precisely on this generally accepted notion that directors from silent days, such as Erich von Stroheim, F. W. Murnau, and Robert Flaherty, have by implication cast a doubt. In their films, montage plays no part, unless it be the negative one of inevitable elimination where reality superabounds. The camera cannot see everything at once but it makes sure not to lose any part of what it chooses to see. What matters to Flaherty, confronted with Nanook hunting the seal, is the relation between Nanook and the animal; the actual length of the waiting period. Montage could suggest the time involved. Flaherty however confines himself to showing the actual waiting period; the length of the hunt is the very substance of the image, its true object. Thus in the film this episode requires one setup. Will anyone deny that it is thereby much more moving than a montage by attraction?

Murnau is interested not so much in time as in the reality of dramatic space. Montage plays no more of a decisive part in *Nosferatu* than in *Sunrise*. One might be inclined to think that the plastics of his image are expressionistic. But this would be a superficial view. The composition of his image is in no sense pictorial. It adds nothing to the reality, it does not deform it, it forces it to reveal its structural depth, to bring out the preexisting relations which become constitutive of the drama. For example, in *Tabu*, the arrival of a ship from left screen gives an immediate sense of destiny at work so that Murnau has no need to cheat in any way on the uncompromising realism of a film whose settings are completely natural.

But it is most of all Stroheim who rejects photographic expressionism and the tricks of montage. In his films reality lays itself bare like a suspect confessing under the relentless examination of the commissioner of police. He has one simple rule for direction. Take a close look at the world, keep on doing so, and in the end it will lay bare for you all its cruelty and its ugliness. One could easily imagine as a matter of fact a film by Stroheim composed of a single shot as long-lasting and as close-up as you like. These three directors do not exhaust the possibilities. We would undoubtedly find scattered among the works of others elements of nonexpressionistic cinema in which montage plays no part – even including Griffith. But these examples suffice to reveal, at the very heart of the silent film, a cinematographic art the very opposite of that which has been identified as "*cinéma par excellence*," a language the semantic and syntactical unit of which is in no sense the Shot; in which the image is evaluated not according to what it adds to reality but what it reveals of it. In the latter art the silence of the screen was a drawback, that is to say, it deprived reality of one of its elements. *Greed*, like Dreyer's *Jeanne d'Arc*, is already virtually a talking film. The moment that you cease to maintain that montage and the plastic composition of the image are the very essence of the language of cinema, sound is no longer the aesthetic crevasse dividing two radically different aspects of the seventh art. The cinema that is believed to have died of the soundtrack is in no sense "*the* cinema." The real dividing line is elsewhere. It was operative in the past and continues to be through thirty-five years of the history of the language of the film.

[. . .]

Thus around 1938 films were edited, almost without exception, according to the same principle. The story was unfolded in a series of set-ups numbering as a rule about 600. The characteristic procedure was by shot-reverse-shot, that is to say, in a dialogue scene, the camera followed the order of the text, alternating the character shown with each speech.

It was this fashion of editing, so admirably suitable for the best films made between 1930 and 1939, that was challenged by the shot in depth introduced by Orson Welles and William Wyler. The influence of *Citizen Kane* cannot be overestimated. Thanks to the depth of field, whole scenes are covered in one take, the camera remaining motionless. Dramatic effects for which we had formerly relied on montage were created out of the movements of the actors within a fixed framework. Of course Welles did not invent the in-depth shot any more than Griffith invented the close-up. All the pioneers used it and for a very good reason. Soft focus only appeared with montage. It was not only a technical must consequent upon the use of images in juxtaposition, it was a logical consequence of montage, its plastic equivalent. If at a given moment in the action the director, as in the scene imagined above, goes to a close-up of a bowl of fruit, it follows naturally that he also isolates it in space through the focusing of the lens. The soft focus of the background confirms therefore the effect of montage, that is to say, while it is of the essence of the storytelling, it is only an accessory of the style of the photography. Jean Renoir had already clearly understood this, as we see from a statement of his made in 1938 just after he had made *La Bête humaine* and *La Grande Illusion* and just prior to *La Règle du jeu*: "The more I learn about my trade the more I incline to direction in depth relative to the screen. The better it works, the less I use the kind of set-up that shows two actors facing the camera, like two well-behaved subjects posing for a still portrait." The truth of the matter is, that if you are looking for the precursor of Orson Welles, it is not Louis Lumière or Zecca, but rather Jean Renoir. In his films, the search after composition in depth is, in effect, a partial replacement of montage by frequent panning shots and entrances. It is based on a respect for the continuity of dramatic space and, of course, of its duration.

5 ■ "A deep focus shot of Charles Foster Kane (Orson Welles) playing in the background while his parents make plans to send him East," from *Citizen Kane*.

To anybody with eyes in his head, it is quite evident that the one-shot sequences used by Welles in *The Magnificent Ambersons* are in no sense the purely passive recording of an action shot within the same framing. On the contrary, his refusal to break up the action, to analyze the dramatic field in time, is a positive action the results of which are far superior to anything that could be achieved by the classical "cut."

[. . .]

It would lie outside the scope of this article to analyze the psychological modalities of these relations, as also their aesthetic consequences, but it might be enough here to note, in general terms:

1 That depth of focus brings the spectator into a relation with the image closer to that which he enjoys with reality. Therefore it is correct to say that, independently of the contents of the image, its structure is more realistic;
2 That it implies, consequently, both a more active mental attitude on the part of the spectator and a more positive contribution on his part to the action in progress. While analytical montage only calls for him to follow his guide, to let his attention follow along smoothly with that of the director who will choose what he should see, here he is called upon to exercise at least a minimum of personal choice. It is from his attention and his will that the meaning of the image in part derives.

3 From the two preceding propositions, which belong to the realm of psychology, there follows a third which may be described as metaphysical. In analyzing reality, montage presupposes of its very nature the unity of meaning of the dramatic event. Some other form of analysis is undoubtedly possible but then it would be another film. In short, montage by its very nature rules out ambiguity of expression. Kuleshov's experiment proves this *per absurdum* in giving on each occasion a precise meaning to the expression on a face, the ambiguity of which alone makes the three successively exclusive expressions possible.

On the other hand, depth of focus reintroduced ambiguity into the structure of the image if not of necessity – Wyler's films are never ambiguous – at least as a possibility. Hence it is no exaggeration to say that *Citizen Kane* is unthinkable shot in any other way but in depth. The uncertainty in which we find ourselves as to the spiritual key or the interpretation we should put on the film is built into the very design of the image.

It is not that Welles denies himself any recourse whatsoever to the expressionistic procedures of montage, but just that their use from time to time in between one-shot sequences in depth gives them a new meaning. Formerly montage was the very stuff of cinema, the texture of the scenario. In *Citizen Kane* a series of superimpositions is contrasted with a scene presented in a single take, constituting another and deliberately abstract mode of story-telling. Accelerated montage played tricks with time and space while that of Welles, on the other hand, is not trying to deceive us; it offers us a contrast, condensing time, and hence is the equivalent for example of the French imperfect or the English frequentative tense. Like accelerated montage and montage of attractions these superimpositions, which the talking film had not used for ten years, rediscovered a possible use related to temporal realism in a film without montage.

If we have dwelt at some length on Orson Welles it is because the date of his appearance in the filmic firmament (1941) marks more or less the beginning of a new period and also because his case is the most spectacular and, by virtue of his very excesses, the most significant.

Yet *Citizen Kane* is part of a general movement, of a vast stirring of the geological bed of cinema, confirming that everywhere up to a point there had been a revolution in the language of the screen.

I could show the same to be true, although by different methods, of the Italian cinema. In Roberto Rossellini's *Paisà* and *Allemania Anno Zero* and Vittorio de Sica's *Ladri di biciclette*, Italian neorealism contrasts with previous forms of film realism in its stripping away of all expressionism and in particular in the total absence of the effects of montage. As in the films of Welles and in spite of conflicts of style, neorealism tends to give back to the cinema a sense of the ambiguity of reality. [. . .]

[. . .]

[. . .] Today we can say that at last the director writes in film. The image – its plastic composition and the way it is set in time, because it is founded on a much higher degree of realism – has at its disposal more means of manipulating reality and of modifying it from within. The film-maker is no longer the competitor of the painter and the playwright, he is, at last, the equal of the novelist.

NOTE

1 There is room, nevertheless, for a study of the psychology of the lesser plastic arts, the molding of death masks for example, which likewise involves a certain automatic process. One might consider photography in this sense as a molding, the taking of an impression, by the manipulation of light.

7

Film, Photography, and Transparency

Kendall L. Walton

There is one clear difference between photography and painting. A photograph is always a photograph of something which actually exists. Even when photographs portray such nonentities as werewolves and Martians, they are nonetheless photographs of actual things: actors, stage sets, costumes. Paintings needn't picture actual things. A painting of Aphrodite, executed without the use of a model, depicts nothing real. But this is by no means the whole story. Those who see a sharp contrast between photographs and paintings clearly think that it obtains no less when paintings depict actual things than when they do not, and even when viewers fully realize that they do. Let's limit our examples to pictures of this kind. The claim before us is that photographs of Abraham Lincoln, for instance, are in some fundamental manner more realistic than painted portraits of him.

I shall argue that there is indeed a fundamental difference between photographs and painted portraits of Lincoln, that photography is indeed special, and that it deserves to be called a supremely realistic medium. But the kind of realism most distinctive of photography is not an ordinary one. It has little to do either with the post-Renaissance quest for realism in painting or with standard theoretical accounts of realism. It is enormously important, however. Without a clear understanding of it, we cannot hope to explain the power and effectiveness of photography.

Painting and drawing are techniques for producing pictures. So is photography. But the special nature of photography will remain obscure unless we think of it in another way as well – as a contribution to the enterprise of seeing. The invention of the camera gave us not just a new method of making pictures and not just pictures of a new kind: it gave us a new way of seeing.

Amidst Bazin's assorted declarations about photography is a comparison of the cinema to mirrors. This points in the right direction. Mirrors are aids to vision, allowing us to see things in circumstances in which we would not otherwise be able to; with their help we can see around corners. Telescopes and microscopes extend our visual powers in other ways, enabling us to see things that are too far away or too small to be seen with the naked eye. Photography is an aid to vision also, and an especially versatile one. With the assistance of the camera, we can see not only around corners and what is distant or small; we can also see into the past. We see long deceased ancestors when we look at dusty snapshots of them. To view a screening of Frederic Wiseman's *Titicut Follies* (1967) in San Francisco in 1984 is to watch events which occurred in 1967 at the Bridgewater State Hospital for the Criminally Insane. Photographs are *transparent*. We see the world *through* them.

I must warn against watering down this suggestion, against taking it to be a colorful, or exaggerated, or not quite literal way of making a relatively mundane point. I am not saying that the person looking at the dusty photographs has the *impression* of seeing his ancestors – in fact, he doesn't have the impression of seeing them "in the flesh," with the unaided eye. I am not saying that photography *supplements* vision by helping us to discover things that we can't discover by seeing. Painted portraits and linguistic reports also supplement vision in this way. Nor is my point that what we see – photographs – are *duplicates* or *doubles* or *reproductions* of objects, or *substitutes* or *surrogates* for them. My claim is that we *see*, quite literally, our dead relatives themselves when we look at photographs of them.

Does this constitute an extension of the ordinary English sense of the word "see"? I don't know; the evidence is mixed. But if it is an extension, it is a very natural one. Our theory needs, in any case, a term which applies both to my "seeing" my great-grandfather when I look at his snapshot and to my seeing my father when he is in front of me. What is important is that we recognize a fundamental commonality between the two cases, a single natural kind to which both belong. We could say that I *perceive* my great-grandfather but do not *see* him, recognizing a mode of perception ("seeing-through-photographs") distinct from vision – if the idea that I do perceive my great-grandfather is taken seriously. Or one might make the point in some other way. I prefer the bold formulation: the viewer of a photograph sees, literally, the scene that was photographed.

Slippery slope considerations give this claim an initial plausibility. No one will deny that we see through eyeglasses, mirrors, and telescopes. How, then, would one justify denying that a security guard sees via a closed circuit television monitor a burglar breaking a window or that fans watch athletic events when they watch live television broadcasts of them? And after going this far, why not speak of watching athletic events via delayed broadcasts or of seeing the Bridgewater inmates via Wiseman's film? These last examples do introduce a new element: they have us seeing past events. But its importance isn't obvious. We also find ourselves speaking of observing through a telescope the explosion of a star which occurred millions of years ago. We encounter various other differences also, of course, as we slide down the slope. The question is whether any of them is significant enough to justify digging in our heels and recognizing a basic theoretical distinction, one which we might describe as the difference between "seeing" (or "perceiving") things and not doing so.

Mechanical aids to vision don't necessarily involve *pictures* at all. Eyeglasses, mirrors, and telescopes don't give us pictures. To think of the camera as another tool of vision is to de-emphasize its role in producing pictures. Photographs are pictures, to be sure, but not ordinary ones. They are pictures through which we see the world.

To be transparent is not necessarily to be invisible. We see photographs themselves when we see through them; indeed it is by looking at *Titicut Follies* that we see the Bridgewater inmates. There is nothing strange about this: one hears both a bell and the sounds that it makes, and one hears the one by hearing the other. (Bazin's remarkable identity claim might derive from failure to recognize that we can be seeing both the photograph and the object: *what we see* are photographs, but we do see the photographed objects; so the photographs and the objects must be somehow identical.)

I don't mind allowing that we see photographed objects only *indirectly*, though one could maintain that perception is equally indirect in many other cases as well: we see objects by seeing mirror images of them, or images produced by lenses, or light reflected or emitted from them; we hear things and events by hearing the sounds that they make. One is reminded of the familiar claim that we see *directly* only our own sense-data or images on our retinas. What I would object to is the suggestion that indirect seeing, in any of these cases, is not really *seeing*, that *all* we actually see are sense-data or images or photographs.

One can see through sense-data or mirror images without specifically noticing them (even if, in the latter case, one notices the mirror); in this sense they *can* be invisible. One may pay no attention to photographic images themselves, concentrating instead on the things photographed. But even if one does attend especially to the photographic image, one may at the same time be seeing, and attending to, the objects photographed.

Seeing is often a way of finding out about the world. This is as true of seeing through photographs as it is of seeing in other ways. But sometimes we learn little if anything about what we see, and sometimes we value the seeing quite apart from what we might learn. This is so, frequently, when we see departed loved ones through photographs. We can't expect to acquire any particularly important information by looking at photographs which we have studied many times before. But we can *see* our loved ones again, and *that* is important to us.

What about paintings? They are not transparent. We do not see Henry VIII when we look at his portrait; we see only a representation of him. There is a sharp break, a difference of kind, between painting and photography.

Granted, it is perfectly natural to say of a person contemplating the portrait that he "sees" Henry VIII. But this is not to be taken literally. It is *fictional*, not true, that the viewer sees Henry VIII. It is equally natural to say that spectators of the Unicorn Tapestries see unicorns. But there are no unicorns; so they aren't really seeing any. Our use of the word "see," by itself, proves nothing.

A photograph purporting to be of the Loch Ness monster was widely published some years ago. If we think the monster really exists and was captured by the photograph, we will speak comfortably of seeing it when we look at the photograph. But the photograph turned out not to be of the monster but (as I recall) of a model, dredged up from the bottom of the lake, which was once used in making a movie about it. With this information we change our tune: what we see when we look at the photograph is not the monster but the model. This sort of seeing is like the ordinary variety in that only what exists can be seen.

What about viewers of the movie (which, let us assume, was a straightforward work of fiction)? They may speak of seeing the monster, even if they don't believe for a moment that there is such a beast. It is fictional that they see it; they actually see, with photographic assistance, the model used in the making of the film. It is fictional also that they see Loch Ness, the lake. And since the movie was made on location at Loch Ness, they really do see it as well.

6 ■ "Cary Grant," from *Notorious*.

Even when one looks at photographs which are not straightforward works of fiction, it can be fictional that one sees. On seeing a photograph of a long forgotten family reunion, I might remark that Aunt Mabel is grimacing. She is not grimacing *now* of course; perhaps she is long deceased. My use of the present tense suggests that it is *fictional* that she is grimacing (now). And it is fictional that I see her grimacing. In addition, I actually see, through the photograph, the grimace that she effected on the long past occasion of the reunion.

We should add that it is fictional that I see Aunt Mabel *directly*, without photographic assistance. Apart from very special cases, when in looking at a picture it is fictional that one sees something, it is fictional that one sees it not through a photograph or a mirror or a telescope but with the naked eye. Fictionally one is in the presence of what one sees.

One such special case is Richard Shirley's beautiful film *Resonant* (1969), which was made by filming still photographs (of an elderly woman, her house, her belongings). Sometimes this is obvious: sometimes, for example, we see the edges of the filmed photographs. When we do, it is fictional that we see the house or whatever through the photographs. But much of *Resonant* is fascinatingly ambiguous. The photographs are not always apparent. Sometimes when they are not, it is probably best to say that fictionally we see things directly. Sometimes we have the impression of fictionally seeing things directly, only to realize later that fictionally we saw them via still photographs. Sometimes, probably, there is no fact of the matter. Throughout, the viewer *actually* sees still photographs, via the film, whether or not he realizes that he does. And he actually sees the woman and the house through the photographs which he sees through the film.

We now have uncovered a major source of the confusion which infects writings about photography and film: failure to recognize and distinguish clearly between the special kind of seeing which actually occurs and the ordinary kind of seeing which only fictionally takes place, between a viewer's *really* seeing something *through a photograph* and his *fictionally* seeing something *directly*. A vague awareness of both, stirred together in a witches' cauldron, could conceivably tempt one toward the absurdity that the viewer is really in the presence of the object.

[. . .]

Film, Photography, and Transparency ■■■ 73

With these objections laid to rest, it is time to tackle directly the question of what it is about photographs that makes them transparent. The reason why we see through photographs but not paintings is related to a difference in how we acquire information from pictures of the two kinds. Suppose an explorer emerges from a central African jungle with a batch of photographic dinosaur-pictures, purportedly shot in the bush and processed straightforwardly. The pictures (together with background information) may convince us that there is a dinosaur lurking in the jungle. Alternatively, suppose that he emerges with a sheaf of dinosaur-sketches, purportedly drawn from life in the field. Again, we may be convinced of the existence of a dinosaur. Perhaps the photographs are more convincing than the drawings, but they needn't be. That is not the crucial difference between them; we *might* have better reason to trust the drawings than the photographs. The important difference is that, in the case of the sketches, we rely on the picture maker's belief that there is a dinosaur in a way in which we don't in the case of the photographs.

The drawings indicate to us what was in the jungle by indicating what the artist *thought* was there. We have reason to believe that the artist set out to draw what he saw and that he is a competent draftsman. Since the sketches show a dinosaur, we judge that he thought he saw one. Taking him to be a reliable observer, we judge that the dinosaur he thought he saw was actually there. We trust *his* judgment – our information about the dinosaur is secondhand.

We don't need to rely on the photographer's judgment in the same way. We may infer that he believes in the dinosaur, knowing that he was looking through the viewfinder when the pictures were taken. We might even assume that it is because he believed there was a dinosaur that the photographs exist or are as they are – we may assume that he aimed the camera where he did and snapped the shutter when he did because he thought he spotted a dinosaur. But no such inferences or assumptions are required for our judgment of the dinosaur's existence. Even if we know or suspect that he didn't see the dinosaur, that he left the camera on a tripod with an automatic triggering device, for instance, we may still infer the existence of the dinosaur from the photographs. In fact, if the photographs *do* convince us that he believed in the dinosaur, they do so because they convince us that there *was* a dinosaur, not the other way around.

We do need to make certain assumptions if we are going to trust the photographs: that the camera was of a certain sort, that no monkey business was involved in the processing, and so on. These may require our accepting the say-so of the photographer; we may have to trust him. And it could be that we are being taken for a ride. It is easy to see that this sort of reliance on the photographer does not mean that we do not see through his photographs. In order to trust the evidence of my senses, I must always make certain assumptions about them and the circumstances in which they operate: that they are not influenced by hallucination-inducing drugs, that they are not being fed misinformation by an evil neurosurgeon, and so forth. I might rely on someone else's word in making these assumptions; I might consult a beneficent doctor. If he assures me that the system is operating normally, and it is, then I am seeing (or perceiving), notwithstanding my reliance on him.

The manner in which we trust the photographer when his photographs convince us of the existence of the dinosaur differs significantly from the manner in which we rely on the artist when we are persuaded by his sketches. Both sets of pictures have a counterfactual dependence on the scene in the jungle. In both cases, if the scene had been different – if there had been no dinosaur, for example – the pictures would have been different (and so would our visual experiences when we look at them). This is why, in both cases, given that the pictures are as they are, we can judge that the scene was as it was. But why are these counterfactuals true? A difference in the scene would have made a difference in the sketches because it would have made a difference in the artist's beliefs (and hence in the way he sketched or whether he sketched at all). But that is not why a difference in the scene would have made a difference in the photographs. *They* would have been different had the scene been different *even if* the photographer believed, and so aimed and snapped his camera, as he actually did. Suppose that the picture maker – artist or photographer – is hallucinating the dinosaur which he attempts to portray. The artist's sketches will show a dinosaur nonetheless, but the photographs will not. What the sketches show depends on what the artist thinks he sees, whether or not he is right; the actual scene in the jungle is, in *this* way, irrelevant to how his pictures turn out. But if the photographer thinks he sees a dinosaur and acts accordingly, what his photographs show is determined by what is really there before him, regardless of what he thinks. The artist draws his hallucination; the camera bypasses the photographer's hallucination and captures what is in the jungle.

A person's belief can be relevantly based on someone else's even if he doesn't realize that it is. If what convinces me of the dinosaur's existence is a painting which I take to be a photograph, I may suppose mistakenly that my belief is independent of the picture maker's and that I see the dinosaur. My grounds for my belief do not include his belief. But still, the absence of the dinosaur would have made a difference in the picture only because it would have made a difference in the artist's belief. Unbeknown to me, my belief is (relevantly) dependent on his, and I am wrong in thinking I see the dinosaur.

Not all theories of perception postulate a strong link between perceiving and believing. We needn't assume such a link. The essential difference between paintings and photographs is the difference in the manner in which they, not the beliefs of those who see them, are based on beliefs of their makers. Photographs are counterfactually dependent on the photographed scene even if the beliefs (and other intentional attitudes) of the photographer are held fixed. Paintings which have a counterfactual dependence on the scene portrayed lose it when the beliefs (and other intentional attitudes) of the painter are held fixed. Both the beliefs and the visual experiences which the viewer derives from a picture are dependent on the picture maker's beliefs in whichever manner the picture itself is. In order to see through the picture to the scene depicted, the viewer must have visual experiences which do not depend on the picture maker's beliefs in the way that paintings do. We can leave open the question of whether, to be seeing the scene, the viewer must have beliefs about it and what connection there may be between his visual experiences and his beliefs.

A familiar pair of science fiction examples may help to convince some that I am on the right track. Suppose that a neurosurgeon disconnects Helen's eyes from her optic nerves and rigs up a device whereby he can stimulate the optic nerves at will. The doctor then stimulates Helen's nerves in ways corresponding to what he sees, with the result that she has "visual" experiences like ones she would have normally if she were using her own eyes. Let us add the assumption that the doctor is conscientious about feeding Helen correct information and that she has every reason to trust him. Helen *seems* to be seeing things, and her visual experiences are caused by the things which she seems to see. But she doesn't really see them; the doctor is seeing for her. This is because her visual experiences are based on his in the way I described. It is only because differences in scenes make for differences in the doctor's beliefs that they make for differences in her visual experiences.

Contrast a patient who receives a double eye transplant or a patient who is fitted with artificial prosthetic eyes. This patient *does* see. He is not relying in the relevant manner on anyone's beliefs about the things he sees, although his visual experiences do depend on the work of the surgeon and on the donor of the transplanted eyes or the manufacturer of the prosthetic ones. In real life, cataract patients owe their visual experiences to others. All of our visual experiences depend on acts of omission by those who have refrained from altering or destroying our visual organs. Obviously these facts do not blind us.

[. . .]

What is photographic realism? Transparency is not the whole story. Realism is a concept with many faces, and photography wears more than one of them. We must not forget how adept photography is at portraying subtleties of texture, shadow, and reflection; how effortlessly it captures the jumbled trivia of ordinary life; how skillfully it uses perspective. The capacity of photography as it is now practiced to "reveal reality" is especially important. Photographic evidence is often very reliable – hence its usefulness in court proceedings and extortion plots. This is no automatic consequence of the "mechanicalness" of the photographic process, however. It derives rather from the fact that our photographic equipment and procedures happen to be standardized in certain respects. (They are not standardized in all respects, of course; so we have to be selective about what conclusions we draw from photographs. We can usually say little beyond gross approximations about the absolute illumination of a scene, for example, on the basis of a photograph, since shutter speeds, film speeds, and lens apertures are so variable.)

But photography's various other talents must not be confused with or allowed to obscure its remarkable ability to put us in perceptual contact with the world, an ability which can be claimed even by a fuzzy and badly exposed snapshot depicting few details and offering little information. It is this – photography's transparency – which is most distinctively photographic and which constitutes the most important justification for speaking of "photographic realism."

8

Non-fictional Cinematic Artworks and Knowledge

Trevor Ponech

I

Even if you have never heard the term "cinematic non-fiction," you are probably familiar with this gigantic cultural category. Television news, investigative reporting, and public affairs programs fit the genre, as do talk, game, and "reality TV" shows. Most people have also seen theatrical release non-fictions, exhibited in movie theaters or at film festivals in roughly the way feature-length fictional movies are distributed. Michael Moore's popular *Bowling for Columbine* is an example of this sort of non-fiction.

Theorists typically use the concept of realism to categorize movies, in all their thematic, stylistic, and formal diversity, as non-fiction. It's claimed that, whatever else they are or do, paradigmatic non-fictions supposedly represent reality, versus the unreal, imaginary entities presented by fictional movies. This definition implies a deep, projectable relationship between a work's ascribed or actual epistemological function and its being non-fiction. Why is *Bowling for Columbine* non-fiction? A careful answer in the realist vein – one not tethered to unattainable standards of perfect truthfulness – might reply: because its makers use its imagery and sounds to assert beliefs that certain entities, states of affairs, situations, and events actually occur(red) or exist(ed) in the actual world, as portrayed.

Conceiving of non-fiction cinema in terms of reality fosters a preoccupation with questions about their reliability as a means of acquiring knowledge – true and justified beliefs – of the world. Hence the great divide within non-fiction theory is that between two epistemological camps. There are those of us who are sanguine about the medium's potential for facilitating epistemic access to reality. The opposing faction contends that since non-fictions are perforce selective, manipulative, and subjective, they cannot escape the vacuum of error, groundless belief, and politically motivated misrepresentation to which all attempts at knowledge are predestined.

Preoccupation with the genre's realism is doubly unfortunate. First, it needlessly weakens the distinction between fiction and non-fiction by giving naysayers of the genre's epistemic fidelity grounds to assert the insubstantial, merely stipulated

7 ■ "Hitler rallying the troops,"
from *Triumph of the Will*.

boundaries separating non-fiction from fiction. For one could say that, despite conventional differences in how it is labeled and treated, non-fiction is ultimately like fiction because it traffics in falsehood and fantasy. Using artifice, narrative, figuration, and symbolism, it offers not a window onto the world but an often rankly ideological contrivance of how someone imagines or desires the world to be.

Secondly, by riveting attention on epistemological matters, the realist preoccupation does a poor job of understanding non-fiction cinema as an artform. A ubiquitous, otherwise heterogeneous group of non-fictions consists of movies resembling fictions insofar as they, too, are works of art and entertainment. They offer audiences pleasures distinct from the satisfaction of learning about reality or gaining information of practical import. Their formal and stylistic properties, narrative, and thematic features are themselves meant to attract viewers' attention and reward contemplation. Reality TV shows compensate for their fatuousness by being highly diverting (so I'm told). *Bowling for Columbine* is surely non-fiction art; as are Leni Riefenstahl's *Triumph of the Will* and Errol Morris's *The Thin Blue Line*, along with experimental works like Dudley Murphey and Fernand Léger's *Ballet mécanique* and Hollis Frampton's (*nostalgia*). Cinematic artworks having no or little cognitive utility are usually ignored by theories of non-fiction. Even when realism does explicitly grapple with non-fiction cinema as art, it tends to view art-making as something that can and should subserve the genre's irreplaceable, stereotypical cognitive function. That function is, however, contingent, not definitive or necessary. Something's being non-fiction, like its being art, has nothing essentially to do with containing knowledge or conveying facts. And art-making, when it coincides with non-fictioneering, is not necessarily consistent with gaining knowledge.

We customarily judge non-fictions as succeeding to the degree they serve cognitive functions to someone's satisfaction. Certain works are appropriately evaluated in this way. Others, being artworks, need have no epistemic value to succeed as non-fictions. If and when they do have a substantive cognitive dimension, its significance is mainly artistic. This claim inverts the arch realist premise that the aim of non-fiction art-making is epistemic access to the world. I'll argue that the cognitive import of many non-fiction movies is secondary to their aesthetic merit, their interest for us often being as artworks, not vehicles for true, justified, illuminating beliefs about reality. In contrast to TV newscasts, *The Thin Blue Line*, *Bowling For Columbine*, and *Ballet mécanique* subordinate or efface epistemic qualities to artistic ones. The challenge, finally, is to show how epistemic qualities can be reasons for aesthetic evaluations, so we might say that *Thin Blue Line* is an excellent work of art in part because of its epistemic strengths, while *Triumph of the Will* is artistically flawed because of its weaknesses.

II

Recording and expressing beliefs or facts about reality are standard goals of some cinematic non-fictions. But my position is that no essential, definitive connection exists between them and a work's being non-fiction. Likewise, a movie can be an abysmal epistemic failure, it can describe imaginary rather than actual entities, express no beliefs, or be full of artifice and figuration, yet be utterly non-fiction. Neither stating nor seeking truth is an essential, constitutive aim of non-fiction. Moreover, to say that a movie, or any other type of communication, is non-fiction is not the same as to say that it makes assertions about reality.

Luckily, there are grounds for labeling a movie non-fiction that are independent of its representing reality. The best current taxonomy of human communicative action comes from speech act theory. A key tenet of that theory is that meaning under-determines illocutionary force. An utterance's illocutionary force is an intention its utterer expresses. It is the utterer's open expression, in a manner intelligible to a target audience, of his or her intention that they adopt a particular attitude toward the utterance's content. At a party, I tell you, "The man with the martini is a renowned documentary filmmaker." I utter this proposition intending you to take the attitude of belief toward its content – that is, mentally assent, perhaps unconsciously, to its truth. You, in turn, more or less by default assume that I am signaling to you to believe what I've said. Your knowledge of the English language, of the context of the utterance, and of my apparent literalness and sincerity support your assumption, which just seems to make the best sense of why I spoke as I did, under the circumstances.

Normally one asserts something in order to trigger a corresponding belief in one's audience. This sort of communication usually involves a mutual interest in indi-viduating what belief is being expressed, the literalness and sincerity with which it is expressed, and whether things in reality are as they are described to be. Contrast assertion with fiction-making: Here the utterance's force is an invitation to fantasize or make-believe that the represented events are real, where this activity is internally motivated, which is to say, one imagines primarily for the pleasure of fantasizing.

An utterance's meaning is indeed a poor guide to its force. Instead of being an asser-tion, "The man with the martini is a renowned documentary filmmaker" could be said as part of a game of make-believe, during which I invite you to imagine the described situation. Or I could be making a kind of joke, speaking non-literally and insincerely, with our shared knowledge that the martini drinker is really just a self-important would-be *auteur*. Likewise, assertions need not be about reality. The martini drinker might only be an obscure poet, in which case I will have failed to refer to reality in quite the way I thought I had. Yet my utterance's force remains unchanged. More dramatically, I could be delusional, hallucinating renowned documentarians where none exists. I am nonetheless signaling assertive illocutionary intent. Calm, level-headed people make assertions about imaginary, fictive, non-actual entities, too. Shake-speare scholars have no trouble making genuine, sincere assertions about Hamlet's motivations. Physicists make speculative assertions about quantum phenomena that they realize might not exist as described in theory. Being about reality is only a contingent property of assertions.

Looking to speech act theory's model, we get the following definition of one major class of cinematic non-fictions. Such a work consists of cinematic imagery having assertive force: its makers explicitly invite their audience to take the attitude of belief toward the represented objects, states of affairs, situations, and events. Using sound as well as pictures, *Bowling for Columbine* presents its director walking into a bank and receiving a free rifle on the spot in return for opening an account. This sequence, like the whole movie, is non-fiction because of something Moore *does*, namely, openly signaling to viewers his intention they adopt the attitude of belief toward the described event.

Not all non-fiction pertains to assertion. The speech act taxonomy also recognizes directives (e.g. requests, prohibitions), commissives (promises, offers), and acknowledgments (apologies, greetings) – all logically distinct from fictioneering. And some non-fiction communication eludes tidy assignment of force, insofar as it is intentionally ambiguous or indeterminate what belief if any is being articulated. Two cinematic examples come to mind. Neither prescribes the attitude of make-believe, so neither is fictional. Yet neither gives its audience reason to assume automatically that the communicator resolutely means for them to assent to any proposition.

Consider highly formalist cinematic works, which needn't have determinate representational content. Many aspiring avant-gardists scratch squiggly lines onto raw film stock then project the results for gatherings of excited connoisseurs. Neither expression nor ascription of any illocutionary force is required to fulfill the point of these experiments: rapt contemplation of the rhythmic jig of patterns on the screen.

Other formalist experiments, like Frampton's (*nostalgia*), go beyond encouraging spectators to notice patterns and make abstract, formal associations. These works are surely about something; but they express their substantive conceptual content non-literally, employing images and sounds figuratively. Like figurative discourse in general, they are designed to provoke audiences to work out some range of ideas, not all of which the author had specifically in mind. Figurative communication is thus an interactive phenomenon of use, the author's role being to manipulate language or imagery in order to guide interpreters toward a somewhat open-ended set of meanings. One strategy is to present a juxtaposition or comparison of things that initially seems incongruous, thereby encouraging an audience to engage in a context-relative process of adjustment and amplification. In (*nostalgia*), twelve separate shots show, one after another photograph being gradually incinerated on a hotplate. While looking at one photo, the spectator hears a narrator's reminiscences about the next to appear, the viewer thus always at a disadvantage to recall the significance of the photograph currently on screen. Taken at face value, with regard only to their literal meanings, the conjunction of images of burning photographs with these verbal utterances is puzzling. Yet the movie's title, along with the fact that we are watching a movie, provide a context in which to explore the implications. It is in this way that we are led to consider the salient respects in which the film's structure and content are like memory; and further, how the succession of burning images is in relevant ways like the cinema itself.

As non-fiction, (*nostalgia*) is a cogitative film. Judging by this work, Frampton entertained various thoughts about cinema's affinity with memory. Using figuration, he encourages us to tease out some of these thoughts, amplifying and expanding them as we go. The filmmaker doesn't thereby assert anything. If a belief is a proposition one sincerely and understandingly affirms, then what exactly he believes about his topic is unspecified. Correspondingly, the film indicates no commitment on Frampton's part to individuate his beliefs and signal an expectation that we adopt an attitude of belief to these propositions. (*nostalgia*) is not thus made fictional – it does not prescribe that we engage in a game of making-believe or fantasizing that the described events are occurring. It is, rather, a cogitative non-fiction. It expresses, indirectly and artfully, a certain line of thinking, a thought being an idea entertained without commitment to asserting or affirming it. Having these thoughts cross our minds, elaborating on them according to the work's cues, are among the chief pleasures of watching this kind of movie.

Though a contingent property, the cognitive function is widespread across the non-fiction genre, making it trivially true that many movies are designed to communicate beliefs and facts about reality. But this function is multifarious. It countenances wildly varying degrees of commitment to the acquisition of knowledge. *F for Fake*, Orson Welles's cunning documentary about art forgery, revels in its own unreliability. Welles delights in gulling viewers with anecdotes, stories, and scenes that he almost simultaneously disavows as misleading, mere conjecture, or wholly false. There's a higher purpose to his chicanery, harnessed to his personal ruminations on the kinship of artists, forgers, filmmakers, and magicians. Welles surely has in mind a few propositions he wants to assert, the content of which he takes to be true or plausible. So playful is his film, though, that it is not obvious that he feels at all responsible for grounding his assertions in any norms of evidence and reasoning beyond those which ordinary interlocutors tacitly appeal to while conversing informally. Least of all does *F for Fake* rigorously *inquire*, as a philosopher would, into the truth of whether art perforce involves illusion.

Other non-fictioneers are thoroughly committed to presenting facts or propositions, observations, or a theory or hypothesis, the truth of which is of focal concern to them. I call these works confirmatives. A confirmative non-fiction results from, and perhaps partly comprises, truth seeking investigative, observational, experimental, and explanatory procedures. These films closely follow an epistemic plan, their makers embracing the task of explicitly presenting evidence and reasoning in support of asserting a clearly articulated belief. By plan, I mean a sort of recipe: an integrated set of goals, plus some steps for realizing them, effectively guiding filmmakers' deliberations and actions in making the movie. This plan is epistemic in that it aims toward goals like instructing or informing; bringing some putative knowledge to an audience's attention; inquiring into a proposition's accuracy or truth; collecting and preserving evidence; observing or recording situations and events, especially with a view to studying, explaining, or interpreting them; reflecting critically on a theme, topic, or epistemic concern, including the perennial subject of cinema's strengths and limitations as a means of acquiring, producing, and conveying knowledge.

While spectators could glean assorted facts (about film technology, aesthetic doctrines, hotplate design, etc.) from abstract and cogitative non-fictions, these movies are unlikely to be the proximal outcome of epistemic plans. Conversely, for all their flaws and biases, television news shows certainly do emerge from such constraints. Although situated at the more commonplace, less scientific end of the spectrum of confirmatives, it is always appropriate to judge these works primarily in terms of their epistemic reliability. Other confirmative works embody epistemic plans writ large: At the far end of the confirmative spectrum are hardcore works, typically integrated with social or natural scientific research and teaching. For instance, Theodore Bestor's *Neighborhood Tokyo* grows out of the anthropologist's field research into the socioeconomic transformations overtaking a closely knit community of small business-owning families; and Frans de Waal's *Social Ethogram of the San Diego Bonobos* is culled from 80 hours of footage that the primatologist shot while studying social behaviors of captive Bonobo chimps. Judging these works' success requires familiarity with the methods, current research, and theories in the pertinent fields, the live debates therein, and the special standards by which explanations are evaluated.

Notice that the non-fiction genre is heterogeneous – a mixed bag of formalist, cogitative, assertive, and confirmative works. No property is shared essentially, necessarily, and exclusively by all exemplars. Not even the absence of fiction is a universal characteristic of non-fiction. Peter Watkins's *The War Game* takes the form of a fictive documentary about a wholly imaginary course of events. He invites us to imagine that we are watching actual news footage of circumstances leading up to and following a Soviet nuclear attack on Britain. Watkins's prescription of these grim imaginings is not intrinsically motivated; it is not for its own sake that he invites audiences into the dramatic, emotionally engrossing experience of making-believe that Kent is incinerated. Instead, his predominant motivation is extrinsic, namely, asserting the likely consequences of a nuclear assault, according to historical records and empirical studies Watkins cites at the end of his film.

A definition of the non-fiction genre as a whole needs to avoid the cognitive fallacy. It must be exclusive enough to be informative and helpful in distinguishing the genre from mere fiction. But it should be inclusive enough to embrace formalist and cogitative movies and to accommodate works arising from very complex, hierarchical arrangements of communicative plans. I suggest, then, that a work is non-fiction if it satisfies either of two conditions pertaining to the expressive goals of its maker(s). Here expression should be construed broadly as any movie-making activity, the purpose of which is to trigger in some audience a certain perception, impression, or affective response, or to indicate to them a certain idea, thought, belief, or proposition. I assume having expressive properties is partly constitutive of being a cinematic work. A cinematic non-fiction therefore results when, in making the work, the maker either (i) fails to express the intention that audiences should imagine or make-believe anything in response to the movie; or (ii) expresses fiction-making intentions, but in subordination to an assertive (directive, commissive, acknowledgment) illocutionary plan.

III

Non-fiction conceptually dissevered from its stereotypical cognitive function, we can now start to examine its adaptability to other ends. My construction of the genre allows for the possibility of filmmakers' expressive goals being mainly artistic. My concept of "non-fiction cinematic artwork" cuts across most other functions, modes, movements, traditions, periods, and subgeneric distinctions. Otherwise dissimilar non-fictions can be alike in being artworks. I take a non-fiction artwork to be one made primarily with the expressed intention of evoking an aesthetic response, that is, an attempt to identify aesthetic value properties in it. Although I leave readers to their own intuitions about what such properties are, my own list would certainly include the likes of beauty, vibrancy, tempo, humorousness, suspense, figuration, narrative (un)reliability, skillfulness, and originality.

My concern with non-fiction cinema as art has an important forerunner in a grand old theory that famously helped shape the history of non-fiction film. This antecedent is, however, highly problematic in ways having to do with the relevance of knowledge to non-fiction art.

John Grierson, the founder of the documentary film movement in the 1930s, is an early and influential exponent of non-fiction cinema as more than mere recording of reality or transmission of facts. He admires non-fictions that are also "creative shapings" of materials drawn from life.[1] This subgenre of non-fiction he calls documentaries. For Grierson, documentary proper pertains to social realities and public issues, and is advocative of reformist, ostensibly progressive social-political goals. It also aspires to rise to the level of poetry. Taking cities, slums, markets, and factories as subjects, documentary gives itself "the job of making poetry where no poet has gone before it, and where no ends, sufficient for the purposes of art, are easily observed."[2]

Griersonian documentary isn't decadent art for art's sake. Explicitly denying that it is art in the Kantian sense of "purposiveness without purpose," he characterizes the genre as having the "quite unaesthetic purpose" of public education in matters of sociological, political, and economic concern.[3] Its artistic properties and merits thus seem pertinent only insofar as they facilitate the maker's expression of a given message or the audience's uptake. Yet Grierson also apparently regards the documentary as occasioning more than art's secondment to non-aesthetic ends, the documentary's artistic value properties somehow depending on or intertwining with its cognitive ones. Documentarians, writes Grierson, produce art by engaging in "laborious, deep-seeing, deep-sympathizing creative effort."[4] Invoking Plato, he suggests that documentarians' capacity for presenting stories, producing drama, and giving poetic form to their material is conditional on their "long intercourse with the thing itself."[5] Contrasted with the fantasy and "shim-sham mechanics" he associates with cinematic fiction, Grierson sees the documentarian's artistic choices and the documentary's aesthetic worth as informed by insights into reality.[6]

Grierson's arguments are polemical and informal, making it hard to identify the premises underlying his envisioned cinematic synthesis of art with knowledge. He refers to documentary's artistic value as a "by-product" of the maker's pursuit of cognitive and ethical-political goals.[7] Yet this effect seems not just a happy coincidence, but intended, since Grierson also urges non-fictioneers to try to create art and recommends a privileged method toward that end. Inspiring though his sentiments are, they never rise beyond expressing an instrumental attitude toward the documentarian's art. He never explicitly indicates whether and, if so, how a documentary's insightful use of materials drawn from life guarantees that it will have poetic qualities. Perhaps he assumes that knowledge is a constitutive property of art, or at least of great art. But that thesis is controvertible and itself begs the relevance question, that is, the question of how cognitive merits improve artworks artistically. At most, Grierson implies that a documentary is good on balance if it is good artistically as well as informative, civically responsible, etc., this latter cohort of epistemic, practical, and moral value properties making it no better or worse artistically.

If ever a cinematic non-fiction is also an artwork, it is inappropriate to link its value overall or in the first instance with its cognitive aims. If one's overriding objectives in making a movie truly are knowledge acquisition and transmission, then treating reality poetically is likely to be of low priority, if not completely unfeasible. Exemplary Griersonian documentaries – Basil Wright's *Song of Ceylon*, Arthur Elton and Edgar Anstey's *Housing Problems*, Wright and Harry Watt's *Night Mail*, Grierson's own *Drifters* – are obviously designed as vehicles of public education. Yet unlike, say, hardcore confirmative movies, none of these evinces a thoroughgoing epistemic commitment.

Song of Ceylon is typical in being a superficial examination of its subject, the harvest and marketing of tea, endowed with aesthetically commendable features, such as its lyrical imagery of Ceylon and complex, densely layered soundtrack. Wright surely wanted to help Britons understand how their tea gets to their cups. But his choice to do so artistically, with the Empire Tea Marketing Expansion Board's support, failed to shed any light on how international market forces disadvantage colonized laborers, to note but one shortcoming. Having cognitive (moral, political) objectives as one's primary reason for art-making thus doesn't guarantee the conduciveness of art-making to serious non-aesthetic goals. On the contrary, it might well be the case that *Song of Ceylon* is made artistically better by its epistemic weakness. Perhaps it would not have been as lyrical in quite the way it is had its maker been genuinely preoccupied with global economics. But if some epistemic faults can improve the work artistically, it follows that others could detract from it artistically. Here we finally raise an idea unaccommodated by Grierson's realist, instrumental doctrine of non-fiction art, namely, that a non-fiction's epistemic properties might be most significant for their conduciveness to artistic values and goals, rather than the other way around.

IV

Cinematic non-fictions – including ones with marked cognitive utility – often matter more as artworks than as contributions to knowledge. Being art, their principal interest is their aesthetic traits, to which knowledge is sometimes a tributary.

The Thin Blue Line presents a story of a man wrongly condemned to death for a Dallas police officer's murder. In making his film, Morris pursued an ambitious epistemic plan of painstaking research into myriad aspects of Randall Adams's case, even acquiring exculpatory evidence along the way. Hence *The Thin Blue Line* falls inside the broad ambit of cinematic confirmatives. Yet not all cinematic confirmatives have an unalloyed interest in truth-seeking. It seems mistaken to conclude that its production, like a hardcore confirmative, is extrinsically motivated by unequivocally cognitive and practical interests. More plausibly, its epistemic plan itself is an input to Morris's attempt to create a work with intrinsic artistic worth. His movie contains no explicitly stated hypothesis or argument. Instead, it offers a story with a theme: how easily irrationality, deception, scapegoating, and indifference can undermine truth-seeking and justice. In narrating its story and bringing us to contemplate its theme, *The Thin Blue Line* adopts various stylistic devices, like the evocation of *film noir* motifs. It makes extensive use of figuration, using, for example, images of city maps as an ironic symbol of how desperately lost Adams, a stranger in Dallas, would become. Thus Morris invites us to respond aesthetically to his style, story, and narrative strategies. We are to engage with his work by teasing out its metaphors and by experiencing the sense of doom and suspense it wrings from its material.

The Thin Blue Line is an excellent non-fiction cinematic artwork; part of its artistic success derives from such epistemic merits as an intelligent exploration of its theme. How are these merits aesthetically relevant? Epistemic and aesthetic values are supposedly different things. Furthermore, artworks per se arguably must possess features only properly appreciated and evaluated independent of their truth or falsity. Someone asking after a work's cognitive utility would thus be missing the point of art, like somebody whose interest in music is whether it cheers him up.

My conception of an epistemic value property includes truth or falsity. Something's serving as or presenting evidence and justification for a belief's truth are also epistemic values. Generally, though, I have such properties in mind as facilitate our gaining knowledge of features of reality, including the cinematic work's photographic properties. One way in which an artwork, fictional or non-fiction, supports epistemic access is by offering a thought-provoking, illuminating perspective on a topic or problem, especially one of abiding if not universal human concern. The work's role in this respect isn't that of a source of decisive evidence or truthful representations of actual, particular events. Its cognitive value derives from its lucidly commenting on and thereby deepening our understanding of a concept, puzzle, situation type, or human concern, taken at a fairly abstract level of description. *The Thin Blue Line*, which vividly models the undermining of truth-seeking by self-interest, desire, and fantasy, thus owes much of its epistemic merit to its capacity to prime our intuitions and refine our thinking about the sources of the sources of breakdowns in human rationality.

Epistemic features could be artistically pertinent to a work's merit in several ways. On one analysis, relevance is secured via "expression-assessment."[8] Here, the truth of ideas contained in a work does not bear directly on aesthetic evaluation. Rather, judgments of truth or falsehood sometimes support properly aesthetic judgments about how well ideas are expressed or how effectively they are put to properly aesthetic uses.

A possible aesthetic evaluation of *Bowling For Columbine* is that its humorous tone is sustained with frequent recourse to cheap and easy laughs. In support, an interpreter could cite jokes constructed from a stereotypical, naive idea of Canada's national peaceableness. Hence the way in which a naive idea is expressed – namely, how it is combined with the aesthetic goal of comedy – is the object of critical assessment. Although the movie's intellectual failure isn't itself artistically interesting – we're neither condemning nor praising it for being wrong about Canadians – it is part of an aesthetic evaluation of the movies' brand of shallow but effective humor.

Another approach to the relevance problem holds that knowledge comes into play artistically by triggering certain responses in the work's audience. All sorts of artworks convey facts and useful information, but that's hardly an aesthetic value. However, some have a cognitive-affective upshot. Art can make knowledge concrete, vivid, salient, and emotionally interesting. In this way, it imparts new concepts and discriminatory skills, triggers the dawning of new perspectives from which hitherto unnoticed aspects of reality become recognizable, and reorders our thoughts and feelings about the world. *The Thin Blue Line*'s epistemic value thus converges with its aesthetic merit to the degree that, by recruiting and focusing our perceptual and imaginative involvement in Adams's predicament, it gives us an intimate sense of how a justice system can devolve to irrational scapegoating.

A third way to secure aesthetic relevance is to allow that epistemic value is partially constitutive of an artwork's identity. Aside from being a physical item, an artwork is an individual's, or group of individuals', personal achievement. This work encompasses actions and efforts, including mental efforts like reasoning, planning, and imagining, that go into the work's execution. Part of understanding and appreciating an artwork consists of recognizing the quality of mind in it. Thus part of what makes *The Thin Blue Line* the movie that it is – part of what establishes its identity as this particular artwork – consists of various skills, talents, and attitudes that Morris and his artistic collaborators effectively acted upon and that the finished work exhibits. Many such skills and talents are guided by, and serve to express, the artists' attitudes toward their subject. Think of the use of Philip Glass's coiling, recursive score to evoke the idea of the ever-tightening trap sprung on Adams. Such attitudes comprise an important object of the audience's aesthetic interest, namely, the work's unique perspective on a given topic or theme.

Unlike philosophical treatises, scientific papers, or hardcore confirmative movies, artworks don't succeed to the extent that they succeed cognitively; despite serious epistemic flaws, they can still be artistically admirable. Yet epistemic value is aesthetically relevant insofar as epistemic plans and skills are proximal conditions of the artwork's emergence, and the work's perspective betokens epistemic attitudes and actions. To contemplate the work's perspective is to evaluate, and admire accordingly, the sophistication, depth, and perceptiveness of the thoughts and ideas presented. To the extent that a work betokens insightful, illuminating thinking, astute observation, and significant truths, we are right to praise it for these epistemic strengths. The object of our admiration is here not restricted to engendered cognitive-affective responses or felicity of expression. It includes the makers' epistemic excellence, a quality of certain of their thoughts and actions, as occasioned by their filmmaking activities and embodied in the resulting movie. Like originality or technical virtuosity, which acquire aesthetic relevance in relation to their historical role in a work's emergence, it is something artists can achieve in making a work. Correspondingly, identification and comprehension of the expressed perspective occur jointly with our epistemic judgments of it.

V

Confirmative *The Thin Blue Line* and cogitative (*nostalgia*) are very different kinds of non-fictions. But they are alike in being art. They issue from their makers' guiding intentions to produce films eliciting aesthetic responses. While only one derives from a properly epistemic plan embedded within an art-making plan, both are aesthetically the better for being epistemically commendable. The insightful perspectives that each affords are objects of contemplation, as well as reasons to admire the artists' work, that is, the thought, reasoning, and action effectively giving rise to these movies.

Discerning epistemic value is like discriminating other aesthetic and aesthetically relevant traits. Beyond art-interpretive competence, it might take critical acumen, background knowledge, and specialized study. It also calls for a little reflection on the norms by which we assess the artwork's epistemic success or failure.

There are two main reasons why we would want to ascertain a cinematic non-fiction's epistemic value. On one hand, we could have a cognitive or practical interest in gaining knowledge of a certain part of reality, looking to that work to help us to acquire that knowledge. On the other, we could be intent on exploring the work itself, its distinctive qualities, and the many attitudes, skills, and talents embodied by it. Looking to the work as an object of and opportunity for contemplation and elaboration, we try to grasp the artist's intellectual achievements as part and parcel of our appreciation.

For works at the hardcore end of the confirmative spectrum, the first motivation is virtually our sole concern, epistemic goals being the predominant impetus for those works. Since we expect them to afford knowledge and serve practical functions in our lives, it is appropriate to assess them almost wholly according to rigorous standards of those truth-seeking disciplines out of which they emerge or whose findings they represent. A newscast, weather forecast, wildlife documentary, ethnographic film, or medical training video typically has aesthetic value properties. But the priority it places on knowledge blocks our claiming that it fails epistemically but is good on balance because it is aesthetically superlative.

During aesthetic engagements with artworks, questions of how things stand in reality are not as central as how things are with respect to the work. What we care most about is having attentive, sensitive cognitive and affective responses to the work such that we discover its aesthetic value. The non-fiction cinematic artwork, if it is in fact art, inherits from art as such if not an independence from epistemic qualities, then at least their relegation to a subordinate role of generating aesthetic value. Rather than a "discourse of sobriety," it is an instance of artistic expression that should not be expected to take a focal, uncompromising interest in epistemic concerns.

It follows that non-fiction cinematic artworks permit greater latitude for weighing aesthetic against epistemic value. Epistemic merits and flaws do not necessarily make a decisive difference to the work's artistic value on the whole. Thanks to its formal complexity, virtuoso technique, and originality, the Dadaist *Ballet mécanique* is a great work of non-fiction, and a wonderful work of art, independent of any conceivable cognitive merit. *Bowling for Columbine* might turn out on examination to be riddled with factual errors and ideologically biased beliefs, but it's still a successful satire, some of its effectiveness doubtless owing to its flagrant biases. What's more, a work can be aesthetically bad to the extent that it has a certain epistemic flaw. But were it improved in this respect, the work need not be ultimately or wholly improved aesthetically. So just as we can make *pro tanto* moral judgments of an artwork – holding it to be good or bad *insofar as* it has a certain property – we can mobilize such principles in judging non-fiction cinematic artworks epistemically.

Triumph of the Will provides a case in point. In assessing her movie, our aim is not to discover from it what Riefenstahl firmly believed about Hitler's leadership and National Socialism's policies. Nor should we identify the movie's content with her actual beliefs. Our focus is on the attitudes and thoughts that her work effectively communicates, and the intellectual as well as practical efforts to express them that she and her collaborators evidently made. It is most important, then, to note this film lacks any critical distance whatsoever from the *Führerprinzip*: the conception, rooted in folk beliefs in myths and magic, of Hitler as a mystical leader embodying the true will of a unified, racially homogeneous German people. It appeals explicitly to those irrational beliefs to compose an image of Hitler as a heroic messiah capable of transcending history to deliver the nation from crisis. *Triumph of the Will*'s epistemic faults are those it takes aboard by expressing attitudes consistent with the *Führerprinzip*.

Judging Riefenstahl's work to be flawed in this way presupposes only moderate, subjectively appropriate norms of epistemic rationality. The movie's trouble is not that it adopts a perspective that we, with our historical knowledge, would have no justification for adopting. The problem is that the ideas the director expresses with apparent sincerity are epistemically irrational *for her* to have entertained at the time of their expression. Identifying them as such and rectifying them would have been both cognitively feasible and preferable for her, had not other, non-epistemic matters been uppermost in her mind. Riefenstahl's cognitive breakdown stems from how she actually went about executing the work, namely, with indifference toward truth-seeking. In settling on how she would represent Hitler, she pursued a line of thinking informed more by myth and doctrine than by a cognitive interest in confirmative activities. Evidently, such ratiocination and action were preempted by powerful non-epistemic motivations. Riefenstahl herself has often professed her aestheticism, stressing her uncompromising intention to create as beautiful a movie as possible. A more rounded account of her motivations would also record her opportunism, which made her a much better vector than critic of the contagion of violent sentiments sweeping Germany. Willfully unconcerned with epistemic matters, Riefenstahl was virtually assured, under the circumstances, of instantiating a perspective on her subject that betokens thinking as poorly informed, ideologically overdetermined, and mystified for her as it was for her audience.

What if Riefenstahl had gotten the facts about Nazism right? Would a wiser *Triumph of the Will* be artistically better? Removing cognitive defects, like excising aesthetically relevant moral flaws, is no guarantee that the work will be made artistically better overall. Although *Triumph of the Will* is artistically bad to the degree that it embodies the maker's irrational thoughts about Hitler, changing the movie to make it more incisive might result, all things considered, in a work that is on balance less aesthetically successful. It might possess aesthetic properties directly dependent upon its perspective. Consider its monumental crowd scenes and visually rhyming montage sequences portraying the epic massification of individual Germans, at last unified and harmonized by the Führer. Such qualities could be lost were the perspective improved epistemically. Perhaps *Triumph of the Will* is the artistic achievement it is because of the indissoluble unity of its form and substance. A faulty viewpoint so skillfully woven into cinematic structure is an artistic accomplishment. But our admiration and pleasure are tempered by the underlying failures.

In their postmodern backlash against Grierson's naively optimistic epistemological hopes for the documentary, contemporary theories of non-fiction cinema often associate artistry with epistemic unreliability. It's tempting, then, to pronounce *Triumph of the Will* flawed by being art; and brought closer to the orbit of fiction by its constructedness and illusory view of Hitler issuing more from the filmmakers' imaginations than reality. I have argued that neither art nor error blurs the boundary between non-fiction and fiction. No aesthetic, structural, formal, referential, or cognitive feature identifies a movie as non-fiction or fiction. That distinction is a property of the work's history, one established when its makers express their intentions regarding illocutionary force.

I have also rejected the notion that artistic and epistemic achievements are either naturally indifferent to or incompatible with each other. Granted, making non-fiction art does not necessitate a substantive commitment to knowledge; and some types of confirmative activities fit badly with aesthetic preoccupations. Otherwise, non-fiction cinematic artworks frequently present beliefs, thoughts, and ideas the epistemic value of which is aesthetically relevant as well. Riefenstahl's artwork stumbles in the respect that its perspective is intellectually defective; it is no great feat for her to have offered audiences the chance to conceive of Hitler as messianic. *The Thin Blue Line*, in contrast, is the more intellectually edifying and artistically admirable for Morris's epistemic accomplishments. A good theory of non-fiction cinema should help discern these kinds of salient differences in artistic and epistemic merit. In doing so, it improves our understanding of a cinematic artform overshadowed by the art of cinematic fiction and obscured by an emphasis on non-fiction's informational, instrumental aspects.

NOTES

1 John Grierson, "Documentary (1)," *Cinema Quarterly* (Winter 1932): 68.
2 John Grierson, "First Principles of Documentary," in Forsyth Hardy, ed., *Grierson on Documentary*, 2nd rev. edn. (London: Faber and Faber, 1979), p. 41.

3 John Grierson, "The Documentary Idea: 1942," in Hardy, ed., *Grierson on Documentary*, pp. 112–13.

4 Grierson, "First Principles of Documentary," p. 41.

5 John Grierson, "Flaherty," in Hardy, ed., *Grierson on Documentary*, p. 33.

6 Grierson, "First Principles of Documentary," p. 37.

7 Ibid., p. 41; see also his "Propaganda and Education," in Hardy, ed., *Grierson on Documentary*, p. 150.

8 Richard Miller, "Truth in Beauty," *American Philosophical Quarterly* 16 (1979): 317–25.

Part III

Do Films Have Authors?

Introduction

Film as an art form is characterized by its cooperative nature. After watching any movie at your local multiplex, don't bolt for the exit when the story is over but remain in your seat and notice the literally scores of people who worked together to make the film you have just watched. To adapt a recent saying, it takes a village to make a movie.

Given the fact that filmmaking is inherently a joint venture with many participants, does it make sense to see just one or perhaps two individuals as the real creative source of the film, those to whom we can trace all of the film's virtues and vices? This is the central issue posed by the question of whether films have authors. And the answer suggested by the *auteur* theory is that the director(s) is (are) the controlling intelligence behind the making of a film.

This ontological question about who or what is responsible for the film's existence is supplemented by two other related issues. The first concerns film interpretation: in interpreting a film, is it possible, given the cooperative nature of film production, to treat the film as the product of a single guiding hand? Or does it make more sense to see films as made by committees – with the concomitant possibility of tensions and incoherences? The second question presses these questions in regard to film evaluation: who (or what) deserves the credit for a film's success or failure?

Given these distinct issues, it is important to determine which version of *auteur* theory – ontological, interpretive, or evaluative – a given theorist is endorsing or questioning. It is possible to deny *auteur*ism in regard to one issue while affirming it in another.

Our first selection comes from François Truffaut, the famous New Wave director who wrote for *Cahiers du Cinéma* before becoming a filmmaker. In order to support his critical evaluation of much of post-World War II French cinema – what he calls the "Cinema of Quality" and which is characterized as adapting literary masterpieces to the screen – Truffaut counterposes the idea of the director as *auteur*. An *auteur* brings his own creative vision to the screen by writing the screenplay as well as directing the shooting. Truffaut asserts that, through this greater control of the creative process, the *auteur* is able to make a film that departs from the standardized pieties of the Cinema of Quality.

In making his argument, Truffaut emphasizes the evaluative *auteur* theory: the films he values are made by *auteur* directors. But this thesis is itself grounded in his claim that the *auteur* — because of his greater control over a film — is responsible for the existence of the film, the ontological version of the theory. Finally, he embraces the interpretive *auteur* theory in saying that these directors bring their own vision to the screen, for it is that which is the object of film interpretation.

Andrew Sarris was a well-known film critic and an important advocate of the academic study of film. He uses the *auteur* theory as the basis for a critical project that he thinks will elevate the study of film from a more or less random process of criticism to a respectable scholarly and academic field. For his purposes, the crucial aspect of the *auteur* theory is its evaluative component: that great films are the product of *auteur* directors.

It is noteworthy that while Sarris, like Truffaut, uses the term "*auteur*" to distinguish the great directors from the mere technicians, the *metteurs en scène*, he goes on to claim that the proper object of study for film scholars should not be individual films but rather the overall output of a director, his or her *oeuvre*. This is because one cannot understand the significance of features of a given film — say its use of a subjective shot to convey a character's feeling — unless one understands its use throughout a director's work. The goal of film scholars is to determine the quality of different directors and to produce, as Sarris does, a pantheon of *auteurs*.

Pauline Kael, one of America's most respected and influential film critics, provides a scathing critique of Sarris's version of the *auteur* theory. Less concerned with philosophical underpinnings, Kael believes that the American and British *auteur* theorists have produced bad film criticism that enshrines inferior films as the work of *auteurs*. Hostile to the academization of film criticism, Kael speaks for an intelligent, committed film criticism she sees embodied in the likes of James Agee, who was for many years the *Nation Magazine*'s film critic.

When Kael attacks what she sees as blatant absurdities in Sarris's claims, she is always focused on the critical judgments he puts forward. Kael thinks that the adherents of *auteur* theory allow their theoretical commitments to distort their critical judgments. Great directors can make bad films and the critic has an obligation to say when this happens. From Kael's point of view, it is a violation of the ethics of criticism to elevate the value of films just because the director who made them belongs to one's sacred pantheon.

Kael concludes her contentious argument with a protofeminist diagnosis. American and British *auteur* critics — she sees the French critics as having a different agenda — attempt to valorize the routine products of Hollywood because they appeal to their regressive masculine desires. The passion behind her critique lies in her conviction that the system that produces such films stands in the way of the existence of a more enlightened mode of producing films that might genuinely meet the needs and desires of the film-going public.

An important contribution to this debate is to be found in Part V of this anthology, in the first section of Seymour Chatman's essay (chapter 19). He returns to a more systematic consideration of the *auteur* theory. Although he believes the theory to be false as a general ontological thesis about the production of films – he provides interesting historical data on how one of John Huston's films was made by committee – he believes that it is a crucial prerequisite for film interpretation. How can this be? The answer involves Chatman's use of the idea of an *implied author*. First put forward by the literary critic Wayne Booth, the implied author of a text is a hypothetical agent whom readers must presuppose in order to interpret a work of art as the product of a single controlling intelligence. Although there are various reasons for accepting this idea, here Chatman points out that many films that were actually produced by many different individuals *appear* to viewers as if they were the product of a single individual's intentions. The implied author is this hypothetical individual who creates the unified films. This is an intriguing idea for thinking about artworks in general and films in particular. It suggests that, despite the falsity of the *auteur* theory as a description of how films are actually made, it grounds the critical practice of film interpretation.

Postmodern literary theory has mounted a challenge to the very idea of a text being the product of a single controlling intelligence. The claim behind their rhetorically bold pronouncement of the "death of the author" is that any use of language takes place through an already constituted linguistic system that both enables and controls the possibility of making claims. Even more telling is an author's being condemned to rely on systems of meaning that elude his or her conscious grasp.

In his contribution, Stephen Heath employs this postmodern perspective to cast doubt on the validity of *auteur* theory in regard to film. Through a critical discussion of some suggestions made by another film theorist, Edward Buscombe, Heath argues that rather than taking films to be produced by a single controlling intelligence – the author – we should develop a "theory of the subject" in relation to film. What he means by this is an investigation that explains why it is that films are taken to be produced by individual *auteurs*, even though it is clear that the author is subject to social forces that structure the possibilities of his creative work. Heath's argument is that we need both to understand and criticize the way in which the *auteur* theory has been used within film theory and philosophy.

Since many of the essays about authorship were written, there have been many technological developments in regard to film as an artistic medium. Indeed, many philosophers think that the digital revolution has affected our most basic sense of the medium of film. One example of such technological change is the fact that many DVDs now come with commentary tracks in which the director or a film scholar or a critic discusses the film on a separate audio track. In their article, Deborah Parker and Mark Parker argue that this development has important implications for our understanding of film authorship and, specifically, what role the filmmakers' intentions play in the creation of a film. Citing a range of distinct commentaries by directors, they argue that theorists need to rethink the level at which they claim films are the products of their makers' intentions. They think that intentions are more "technical and local" than theorists would have it, that directors are thinking about much more specific issues than those normally posited by *auteur* theorists.

The Parkers' claims bring us full circle on the idea of authorship. We must ask whether the idea that certain films are the product of an *auteur* – first proposed to justify a new type of cinematic practice – has been made obsolete by new understandings of the nature of film production and new practices involved in film distribution.

Study Questions

1. Explain the distinction between an *auteur* and a *metteur en scène*. What is the basis for making this distinction? What use is made of it by Truffaut? by Sarris? Do you think it is a useful distinction? In what way?

2. The *auteur* theory has more than one form. What are its different aspects? Do you think that any form of the *auteur* theory is valid? Why or why not?

3. Sarris has a particular conception of how the academic study of film should be conducted. What is it? What aspect of the study of film does it emphasize? Do you think there are problems with his view?

4. Who belongs to your pantheon of great directors? Why?

5. Kael has a conception of how film should be studied that is very different than Sarris's. What is her view? Which view, if either, do you support?

6. Explain the idea of an implied author of a film. Do you agree with Chatman that it makes sense to see films as the products of their implied authors? Do you see any problems with this idea?

7. Do you think that the idea of an implied author solves the contradiction between a film being a group product and a unified work? Why or why not?

8. Heath takes a very different approach to the interpretation of films than do the other authors. How would you characterize his approach? What features of a film is he interested in?

9. Heath argues that, rather than focusing on *auteurs*, film scholars need to develop a "theory of the subject." What does he mean by this? How would it affect our understanding of films?

10. Deborah and Mark Parker say that DVDs show the "limits of intention." What do they mean by that phrase? What about DVDs demonstrate this, according to them? Do you agree?

11. The authors present the comments of a variety of different film directors. What do they say these commentaries show us about the relationship between a film director's intentions and the films we see?

12. Do you accept the idea that, at least in the case of films, the directors' intentions are more "local and technical" than philosophers have argued?

13. Do you find any of the different approaches to the interpretation of films put forward in this section convincing? If so, why? If not, why not?

9

La Politique des Auteurs

François Truffaut

These notes have no other object than to attempt to define a certain tendency of the French cinema – a tendency called "psychological realism" – and to sketch its limits.

[. . .]

There are scarcely more than seven or eight scenarists working regularly for the French cinema. Each one of these scenarists has but one story to tell, and, since each only aspires to the success of the "two greats," it is not exaggerating to say that the hundred-odd French films made each year tell the same story: it's always a question of a victim, generally a cuckold. (The cuckold would be the only sympathetic character in the film if he weren't always infinitely grotesque: Blier-Vilbert, etc. . . .) The

8 ■ "Jean Renoir (pictured here) sometimes acted in the films he directed," from *Rules of the Game* (*Règle du jeu*).

knavery of his kin and the hatred among the members of his family lead the "hero" to his doom; the injustice of life, and for local color, the wickedness of the world (the curés, the concierges, the neighbors, the passers-by, the rich, the poor, the soldiers, etc. . . .).

For distraction, during the long winter nights, look for titles of French films that do not fit into this framework and, while you're at it, find among these films those in which this line or its equivalent does not figure, spoken by the most abject couple in the film: "It's always they that have the money (or the luck, or love, or happiness). It's too unjust, in the end."

This school which aspires to realism destroys it at the moment of finally grabbing it, so careful is the school to lock these beings in a closed world, barricaded by formulas, plays on words, maxims, instead of letting us see them for ourselves, with our own eyes. The artist cannot always dominate his work. He must be, sometimes, God and, sometimes, his creature. You know that modern play in which the principal character, normally constituted when the curtain rises on him, finds himself crippled at the end of the play, the loss of each of his members punctuating the changes of acts. Curious epoch when the least flash-in-the-pan performer uses Kafkaesque words to qualify his domestic avatars. This form of cinema comes straight from modern literature – half-Kafka, half-Bovary!

A film is no longer made in France that the authors do not believe they are re-making Madame Bovary.

For the first time in French literature, an author adopted a distant, exterior attitude in relation to his subject, the subject becoming like an insect under the entomologist's microscope. But if, when starting this enterprise, Flaubert could have said, "I will roll them all in the same mud – and be right" (which today's authors would voluntarily make their exergue), he could declare afterwards "I am Madame Bovary" and I doubt that the same authors could take up that line and be sincere!

The object of these notes is limited to an examination of a certain form of cinema, from the point of view of the scenarios and scenarists only. But it is appropriate, I think, to make it clear that the *metteurs-en-scène* are and wish to be responsible for the scenarios and dialogues they illustrate.

Scenarists' films, I wrote above, and certainly it isn't Aurenche and Bost who will contradict me. When they hand in their scenario, the film is done; the *metteur-en-scène*, in their eyes, is the gentleman who adds the pictures to it and it's true, alas! I spoke of the mania for adding funerals everywhere. And, for all that, death is always juggled away. Let us remember Nana's admirable death, or that of Emma Bovary, presented by Renoir; in *La Pastorale*, death is only a make-up job and an exercise for the camera man: compare the close-ups of Michèle Morgan in *La Pastorale*, Dominique Blanchar in *Le Secret de Mayerling* and Madeleine Sologne in *L'Eternel Retour*: it's the same face! Every-thing happens *after* death.

Let us cite, lastly, that declaration by Delannoy that we dedicate, with perfidy, to the French scenarists: "When it happens that authors of talent, whether in the spirit of gain or out of weakness, one day let themselves go to 'write for the cinema,' they do it with the feeling of lowering themselves. They deliver themselves rather to a curious temptation towards mediocrity, so careful are they to not compromise their talent and certain that, to write for the cinema, one must make oneself understood by the lowliest." ("*La Symphonie Pastorale* ou L'Amour Du Métier," revue Verger, November 1947.)

I must, without further ado, denounce a sophism that will not fail to be thrown at me in the guise of argument: "This dialogue is spoken by abject people and it is in order to better point out their nastiness that we give them this hard language. It is our way of being moralists."

To which I answer: it is inexact to say that these lines are spoken by the most abject characters. To be sure, in the films of "psychological realism" there are nothing but vile beings, but so inordinate is the authors' desire to be superior to their characters that those who, perchance, are not infamous are, at best, infinitely grotesque.

Well, as for these abject characters, who deliver these abject lines – I know a handful of men in France who would be INCAPABLE of conceiving them, several cinéastes whose world-view is at least as valuable as that of Aurenche and Bost, Sigurd and Jeanson. I mean Jean Renoir, Robert Bresson, Jean Cocteau, Jacques Becker, Abel Gance, Max Ophuls, Jacques Tati, Roger Leenhardt; these are, nevertheless, French cinéastes and it happens – curious coincidence – that they are *auteurs* who often write their dialogue and some of them themselves invent the stories they direct.

"But why," they will say to me, "why couldn't one have the same admiration for all those cinéastes who strive to work in the bosom of this 'Tradition of Quality' that you make sport of so lightly? Why not admire Yves Allégret as much as Becker, Jean Delannoy as much as Bresson, Claude Autant-Lara as much as Renoir?"[1]

Well – I do not believe in the peaceful co-existence of the "Tradition of Quality" and an "*auteur's* cinema."

Basically, Yves Allégret and Delannoy are only caricatures of Clouzot, of Bresson.

It is not the desire to create a scandal that leads me to depreciate a cinema so praised elsewhere. I rest convinced that the exaggeratedly prolonged existence of *psychological realism* is the cause of the lack of public comprehension when faced with such new works as *Le Carrosse d'Or* (*The Golden Coach*), *Casque d'Or*, not to mention *Les Dames Du Bois De Boulogne* and *Orphée*.

Long live audacity, to be sure, still it must be revealed as it is. In terms of this year, 1953, if I had to draw up a balance-sheet of the French cinema's audacities, there would be no place in it for either the vomiting in *Les Orgueilleux* (*The Proud And The Beautiful*) or Claude Laydu's refusal to be sprinkled with holy water in *Le Bon Dieu Sans Confession* or the homosexual relationships of the characters in *Le Salaire De La Peur* (*The Wages Of Fear*), but rather the gait of *Hulot*, the maid's soliloquies in *La Rue De L'Estrapade*, the *mise-en-scène* of *La Carrosse d'Or*, the direction of the actors in *Madame de* (*The Earrings Of Madame De . . .*), and also Abel Gance's studies in Polyvision. You will have understood that these audacities are those of *men of the cinema* and no longer of scenarists, directors and litterateurs.

[. . .]

It is always good to conclude, that gives everyone pleasure. It is remarkable that the "great" *metteurs-en-scène* and the "great" scenarists have, for a long time, all made minor films, and the talent they have put into them hasn't been sufficient to enable one to distinguish them from others (those who don't put in talent). It is also remarkable that they all came to "Quality" at the same time, as if they were giving themselves a good address. And then, a producer – even a director – earns more money making *Le Blé En Herbe* than by making *Le Plombier Amoureux*. The "courageous" films are revealed to be very profitable. The proof: someone like Ralph Habib abruptly renounces demipornography, makes *Les Compagnes De La Nuit* and refers to Cayatte. Well, what's keeping the André Tabets, Companeer, the Jean Guittons, the Pierre Vérys, the Jean Lavirons, the Ciampis, the Grangiers, from making, from one day to the next, intellectual films, from adapting masterpieces (there are still a few left) and, of course, adding funerals, here, there and everywhere?

Well, on that day we will be in the "Tradition of Quality" up to the neck and the French cinema, with rivalry among "psychological realism," "violence," "strictness," "ambiguity," will no longer be anything but one vast funeral that will be able to leave the studio in Billancourt and enter the cemetery directly – it seems to have been placed next door expressly, in order to get more quickly from the producer to the grave-digger.

Only, by dint of repeating to the public that it identified with the "heroes" of the films, it might well end by believing it, and on the day that it understands that this fine big cuckold whose misadventures it is solicited to sympathize with (a little) and to laugh at (a lot), is not, as had been thought, a cousin or neighbor down the hall but ITSELF, that abject family ITS family, that scoffed-at religion ITS religion – well, on that day it may show itself to be ungrateful to a cinema that will have labored so hard to show it life as one sees it on the fourth floor in Saint-Germin-des-Près.

To be sure, I must recognize it, a great deal of emotion and taking-sides are the controlling factors in the deliberately pessimistic examination I have undertaken of a certain tendency of the French cinema. I am assured that this famous "school of psychological realism" had to exist in order that, in turn, *The Diary Of A Country Priest*, *Le Carrosse d'Or*, *Orpheus*, *Casque d'Or*, *Mr. Hulot's Holiday* might exist.

But our authors who wanted to educate the public should understand that perhaps they have strayed from the primary paths in order to become involved with the more subtle paths of psychology; they have passed on to that sixth grade so dear to Jouhandeau, but it isn't necessary to repeat a grade indefinitely!

NOTE
1 "Taste is made of a thousand distastes" – Paul Valéry.

10

Auteur Theory and Film Evaluation

Andrew Sarris

An exhibitor once asked me if an old film I had recommended was *really* good or good only according to the *auteur* theory. I appreciate the distinction. Like the alchemists of old, *auteur* critics are notorious for rationalizing leaden clinkers into golden nuggets. Their judgments are seldom vindicated, because few spectators are conditioned to perceive in individual works the organic unity of a director's career. On a given evening, a film by John Ford must take its chances as if it were a film by Henry King. Am I implying that the weakest Ford is superior to the strongest King? Yes! This kind of unqualified affirmation seems to reduce the *auteur* theory to a game of aesthetic solitaire with all the cards turned face up. By *auteur* rules, the Fords will come up aces as invariably as the Kings will come up deuces. Presumably, we can all go home as soon as the directorial signature is flashed on the screen. To those who linger, *The Gunfighter* (King 1950) may appear worthier than *Flesh* (Ford 1932). (And how deeply one must burrow to undermine Ford!) No matter. The *auteur* theory is unyielding. If, by definition, Ford is invariably superior to King, any evidence to the contrary is merely an optical illusion. Now what could be sillier than this inflexible attitude? Let us abandon the absurdities of the *auteur* theory so that we may return to the chaos of common sense.

My labored performance as devil's advocate notwithstanding, I intend to praise the *auteur* theory, not to bury it. At the very least, I would like to grant the condemned system a hearing before its execution. The trial has dragged on for years, I know, and everyone is now bored by the abstract reasoning involved. I have little in the way of new evidence or new arguments, but I would like to change some of my previous testimony. What follows is, consequently, less a manifesto than a credo, a somewhat disorganized credo, to be sure, expressed in formless notes rather than in formal brief.

I. Aimez-vous Brahms?

[. . .]

It can be argued that any exact ranking of artists is arbitrary and pointless. Arbitrary up to a point, perhaps, but pointless, no. Even Bazin concedes the polemical value of the *politique*. Many film critics would rather not commit themselves to specific rankings ostensibly because every film should be judged on its own merits. In many instances, this reticence masks the critic's condescension to the medium. Because it has not been firmly established that the cinema is an art at all, it requires cultural audacity to establish a pantheon for film directors. Without such audacity, I see little point in being a film critic. Anyway, is it possible to honor a work of art without honoring the artist involved? I think not. Of course, any idiot can erect a pantheon out of hearsay and gossip. Without specifying any work, the Saganesque seducer will ask quite cynically, "Aimez-vous Brahms?" The fact that Brahms is included in the pantheon of high-brow pickups does not invalidate the industrious criticism that justifies the composer as a figure of speech.

Unfortunately, some critics have embraced the *auteur* theory as a short-cut to film scholarship. With a "you-see-it-or-you-don't" attitude toward the reader, the particularly lazy *auteur* critic can save himself the drudgery of communication and explanation. Indeed, at their worst, *auteur* critiques are less meaningful than the straightforward plot reviews that pass for criticism in America. Without the necessary research and analysis, the *auteur* theory can degenerate into the kind of snobbish racket that is associated with the merchandising of paintings.

It was largely against the inadequate theoretical formulation of *la politique des auteurs* that Bazin was reacting in his friendly critique. (Henceforth, I will abbreviate *la politique des auteurs* as the *auteur* theory to avoid confusion.) Bazin introduces his arguments within the context of a family quarrel over the editorial policies of *Cahiers*. He fears that, by assigning reviews to admirers of given directors, notably Alfred Hitchcock, Jean Renoir, Roberto Rossellini, Fritz Lang, Howard Hawks, and Nicholas Ray, every work, major and minor, of these exalted figures is made to radiate the same beauties of style and meaning. Specifically, Bazin notes a distortion when the kindly indulgence accorded the imperfect work of a Minnelli is coldly withheld from the imperfect work of Huston. The inherent bias of the *auteur* theory magnifies the gap between the two films.

I would make two points here. First, Bazin's greatness as a critic (and I believe strongly that he was the greatest film critic who ever lived) rested in his disinterested conception of the cinema as a universal entity. It follows that he would react against a theory that cultivated what he felt were inaccurate judgments for the sake of dramatic paradoxes. He was, if anything, generous to a fault, seeking in every film some vestige of the cinematic art. That he would seek justice for Huston vis-à-vis Minnelli on even the secondary levels of creation indicates the scrupulousness of his critical personality.

However, my second point would seem to contradict my first. Bazin was wrong in this instance, insofar as any critic can be said to be wrong in retrospect. We are dealing here with Minnelli in his *Lust for Life* period and Huston in his *Moby Dick* period. Both films can be considered failures on almost any level. The miscasting alone is disastrous. The snarling force of Kirk Douglas as the tormented Van Gogh, the brutish insensibility of Anthony Quinn as Gauguin, and the nervously scraping tension between these two absurdly limited actors, deface Minnelli's meticulously objective decor, itself inappropriate for the mood of its subject. The director's presentation of the paintings themselves is singularly unperceptive in the repeated failure to maintain the proper optical distance from canvases that arouse the spectator less by their detailed draughtsmanship than by the shock of a *gestalt* wholeness. As for *Moby Dick*, Gregory Peck's Ahab deliberates long enough to let all the demons flee the Pequod, taking Melville's Lear-like fantasies with them. Huston's epic technique with its casually shifting camera viewpoint then drifts on an intellectually becalmed sea toward a fitting rendezvous with a rubber whale. These two films are neither the best nor the worst of their time. The question is: Which deserves the harder review? And there's the rub. At the time, Huston's stock in America was higher than Minnelli's. Most critics expected Huston to do "big" things, and, if they thought about it at all, expected Minnelli to stick to "small" things like musicals. Although neither film was a critical failure, audiences stayed away in large enough numbers to make the cultural respectability of the projects suspect. On the whole, *Lust for Life* was more successful with the audiences it did reach than was *Moby Dick*.

In retrospect, *Moby Dick* represents the turning downward of Huston as a director to be taken seriously. By contrast, *Lust for Life* is simply an isolated episode in the erratic career of an interesting stylist. The exact size of Minnelli's talent may inspire controversy, but he does represent something in the cinema today. Huston is virtually a forgotten man with a few actors' classics behind him surviving as the ruins of a once-promising career. Both Eric Rohmer, who denigrated Huston in 1957, and Jean Domarchi, who was kind to Minnelli that same year, somehow saw the future more clearly on an *auteur* level than did Bazin. As Santayana has remarked: "It is a great advantage for a system of philosophy to be substantially true." If the *auteur* critics of the 1950s had not scored so many coups of clairvoyance, the *auteur* theory would not be worth discussing in the 1960s. [. . .]

[. . .]

Some of Bazin's arguments tend to overlap each other as if to counter rebuttals from any direction. He argues, in turn, that the cinema is less individualistic an art than painting or literature, that Hollywood is less individualistic than other cinemas, and that, even so, the *auteur* theory never really applies anywhere. In upholding historical determinism, Bazin goes so far as to speculate that, if Racine had lived in Voltaire's century, it is unlikely that Racine's tragedies would have been any more inspired than Voltaire's. Presumably, the Age of Reason would have stifled Racine's neoclassical impulses. Perhaps. Perhaps not. Bazin's hypothesis can hardly be argued to a verifiable conclusion, but I suspect somewhat greater reciprocity between an artist and his *zeitgeist* than Bazin would allow. He mentions, more than once and in other contexts, capitalism's influence on the cinema. Without denying this influence, I still find it impossible to attribute X directors and Y films to any particular system or culture. Why should the Italian cinema be superior to the German cinema after one war, when the reverse was true after the previous one? As for artists conforming to the spirit of their age, that spirit is often expressed in contradictions, whether between Stravinsky and Sibelius, Fielding and Richardson, Picasso and Matisse, Chateaubriand and Stendhal. Even if the artist does not spring from the idealized head of Zeus, free of the embryonic stains of history, history itself is profoundly affected by his arrival. If we cannot imagine Griffith's *October* or Eisenstein's *Birth of a Nation* because we find it difficult to transpose one artist's unifying conceptions of Lee and Lincoln to the other's dialectical conceptions of Lenin and Kerensky, we are, nevertheless, compelled to recognize other differences in the personalities of these two pioneers beyond their respective cultural complexes. It is with these latter differences that the *auteur* theory is most deeply concerned. If directors and other artists cannot be wrenched from their historical environments, aesthetics is reduced to a subordinate branch of ethnography.

I have not done full justice to the subtlety of Bazin's reasoning and to the civilized skepticism with which he propounds his own arguments as slight probabilities rather than absolute certainties. Contemporary opponents of the *auteur* theory may feel that Bazin himself is suspect as a member of the *Cahiers* family. After all, Bazin does express qualified approval of the *auteur* theory as a relatively objective method of evaluating films apart from the subjective perils of impressionistic and ideological criticism. Better to analyze the director's personality than the critic's nerve centers or politics. Nevertheless, Bazin makes his stand clear by concluding: "This is not to deny the role of the author, but to restore to him the preposition without which the noun is only a limp concept. 'Author,' undoubtedly, but of what?"

Bazin's syntactical flourish raises an interesting problem in English usage. The French preposition "de" serves many functions, but among others, those of possession and authorship. In English, the preposition "by" once created a scandal in the American film industry when Otto Preminger had the temerity to advertise *The Man With the Golden Arm* as a film "by Otto Preminger." Novelist Nelson Algren and the Screenwriters' Guild raised such an outcry that the offending preposition was deleted. Even the noun "author" (which I cunningly mask as "*auteur*") has a literary connotation in English. In general conversation, an "author" is invariably taken to be a writer. Since "by" is a preposition of authorship and not of ownership like the ambiguous "de," the fact that Preminger both produced and directed *The Man with the Golden Arm* did not entitle him in America to the preposition "by." No one would have objected to the possessive form: "Otto Preminger's *The Man with the Golden Arm*." But, even in this case, a novelist of sufficient reputation is usually honored with the possessive designation. Now, this is hardly the case in France, where *The Red and the Black* is advertised as "un film de Claude Autant-Lara." In America, "directed by" is all the director can claim, when he is not also a well-known producer like Alfred Hitchcock or Cecil B. de Mille.

Since most American film critics are oriented toward literature or journalism, rather than toward future film-making, most American film criticism is directed toward the script instead of toward the screen. The writer-hero in *Sunset Boulevard* complains that people don't realize that someone "writes a picture; they think the actors make it up as they go along." It would never occur to this writer or most of his colleagues that people are even less aware of the director's function.

Of course, the much-abused man in the street has a good excuse not to be aware of the *auteur* theory even as a figure of speech. Even on the so-called classic level, he is not encouraged to ask "Aimez-vous Griffith?" or "Aimez-vous Eisenstein?" Instead, it is which Griffith or which Eisenstein? As for less acclaimed directors, he is lucky to find their names in the fourth paragraph of the typical review. I doubt that most American film critics really believe that an indifferently directed film is comparable to an indifferently written book. However, there is little point in wailing at the Philistines on this issue, particularly when some progress is being made in telling one director from another, at least when the film comes from abroad. The Fellini, Bergman, Kurosawa, and Antonioni promotions have helped push more directors up to the first paragraph of a review, even ahead of the plot synopsis. So, we mustn't complain.

Where I wish to redirect the argument is toward the relative position of the American cinema as opposed to the foreign cinema. Some critics have advised me that the *auteur* theory only applies to a small number of artists who make personal films, not to the run-of-the-mill Hollywood director who takes whatever assignment is available. Like most Americans who take films seriously, I have always felt a cultural inferiority complex about Hollywood. Just a few years ago, I would have thought it unthinkable to speak in the same breath of a "commercial" director like Hitchcock and a "pure" director like Bresson. Even today, *Sight and Sound* uses different type sizes for Bresson and Hitchcock films. After years of tortured revaluation, I am now prepared to stake my critical reputation, such as it is, on the proposition that Alfred Hitchcock is artistically superior to Robert Bresson by every criterion of excellence and, further, that, film for film, director for director, the American cinema has been consistently superior to that of the rest of the world from 1915 through 1962. Consequently, I now regard the *auteur* theory primarily as a critical device for recording the history of the American cinema, the only cinema in the world worth exploring in depth beneath the frosting of a few great directors at the top.

These propositions remain to be proven and, I hope, debated. The proof will be difficult because direction in the cinema is a nebulous force in literary terms. In addition to its own jargon, the director's craft often pulls in the related jargon of music, painting, sculpture, dance, literature, theatre, architecture, all in a generally futile attempt to describe the indescribable. What is it the old jazz man says of his art? If you gotta ask what it is, it ain't? Well, the cinema is like that. Criticism can only attempt an approximation, a reasonable preponderance of accuracy over inaccuracy. I know the exceptions to the *auteur* theory as well as anyone. I can feel the human attraction of an audience going one way when I am going the other. The temptations of cynicism, common sense, and facile culture-mongering are always very strong, but, somehow, I feel that the *auteur* theory is the only hope for extending the appreciation of personal qualities in the cinema. By grouping and evaluating films according to directors, the critic can rescue individual achievements from an unjustifiable anonymity. If medieval architects and African sculptors are anonymous today, it is not because they deserved to be. When Ingmar Bergman bemoans the alienation of the modern artist from the collective spirit that rebuilt the cathedral at Chartres, he is only dramatizing his own individuality for an age that has rewarded him handsomely for the travail of his alienation. There is no justification for penalizing Hollywood directors for the sake of collective mythology. So, invective aside, "Aimez-vous Cukor?"

II. What Is the *Auteur* Theory?

As far as I know, there is no definition of the *auteur* theory in the English language, that is, by any American or British critic. Truffaut has recently gone to great pains to emphasize that the *auteur* theory was merely a polemical weapon for a given time and a given place, and I am willing to take him at his word. But, lest I be accused of misappropriating a theory no one wants anymore, I will give the *Cahiers* critics full credit for the original formulation of an idea that reshaped my thinking on the cinema. First of all, how does the *auteur* theory differ from a straightforward theory of directors. Ian Cameron's article "Films, Directors, and Critics," in *Movie* of September, 1962, makes an interesting comment on this issue: "The assumption that underlies all the writing in *Movie* is that the director is the author of a film, the person who gives it any distinctive quality. There are quite large exceptions, with which I shall deal later." So far, so good, at least for the *auteur* theory, which even allows for exceptions. However, Cameron continues: "On the whole, we accept the cinema of directors, although without going to the farthest-out extremes of the *la politique des auteurs*, which makes it difficult to think of a bad director making a good film and almost impossible to think of a good director making a bad one." We are back to Bazin again, although Cameron naturally uses different examples. That three otherwise divergent critics like Bazin, Roud, and Cameron make essentially the same point about the *auteur* theory suggests a common fear of its abuses. I believe there is a misunderstanding here about what the *auteur* theory actually claims, particularly since the theory itself is so vague at the present time.

First of all, the *auteur* theory, at least as I understand it and now intend to express it, claims neither the gift of prophecy nor the option of extracinematic perception. Directors, even *auteurs*, do not always run true to form, and the critic can never assume that a bad director will always make a bad film. No, not always, but almost always, and that is the point. What is a bad director, but a director who has made many bad films? What is the problem then? Simply this: The badness of a director is not necessarily considered the badness of a film. If Joseph Pevney directed Garbo, Cherkassov, Olivier, Belmondo, and Harriet Andersson in *The Cherry Orchard*, the resulting spectacle might not be entirely devoid of merit with so many subsidiary *auteurs* to cover up for Joe. In fact, with this cast and this literary property, a Lumet might be safer than a Welles. The realities of casting apply to directors as well as to actors, but the *auteur* theory would demand the gamble with Welles, if he were willing.

Marlon Brando has shown us that a film can be made without a director. Indeed, *One-Eyed Jacks* is more entertaining than many films with directors. A director-conscious critic would find it difficult to say anything good or bad about direction that is nonexistent. One can talk here about photography, editing, acting, but not direction. The film even has personality, but, like *The Longest Day* and *Mutiny on the Bounty*, it is a cipher directorially. Obviously, the *auteur* theory cannot possibly cover every vagrant charm of the cinema. Nevertheless, the first premise of the *auteur* theory is the technical competence of a director as a criterion of value. A badly directed or an undirected film has no importance in a critical scale of values, but one can make interesting conversation about the subject, the script, the acting, the color, the photography, the editing, the music, the costumes, the decor, and so forth. That is the nature of the medium. You always get more for your money than mere art. Now, by the *auteur* theory, if a director has no technical competence, no elementary flair for the cinema, he is automatically cast out from the pantheon of directors. A great director has to be at least a good director. This is true in any art. What constitutes directorial talent is more difficult to define abstractly. There is less disagreement, however, on this first level of the *auteur* theory than there will be later.

The second premise of the *auteur* theory is the distinguishable personality of the director as a criterion of value. Over a group of films, a director must exhibit certain recurring characteristics of style, which serve as his signature. The way a film looks and moves should have some relationship to the way a director thinks and feels. This is an area where American directors are generally superior to foreign directors. Because so much of the American cinema is commissioned, a director is forced to express his personality through the visual treatment of material rather than through the literary content of the material. A Cukor, who works with all sorts of projects, has a more developed abstract style than a Bergman, who is free to develop his own scripts. Not that Bergman lacks personality, but his work has declined with the depletion of his ideas largely because his technique never equaled his sensibility. Joseph L. Mankiewicz and Billy Wilder are other examples of writer-directors without adequate technical mastery. By contrast, Douglas Sirk and Otto Preminger have moved up the scale because their miscellaneous projects reveal a stylistic consistency.

The third and ultimate premise of the *auteur* theory is concerned with interior meaning, the ultimate glory of the cinema as an art. Interior meaning is extrapolated from the tension between a director's personality and his material. This conception of interior meaning comes close to what Astruc defines as *mise en scène*, but not quite. It is not quite the vision of the world a director projects nor quite his attitude toward life. It is ambiguous, in any literary sense, because part of it is imbedded in the stuff of the cinema and cannot be rendered in noncinematic terms. Truffaut has called it the temperature of the director on the set, and that is a close approximation of its professional aspect. Dare I come out and say what I think it to be is an *élan* of the soul?

Lest I seem unduly mystical, let me hasten to add that all I mean by "soul" is that intangible difference between one personality and another, all other things being equal. Sometimes, this difference is expressed by no more than a beat's hesitation in the rhythm of a film. In one sequence of *La Règle du Jeu*, Renoir gallops up the stairs, turns to his right with a lurching movement, stops in hop-like uncertainty when his name is called by a coquettish maid, and, then, with marvelous postreflex continuity, resumes his bearishly shambling journey to the heroine's boudoir. If I could describe the musical grace note of that momentary suspension, and I can't, I might be able to provide a more precise definition of the *auteur* theory. As it is, all I can do is point at the specific beauties of interior meaning on the screen and, later, catalogue the moments of recognition.

The three premises of the *auteur* theory may be visualized as three concentric circles: the outer circle as technique; the middle circle, personal style; and the inner circle, interior meaning. The corresponding roles of the director may be designated as those of a technician, a stylist, and an *auteur*. There is no prescribed course by which a director passes through the three circles. Godard once remarked that Visconti had evolved from a *metteur en scène* to an *auteur*, whereas Rossellini had evolved from an *auteur* to a *metteur en scène*. From opposite directions, they emerged with comparable status. Minnelli began and remained in the second circle as a stylist; Buñuel was an *auteur* even before he had assembled the technique of the first circle. Technique is simply the ability to put a film together with some clarity and coherence. Nowadays, it is possible to become a director without knowing too much about the technical side, even the crucial functions of photography and editing. An expert production crew could probably cover up for a chimpanzee in the director's chair. How do you tell the genuine director from the quasichimpanzee? After a given number of films, a pattern is established.

In fact, the *auteur* theory itself is a pattern theory in constant flux. I would never endorse a Ptolemaic constellation of directors in a fixed orbit. At the moment, my list of *auteurs* runs something like this through the first twenty: Ophuls, Renoir, Mizoguchi, Hitchcock, Chaplin, Ford, Welles, Dreyer, Rossellini, Murnau, Griffith, Sternberg, Eisenstein, von Stroheim, Buñuel, Bresson, Hawks, Lang, Flaherty, Vigo. This list is somewhat weighted toward seniority and established reputations. In time, some of these *auteurs* will rise, some will fall, and some will be displaced either by new directors or rediscovered ancients. Again, the exact order is less important than the specific definitions of these and as many as two hundred other potential *auteurs*. I would hardly expect any other critic in the world fully to endorse this list, especially on faith. Only after thousands of films have been revaluated, will any personal pantheon have a reasonably objective validity. The task of validating the *auteur* theory is an enormous one, and the end will never be in sight. Meanwhile, the *auteur* habit of collecting random films in directorial bundles will serve posterity with at least a tentative classification.

Although the *auteur* theory emphasizes the body of a director's work rather than isolated masterpieces, it is expected of great directors that they make great films every so often. The only possible exception to this rule I can think of is Abel Gance, whose greatness is largely a function of his aspiration. Even with Gance, *La Roue* is as close to being a great film as any single work of Flaherty's. Not that single works matter that much. As Renoir has observed, a director spends his life on variations of the same film.

Two recent films — *Boccaccio '70* and *The Seven Capital Sins* — unwittingly reinforced the *auteur* theory by confirming the relative standing of the many directors involved. If I had not seen either film, I would have anticipated that the order of merit in *Boccaccio '70* would be Visconti, Fellini, and De Sica, and in *The Seven Capital Sins* Godard, Chabrol, Demy, Vadim, De Broca, Molinaro. (Dhomme, Ionesco's stage director and an unknown quantity in advance, turned out to be the worst of the lot.) There might be some argument about the relative badness of De Broca and Molinaro, but, otherwise, the directors ran true to form by almost any objective criterion of value. However, the main point here is that even in these frothy, ultracommercial servings of entertainment, the contribution of each director had less in common stylistically with the work of other directors on the project than with his own previous work.

Sometimes, a great deal of corn must be husked to yield a few kernels of internal meaning. I recently saw *Every Night at Eight*, one of the many maddeningly routine films Raoul Walsh has directed in his long career. This 1935 effort featured George Raft, Alice Faye, Frances Langford, and Patsy Kelly in one of those familiar plots about radio shows of the period. The film keeps moving along in the pleasantly unpretentious manner one would expect of Walsh until one incongruously intense scene with George Raft thrashing about in his sleep, revealing his inner fears in mumbling dream-talk. The girl he loves comes into the room in the midst of his unconscious avowals of feeling and listens sympathetically. This unusual scene was later amplified in *High Sierra* with Humphrey Bogart and Ida Lupino. The point is that one of the screen's most virile directors employed an essentially feminine narrative device to dramatize the emotional vulnerability of his heroes. If I had not been aware of Walsh in *Every Night at Eight*, the crucial link to *High Sierra* would have passed unnoticed. Such are the joys of the *auteur* theory.

11

The Idea of Film Criticism

Pauline Kael

It should be pointed out that Sarris's defense of the *auteur* theory [see chapter 10] is based not only on aesthetics but on a rather odd pragmatic statement: "Thus to argue against the *auteur* theory in America is to assume that we have anyone of Bazin's sensibility and dedication to provide an alternative, and we simply don't." Which I take to mean that the *auteur* theory is necessary in the absence of a critic who wouldn't need it. This is a new approach to aesthetics, and I hope Sarris's humility does not camouflage his double-edged argument. If his aesthetics is based on expediency, then it may be expedient to point out that it takes extraordinary intelligence and discrimination and taste to *use* any theory in the arts, and that without those qualities, a theory becomes a rigid formula (which is indeed what is happening among *auteur* critics). The greatness of critics like Bazin in France and Agee in America may have something to do with their using their full range of intelligence and intuition, rather than relying on formulas. Criticism is an art, not a science, and a critic who follows rules will fail in one of his most important functions: perceiving what is original and important in *new* work and helping others to see.

The Outer Circle

> . . . the first premise of the *auteur* theory is the technical competence of a director as a criterion of value.

This seems less the premise of a theory than a commonplace of judgment, as Sarris himself indicates when he paraphrases it as, "A great director has to be at least a good director." But this commonplace, though it *sounds* reasonable and basic, is a shaky premise: sometimes the greatest artists in a medium bypass or violate the simple technical competence that is so necessary for hacks. For example, it is doubtful if Antonioni could handle a routine directorial assignment of the type at which John Sturges is so proficient (*Escape from Fort Bravo* or *Bad Day at Black Rock*), but surely Antonioni's

L'Avventura is the work of a great director. And the greatness of a director like Cocteau has nothing to do with mere technical competence: his greatness is in being able to achieve his own personal expression and style. And just as there were writers like Melville or Dreiser who triumphed over various kinds of technical incompetence, and who were, as artists, incomparably greater than the facile technicians of their day, a new great film director may appear whose very greatness is in his struggling toward grandeur or in massive accumulation of detail. An artist who is not a good technician can indeed create new standards, because standards of technical competence are based on comparisons with work already done.

Just as new work in other arts is often attacked because it violates the accepted standards and thus seems crude and ugly and incoherent, great new directors are very likely to be condemned precisely on the grounds that they're not even good directors, that they don't know their "business." Which, in some cases, is true, but does it matter when that "business" has little to do with what they want to express in films? It may even be a hindrance, leading them to banal slickness, instead of discovery of their own methods. For some, at least, Cocteau may be right: "The only technique worth having is the technique you invent for yourself." The director must be judged on the basis of what he produces – his films – and if he can make great films without knowing the standard methods, without the usual craftsmanship of the "good director," then that is the way he works. I would amend Sarris's premise to, "In works of a lesser rank, technical competence can help to redeem the weaknesses of the material." In fact it seems to be precisely this category that the *auteur* critics are most interested in – the routine material that a good craftsman can make into a fast and enjoyable movie. What, however, makes the *auteur* critics so incomprehensible is not their *preference* for works of this category (in this they merely follow the lead of children who also prefer simple action films and westerns and horror films to works that make demands on their understanding) but their truly astonishing inability to exercise taste and judgment *within* their area of preference. Moviegoing kids are, I think, much more reliable guides to this kind of movie than the *auteur* critics: every kid I've talked to knows that Henry Hathaway's *North to Alaska* was a surprisingly funny, entertaining movie and *Hatari!* (classified as a "masterpiece" by half the *Cahiers* Conseil des Dix, Peter Bogdanovich, and others) was a terrible bore.

The Middle Circle

   . . . the second premise of the *auteur* theory is the distinguishable personality of
   the director as a criterion of value.

Up to this point there has really been no theory, and now, when Sarris begins to work on his foundation, the entire edifice of civilized standards of taste collapses while he's tacking down his floorboards. Traditionally, in any art, the personalities of all those involved in a production have been a factor in judgment, but that the *distinguishability* of personality should in itself be a criterion of value completely confuses *normal* judgment. The smell of a skunk is more distinguishable than the perfume of a rose; does that make it better? Hitchcock's personality is certainly more distinguishable in *Dial M for Murder*, *Rear Window*, *Vertigo*, than Carol Reed's in *The Stars Look Down*, *Odd Man Out*, *The Fallen Idol*, *The Third Man*, *An Outcast of the Islands*, if for no other reason than because Hitchcock repeats while Reed tackles new subject matter. But how does this distinguishable personality function as a criterion for judging the works? We recognize the hands of Carné and Prévert in *Le Jour se Lève*, but that is not what makes it a beautiful film; we can just as easily recognize their hands in *Quai des Brumes* — which is not such a good film. We can recognize that *Le Plaisir* and *The Earrings of Madame de . . .* are both the work of Ophuls, but *Le Plaisir* is not a great film, and *Madame de . . .* is.

Often the works in which we are most aware of the personality of the director are his worst films — when he falls back on the devices he has already done to death. When a famous director makes a good movie, we look at the movie, we don't think about the director's personality; when he makes a stinker we notice his familiar touches because there's not much else to watch. When Preminger makes an expert, entertaining whodunit like *Laura*, we don't look for his personality (it has become part of the texture of the film); when he makes an atrocity like *Whirlpool*, there's plenty of time to look for his "personality" — if that's your idea of a good time.

It could even be argued, I think, that Hitchcock's uniformity, his mastery of tricks, and his cleverness at getting audiences to respond according to his calculations — the feedback he wants and gets from them — reveal not so much a personal style as a personal theory of audience psychology, that his methods and approach are not those of an artist but a prestidigitator. The *auteur* critics respond just as Hitchcock expects the gullible to respond. This is not so surprising — often the works *auteur* critics call masterpieces are ones that seem to reveal the contempt of the director for the audience.

It's hard to believe that Sarris seriously attempts to apply "the distinguishable personality of the director as a criterion of value" because when this premise becomes troublesome, he just tries to brazen his way out of difficulties. For example, now that John Huston's work has gone flat Sarris casually dismisses him with: "Huston is virtually a forgotten man with a few actors' classics behind him . . ." If *The Maltese Falcon*, perhaps the most high-style thriller ever made in America, a film Huston both wrote and directed, is not a director's film, what is? And if the distinguishable personality of the director is a criterion of value, then how can Sarris dismiss the Huston who comes through so unmistakably in *The Treasure of Sierra Madre, The African Queen*, or *Beat the Devil*, or even in a muddled Huston film like *Key Largo*? If these are actors' movies, then what on earth is a director's movie?

Isn't the *auteur* theory a hindrance to clear judgment of Huston's movies and of his career? Disregarding the theory, we see some fine film achievements and we perceive a remarkably distinctive directorial talent; we also see intervals of weak, half-hearted assignments like *Across the Pacific* and *In This Our Life*. Then, after *Moulin Rouge*, except for the blessing of *Beat the Devil*, we see a career that splutters out in ambitious failures like *Moby Dick* and confused projects like *The Roots of Heaven* and *The Misfits*, and strictly commercial projects like *Heaven Knows, Mr. Allison*. And this kind of career seems more characteristic of film history, especially in the United States, than the ripening development and final mastery envisaged by the *auteur* theory – a theory that makes it almost de rigueur to regard Hitchcock's American films as superior to his early English films. Is Huston's career so different, say, from Fritz Lang's? How is it that Huston's early good – almost great – work, must be rejected along with his mediocre recent work, but Fritz Lang, being sanctified as an *auteur*, has his bad recent work praised along with his good? Employing more usual norms, if you respect the Fritz Lang who made *M* and *You Only Live Once*, if you enjoy the excesses of style and the magnificent absurdities of a film like *Metropolis*, then it is only good sense to reject the ugly stupidity of *Journey to the Lost City*. It is an insult to an artist to praise his bad work along with his good; it indicates that you are incapable of judging either.

[. . .]

Sarris believes that what makes an *auteur* is "an élan of the soul." (This critical language is barbarous. Where else should élan come from? It's like saying "a digestion of the stomach." A film critic need not be a theoretician, but it is necessary that he know how to use words. This might, indeed, be a first premise for a theory.) Those who have this élan presumably have it forever and their films reveal the "organic unity" of the directors' careers; and those who don't have it – well, they can only make "actors' classics." It's ironic that a critic trying to establish simple "objective" rules as a guide for critics who he thinks aren't gifted enough to use taste and intelligence, ends up – where, actually, he began – with a theory based on mystical insight. This might really make demands on the *auteur* critics if they did not simply take the easy way out by arbitrary decisions of who's got "it" and who hasn't. Their decisions are not merely not based on their theory; their decisions are *beyond* criticism. It's like a woman's telling us that she feels a certain dress *does* something for her: her feeling has about as much to do with critical judgment as the *auteur* critics' feeling that Minnelli *has* "it," but Huston never had "it."

[. . .]

The Inner Circle

> The third and ultimate premise of the *auteur* theory is concerned with interior meaning, the ultimate glory of the cinema as an art. Interior meaning is extrapolated from the tension between a director's personality and his material.

This is a remarkable formulation: it is the opposite of what we have always taken for granted in the arts, that the artist expresses himself in the unity of form and content. What Sarris believes to be "the ultimate glory of the cinema as an art" is what has generally been considered the frustrations of a man working against the given material. Fantastic as this formulation is, it does something that the first two premises didn't do: it clarifies the interests of the *auteur* critics. If we have been puzzled because the *auteur* critics seemed so deeply involved, even dedicated, in becoming connoisseurs of trash, now we can see by this theoretical formulation that trash is indeed their chosen province of film.

9 ■ "The Dance of Death," from
The Seventh Seal.

Their ideal *auteur* is the man who signs a long-term contract, directs any script that's handed to him, and expresses himself by shoving bits of style up the crevasses of the plots. If his "style" is in conflict with the story line or subject matter, so much the better – more chance for tension. Now we can see why there has been so much use of the term "personality" in this aesthetics (the term which seems so inadequate when discussing the art of Griffith or Renoir or Murnau or Dreyer) – a routine, commercial movie can sure use a little "personality."

Now that we have reached the inner circle (the bull's eye turns out to be an empty socket) we can see why the shoddiest films are often praised the most. Subject matter is irrelevant (so long as it isn't treated sensitively – which is bad) and will quickly be disposed of by *auteur* critics who know that the smart director isn't responsible for that anyway; they'll get on to the important subject – his *mise-en-scène*. The director who fights to do something he cares about is a square. Now we can at least begin to understand why there was such contempt toward Huston for what was, in its way, a rather extraordinary effort – the *Moby Dick* that failed; why *Movie* considers Roger Corman a better director than Fred Zinnemann and ranks Joseph Losey next to God, why Bogdanovich, Mekas, and Sarris give their highest critical ratings to *What Ever Happened to Baby Jane?* (mighty big crevasses there). If Carol Reed had made only movies like *The Man Between* – in which he obviously worked to try to make something out of a ragbag of worn-out bits of material – he might be considered "brilliant" too. (But this is doubtful: although even the worst Reed is superior to Aldrich's *Baby Jane*, Reed would probably be detected, and rejected, as a man interested in substance rather than sensationalism.)

I am angry, but am I unjust? Here's Sarris:

> A Cukor who works with all sorts of projects has a more developed abstract style than a Bergman who is free to develop his own scripts. Not that Bergman lacks personality, but his work has declined with the depletion of his ideas largely because his technique never equaled his sensibility. Joseph L. Mankiewicz and Billy Wilder are other examples of writer-directors without adequate technical mastery. By contrast, Douglas Sirk and Otto Preminger have moved up the scale because their miscellaneous projects reveal a stylistic consistency.

How neat it all is – Bergman's "work has declined with the depletion of his ideas largely because his technique never equaled his sensibility." But what on earth does that mean? How did Sarris perceive Bergman's sensibility except through his technique? Is Sarris saying what he seems to be saying, that if Bergman had developed more "technique," his work wouldn't be dependent on his ideas? I'm afraid this *is* what he means, and that when he refers to Cukor's "more developed abstract style" he means by "abstract" something unrelated to ideas, a technique not dependent on the content of the films. This is curiously reminiscent of a view common enough in the business world, that it's better not to get too involved, too personally interested in business problems, or they take over your life; and besides, you don't function as well when you've lost your objectivity. But this is the *opposite* of how an artist works. His technique, his *style*, is determined by his range of involvements, and his preference for certain themes. Cukor's style is no more *abstract*(!) than Bergman's: Cukor has a range of subject matter that he can handle and when he gets a good script within his range (like *The Philadelphia Story* or *Pat and Mike*) he does a good job; but he is at an immense *artistic* disadvantage, compared with Bergman, because he is dependent on the ideas of so many (and often bad) scriptwriters and on material which is often alien to his talents. It's amusing (and/or depressing) to see the way *auteur* critics tend to downgrade writer-directors — who are in the *best* position to use the film medium for personal expression.

Sarris does some pretty fast shuffling with Huston and Bergman; why doesn't he just come out and admit that writer-directors are disqualified by his third premise? They can't arrive at that "interior meaning, the ultimate glory of the cinema" because a writer-director has no tension between his personality and his material, so there's nothing for the *auteur* critic to extrapolate from.

[. . .]

I assume that Sarris's theory is not based on his premises (the necessary causal relationships are absent), but rather that the premises were devised in a clumsy attempt to prop up the "theory." (It's a good thing he stopped at three: a few more circles and we'd really be in hell, which might turn out to be the last refinement of film tastes — Abbott and Costello comedies, perhaps?) These critics work embarrassingly hard trying to give some semblance of intellectual respectability to a preoccupation with mindless, repetitious commercial products — the kind of action movies that the restless, rootless men who wander on Forty-second Street and in the Tenderloin of all our big cities have always preferred just because they could respond to them without thought. These movies soak up your time. I would suggest that they don't serve a very different function for Sarris or Bogdanovich or the young men of *Movie* — even though they devise elaborate theories to justify soaking up their time. An educated man must have to work pretty hard to set his intellectual horizons at the level of *I Was a Male War Bride* (which, incidentally, wasn't even a good *commercial* movie).

"Interior meaning" seems to be what those in the know know. It's a mystique — and a mistake. The *auteur* critics never tell us by what divining rods they have discovered the élan of a Minnelli or a Nicholas Ray or a Leo McCarey. They're not critics; they're inside dopesters. There must be another circle that Sarris forgot to get to — the one where the secrets are kept.

Outside the Circles, or What Is a Film Critic?

I suspect that there's some primitive form of Platonism in the underbrush of Sarris's aesthetics. He says, for example, that "Bazin's greatness as a critic . . . rested in his disinterested conception of the cinema as a universal entity." I don't know what a "universal entity" is, but I rather imagine Bazin's stature as a critic has less to do with "universals" than with intelligence, knowledge, experience, sensitivity, perceptions, fervor, imagination, dedication, lucidity – the traditional qualities associated with great critics. The role of the critic is to help people see what is in the work, what is in it that shouldn't be, what is not in it that could be. He is a good critic if he helps people understand more about the work than they could see for themselves; he is a great critic, if by his understanding and feeling for the work, by his passion, he can excite people so that they want to experience more of the art that is there, waiting to be seized. He is not necessarily a bad critic if he makes errors in judgment. (Infallible taste is inconceivable; what could it be measured against?) He is a bad critic if he does not awaken the curiosity, enlarge the interests and understanding of his audience. The art of the critic is to transmit his knowledge of and enthusiasm for art to others.

[. . .]

I believe that we respond most and best to work in any art form (and to other experience as well) if we are pluralistic, flexible, relative in our judgments, if we are eclectic. But this does not mean a scrambling and confusion of systems. Eclecticism is not the same as lack of scruple; eclecticism is the selection of the best standards and principles from various systems of ideas. It requires more care, more orderliness to be a pluralist than to apply a single theory. Sarris, who thinks he is applying a single theory, is too undisciplined to recognize the conflicting implications of his arguments. If he means to take a Platonic position, then is it not necessary for him to tell us what his ideals of movies are and how various examples of film live up to or fail to meet his ideals? And if there is an ideal to be achieved, an objective standard, then what does élan have to do with it? (The ideal could be achieved by plodding hard work or by inspiration or any other way; the method of achieving the ideal would be as irrelevant as the "personality" of the creator.) As Sarris uses them, vitalism and Platonism and pragmatism do not support his *auteur* theory; they undermine it.

Those, like Sarris, who ask for objective standards seem to want a theory of criticism which makes the critic unnecessary. And he *is* expendable if categories replace experience; a critic with a single theory is like a gardener who uses a lawn mower on everything that grows. Their desire for a theory that will solve all the riddles of creativity is in itself perhaps an indication of their narrowness and confusion; they're like those puzzled, lost people who inevitably approach one after a lecture and ask, "But what is your basis for judging a movie?" When one answers that new films are judged in terms of how they extend our experience and give us pleasure, and that our ways of judging how they do this are drawn not only from older films but from other works of art, and theories of art, that new films are generally related to what is going on in the other arts, that as wide a background as possible in literature, painting, music, philosophy, political thought, etc., helps, that it is the wealth and variety of what he has to bring to new works that makes the critic's reaction to them valuable, the questioners are always unsatisfied. They wanted a simple answer, a formula; if they approached a chef they would probably ask for the one magic recipe that could be followed in all cooking.

[. . .]

This range of experience, and dependence on experience, is pitifully absent from the work of the *auteur* critics; they seem to view movies, not merely in isolation from the other arts, but in isolation even from their own experience. Those who become film specialists early in life are often fixated on the period of film during which they first began going to movies, so it's not too surprising that the *Movie* group [an English group of *auteur* critics] — just out of college and some still in — are so devoted to the films of the forties and fifties. But if they don't widen their interests to include earlier work, how can they evaluate films in anything like their historical continuity, how can they perceive what is distinctive in films of the forties? And if they don't have interests outside films, how can they evaluate what goes on in films? Film aesthetics as a distinct, specialized field is a bad joke: the *Movie* group is like an intellectual club for the intellectually handicapped. And when is Sarris going to discover that aesthetics is indeed a branch of ethnography; what does he think it is — a sphere of its own, separate from the study of man in his environment?

Some Speculations on the Appeal of the *Auteur* Theory

[. . .]

The French *auteur* critics, rejecting the socially conscious, problem pictures so dear to the older generation of American critics, became connoisseurs of values in American pictures that Americans took for granted, and if they were educated Americans, often held in contempt. The French adored the American gangsters, and the vitality, the strength, of our action pictures — all those films in which a couple of tough men slug it out for a girl, after going through hell together in oil fields, or building a railroad, or blazing a trail. In one sense, the French were perfectly right — these were often much more skillfully made and far more interesting visually than the movies with a message which Americans were so proud of, considered so *adult*. Vulgar melodrama with a fast pace can be much more exciting — and more honest, too — than feeble, pretentious attempts at drama — which usually meant just putting "ideas" into melodrama, anyway. Where the French went off was in finding elaborate intellectual and psychological meanings in these simple action films. (No doubt we make some comparable mistakes in interpreting French films.)

Like most swings of the critical pendulum, the theory was a *corrective*, and it helped to remind us of the energies and crude strength and good humor that Europeans enjoyed in our movies. The French saw something in our movies that their own movies lacked; they admired it, and to some degree, they have taken it over and used it in their own way (triumphantly in *Breathless* and *Shoot the Piano Player*, not very successfully in their semi-American thrillers). Our movies were a product of American industry, and in a sense, it was America itself that they loved in our movies — our last frontiers, our robber-barons, our naiveté, our violence, our efficiency and speed and technology, our bizarre combination of sentimentality and inhuman mechanization.

But for us, the situation is different. It is good for us to be reminded that our mass culture is not altogether poisonous in its effect on other countries, but what is appealingly exotic – "American" – for them is often intolerable for us. The freeways of cities like Los Angeles may seem mad and marvelous to a foreign visitor; to us they are the nightmares we spend our days in. The industrial products of Hollywood that we grew up on are not enough to satisfy our interests as adults. We want a great deal more from our movies than we get from the gangster carnage and the John Ford westerns that Europeans adore. I enjoy some movies by George Cukor and Howard Hawks but I wouldn't be much interested in the medium if that were all that movies could be. We see many elements in foreign films that *our* movies lack. We also see that our films have lost the beauty and innocence and individuality of the silent period, and the sparkle and wit of the thirties. There was no special reason for the French critics, preoccupied with *their* needs, to become sensitive to *ours*. And it was not surprising that, in France, where film directors work in circumstances more comparable to those of a dramatist or a composer, critics would become fixated on American directors, not understanding how confused and inextricable are the roles of the front office, the producers, writers, editors, and all the rest of them – even the marketing research consultants who may pretest the drawing powers of the story and stars – in Hollywood. For the French, the name of a director *was* a guide on what American films to see; if a director was associated with a certain type of film that they liked, or if a director's work showed the speed and efficiency that they enjoyed. I assume that anyone interested in movies uses the director's name as some sort of guide, both positive and negative, even though we recognize that at times he is little more than a stage manager. [. . .]

But what has happened to the judgment of the English and New York critics who have taken over the *auteur* theory and used it to erect a film aesthetics based on those commercial movies that answered a need for the French, but which are not merely ludicrously inadequate to our needs, but are the results of a system of production that places a hammerlock on American directors? And how can they, with straight faces, probe for deep meanings in these products? Even the kids they're made for know enough not to take them seriously. How can these critics, sensible enough to deflate our overblown message movies, reject the total content of a work as unimportant and concentrate on signs of a director's "personality" and "interior meaning"? It's understandable that they're trying to find movie art in the loopholes of commercial production – it's a harmless hobby and we all play it now and then. What's incomprehensible is that they *prefer* their loopholes to unified film expression. If they weren't so determined to exalt products over works that attempt to express human experience, wouldn't they have figured out that the *mise-en-scène* which they seek out in these products, the director's personal style which comes through despite the material, is only a mere suggestion, a hint of what an artist can do when he's in control of the material, when the whole film becomes expressive? Isn't it obvious that *mise-en-scène* and subject material – form and content – can be judged separately only in bad movies or trivial ones? It must be black comedy for directors to read this new criticism and discover that films in which they felt trapped and disgusted are now said to be their masterpieces. It's an aesthetics for 1984: failure is success.

[. . .]

Isn't the anti-art attitude of the *auteur* critics, both in England and here, implicit also in their peculiar emphasis on virility? (Walsh is, for Sarris, "one of the screen's most virile directors." In *Movie* we discover: "When one talks about the heroes of *Red River*, or *Rio Bravo*, or *Hatari!* one is talking about Hawks himself. . . . Finally everything that can be said in presenting Hawks boils down to one simple statement: here is a man.") I don't think critics would use terms like "virile" or "masculine" to describe artists like Dreyer or Renoir; there is something too *limited* about describing them this way (just as when we describe a woman as sensitive and feminine, we are indicating her *special* nature). We might describe Kipling as a virile writer but who would think of calling Shakespeare a virile writer? But for the *auteur* critics calling a director virile is the highest praise because, I suggest, it is some kind of assurance that he is not trying to express himself in an art form, but treats moviemaking as a professional job. (*Movie*: Hawks "makes the very best adventure films because he is at one with his heroes. . . . Only Raoul Walsh is as deeply an adventurer as Hawks. . . . Hawks' heroes are all professionals doing jobs – scientists, sheriffs, cattlemen, big game hunters: real professionals who know their capabilities. . . . They know exactly what they can do with the available resources, expecting of others only what they know can be given.") The *auteur* critics are so enthralled with their narcissistic male fantasies (*Movie*: "Because Hawks' films and their heroes are so genuinely mature, they don't need to announce the fact for all to hear") that they seem unable to relinquish their schoolboy notions of human experience. (If there are any female practitioners of *auteur* criticism, I have not yet discovered them.) Can we conclude that, in England and the United States, the *auteur* theory is an attempt by adult males to justify staying inside the small range of experience of their boyhood and adolescence – that period when masculinity looked so great and important but art was something talked about by poseurs and phonies and sensitive-feminine types? And is it perhaps also their way of making a comment on our civilization by the suggestion that trash is the true film art? I ask; I do not know.

12

Against Authorship

Stephen Heath

Edward Buscombe's paper[1] outlines clearly the issues raised by the development of the *auteur* theory in the *Cahiers du Cinéma* and in subsequent extensions (Sarris) and considerations (Wollen). This comment is intended simply to raise one or two further questions and to shift the perspective a little by offering something of a different articulation of the elements of Buscombe's conclusion.

The idea of authorship carries within it some assumption of the author as originator of discourse: it is as its source that the author is given as a unity of discourse. Immediately, certain qualifications impose themselves. Not all discourse has an author; nor do we demand it, surrounded as we are in our everyday living by a whole tissue of discourse to the varying interweaving strands of which we would not even know how to begin to pose the demands of authorship. These demands are, indeed, limited in relation to film; leaving aside the mass of material presented by television, think merely in this respect of the range of documentary, educational, medical, newsreel works for which only exceptionally do we bring into play any notion of the author. Even within the very area of the book (to which the assumptions and models of authorship are so closely connected), similar kinds of limitation can be seen to apply. Many scientists, for example, produce books; only a very few (a Heisenberg or a Bronowski), however, achieve the accepted status of an author: the validity of science, in fact, is that it is assumed as being without author, nowise particular but a clear and general demonstration of reality (something of the same assumption lies behind conventional conceptions of film documentary, though film also knows a convention of personal documentary, the cineast as witness, – Marker on Cuba). Where the idea of authorship is firmly established, doubts and limitations still persist: how are we to deal with films on which a director – an author – may have been involved in some other capacity (scenarist, assistant director) or which he may have realised in collaboration or to which he may have contributed no more than a brief sequence (Resnais's contribution to *L'An 01*)? What of the problem of *control* which the *auteur* theory confronted in its applications to Hollywood directors? (Similar questions arise with regard to the idea of authorship in literature.)

Such questions confirm the assumption of the author as originator, as source, and these ideas are then traditionally theorised, more or less sophisticatedly, through notions of the 'creative imagination', of 'personality', 'spontaneity', 'originality', or whatever. As source, the author produces 'works', closed units of discourse from without himself, the series of which will have a further unity that will be available for discussion in terms of the author's development, his 'maturity' and so on. [. . .]

What can it mean, however, to speak of the author as a source of discourse? The author is constituted only in language and a language is by definition social, beyond any particular individuality and, as Saussure put it in respect of natural language, 'to be accepted such as it is'. One can see how the question and the objection are, in fact, answered in the distinction between language and discourse, between general *langue* and singular usage. There is support for this in linguistics in the recognition formulated by Jakobson of increased freedom in individual language use proportionate to the increased size of the linguistic unit: in the combination of distinctive traits into phonemes, the user's liberty is nil; in the combination of phonemes into words, his liberty is heavily circumscribed; in the formation of sentences, he is much less constrained, though his 'creativity' depends on the formal constraint of the set of syntactic structures that transformational generative grammar seeks to describe in its model of competence; in the combination of sentences into blocks of discourse, finally, his liberty grows very substantially indeed and so the sentence becomes the upper limit of linguistics as a science, the threshold beyond which lies the individual and hence the unformalisable.

The dangers of this account can be readily seen: it tends to instrumentalise language and it is precisely this instrumentalisation that supports the idea of authorship in its conventional terms; consciousness and language are confused as an immediate unity in the flow of expression (this immediacy of consciousness is that bourgeois conception of 'man' as the punctual subject of history which Marx attacked in, for example, the *German Ideology*; 'man' and 'author' go hand in hand, the latter a particular instance of the former). In connection with cinema, an account of this kind is especially tempting since the straight application of the *langue/parole* model to film has led to the idea of cinema as a realm of pure performance, as being a language without a *langue*, the perfect expressive medium. [. . .] Classically, the *auteur* theory cannot but confirm this expressionism; the author is constituted *at the expense of* language, of the orders of discourse (he is what the texts can be stripped away to reveal). The effect of this confirmation can be seen at its clearest when the theory functions – and it seems inevitably always finally so to function – as a mode of evaluation.

To combat this, Edward Buscombe proposes other ways of looking at the cinema: '(a) the examination of the effects of the cinema on society (mass media research, etc.); (b) the effects of society on the cinema (the influence of ideology, of economics, of history, etc.); (c) a sub-division of (b), the effects of films on other films'. There will probably be an overall agreement with these as general emphases of areas with which reflection on cinema should be concerned. What is perhaps limiting is the formulation of these emphases in terms of a simple process of addition, as so many approaches that can be added to *auteur* theory. It would seem rather that the development of these emphases must constitute a radical criticism of *auteur* theory; one cannot merely consider the 'influence of ideology' alongside that theory, retaining both as different 'approaches', for the notion of the author is itself a major ideological construction (like, for example, the 'realism' of film) and any attention to cinema as ideological articulation must come back on that notion and its assumptions. The force of Buscombe's proposals cannot be limited to a plea for a variety of independent and pacific approaches the sum of which will give a better insight into film (better because of the disposition of a quantitatively greater number of separate insights); what is in question is the production, through the development of these proposals, of new objects the formalisation of which will provide not so much an insight as a theoretical grasp of film as signifying practice, a new problematic in which traditional notions are radically displaced.

Buscombe's paper effectively recognises the necessity of such a displacement. In relation to the idea of authorship, the theoretical object that the development of such a recognition entails is the *subject*; the need is for the construction of a theory of the subject with regard to the specific signifying practice of film. It is just such a theory that the notion of the author forecloses, determining a history of the cinema (how that history is conceived and written) and the history of cinema (operating an effective determination). Thus, for instance, the liberation of the camera is the evolution of its instrumental perfection (Balzac could declare an exactly similar view towards language); constructed to reproduce the centrality of the subject as punctual source (to sustain the ignorance of his subjection), it is given more and more as the point of his expression: the subject-author expresses himself in an immediate independence.

One or two elements of the displacement that a theory of the subject would operate may be worth briefly mentioning here.

The function of the author (the effect of the idea of authorship) is a function of unity; the use of the notion of the author involves the organicisation of the film (as 'work') and, in so doing, it avoids – this is indeed its function – the thinking of the articulation of the film text in relation to ideology. A theory of the subject represents precisely an attempt, at one level, to grasp the constructions of the subject in ideology (the modes of subjectivity); it thus allows at once the articulation of contradictions in the film text other than in relation to an englobing consciousness, in relation now, that is, to a specific historico-social process, and the recognition of a heterogeneity of structures, codes, languages at work in the film and of the particular positions of the subject they impose. (It is evident that a theory of the subject will then question the simple use of the *langue/parole* model.)

[. . .]

The equation of unconscious themes and outside pressures (with its corollary of conscious intention and independence as the alternative) seems especially significant in the emphases and developments of *auteur* theory. On the one hand, we find ideas of personality, free-wheeling creativity, independent intention; on the other, those of unconscious structures, constraints, effects from 'outside'. In theory, one might assign different procedures to these two emphases: stylistic analysis and structural analysis (of the kind developed by Lévi-Strauss). In practice, *auteur* theory seems to mix the two (the proportions vary as Buscombe shows in his account) in a confused strategy that generally refuses to develop theoretically the results it produces. The themes and shifting antinomies which *auteur* theory so often traces – think, for example, of Wollen's description of Ford and Hawks in the second chapter of *Signs and Meaning* – are ideological formations; it determines, in other words, the particular inscriptions of ideology by a corpus of films (the principle of pertinence for the corpus being that of authorship). If this recognition is held, new problems arise which it becomes increasingly important to consider. One such problem is that of the inscription of the subject in ideological formations and this cannot be formulated simply as the question of 'outside pressures'. Indeed, if we look at the work of Dickens, Buscombe's example of a relative freedom from 'outside pressures', it can be seen that it responds to almost every ideological pressure of the age, so much so that it reads as a massive *dispositif* of the ideological formations then current (not a form of discourse that is not somewhere assumed, even where this leads to what is defined as 'contradiction' and finally, in the later texts, overspills the given assumptions of representation to produce something of a frantic – the theme of negation, of endless circulation, of disorigination – dramatisation of the discursive orders of these formations). What is crucial is the focus on the languages, codes, orders of discourse that 'cross' the text and the analysis of the activity it brings to bear on them. The *text*, the new object that provides the necessity for a theory of the subject in relation to film, is precisely the space of the breakdown of the opposition between 'inside' and 'outside', 'dependent' and 'independent' and so on. [. . .] Another problem is that of the construction of the ideological subject, the production of the subject as support for ideological formations, and it is here that psychoanalysis plays a fundamental theoretical role as description of the setting in position of the individual subject. As far as the specific practice of film is concerned, it would seem that the psychoanalytical intervention in a general theory of the subject needs at once to be focussed as a critical perspective on the use of the idea of authorship and its assumptions and to be employed to disengage within that idea, and hence to operate its methodological displacement, 'individual' and 'person'; where the latter is the ideological construction of the author, the former marks a configuration of elements, the subject in his particularity the determination of which, its 'history', is the task of pyschoanalysis. The interrogation of a group of films within this history is not the revelation of the author but the tracing in the series of texts of the insistence of the unconscious (in the Freudian sense of the term). Such an interrogation meets difficulties similar to those encountered by the attempt to place literary texts in this perspective – absence of analytical situation, associations, transference, etc. – and it seems clear that the work that needs to be done at the moment is the close analysis of the systems of particular texts ('textual systems' in Metz's terminology) in relation to the ideological formations they reflect or articulate and the positions in which they inscribe the subject and, overall, to the whole process of subject and sense in the text. (We need, for example, to begin to reflect on the modes of relation and displacement between subject of *énonciation* and subject of *énoncé* in film.)

The list of problems could be extended and their consideration, together with that of those mentioned, is the development of that new problematic to which Edward

Buscombe's proposals point and within which the question of the *auteur* theory is re-cast. What then remains, if anything, of that theory? The passage quoted by Buscombe from Wollen's postscript to the revised edition of *Signs and Meaning* perhaps provides one answer, though preceding formulations there tend to pull it back into rather traditional terms, in its distinction of Fuller and 'Fuller': 'But Fuller or Hawks, or Hitchcock, the directors, are quite separate from "Fuller" or "Hawks" or "Hitchcock" the structures named after them, and should not be methodologically confused.' The author, that is may return as a *fiction*, figure – fan of elements – of a certain pleasure which begins to turn the film, or series of films the ones over the others, into a plural-ity, a play of assemblage and dispersion. Grasped thus, the author, like its corollary the reader as passive receiver, now becomes part of an activity of writing-reading; we come back once again, in other words, to the new object of the text, space of the process of sense and subject.

NOTE

1 'Ideas of Authorship', *Screen* 14.3 (Autumn 1973): 75–85.

13

DVDs and the Director's Intentions

Deborah Parker and Mark Parker

Midway through the commentary track to the DVD of *Fitzcarraldo*, Werner Herzog reveals that the Amazonian Indians offered to kill his star Klaus Kinski. Herzog jokingly adds that he wanted to kill the actor himself while working on an earlier movie with Kinski, whose manic tirades were famous in the industry, and that he briefly considered the present offer. This is an amusing and memorable anecdote, told with great brio by Herzog. However, it adds another layer to the film itself, as Herzog, moving from raconteur to director, explains how he took artistic advantage of the situation. The smoldering hostility registered on the faces of the Indians as they surround Fitzcarraldo and his remaining crew during a meal on the ship provides a powerful expression – perhaps a culmination – of the menace with which Herzog tried to imbue his film. The anecdote also reveals the complications in Herzog's stated project of recording the faces of the Peruvian Indians, whom he well knew would be changed forever by the incursion of other cultures and modernity. To render a reality and to create an artistic object are not so easily separable.

Herzog's story about the trials of working with Klaus Kinski is but one example of the kind of information that emerges in discussions of film on digital video discs (DVDs). Such an anecdote, drawn from a printed book, would be suggestive, but in this particular form, as part of the commentary track to the scene that it describes, it has an unusual immediacy. It becomes another text, intimately related to the film, complicating the experience of the film, but nevertheless not quite the film. With it come considerations barely discernible in the film, more abstract, but just as compelling, as Herzog reorients the viewer's relation to the material.

Such moments will soon be much more common in the study and appreciation of film, as the DVD medium permeates the market. Boasting the same high visual and sound quality as laser discs, but more practical, DVDs are rapidly becoming a household staple. Recent statistics show that between 16% and 25% of U.S. homes have a DVD player, and as of August 28, 2001, DVD sales in the United States had jumped to $127.7 million, more than double the previous year's $58.8 million. The advantages of the format – durability, compactness, cost – have driven the switch from videotape to digital media, but with the new format have come other opportunities. The storage capacity of the DVD (an astonishing 8.5 gigabytes achieved by a remarkable combination of compression and the addition of a second layer of data) allows for much more than a copy of the film, and a host of supplementary materials now accompanies each title. The medium, as in other cases of technological transformation, may well be the message. However, what we wish to address here is the way this new medium allows for certain new messages and new approaches not only in the formal study of film but in the experience of film more generally.

The first DVDs, introduced in March 1997, contained just the film and subtitled versions in French or Spanish. Current special edition DVDs brim with supplementary materials. The two-disc set of *The Fight Club* contains four audio commentary tracks, three theatrical trailers, twelve American TV spots, seven deleted/alternate scenes, a behind-the-scenes featurette, fourteen segments on production and video effects with alternate video and audio tracks, storyboards, the film's press kit, the transcript of an interview with Edward Norton, and cast and crew bios – and this is just a partial list. The time required for taking in these materials far exceeds the viewing time of the film.

Some of this supplementary material is simply recycled, such as electronic press kits, trailers from theatrical release, or deleted scenes. Other features are specifically commissioned for the DVD release. The production and packaging of these extra features has become an industry in itself. Larger studios such as Paramount and Dream Works have been producing documentary-style behind-the-scenes features during the shooting of a film for at least three years. Other supplementary material is created by smaller, independent film companies after the film is shot and edited. Once a film is "locked" or given its final edit, such companies make requests for deleted scenes. Their staffs then convene to determine further packaging details, which can vary widely from creative re-editing of materials to imaginative extensions of the film. [. . .] Most interesting for students of film is the production of a commentary track, an audio track that runs the length of the film. Typically the director, writer, or sundry crew members assemble to record the commentary track, but some editions of DVDs – often re-releases of older films – provide critical and scholarly analysis.

It would be easy to dismiss much of this supplementary material as superfluous, as second-rate entertainment, or simply as redundant promotional materials. Somewhat obscured in this rush of additional material and the marketing hype that surrounds it, however, is the transformative nature of this change in format. One index of this change is the bibliographic terminology newly appropriated for DVDs, which present themselves as "special editions" or "anthologies," and that generally divide the film not into "scenes" but into "chapters." Films, even as they have increasingly taken the place of books in culture, have routinely adopted, somewhat anxiously, the trappings of literature and the book, and the application of this vocabulary to DVDs extends this familiar practice. But these bibliographic terms are worth pondering in another sense as well, one in which the applicability of such a description should be carefully considered. DVDs are no longer simply copies of films, like videotapes; they have been physically changed by the process of digitization. There is an obvious sense in which this is so. Digitization affords the opportunity of cleaning up scratches and blots in the visual track as well as sonic imperfections. The color is routinely enhanced as well, especially in the case of digitization of older prints. All this comes, however, with some loss of data during compression. Hence, in the most rudimentary, physical sense, the DVD version is a reconstruction. Even more transformative, however, is the new relation between film and audience offered by the DVD. The effect of the film is now, at least potentially, intensely mediated by "supplementary materials," which include extensive commentary by directors and writers, the reminiscence of actors, the technical remarks of cameramen and set designers, and the critical remarks of scholars. The DVD edition is essentially a reorientation of the film, often carried out by a variety of agents, and subject to a wide variety of choices made by the eventual viewers. Consciously or not, the DVD constitutes a new edition, and it should be seen in these terms.

The dichotomy between entertainment and critical apparatus is evident to the participants themselves. DVD producers, at least publicly, are unanimous in claiming that the extra features are intended to enhance viewers' appreciation and understanding of a film. As Jay Douglas, vice-president of Anchor Bay Entertainment, observes, the special features "open up contact" with the talent behind a film, enabling viewers to "hear the enthusiasm of the directors" and to learn "the story of how the film got made." Yet Tim Allen, who has edited many commentary tracks, reports that directors routinely quip, "Who is going to listen to this except a bunch of film students?" In his commentary to *Out of Sight* Steven Soderbergh seems even more doubtful about the audience, wondering aloud "Do people actually listen to this stuff?" While the sales figures for DVDs show that purchasers extend far beyond the world of film buffs, determining the audience for the extra materials is not easy. According to a recent *Wall Street Journal* article, viewers are just as likely to claim that they are "disappointed" if a disc contains no bonus materials as to admit they watch them "very rarely." In the face of uncertainty about the audience for these materials, many studios are simply piling on the extras. The result, as Guido Henkel, editor of *DVD Review* wryly observes, can resemble "a landfill in which everything is dumped in without any sort of vision, simply to create selling points on the back of the packaging."

One might note the precarious nature of the anthologizing venture. It emerges as a kind of fold in the film market, a space created by technological innovation and the ambiguities of an emerging market. What drives the market for DVDs, clearly, is improved image and sound quality, both immediately and over repeated viewings, as well as economies of manufacture and distribution. Increased capacity, in excess of what is necessary to present the film itself, is a secondary benefit of digitization, not the goal that drove development of the medium. In itself, the opportunity provided by such an increase is a spare one. It affords space for certain materials, but it cannot, in itself, provide a rationale for creating them. One expects market demand to do that. But in this case, as the comments of various producers and performers suggest, there is no clearly articulated demand. Consumers expect these "bonus" features, although it is not clear that the absence of such features would cause them not to buy digitized versions of a film, and larger studios, almost defensively, provide them. This structures the product, and the volume of mass market DVDs, chock full of supplementary materials, reinforces this particular format. This structure enables the production of more serious or scholarly supplementary materials.

As is often the case in the history of criticism and art in the last 200 years, the space for this kind of cultural life is found on the margins of technological advance and the market. At its best, commentary by directors and screen writers can afford a glimpse of the care and deliberation behind the production of movies: how details are carefully weighed for significance, how patterns of meaning are built up and maintained, and how the editing process shapes meaning out of conflicting visions. It also shows the limits of intention, that is, the ways in which contingency and chance in shooting a film can become part of meaning. For those unaccustomed to thinking in terms of the deliberate processes of construction, selection, and concentration crucial to art, these commentaries, delivered by authoritative figures such as directors, writers, and set designers, can be a valuable, pragmatic introduction to the study and enjoyment of film.

A complete study of the DVD as a form for film would require a more extensive review of the history of the transmission of film than is possible here; one in which different kinds of projection, different kinds of reconstruction, and the videotape format would only be the most obvious – and perhaps not the most important – topics. [. . .] In the remainder of this essay, we would like to examine one facet of the DVD's reorientation of film, the new prominence it gives to questions of intention, both directorial and cinematographical, and to speculate on the curious fitness of this recrudescence for the present moment.

Intention is as vexed a concept in film studies as it has been in the study of literary texts. Nevertheless, in both fields the last twenty to thirty years have seen a decided retreat from authorial or directorial intention toward analysis of interpretive conventions. Meaning is not inherent to a text, but something a community of readers or viewers, acting in loose accord with various interpretive protocols, agree to infer. More recent scholarly turns to history, while applying specific historical contexts, have at the same time conceded that these very contexts are multiple, if not endless. Such reflexivity, which brings with it a plurality of meanings, is the hallmark of post-structuralist interpretation. Directorial commentary tracks have a peculiar salience at such a moment. While directors, like authors, are not always the most accurate or reliable commentators on their own work, many directors provide a consistent set of protocols for their films and display a self-consciousness at least as well-developed as that of most critics.

In addition to providing a splendid enhancement of Bertrand Tavernier's 1988 *Coup de Torchon*, the Criterion Collection's 2001 edition of the film offers a series of interviews with the director that incorporates and comments upon specific scenes. In his adaptation to film of Jim Thompson's novel *Pop. 1280*, Tavernier lucidly sets out some of his intentions in abstract terms as well as in terms of the minute particularities of production. He speaks compellingly of the relation of *Coup de Torchon* to the genre of French film noir ("a film noir which refuses the conventions of the film noir") as well as his reliance on the steady cam (and complete avoidance of tracking shots) in order to create a thematically central "slight feeling of unbalance" and instability. His commentary on specific scenes insistently links his intention to formal features. For instance, his remarks on a scene in which the protagonist, a seemingly dimwitted policeman (Philippe Noiret), discusses his difficulties with the local priest, clearly set out the means by which the film makes its critique of the French presence in Africa. As the priest puts the last touches on the task of replacing a termite-infested cross, carefully hammering nails through Christ's feet, his advice ("all in good time, each thing in turn, and one thing after the other") combines with the rich irony of his action to show at once the stupid, redundant, and complicit posture of the clergy. In discussing (in fact, defending) a troubling scene in which the sheriff murders a black man who has witnessed another of his murders, Tavernier not only outlines his intentions but links them to Thompson's aims in *Pop. 1280*. Tavernier's intentions in the film are sharply delimited and clearly articulated throughout the commentary.

Much less pointed are the intentions that emerge in Alexander Payne's commentary to *Election*. Payne's discussion of the film presupposes a different notion of intention, one far more open in application. A comparison to Tavernier is revealing. Payne notes, for instance, the persistence of certain visual cues in the film – Jim McAllister's (Matthew Broderick) repeated frustration as he walks through circular enclosures, the appearance of garbage trucks behind the main action – which function less as determinate objective correlatives than indications of atmosphere. The circles traced by the protagonist culminate in his return, at the end of the film, to something of his original, frustrated position, and the garbage motif slyly prefigures McAllister's ultimate demise, when the ballot he has stolen to change the outcome of the school election is found in the trash can near his desk by a janitor he had earlier annoyed by carelessly littering. Payne's intentions are more suggestive, that a kind of rubbish persists in our lives, our attempts to beautify them notwithstanding, and that something of a trashy dark nemesis stalks McAllister in his pathetic attempts to transcend his mundane life. Intention, for these two directors, means quite different things.

These two ways of talking about intention are far different from that of Paul Verhoeven, whose commentary to the restored director's cut of *RoboCop* promulgates an entirely different set of interpretive protocols. Verhoeven's analysis of various images requires a much more energetic viewer, one thoroughly versed in what often goes without saying in a culture. For instance, the commentary on the introduction of the ED 209 – a policing robot built for what one of the executives terms "urban pacification" – at a corporate meeting, connects the ED 209 with Vietnam, first by the term "urban pacification" itself, then by the shape of the robot – which recalls a Bell Huey helicopter – and finally by the name of the presiding scientist, McNamara. Robert McNamara was Secretary of Defense (1961–1981) under presidents Kennedy and Johnson. Edward Neumeier, one of the film's co-writers, describes the scene as "the American attitude in Vietnam brought to an urban situation." [. . .] Through such commentary, what appears to be an extreme parody takes on a more discursive form. We perceive an argument, a method, beneath the apparent mayhem and madness. In fact, the speed and ubiquity of such allusions to contemporary events and culture make even humorous commentary seem more plausible. Neumeier's comments on a part of a scene in which Emile, a member of the murderous gang that tortures and murders Murphy (the policeman who later becomes RoboCop), watches television through a store window, links Emile's actions to contemporary debates on the effect of television on criminality. As Emile, surrounded by rampaging gangs along the street, rises to throw his half-finished bottle of whiskey through the glass, the debate is rehearsed and satirized. Neumeier may well be joking here – the comment is very funny in context – but the structure of the parodic reading is really no different from the more serious reading of parody encouraged at other moments in the commentary. The movie is flooded with such lightning references – linking the decline in the quality of manufactures to the military-industrial complex; translating the warrior ethos of corporate boardrooms to an execution of a rival co-worker, a ghastly accidental murder of an employee during the demonstration of the ED 209, and a climactic shootout between RoboCop and a particularly villainous executive; and repeatedly conflating persons with products.

The discussions of intention that emerge in these three commentaries are notable for their avoidance of abstraction. In each case, the director lays out a set of consistent and coherent protocols for working through his film, but in each case intention is invoked only in terms of specific situations. These accounts of intent are more pragmatic than those in most critical discussions – less rigid, more descriptive of certain choices made within specific contexts, and perhaps more thoughtful about how an audience might actually perceive a given sequence and the objects that make it up. In a sense, it is not so much that each director talks about intention itself than that the commentary track provides us with an opportunity to follow the director's application of such a concept to his work. Payne, one might note, is not nearly so purposeful in his selection of objects and in his recollection of past films as Tavernier. Tavernier is more likely to articulate more fully the context for some of his ideas than Verhoeven, who expects the reader to bring more of a contemporary sense of history and popular culture to his suggestive images. Payne's material, being less complicated than that of Tavernier and less time-bound than that of Verhoeven, is more likely to reach a larger audience. We can, through these commentaries, begin to think of intention as denoting a wide variety of practices, and to see that there are several kinds of intention. One might, over time, develop an effective typology of interpretive protocols.

Other commentary tracks complicate this picture of intention in productive ways. Tracks with multiple commentators often prompt a consideration of instances in which intention becomes collaborative – sometimes happily, as in the *RoboCop* commentary track, and sometimes with a residue of conflict. *The Limey* features an animated debate between director Steven Soderbergh and the screenwriter Lem Dobbs over the eventual shape of the film. Their two competing visions of the material as conceived and shot are resolved only, and then not fully, by the editing process. Dobbs, at times showing some exasperation, laments the excision of material that would have made the film a meditation on the spirit of the 1960s – long sequences that would not only have developed the characters more fully, but would have articulated something about the legacy of this era. Clearly the film was planned around such ideas, as the casting of such diverse 1960s icons as Peter Fonda, Barry Newman, and Terence Stamp suggests. In critical terms, the dispute between Soderbergh and Dobbs could be described as rival plottings of the same story, that is, a question of narration. [. . .] The exchange [. . .] asks that we distinguish dominant, suppressed, and residual intentions, that we perform an act of recovery that is less critical than historical or archaeological.

Such discussions need not have the tension Dobbs and Soderbergh display. The supplementary materials to the DVD of *American Beauty* include a pleasant exchange between director Sam Mendes and cinematographer Conrad L. Hall that illuminates a complicated play of intention and chance in the production of the film. The conversation is efficiently realized throughout by the use of storyboards and frames from the movie. The mood is justifiably congratulatory and amiable, but as the conversation develops, a certain gap emerges between the stated intentions of each party. Hall often deflates the very intention that Mendes praises in Hall's realization of the storyboards, offering purely visual pleasure or expedience as motivation for what Mendes infers as thematic. [. . .]

The commentary tracks to *American Beauty* and to *The Limey*, unlike those to *Coup de Torchon*, *Election*, and *RoboCop*, do more than provide a set of coherent interpretive protocols. They provide a vivid picture of the complications that collaboration inevitably imposes upon the application of the concept of intention. The problems do not, however, disrupt or preclude the discussion of intention so much as require, at least for critics and scholars, a self-consciousness about the discursive use of the term. Other commentary tracks, however, do explore such contradictions and inconsistencies. Nevertheless, they pose these questions in pragmatic rather than theoretical terms, as a special kind of discourse on intention.

In his commentary to *Dead Ringers*, David Cronenberg provides a most consistent and well-delimited discussion of intention, meticulously setting out not only his specific intentions, but the means by which he sought to communicate them. One considerable challenge in filming the movie was to find a way of showing the psychological deterioration of the protagonists (identical twin gynecologists Beverly and Elliot Mantle, played by Jeremy Irons in a virtuosic display of craft). Cronenberg's solution is a version of what T. S. Eliot famously termed the "objective correlative," that is, "a set of objects, a situation, a chain of events which shall be the formula for that *particular* emotion." Cronenberg, through a series of shots, very deliberately emphasizes a "set of objects" in the film, the twins' strikingly modern apartment and offices, and he painstakingly follows the degradation of these environments through the film. The cold, "bruised" color of the rooms, the austerity of the modernist furniture, and the precise ordering of the objects, all become readable signs of the twins' state of mind and their gradual deterioration. Cronenberg sets out a kind of grammar for the film, authorizing a coherent and deliberate approach to reading the psychology of his characters. For example, just as the twins' rationalist bias is challenged by the warmer, emotional Claire Niveau (Geneviève Bujold), so does her apartment present a far more complex play of textures, colors, and curved lines. Hence as Beverly falls in love with Claire we have more than a simple love story; we are also aware of this attachment as the eruption of Beverly's emotional life, a movement from an ordered, objective viewpoint to the messier world of subjectivity and affect. (The pattern is made emphatic by

Claire's occupation as an actress, which clashes with the scientific work done by the twins.) [. . .]

Most evocative, however, are the tools designed by Beverly, the famous "Mantle Retractor" he builds while a medical student and the frightening set of "Instruments for Operating on Mutant Women" he designs and commissions later. These objects, examined in sequence, encapsulate the film's main themes. As Cronenberg explains, the first of these inventions expresses the twins' deepest desire, to analyze and to master nature: "I felt that I needed a physical symbol of the twins' efforts to deal with reality by their own version of creativity, by their own attempt to create something that could modify the human body and control it." The "Mantle Retractor" earns the twins professional accolade and prestige, which the "gold-plated" trophy they receive embodies; the latter tools bespeak "a man whose rationality is failing but in its failing is producing these strange kind[s] of works of art, horrific works of art." On one level, this sequence, like the gradual deterioration of the apartment, seems to reveal Beverly's disorientation and madness clearly. Cronenberg's commentary paradoxically invests the irrationality of this sequence with an airtight, Cartesian logic. The objects speak clearly and compellingly of Beverly's descent into a pitiable madness, one that fulfills all the tragic depths of Aristotle's famous formulation of "fear and pity." Yet, on another level, this sequence of objects, which embody the thematic core of the film, is disrupted by the director's commentary. Cronenberg opens the discussion of these objects by revealing that, while working as an artist in France years before the film was conceived, he had created, in cast aluminum, an "Instrument for Operating on Mutants." Hence the well-delimited sequence of the film, with its clear implications and intentions, is extended by an autobiographical revelation. The audio commentary track, with its insistent immediacy, distends the precise formulations of a formal reading of the film to include the imprecision, silences, and ambiguities of an autobiographical approach. Viewed in these terms, Cronenberg's opening words on the commentary track take on much greater implication: "This is gonna be maybe a lot more traumatic for me than for you, reliving the film." As we have seen in the instance of Herzog's commentary on *Fitzcarraldo*, the commentary track allows Cronenberg to create another, and perhaps a more complicated, text, one that even as it resolutely pursues a formal reading of *Dead Ringers*, unsettles that reading with an equally powerful, if sketchier, autobiographical one. Cronenberg's audio commentary retraces and transposes the movie's central conflict, as formal analysis (cold, detached, technical) is opposed yet again to the ambiguities, subjectivities, and perhaps ineffabilities, of affect.

[. . .]

This selection – by no means an exhaustive one – of commentary tracks amply demonstrates the pervasive recourse to intention when directors explain or analyze film. The means of recovering or ascertaining intention may vary, intention may involve accident or seem curiously after the fact, and intentions may be multiple, but, just as there are no atheists in foxholes, there seems to be no doubt about the utility of intentionality among the producers of film. Each director wields the term with a canny sense of its potential for analysis and criticism as well as a sharply defined awareness of its limitations. [. . .] Viewed solely in these terms, the evidence from DVD commentaries by directors seems simply to support conventional and pluralistic notions of intention employed by critics and scholars of film, who have typically had recourse in their analyses to commentary by directors and others involved in production. DVD commentaries would thus seem to offer more evidence of the same kind – richer, perhaps, but no more conclusive or compelling.

To view DVD commentary in this way, however, is to mistake the particular virtues of this form. By its very nature, the DVD commentary track enforces a heightened attention to intricacies of intention as it plays out over the course of the film. Directorial comment returns again and again to questions of intention that are local and technical, and the discussion has an unusual immediacy and density. Intention in these tracks is not used in the abstract and broadly thematic sense in which it is invoked in other forms, such as interviews, *manifesti*, or more general statements by directors. Rather, what emerges in this form is the intentional practice carried out by a particular director from scene to scene, what we might call the specifics of intention. The informal and at times desultory quality of the commentary allows us to see how each director uses the concept, not so much how he might wish to use it, and it allows us, if we wish, to address other moments in the film in terms of the particular use of intention practiced by its director.

Taken altogether, commentary tracks exemplify a practice urged by Wittgenstein in *Philosophical Investigations*: "to bring back words from their metaphysical to their everyday use." These discussions treat intention as a particularly useful kind of language game, one that organizes the production and experience of film, but which is capable of transformation as interpreters adopt different roles in the game, such as director, writer, cinematographer, critic, or fan. Their commentary sketches what Wittgenstein calls the "original home" in which the language game of intention abides. Commentary tracks create another text, one overrun with intentions, and one that, as it maps coherent and recoverable intention according to consistent and seemingly authoritative protocols, may bring the pragmatics of intention into renewed prominence.

How Do Films Engage Our Emotions?

Introduction

Have you ever come back from a movie feeling disappointed that the characters failed to move you? Or, have you felt manipulated when you found yourself crying in response to a character's plight, perhaps against your better judgment? Could you find that *Scream* (Wes Craven, 1996) is a good horror movie, even though you did not feel frightened while watching it? These questions prompt us to consider how the evocation of emotions, of one kind or another, is central to our experience of watching films.

The essays in Part IV reflect on the diverse ways in which films engage our emotions. These discussions in the philosophy of film are part of a long tradition in which philosophers, going back to the time of Plato, have examined the central role that the emotions play in our experience of art. For Plato, in his work *The Republic*, this meant that an art form like tragedy was an invitation to irrationality, since it "watered" the emotions when, instead, reason should be dominant in a person's soul. The authors in this section engage with the worries that some philosophers and film theorists have had regarding the emotional appeal of movies.

In his essay Gregory Currie looks closely at the ways in which works of fiction, such as fictional film, produce logically distinct kinds of desires in the viewer. He also considers whether these desires elicited by the film may carry over and affect our desires in real life. Works of fiction engender what Currie calls "character desires" and also "narrative desires." Viewers of *Casablanca* (Michael Curtiz, 1942) desire, for example, that the lovers, Rick and Ilsa, stay together. This is a "character desire" within what Currie calls the "scope of imagination," for it pertains to the characters in a work of fiction, not to real people, and this desire can be satisfied if in the film's narrative Rick and Ilsa do stay together. On the other hand, viewers desire that the narrative of *Casablanca* conclude with Ilsa leaving with her husband Victor, and Rick staying to fight the Nazis alongside Captain Renault. Here we have a desire with respect to the way that the narrative of *Casablanca* should end: this is what Currie calls a "narrative desire." Currie argues that it is not uncommon for films to create a conflict between character desires as well as a conflict between character desires and narrative desires. A tragedy such as *Othello* is an illustration of the latter, for our character desire that Desdemona flourish conflicts with our narrative desire that Othello not realize that Desdemona is faithful to him. *Casablanca* illustrates the former conflict, for we desire that Rick and Ilsa stay together. But we also desire that Ilsa stay with her husband to support his work in the war effort, creating a conflict in our desires with respect to these characters.

Currie applies the concepts of narrative desire and character desire to real-life events and people. We evoke non-fictional narratives to explain and understand our lives, and actual people can become characters in these narratives. In this case we can have character desires and narrative desires with respect to these non-fictional narratives as well. How then might filmic fictions affect the narrative desires we have concerning real people and events? Currie speculates that desiring something in the imagination might make one more prone to desire it in real life and also prone to try to satisfy that desire. In this circumstance, the desires that are unproblematic in a fictional context may become problematic in a real-life setting.

Carl Plantinga responds to scholars in film studies who argue that mainstream films positions viewers to adopt an "ideology," or a distorted view of social reality through its use of narratives and characters that evoke certain emotions in the audience. A central influence on these theorists is the writing of Bertolt Brecht, the famous German playwright, producer, and poet (1898–1956). Brecht lived during World War II and saw Hitler using art and film to whip up the emotions of the German people to support the Nazi movement. Brecht's own "epic theatre" utilized dramatic practices ("alienation devices") that affected an emotional distance between the audience and the characters and action of the play. His goal was to prompt viewers to think critically and form a rational judgment about what they were seeing on stage. Neo-Brechtian film scholars argue that the evocation of emotion characteristic of many mainstream film genres is incompatible with the viewer adopting a critical attitude toward the films' representations.

Plantinga questions the opposition between reason and the emotions that is central to the neo-Brechtians' analysis. Working within a cognitive film theoretic framework, Plantinga argues that emotions are not simply related to private feelings or physiological responses: they are also connected to cognitions – inferences, judgments, and hypotheses. This cognitive analysis of the emotions goes back at least to Aristotle, who said in the *Rhetoric* that feeling the emotion of pity for Oedipus, for example, requires a judgment that Oedipus suffers a misfortune greater than he deserves. If emotions are partially constituted by judgments, then emotions can be rational or irrational. In this way the evocation of emotion in a viewer is not automatically an invitation to irrationality. Plantinga concludes that the elicitation of emotion in a viewer is therefore not, in itself, problematic – it is the particular evocations of the emotions by films in specific contexts that may be questionable from the point of view of ideological film criticism. He illustrates this idea with an analysis of the sentimental ending of Charlie Chaplin's *City Lights* (1931), suggesting that the use of sentiment in this context does not prevent the viewer from taking a critical perspective on the social realities the film depicts.

Murray Smith's essay is taken from a central chapter in his book, *Engaging Characters: Fiction, Emotion, and the Cinema.* Many of us will criticize a film if it fails to feature characters with which we can "identify." In the *Poetics*, Aristotle made a related point in saying that we will emotionally engage with characters in tragedy only if they are "like us." From these observations we might conclude that we "identify" with a character in a fictional film when we (1) engage with a central character who possesses qualities we either do possess or would like to possess, and (2) experience feelings that are congruent to those experienced by the central protagonist.

Smith breaks new ground in arguing that what is commonly called "identification" with a character is actually three distinct responses: (1) recognition; (2) alignment; (3) allegiance. First, we engage in "recognition" of a character when we construct a character based on the perception of textual elements, including character traits, physical characteristics, and emotions, which come together around the image of a body. Second, a film "aligns" viewers with a character when the film gives the viewers access to the character's actions, feelings, and thoughts. Sometimes a film restricts our knowledge of what is going on to what it is that a character knows or believes is going on. Or a film may align us with a character, while also shifting to the perspective of another character, giving us a viewpoint that is not restricted to what it is that the central character knows or believes.

Recognition and alignment with a character require that the viewer have access to and understand the point of view of the person. But Smith argues that these two modes of engagement fall short of evaluating and endorsing the moral traits, emotions, and actions of the character. When we engage in this way, we develop an "allegiance" toward the character. This way of relating to a character comes close to what we commonly or loosely think of as "identifying" with a character. Smith argues that all three modes of engagement are different aspects of what he calls "the structure of sympathy." He applies these concepts to analyze Hitchcock's *The Man Who Knew Too Much* (1956), arguing that the film engages the viewer in a strong allegiance with the central characters, Jo and Ben McKenna. Yet at the same time it complicates this allegiance through a shifting structure of alignments with these and other central characters. Rather than providing an experience in which the film engages the viewer with one primary protagonist, the film expands the viewer's knowledge through "plural engagement" with multiple characters. Smith suggests that the phenomenon of plural engagement is not unique to this film, but is the typical mode in which most Hollywood films emotionally connect with viewers.

The last selection is from Noël Carroll's *The Philosophy of Horror; or Paradoxes of the Heart.* Carroll, a leading philosopher of film and a connoisseur of horror films, discusses a paradox regarding our emotional engagement with horror films. It seems that horror films evoke conflicting emotional responses from the audience: revulsion and pleasurable fascination. For monsters, of one sort or another, are at the center of most, if not all, horror films. The monster is a creature that is dangerous, disgusting, and fearsome. Yet people obviously take pleasure in watching horror films – why else do they go to them? The paradox of horror, then, is the puzzle of how viewers of horror films can be attracted by what is repulsive. This paradox is an instance of a more general philosophical problem: how is it that the aesthetic representation of normally disturbing events and objects can compel our interest and please us?

Carroll argues that horror induces a dichotomous emotional response: on the one hand, there is disgust and revulsion evoked by the monster. Think, for example of the horrific man/insect, "BrundleFly," which the scientist, Seth Brundle, turns into in David Cronenberg's remake of the 1958 horror film classic, *The Fly*. Carroll argues that the reason the monster is disgusting is that it is a being that violates our conceptual categories by crossing species barriers. Yet, on the other hand, horror movies also induce pleasure in the viewer. Carroll argues that this pleasure is primarily *cognitive*, for viewers get pleasurable fascination from discovering, tracking, and confirming the existence of the monster in these films.

These observations lead to Carroll's solution to the paradox: the audience of horror films both feels disgust and experiences pleasure; but this is not paradoxical. The disgust felt by the audience for the monster is the price they must pay for the cognitive pleasures provided by the horror film narrative.

The essays in Part IV help us to understand the emotional power of movies. As Currie notes, films may shape our desires in our ordinary lives. But these readings also bring out an important cognitive aspect to our emotional response to films. By attending to our emotional responses to films we can, therefore, enrich our understanding of the characters and situations depicted and of the emotions and desires we experience in our everyday lives.

Study Questions

1. What is the distinction Currie draws between character desires and narrative desires with respect to a work of fiction such as a film? How do these two kinds of desire apply to real-life situations as well?
2. How does a film such as *Casablanca* engage the viewer in a conflict of her or his desires? Contrast what Currie says about *Casablanca* with his view that *Othello* involves the viewer in a conflict between character and narrative desires. Do you agree with Currie that the viewer's conflict in relation to *Casablanca* pertains to character desires and is not also a conflict between character desires and narrative desires?
3. Why does Currie argue that desiring something in the imagination might make one more prone to desire it in reality? Do you agree with him that narrative desires with respect to fiction films can carry over to real life in ways that are harmful? What are some examples?
4. What are the criticisms of the emotions elicited by mainstream films offered by neo-Brechtian theories? What is Plantinga's response to these criticisms?
5. Why does Plantinga think that a cognitive film theoretic approach is useful in accounting for how films move us emotionally? What does he see as the main difference between cognitivism and neo-Brechtian theories on this topic?
6. Plantinga says that when we become absorbed in the narrative of a fiction film we accept an emotional role. What are some examples of films and film genres that illustrate this idea?

7. Do you agree with Plantinga that it is possible for a film to affect you emotionally yet not manipulate your ability to think critically about the message of the film?

8. Smith describes a "structure of sympathy" that consists of three aspects: (1) recognition; (2) alignment; and (3) allegiance. Explain the difference between these modes of engaging with characters in fictional films.

9. What shifts in the structure of alignment take place in *The Man Who Knew Too Much*, according to Smith? Why does he argue that these shifting alignments complicate the viewer's assessment of the moral values embodied by the characters?

10. Do you agree with Smith that most films, including mainstream Hollywood films, engage the viewer in a shifting pattern of recognition, alignment, and allegiance? What would be some examples of films you have seen that exhibit this pattern of engagement?

11. Why is the monster an object of both fascination and disgust, on Carroll's view?

12. Carroll says that the disgust we feel toward the monster is the price we must pay for having our curiosity satisfied. Is he right that the disgusting and the revolting cannot give us pleasure? Or is it disgust we crave when we go to see horror films?

13. Would Carroll's account explain why it is that people watch horror films over and over again?

14

Narrative Desire

Gregory Currie

The ending is inevitable: dramatically, commercially, morally, geopolitically. Ilsa (Ingrid Bergman) must stay with Victor (Paul Henreid). This is wartime and sacrifices must be made, and Rick (Humphrey Bogart) has the compensation of an exciting future resisting the Nazis alongside a morally braced Captain Renault (Claude Rains). The idea that it was unclear to anyone – let alone the writers – how the story would end is as incredible as it is appealing, and Richard Maltby has demonstrated its falsehood.[1]

10 ■ "Rick (Humphrey Bogart) and Ilse (Ingrid Bergman) driving in Paris," from *Casablanca*.

But for all its evident rightness, the ending does not satisfy all our desires. After all, we want Ilsa and Rick to be together, and our sustained interest in the narrative depends largely on this being so. There is here, as in so much filmic and other fiction, a conflict of desire, the logical structure of which I hope to tease out.

There are conflicts of desire which we experience in connection with nonfictional things, and I will say something about the structural relations between the conflicts which arise in these different settings. But there are causal relations as well: in particular, film can engender desires that look outward at the world: a benign example is Woody Allen/Allan Felix, the Bogart/Rick-fixated character in *Play It Again, Sam* (1972). There are also claims of media-inspired misogyny and violence.[2]

I don't aim to decide here what the causal connections are, and as a philosopher I am not especially well placed to contribute to what is, after all, a complex empirical question. My questions – or two of them – are more guarded: how *might* films and other fictions engender desirings? How *might* the desires so engendered be harmful?[3] And I shall suggest that some of what we regard as healthy, even aesthetically sophisticated desiring with respect to fiction would be highly undesirable desiring with respect to the real world.

A great deal of recent film theory has been concerned with desire. But most of that work neglects two central issues. First, no serious attempt is made to clarify the logical structure of desire, its relations to other kinds of states, and the kinds of relations there can be between different desires. Accordingly, I want to spend a good deal of time focusing on conceptual issues. Second, no serious attempt is made to develop theories of filmic desire in a way that would render them empirically testable, or to find empirical support for the background psychological assumptions (often drawn from psychoanalytic theorizing) used in building theories of filmic desire. Accordingly, I shall place some of this discussion in the context of evidence we have concerning the emotional and other reactions of subjects to fictional narratives. I shall also cite some evidence for the thesis that what we imagine can affect how we behave.

Having been so critical of the opposition, it would be delightful to wheel in a complete and convincing alternative. Unfortunately I do not have one. What follows is, at best, a series of vague suggestions about the direction in which we ought to proceed.

The Framework

One difficulty that the following discussion poses is that of finding the right terms in which to represent a complex set of distinctions. I want to distinguish what I shall call *character desires* and *narrative desires*, to distinguish, say, wanting Ilsa and Rick to stay together and wanting *Casablanca* (1942) to be a narrative that has Rick and Ilsa staying together. These are two kinds of desires that one can have when one confronts a work of fiction. But then I want to make a further distinction between the kinds of desires that we have when we confront the fictional and the kinds of desires we have concerning our family, friends, and fellow citizens, trees, books, and cars, ourselves and the really occurring events that all these things are caught up in. It is tempting to think of this distinction as the distinction between fiction-focused and world-focused desires, with the two halves of the previous distinction (character and narrative desires) fitting neatly into the fiction half of *this* distinction [see figure 1].

But this will not do. One reason is that fictional narratives, and sometimes fictional characters, too, are things of the real world. Othello may be a creature of imagination, something that simply does not exist, but *Othello* is a real thing, and wanting, say, for *Othello* to end happily is as much desiring something about the real world as wanting the friendship and respect of your fellow creatures. We can get around this difficulty by distinguishing, instead, between fiction-focused and nonfiction-focused desires, with reality crossing the boundary between the two, since *Othello* would count as belonging

Figure 1

Figure 2

to the fictional-but-real. And those real people who appear in fictions, as Christopher Wren appears in *Hawksmoor*, would belong to the same category.

But there is another dimension we need to take into account. I shall suggest later that it is important to see a role for the interplay between character desires and narrative desires outside the realm of the fictional altogether; we construct and tell narratives about ourselves and about each other, and we have certain desires concerning the outcomes of those narratives – desires that can be in conflict with the desires we have concerning ourselves and each other. So we need to recognize the categories [as given in figure 2].

This has the advantage of displaying a symmetry between the fiction and the nonfiction cases that I shall come back to when I talk about immoral and pathological desires. But I need to represent yet another distinction. The desires I have concerning my friends and those I have concerning fictional characters differ not merely in belonging to different focus-groups; they differ also in such a way that one hesitates to call the ones concerning fictional characters *desires* at all. The problem is a familiar one: desires require a background of belief, which is lacking in the case of, say, Anna Karenina. I don't believe she exists, so I don't believe she can be harmed, so how can I desire her not to be harmed? And even if the fictional character is real, as with Wren, the character's plight in the story is one I don't believe the character concerned really was in. How can I worry/be concerned about someone in situation *S* when I don't believe they ever were in *S*?

This is a problem I've had my say on elsewhere, and I don't wish to impose an uncomfortable burden of theory by repeating that here.[4] Instead, I shall simply distinguish between desires *in the scope of an imagining*, and desires not so restricted. My desire that Anna Karenina thrive is in the scope of an imagining; my desire that my child thrive is not. There are additional complexities here: for example, I can have desires in the scope of imagining concerning my child, if my child becomes the subject of a little fictional story I tell myself about him. But to keep the picture manageable I will be satisfied with the [categories shown in figure 3], which could be further articulated.

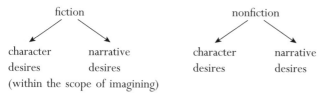

Figure 3

Notice that my narrative desires on the fiction side are never within the scope of an imagining (or so at least I shall assume, once again for the sake of a manageable taxonomy). My desires concerning fictional narratives are desires backed by the right kinds of beliefs: I rightly believe *Casablanca* to be a real thing, and I have all sorts of appropriate beliefs about it.

A second issue that needs to be confronted in order to give us an adequate framework is the relation between desire and emotion. I focus here on desires, but much of what I shall say generalizes to cover at least many emotions. How are desire and emotion related? The question is complicated by the fact that "emotion" names a heterogeneous class of states, not all the members of which have essential connections with desires. Certain low-level emotions, like the startle response, for example, have causes and effects that bypass the cognitive parts of the mind (those that lead to decision and action), and hence are explicable without reference to desire or to belief.[5] At the other end of the scale, emotions become hard to distinguish from pure evaluations, as with deploring Michael Corleone's (Al Pacino) progressive moral anesthesia while at the same time somewhat unwillingly admiring his icy resourcefulness. At this end, emotions look like beliefs of an evaluative kind. In thinking about desire and the emotions it will be useful, therefore, to concentrate on certain cases of emotion: my rationally explicable fear of large, fierce, and unrestrained dogs, your anxiety about getting the Chair of Cultural Hermeneutics, Albert's jealousy of the handsome, wealthy, and talented Gustave.

One thing common to these cases is that they involve beliefs and desires: I believe the dog is a likely cause of harm to me and desire not to be harmed, you desire the chair and believe you have only a limited chance of getting it, Albert desires possession of the qualities Gustave has and to which he, Albert, believes himself entitled. But in these cases, an emotion is not just a combination of beliefs and desires. It involves feelings as well, that is, states with *phenomenology*. It makes sense to ask, "What is it like to be afraid of that dog, anxious about the job, jealous of Gustave?"[6] Different feelings go with different emotions, and there is a debate about the extent to which a given emotion can have a feeling (or correlated activity in the nervous system) uniquely its own.[7] But once we take into account states with content (beliefs and desires) as well as states with phenomenology, we can discriminate emotions more finely than any plausible taxonomy of feeling can. Fearing the dog may feel no different from fearing a burglar or ill health, yet they are discriminable emotions. So feelings are, at most, constitutive of emotions; they are not identical with them.

If my fear of the dog gives me an unpleasant feeling, it is presumably in virtue of my believing that I am in danger from it and wishing not to be (simply imagining a threatening dog might do it as well: the kind of case I would describe as an emotion "within the scope of imagination"). So we might say that an emotion of this kind (in the occurrent rather than the dispositional sense) is an episode of causation: contentful states (beliefs and desires) causing states of feeling. And so desires are part of what we have to specify when we describe an episode of emotional disturbance.

But while desires are essential to emotions (or at least to the emotions I am concerned with here), desires can exist independently of emotions. They do so when they fail, as they often do, to cause significant feeling or affect. Desire is therefore a more basic category of mental state than emotion is. But desire and belief, while distinct, are not so easily separated, either in definition or in fact. An explanation of belief presupposes the notion of desire, and vice versa,[8] and a creature with beliefs must necessarily have desires as well. A creature capable of actions needs two things: a representation of what the world is like and a representation of what it wants the world to be like. Only with those two things in place is it sensible to speak of the creature seeking to bring about a change in the world. The first representation constitutes the creature's belief-state (the totality of its beliefs), the second its desire-state. Take away either, and action is impossible, and without the capacity for action there is no room for either belief or desire.

Like desires, beliefs and emotions can lie within the scope of an imagining. Thinking I shall attend the faculty lunch today, wanting to stay in my room and work, and getting upset at the thought of the time wasted are examples of, respectively, real belief, desire, and emotion; thinking that Captain Renault underrates himself morally, wanting Rick not to give Victor away, and getting upset at the thought that he might are examples of, respectively, belief, desire, and emotion within the scope of imagining. So what I am going to say about desire, within and without the scope of imagining, could be said all over again about belief, and about emotion.

Character Desires, Narrative Desires

Go back to *Casablanca* and the satisfaction of desire. We want Ilsa and Rick to stay together, but we would be dissatisfied if things turned out that way. So we have a conflict in our desires – something that is relatively common. What sort of conflict is this? Perhaps it is of the common kind: we desire that lovers be united, but also that a marriage survive. We may also suspect that Victor will be a more effective opponent of the Nazis with Ilsa, and Rick a more effective one without her. All that conflict is describable within the confines of our thoughts about the action of the film: its events and characters. It is a conflict within what I am calling "character desires." It is also a case of what I called "desiring in imagination": Ilsa and Rick don't exist, their meeting in Paris never occurred, and we know that. We imagine these things, and it is within the scope of that imagining that we desire conflicting outcomes. But otherwise, the case as I describe it is structurally like the kind of conflict of desire we experience in real life, where there is a range of (real) alternatives that confront a group of (real) people, but where each alternative involves something we don't want.

Casablanca would be a more interesting case from my perspective if the viewer's conflict in desire was one that went beyond characters to include narrative. The cases that most obviously do this are cases of tragedy. We desire that Desdemona flourish, and that Othello see how Iago is duping him. But an *Othello* in which these things happened would, other things being equal, be a worse play than the *Othello* we have. Here, the fact that we want Desdemona to flourish but would be disappointed if things turned out that way is not easily explained as a conflict within character desires. It is not as if there is strong reason describable in terms of the characters and events of the story for Desdemona being destroyed; she has, after all, done nothing wrong. To the extent that we desire the outcome that the play actually gives us – an outcome involving Desdemona's destruction – our desiring concerns narrative. It is the desire for a tragic narrative. We thus desire something which, if it is to be satisfied, requires the destruction of Desdemona, though that is not something we desire in itself. Here the conflict in desire is not a conflict structurally like the kinds of conflicts we most commonly find in our desires concerning real events and people, for it is a conflict between desiring something for a character and desiring something for a narrative.

The conflict is also notable insofar as *it is a conflict we find desirable*. A typical reaction to *Othello* is not adequately described by saying that the disappointment and anguish caused by witnessing Desdemona's destruction are compensated for by the satisfaction of our narrative desire, for the success of the play does not depend merely on the strength of our narrative desire being greater than that of our character desire. Rather, we seem to experience a further, higher order desire for there to be such a conflict, and for the conflicting desires to be resolved as the play resolves them. That desire is then wholly satisfied. Again, this is not commonly thought to be a feature of desire concerning real-world outcomes, whatever other complexities such desires may involve.

If a conflict in desire is wholly a matter of conflict within the class of character desires, then it is also wholly a matter of conflict among desires within the scope of the imagination. But if the conflict is, as with *Othello*, a conflict between character and narrative desires, then it is going to involve both real desires and desires within the scope of imagination. For narratives are real things and the desires we have concerning them are real desires. To desire that *Othello* be a narrative with a tragic ending is to desire a real-world outcome, one the satisfaction conditions of which are that a certain proposition, namely that *Othello* have a tragic ending, be true. And indeed this proposition is true. But character desires are not like that. My desiring that Desdemona flourish is not a desire that is satisfied if it is true that Desdemona flourishes: since Desdemona doesn't exist, that proposition isn't – and couldn't be – true. That desire is satisfied if it is part of the narrative of *Othello* that Desdemona flourish. This distinction gives us a way of characterizing what it is for a desire to be within the scope of imagining. A desire that P occur is within the scope of imagining if and only if the satisfaction of the desire depends, not on it being true that P, but on it being part of a narrative that P.

[. . .]

Changing Desire

So far I have considered narrative desires in a fictional setting, and in the setting of real people and events. Let us, finally, bring these two together. How might the experience of fiction change our desires outside the context of the fictions they present? How, in particular, might fiction (especially filmic fiction) change the desires I have concerning real people and events? In many ways: By making available thought-contents that were not previously available to the subject; by vividly depicting a state of affairs and thus giving specificity to a previously inchoate desire; by depicting a certain state of affairs and eliciting a pleasurable sensation from the viewer, causing the viewer to desire a state of affairs relevantly similar to the depicted one. I would like to focus here on one other way that movies can bring about change in desire, because it connects with what I take to be an important fact about the nature of imagination.

If we think of the imagination as a private inner world quite cut off from reality and without implications for behavior, it is possible to defend a strongly liberal conception of the mimetic arts by insisting that such arts engage the imagination alone. But if we think once again in evolutionary terms, this is unlikely. A complex mental organ like the imagination is not likely to be disconnected from our capacity to act; if it were, it is hard to see how the imagination could have contributed to our fitness. True, not every feature so contributes: the heaviness of the polar bear's coat slows him down and makes it harder to catch prey; it is there because engineering a warm coat required weight.[9] But it does not seem that way with the imagination. I suggest that the imagination is a mechanism designed to help us improve our performance.

It is worth noting, first of all, that the imagination is a capacity not wholly divorced from our capacity to act. Sometimes what we can imagine reflects our own physical limitations. [. . .] When patients with impairment on one side of the body due to Parkinson's disease are asked to report the speed at which they can imagine performing a finger-sequencing exercise for both hands, they report a slower speed in imagination for the impaired hand, and the time differences for these imagined cases closely match the time differences for their actual performance. [. . .] Astonishingly, imagining undertaking physical exercise can, in the right circumstances, result in increases in maximal muscle force comparable to (though less than) the increases produced by actually exercising! And there are many skills besides directly athletic ones which seem to benefit from practice *in imagination* as well as in reality.[10] These connections between imagining moving and really moving are paralleled in the case of imagined experience: imagining seeing and attending to things has all sorts of effects on one's capacity actually to see and attend to them.[11] In that case it might be (though I know of no direct evidence for this) that *desiring* things in the imagination (the sort of desiring involved in narrative desires) has connections with one's tendency actually to desire them. In particular, desiring something in imagination might make one more prone to desire it in reality. If we suppose, plausibly, that it is relatively common for people to desire, to some (perhaps very limited) degree, to do things they know or believe are wicked, then works of fiction that encourage us to desire wicked things in imagination (to desire that someone suffer or be humiliated) may have the effect of strengthening those wicked desires to the point where they become the desires on which the agent is prepared to act.

There are further possibilities. Might narrative desires be harmful in themselves rather than because they lead to other directly harmful desires? If we focus on cases like wanting *Othello* to be a narrative in which Desdemona suffers, the answer seems to be no: there is nothing directly harmful about that. But suppose the narratives we read and watch suggest to us *other* narratives: narratives in which *we* play roles, and in which *others* play roles at our behest, perhaps in situations of coercion? [. . .] Now in any case where we recruit a person to our purpose, the possibility arises that there is coercion involved. If certain kinds of movies and other fictions (examples come readily to mind) are capable of prompting the desire to reenact that narrative, and if the narrative involved requires or would at least be rendered more vivid by the participation of someone in a degrading role, then there could be cases where a person's degradation arises, coerced or not, from a narrative desire.

Conclusion

In thinking about film and desire it is important to be clear what kinds of desires we have in mind. I have suggested a taxonomy of such kinds, and some connections between them. And I have also suggested that desiring in relation to filmic and other fictional narratives needs to be seen in the context of a theory about the natural capacities and functions of the imagination.

NOTES

1 See Richard Maltby, "A Brief Romantic Interlude: Dick and Jane Go to $3^1/_2$ Seconds of the Classical Hollywood Cinema," in *Post-Theory: Reconstructing Film Studies*, ed. David Bordwell and Noël Carroll (Madison: University of Wisconsin Press, 1996), pp. 434–59.

2 See, e.g., Rae Langton, "Sexual Solipsism," *Philosophical Topics* 23 (1995): 149–87, and his "Love and Solipsism," in *Love Analysed*, ed. Roger Lamb (Boulder, Colo.: Westview Press, 1997).

3 This essay continues the project of "The Moral Psychology of Fiction," *Australasian Journal of Philosophy* 73 (1995): 250–9, and "Realism of Character and the Value of Fiction," in *Ethics and Aesthetics*, ed. Jerrold Levinson (Cambridge: Cambridge University Press, 1998).

4 See my "The Paradox of Caring: Fiction and the Philosophy of Mind," in *Emotion and the Arts*, ed. Mette Hjort and Sue Laver (Oxford: Oxford University Press, 1997). Later I shall give a simple and intuitive test for whether a desire is real or imaginary.

5 "Startle" refers to the specifically reflex reaction caused by, say, hearing a loud noise. The duration of the response is about half a second, and involves certain characteristic facial and bodily movements, as well as changes in the autonomic nervous system. It is involuntary, people are often unaware of engaging in it, and the reaction does not depend on the stimulus being unexpected. It is common to humans and a number of other species. There is some uncertainty as to whether startle should be thought of as a primitive version/ancestor of fear or of surprise, or of both. See Jenefer Robinson, "Startle," *Journal of Philosophy* 92 (1995): 53–74.

6 See Thomas Nagel, "What Is It Like to Be a Bat?," in his *Mortal Questions* (Cambridge: Cambridge University Press, 1979).

7 See, e.g., Paul Ekman et al., "Autonomous Nervous System Activity Distinguishes among the Emotions," *Science* 221 (1983): 1208–10.

8 See, e.g., Robert Stalnaker, *Inquiry* (Cambridge: MIT Press, 1984).

9 See Frank Jackson, "Epiphenomenal Qualia," *Philosophical Quarterly* 32 (1982): 127–36.

10 See Gregory Currie and Ian Ravenscroft, "Mental Simulation and Motor Imagery," *Philosophy of Science* 64 (1997): 161–80, for discussion and references.

11 See my "Mental Imagery as the Simulation of Vision," *Mind and Language* 10 (1995): 25–44.

15

Spectator Emotion and Ideological Film Criticism

Carl Plantinga

Many of us occasionally practise ideological criticism, when we consider the ideological issues raised by viewing films. We often believe that films have moral and ideological significance and that they are not merely consumed, discarded, and forgotten but have psychological and cultural effects. Whether it be concern with screen violence, racism, Oliver Stone's revisionist histories, or the promotion of shallow emotional lives, ideological criticism appraises the moral and ideological import of experiences offered by films.

The purpose of this chapter is not primarily to chart a particular ethical position toward the emotions mainstream films are designed to elicit, but to suggest how emotions should be understood in ideological criticism. That being said, I do argue for one substantive ideological claim – that while we should certainly be aware of the rhetorical uses of spectator emotions, it makes little sense to condemn such emotions *tout court*. I begin by criticizing two tenets of ideological film criticism widely assumed in film studies. The first, deriving from Bertolt Brecht, argues that experiencing emotion in mainstream films is inherently mystifying and politically regressive, because emotion clouds a certain kind of critical judgement. The second tenet, a legacy of neo-Freudian film theory, assumes that the critic can make universal claims about the ideological effect of various formal strategies, irrespective of a film's propositional content.

The chapter goes on to characterize spectator emotion, with a view toward conceptual clarification. It argues that the *kind* of emotional experience a film offers, and not emotion *per se*, is a proper target of ideological investigation. It holds that a cognitive approach to emotion is useful in describing kinds of spectator emotions. In its second half, the essay examines two families of screen emotions – (1) sentiment and sentimentality, and (2) the emotions which accompany screen violence – to demonstrate how spectator emotion is related to ideological criticism.

Ideological Stoicism

At least since Plato, critics have worried about the affective nature of art. The pleasurable affect and emotion elicited by films has also been a central concern of film criticism. Some critics presume a duality between an emotional response deemed naive, self-indulgent, or even perverse, and an intellectual, vigilant, cognitive response based on reason and critical judgement. An emotional or pleasurable experience is often thought to be harmful or naive of itself, while an alienated, distanced response becomes the mark of a knowing spectator.

Both the neo-Brechtian and neo-Freudian approaches in film theory distrust the affective pleasures offered by mainstream films. While Brecht and neo-Brechtians characterize emotion negatively, in 'common sense' terms, neo-Freudians refer to pleasures resulting from the arousal and fulfilment of unconscious desire. Such 'desire' is not for this or that narrative outcome, or for any explicit referential occurrence; rather it relates to 'the symbolic circulation of unconscious wishes through signs bound to our earliest forms of infantile satisfaction'.[1] I classify these views as forms of *ideological stoicism* because they call for a retreat from affective experience *tout court* – be it emotion or pleasure – on moral principle. For both Brecht and many neo-Freudian theorists, this retreat must occur through distancing and alienating techniques which short-circuit emotion, pleasure, and 'desire', and thus allow reason to work, unencumbered, in the landscape of our minds.

The facile duality between reason and emotion lies as the unspoken premiss behind many discussions of affect and the spectator, as though emotion must be 'bridled' or 'mastered' to allow reason to function adequately. This duality animates much of Bertolt Brecht's writing about the epic theatre, and since Brecht's ideological criticism has become a model for critical theory, the legacy of this dualism lives on. Brecht embraces a traditional Western perspective in his distrust of the 'soft' emotions; he expresses contempt for the 'scum who want to have the cockles of their hearts warmed' at the theatre.[2] At times Brecht seems to castigate both emotion and empathy as inherently problematic in theatre spectatorship. He writes, for example, that feelings 'are private and limited', and that reason is 'fairly comprehensive and to be relied on' (15). He promotes a distanced and alienated spectator response which encourages psychic distance and critical judgement rather than involved experience, as though involvement and judgement were mutually exclusive, and alienation were inherently superior to affective participation.[3]

Brecht's stoicism has limits, however. Elsewhere, Brecht clearly realizes that this simplistic emotion/reason duality will not hold and that the proper target of his criticism is not emotion *per se* but emotional experiences *of certain types*. He says that the goal of the practitioner of epic theatre must not be to eliminate emotional experience but to encourage the spectator to 'adopt a critical approach to his emotions, just as [he] does to his ideas' (101). Brecht's followers have sometimes ignored the subtleties he recognized, in part because Brecht merely alludes to this critical approach rather than describing it in any detail. Brechtian concepts such as alienation or distancing, plus his frequently drawn, moralistic opposition between 'feeling' and 'reason' (e.g. 37), reinforce the simplistic duality that, in his better moments, he realized is superficial.

Brecht wished to encourage a kind of judgement whereby the spectator takes a critical perspective toward the play. Rather than empathizing with characters or experiencing the emotions the play intends to elicit, the spectator should consider and criticize the larger social and cultural forces the play presumes. Brecht's perspective can be criticized from many directions. Notice that Brecht values a kind of alienated, intellectualized response to the theatre, as though there were no legitimate place for compassion, sympathy, empathy, or any of the emotions which might warm the 'cockles' of one's heart. A feminist critique, expanded on below, could well take this as a masculinist response to discomfort with those emotions sometimes denigrated as feminine, or an assumption of the importance of the political and the triviality of the personal. If Brecht's claim is that we must encourage plays which raise social consciousness, we have no quarrel. If he means to eliminate a whole class of spectator responses, then we must question him.

Brechtian theory also neglects the extent to which critical judgement of the sort Brecht recommends is not only compatible with an emotional response congruent with the play's intentions, but is also often implicated in it. For the cognitivist, emotions have reasons, or objects. For example, the object of my fear could be a lion I imagine to threaten my life. The object of my shame might be the obnoxious behaviour of a friend or relative at a social gathering. *Spectator* emotions also have objects or reasons. Some spectator emotions seem especially designed to accompany a Brechtian sort of critical response. The amusement which emerges from satire, for example, contributes to the spectator's questioning of the object of the satire.[4] In *Dr Strangelove or; How I Learned to Stop Worrying and Love the Bomb* (1964), the target of the satire is the American military-industrial complex. The brilliance of the concluding sequence stems in part from the mixed emotions it fosters. As the sympathetically portrayed pilots approach their target, the suspense and excitement build. The film encourages us to share that excitement, despite our simultaneous knowledge that the mission is misguided and its consequences, should it succeed, apocalyptic. Thus *Dr Strangelove* throws into question every war film which celebrates blind patriotism, heroism, and doing one's duty, and it asks, 'To what end?' Here my amusement depends on my judgement of the film's social and political representations. Moreover, *Dr Strangelove* simultaneously displays the attractiveness and the folly of the actions it represents, eliciting mixed emotions which encourage reflection.

[. . .]

The neo-Brechtian could argue that films such as *Dr Strangelove* and *El Norte* are the exception, and that Hollywood products like *Pretty Woman*, which *do* mystify the social relations they embody, are the rule. We can grant that point. Many films use emotions in harmful and manipulative ways. Nonetheless, what films such as *Dr Strangelove* and *El Norte* show is that the ideological critic must not condemn spectator emotion *per se* but should examine the *kind* of emotional experience a film offers and the way spectator emotions function in the film's rhetorical project.

[. . .]

While Brecht tends to dismiss emotion as mystifying, neo-Freudian theory some-times posits particular psychic phenomena as *essential* to film pleasure, such as maso-chism for Gaylyn Studlar and voyeurism and scopophilia for Laura Mulvey. I have argued elsewhere that there exists no single, essential pleasure in viewing mainstream films, but rather many varied pleasures. Surely the emotions, pleasures, and affect generated at the cinema are more complex than the above theories imply.

As a substantive ideological theory, ideological stoicism is suspect due to its con-ceptual shortcomings. Given the limitations of ideological stoicism, together with a contemporary understanding of the relationship between judgement and emotion, it is incumbent upon the stoicist to provide compelling arguments for taking the eliciting of all spectator emotion to be inherently unethical.

Thinking About Spectator Emotion

V. F. Perkins notes that because when we view films 'our satisfaction is so directly involved, our experience is the more likely to contradict the film-maker's statement wherever the meaning which he offers is less attractive than the one which we can take'. He gives the example of *The Bridge on the River Kwai* (1957), in which screen-writer Carl Foreman's dialogue repeatedly argues the futility of war and the hollowness of victory, while the film's emotional dynamics invite us 'to share in the excitements, tensions and triumphs offered by the action.'[5] The film establishes a contradiction between what is said to be futile and felt to be magnificent.

We need a language and a method to enable us to understand better the spectator's involvement in movies. I suggest the utility of a broadly cognitive approach, simply because it ties spectator emotion not only to private feelings and/or physiological responses, but to cognition – inferences, appraisals, judgements, hypotheses, etc. This approach to emotion was not born with cognitive theory, narrowly considered. While the cognitive science movement rose during the 1970s, the cognitive approach to emo-tion dates back at least to the ancients. Aristotle defines emotions as kinds of feeling caused by kinds of thinking. He defines fear, for example, as 'a sort of pain or agitation derived from the imagination of a future destructive or painful evil'.[6] A cognitive approach, broadly considered, allows for differences in methodology and assumptions in the tradition of piecemeal theorizing advocated by Noël Carroll and others.[7] The cognitivist assumptions here, for example, differ from mainstream cognitive science of the early 1980s, which bracketed emotions in relation to cognition and modelled the human mind after the electronic computer.[8]

A cognitive approach will be useful, in the first instance, because it transcends reductive characterizations of emotion. Much recent philosophy and psychology of the emotions has rejected the traditional assumption that emotion is the enemy of reason and critical judgement. It was once commonly thought that emotions were coextens-ive with feelings. Currently, many philosophers and psychologists would agree that no particular felt physical state represents either a necessary or sufficient condition for a specific emotional state. A cognitive approach holds that an emotional state is one in which some physical state of felt agitation is caused by an individual's construal and evaluation of his situation.[9] In other words, my galvanic skin response and heart palpitations cannot define my emotions; what *particular* emotion I experience depends on my cognitions about my situation.[10]

Not only does thinking accompany and in many cases determine emotion, but emotions can themselves be rational or irrational. In the realm of practical reason, emotional response in some cases *just is* a rational (or appropriate) response to an event or circumstance, while lack of emotion may in some situations be irrational. Ronald de Sousa claims that emotion can be rational because it has the ability to guide reason, to make salient what needs attending to in a specific situation, and to initiate a response.[11] If we accept this, then we must grant that some emotions may be beneficial to the self and society. The relevant ideological issue then becomes not emotions *per se*, but distinguishing those which are benign or beneficial from those which are manipulative or harmful. While we should be suspicious of the manipulative nature of emotions, as Brecht is, a contemporary understanding of emotion leaves little ground for condemning emotion *tout court* as the enemy of reason.

Moreover, rather than positing universal ideological effects for film forms and styles, we should more usefully relate film form to narrative representations and to the kinds of cognitions and emotions such forms encourage. The fundamental tenet of a cognitive approach is that the spectator's affective experience is dependent on cognition, on mental activity cued not only by film form but also by story content. In viewing films, cognition would include inferences, hypotheses, and evaluative judgements. [. . .]

To develop such an approach, we must first describe the film viewing situation. Emotion in film viewing can be understood only in light of the context in which it occurs – consisting of the situation of the spectator in the theatre or before a monitor, the spectator's understanding of that situation, and various physiological, cognitive, and emotional responses to the images and sounds and what they represent. [. . .]

When we view a fiction film we participate in a ritual designed by the institutions that bring us movies.[12] When we assent to the narrative of a film and become 'absorbed' or 'immersed', we accept an emotional role. We entertain the fiction in our imagination, and it moves us, yet we have a consistent background awareness of its artificiality. This concurrent and dual awareness might be compared to that of an actor who may experience emotions similar to those of the character he plays, but who cannot relinquish his sense of a self separate from the role. This dual and concurrent awareness enables the actor to *act* the role, since a loss of awareness of the acting situation would also entail loss of the ability to act the role. Similarly, a spectator who loses awareness of his ritual situation would have a harder time sitting still when pursued by the Tyrannosaurus Rex in *Jurassic Park*, or abiding any narrative event which, in absence of an awareness of its artificiality, would cause unbearable emotional stress.

[. . .]

Murray Smith argues that the cinema blends on the one hand, complex narrative scenarios with which we engage imaginatively and, on the other, a striking sensual and perceptual experience not found in literature.[13] Moreover, the photographic and sonic qualities of this experience, although representing fictional and sometimes fantastical events, can have a remarkable quality of perceptual realism. Faced with moving photographs of a toe being smashed (coupled with the appropriate crunching noise), the perceptual realism of the representation makes my wincing almost involuntary.

We 'enter' the fictional world in part through developing a bond of allegiance with one or more characters. This orients us toward the narrative events and is essential in eliciting the desired emotional response. Whether we laugh or cry or feel suspense during a scene often depends on our estimation of its significance for characters. Smith describes what he calls a structure of sympathy, consisting of three aspects: (1) the viewer's recognition of character traits and emotions, (2) alignment with characters through perceptual and epistemic means (point-of-view structures or voice-over narration, for example), and (3) an allegiance toward characters that is based on a moral evaluation.[14]

Critics sometimes assume that character identification is an either/or phenomenon, such that either we identify with a character, in which case we unproblematically lend him our complete allegiance, or we do *not* identify and take an attitude ranging from antipathy to indifference. Some notions of identification attribute a kind of identity of thought and emotion between spectator and character, during which the spectator loses a sense of separate selfhood. Smith's analysis of the structures of sympathy shows that our response to characters is typically exterior, from the standpoint of an evaluating self outside the fictional world, that our perceptual or epistemic alignment with characters does not necessarily imply allegiance toward them, and that, as a key component in determining emotional response to a scene, our allegiance with a character (or antipathy toward him or her) may be complex, ambiguous, and may change over the course of the narrative. If our engagement with a character is conflicted, then our emotions and judgements will be so as well.

In mainstream films, allegiances with and antipathy toward characters orient us. What we are oriented *toward*, and respond to, are characters in narrative situations. Emotional response both inside and outside the theatre depends in part on our evaluation of a situation or scenario. For example, two persons stand in a dark alley. A figure approaches from the shadows. Person A recognizes him as a friend and responds with relief, while Person B thinks him a sinister-looking stranger and becomes fearful. Clearly, these different emotional responses depend on contrary evaluations of the situation. [. . .]

A film also presents a continuously evolving narrative situation, a script or scenario, for the appraisal of the audience. We experience diverse emotions based on these paradigmatic scenarios. One may be curious during a mystery, feel suspense during a thriller, be sad during an unhappy ending, be fearful when the jeep is chased by the Tyrannosaurus Rex in *Jurassic Park*, be shocked during the murder sequence of *Psycho*, be compassionate and angry during *El Norte*, or be sentimental when Rock Hudson restores Jane Wyman's sight and the lovers look forward to a promising 'tomorrow' in *Magnificent Obsession*. It is unlikely that a narrative scenario will elicit a single emotion; more often our response is mixed and complex. In *Rear Window*, for example, an audience may experience a mixture of interest, curiosity, and guilt about Jeff (James

Stewart) spying on his neighbours. Thus emotional response depends not only on film form and style but also on narrative 'content' – our evaluation of character, narrative situation, theme, etc.

One issue still to be addressed is spectator difference. Many film scholars have rejected the model of the spectator as passive and defenceless against a film which 'positions them'. [. . .]

However, when we justifiably reject the claim that films *determine* spectator response, we should not characterize films as 'blank pages' or 'empty receptacles' and spectator response as wholly determined by contextual and individual factors. When viewing a film, spectators may have a wide variety of responses. Yet any examination of spectator psychology must assume that one important kind of response will be congruent with the implicit intentions of the film, even while recognizing the possibility of incongruent and even oppositional responses. It should not be a matter of determining whether text or context is most important, as though one should reign supreme. Audience response lies at the intersections of individual and general spectator characteristics, specific context, and textual cues.

Spectator Emotions and Ideology

[. . .]

We rarely view films indiscriminately, but decide what films to view in part for the kind of experience they offer. This sometimes has little to do with aesthetics; while I may admire Martin Scorsese's *Raging Bull* as a work of art, I may nonetheless limit my viewings because its brutality and graphic violence disturb me. Alternatively, the sentimental pleasures of films such as *Mr Holland's Opus* could offer the kind of experience I seek, even if I do not expect a first-rate film. The emotional roles movies afford are not only something to which we are subjected; we choose to subject ourselves to them.

Hollywood has concocted various means for advertising the kind of emotional role each film offers – through genres which repeat similar experiences, sequels, the typecasting of stars, previews, and advertising. Whether a movie will offer a story of hatred and revenge, 'dangerous' sex, family melodrama, the pleasures of curiosity associated with mystery, or the ironic distance combined with graphic violence of a Quentin Tarantino film, we often have a general sense of the kind of experience it may offer, before we view the film. Some of my female students report having difficulty getting their male friends to see what are derogatorily called 'chick flicks'; these films offer experiences these young men think inappropriate or uninteresting for males. In fact, one could characterize Hollywood genres in part according to the basic emotional responses they afford. The melodrama offers sentiment, the horror film elicits what Noël Carroll calls 'art horror',[15] certain westerns satisfy vengeance, comedies amuse, mysteries encourage curiosity and suspense, adventures excitement, etc.

However circumscribed by social convention, we nonetheless choose from a diverse palette of emotions at the cinema, ranging from compassion and pity to vengefulness and contempt. Amidst this diversity, I should like to examine two kinds of experiences with a view toward initiating a discussion of their ideological import. They are, first, sentiment and sentimentality and, second, the emotions which accompany screen violence. My purpose is not primarily to take a particular ideological stance toward these. Rather, I wish to show how we might think of emotion in relation to ideology without resorting to [. . .] stoicism. Emotion, as these examples show, depends on *and* informs belief.

Sentimentality

It is sentimentality, rather than vengeance, contempt, or hatred, that has sparked the most interest among aestheticians, and suffered the heaping scorn of critics. While sentimentality (*false* or *unearned* sentiment) is often the object of condemnation, even sentiment more broadly considered (any tender, romantic, or nostalgic response) is also held under suspicion. Sentiment is most often associated with the family melodrama and especially the 'woman's film'. [. . .]

[. . .]

[. . .] False or unearned sentiment has been maligned as not only distasteful but immoral. 'Being sentimental', Mary Midgeley writes, 'is misrepresenting the world in order to indulge our feelings.' It is a 'howling self-deception', she goes on, and a 'distortion of the world'.[16] Mark Jefferson adds that sentimentality is grounded in a fiction of innocence, emphasizing the 'sweetness, dearness, littleness, blamelessness, and vulnerability of the emotion's objects'.[17] And as Anthony Savile writes, sentimentality not only requires the idealization of the object but also contributes to self-righteousness or self-deception in encouraging a 'gratifying image of the self as compassionate, righteous, or just'.[18]

[. . .]

It is one thing, however, to say what sentimentality *is* and another to determine whether a particular scene or film is sentimental. Since it involves charges of misrepresentation, distortion, and self-deception, sentimentality is a matter of interpretation. In *City Lights*, Chaplin's character falls in love with a blind flower vendor, who thinks him a benevolent millionaire. Through many trials and tribulations, he raises the money needed for an operation to restore her sight. After a stint in jail, he is set free and discovers that she can now see. Now running a flower shop, the cured woman offers the ragged tramp a coin. After touching his hands and face, she realizes who he is. Her look of disappointment is followed by Chaplin's poignant smile, and the film ends.

11 ■ 'The Blind Flower Girl and the Tramp,' from *City Lights*.

If her response had been one of unambiguous joy in rediscovering her benefactor, and the film had implied the usual romance 'happily ever after', then it would clearly be sentimental, a self-deceptive denial that economic class, power, and appearances do compromise romantic love. However, the film implies that although the tramp's love is sincere and selfless, his social standing will probably interfere with any future relationship. On this interpretation, *City Lights* escapes sentimentality. Yet matters are not so simple, and the cynic might reply that the scene is nonetheless sentimental in its representation of the tramp's love as blameless, sweet, vulnerable, and pure. Through our allegiance with the tramp and our experience of congruent emotions, we celebrate a gratifying image of ourselves as compassionate, righteous, and just – because we recognize his selfless love in a cruel world and respond to it emotionally. My point is not to come to a final determination about whether *City Lights* is or is not sentimental. Rather it is to suggest that this type of discussion is useful because it relates emotion to belief and value.

Emotion is a process. The ideological criticism of spectator emotion must consider not simply individual occurrences of spectator emotion, but the trajectory of responses a film elicits. Any spectator emotion, whether 'good' or 'bad' in itself, can be used for unfortunate rhetorical ends. That is, if we grant that sentiment is in itself ideologically neutral or even beneficial, sentiment can play a part in a questionable ideological project. The above discussion of sentimentality and sentiment implies that some emotions are by definition ideologically problematic. Yet a film may elicit sentimentality (or envy, jealousy, etc.) for the purpose of criticizing it. Ideological criticism may begin with considerations of individual spectator emotions, but must then appraise those emotions in narrative context.

Violence

The consistent attention in the popular press to screen violence tends to cast the problem as one of the sheer numbers of violent acts represented. Thus researchers and journalists often count the murders and assaults a teenager is likely to view over a span of time. Certainly this is one important aspect of screen violence and it relates to the issue of 'desensitization'. More telling, however, are considerations of how the spectator's involvement and affective experience are played into narratives of violence. What kind of affective experience do we have, for example, when absorbed in a narrative of revenge and killing? If we have allegiance with a protagonist who has been horribly wronged and becomes vengeful, do we become vengeful toward the wrongdoers?

In the *Death Wish* series (1974–87), for example, the narratives are designed to offer the pleasures of vengeance. In the first film, the wife of Paul Kersey (Charles Bronson) is killed and his daughter assaulted by street thugs. In this and the next three films (*Death Wish II, III*, and *IV*), Kersey exacts revenge on the thugs and then, seeking new targets for further vengeance, attacks any wrongdoer who falls across his path. Kersey's vengeance is represented as 'just', and the criminals so unproblematically evil and unattractive that the spectator is cued to experience emotions such as hatred, disgust, contempt, and vengefulness. Yet these are *spectator* emotions in that they are tempered by a knowledge of the ritual viewing situation and by an implicit awareness that events are guided by a narration.[19]

Nonetheless, although our vengeance at the movies is *spectator vengeance*, it is cued by scenarios that have a counterpart in actual events and may encourage a kind of thinking similar in some respects to that of sentimentality. For in cueing the contempt necessary to warrant the protagonist's extreme violence, the viewer must deny both the banality and the complexity of evil. To encourage our unmitigated hatred, the wrongdoing must be excessively obvious and the wrongdoers beneath contempt. Accordingly, both vengefulness and contempt may be rooted in epistemic distortions related to those that allow for sentimentality.

Richard Slotkin, in *Gunfighter Nation*, has claimed that all traditional westerns embody a myth of regenerative and purgative violence.[20] In the western, the means of cleansing the self and society of the Other is through ritual violence, typically reaching its climax in the final confrontation at the film's end. What I would add is that this climactic violent scene, so common in the western, is regenerative not only thematically but also through its function in the spectator's affective trajectory. In *High Noon*, for example, Sheriff Kane (Gary Cooper) is not only shown to be good and just while his opponents are shown to be evil and unlawful. The film also builds up intense suspense through an emphasis on clocks, deadlines, the danger to Kane's life, and conflicts with his wife. The shoot-out not only resolves a moral tension but also becomes a purgative release from the tensions the film cultivates. Thus violence plays into the spectator's release and satisfaction, a satisfaction that depends on both cognitive *and* affective factors. This is in part how westerns make violence seem attractive.

In the western, violence can become a spectacle, pleasurable for its own sake. But this requires conventional treatment. In this regard, the treatment of violence in *Unforgiven* warrants special attention. *Unforgiven* treats violence differently from most westerns, at least until the obligatory shoot-out at its end. In the film, William Munny (Clint Eastwood) and two sidekicks have come to Big Whiskey to kill two cowboys for assaulting a woman. The motive of Munny and company is bounty money, but they have been exaggerating stories about the assault to rationalize their intentions. Several scenes in *Unforgiven* complicate our response to violence through ambiguous allegiances and confusing event-scenarios. Most notable is the scene where Munny and his two assistants ambush and kill 'Davey Boy', as Davey and his friends rope cattle in a canyon.

The scene withholds many of the psychological props that normally justify the hero's killing in westerns and make it satisfying and pleasurable. Although Davey played an ambiguous role in the brutal assault on Delilah, he has attempted to make amends by offering the victim his finest pony; our sympathies are with him on some level, complicating appeals to 'just deserts'. Munny and company ambush the cowboy, shooting him with a rifle from some rocks above; gone are all notions of the fair fight to which most westerns appeal. Killing is often made fun through the talent of the hero, whose skilful gunplay becomes a kind of fetish which distracts our attention from the import of his actions; Munny's killing here is almost inept, since he is a bad shot and requires all his ammunition to finish off the cowboy. Unlike scenes of killing in most westerns, here we concentrate on the suffering of the victim, as Davey, realizing he is dying, pleads for water. Munny's response is itself conflicted, as is that of his cohorts. If Munny himself is unsure about what he has done, then how can we be satisfied with it?

In this scene *Unforgiven* problematizes our reaction to violence on a thematic and affective level, by presenting a narrative event which withholds the typical justifications of violence, and the pleasures violence affords the spectator. Unfortunately, the climactic shoot-out at the end of the film participates in the same myth of regeneration through violence that the typical western promotes and which the film had criticized up to that point.

Screen violence is prevalent in part because it is a sure method to generate affect, and the pleasurable affect films typically use to promote screen violence in turn ensures that the practice will continue. Violence has become such a prevalent subject in mainstream film that many of us consider it a 'natural' subject for the movies. We must reclaim our sense that we may legitimately demand more humane popular art, less dependent on spectator emotions such as simplistic contempt and vengefulness.

The Rhetoric of Spectator Emotion

A 'weak' social constructionist approach to emotion would argue that although some emotions may be 'natural' or universal, our emotional lives are learned and culture-bound. Cognitive approaches to affect are useful in charting the paradigm scenarios, or emotion schemata, into which a culture 'educates' its members.[21] The cognitive approach also suggests how films might figure into that process, by creating, altering, and/or promoting scenarios for behaviour and emotional response. Narrative schemata such as the revenge plot of the *Death Wish* series can become stereotypes just as character types can, presenting a 'script' for vengefulness. Noël Carroll suggests that paradigm scenarios in film may also affect male emotional responses to women. For example, what Carroll calls the '*Fatal Attraction* scenario' tends to 'demote the exlover to the status of an irrational creature and to regard her claims as a form of persecution'.[22]

Through repetition and promotion (making the scenario seem natural, morally correct, or in accordance with 'advanced' tastes and attitudes), narrative paradigm scenarios influence our emotional lives. Our emotional experience at the movies may affect our ways of thinking and thus reinforce or alter the emotion schemata we apply to actual situations. Our responses to films depend on our culture's moral order and can function to prescribe and proscribe thought, feeling, behaviour, and values.

In this chapter I have argued for a cognitive approach to the rhetoric of spectator emotion. My discussion of sentimentality and screen violence is meant to suggest how such an approach would begin a discussion of the ideological import of spectator emotions. Spectator emotions have a powerful rhetorical force because they involve thinking, belief, and evaluation. In fact, one cannot have spectator emotions without the kinds of evaluations that relate narratives to our ideological concerns.

NOTES

1 Robert Stam, Robert Burgoyne, and Sandy Flitterman-Lewis, *New Vocabularies in Film Semiotics* (London: Routledge, 1992), p. 124.

2 *Brecht on Theater*, ed. and trans. John Willet (New York: Hill & Wang, 1964), p. 14. References to Willet's translation are made parenthetically within the text.

3 See also Murray, Smith, 'The Logic and Legacy of Brechtianism', in David Bordwell and Noël Carroll (eds.), *Post-Theory: Reconstructing Film Studies* (Madison: University of Wisconsin Press, 1996), pp. 130–48.

4 Here I am bracketing the question of whether amusement is, strictly speaking, an emotion. It is at least an affective state, and thus has the same rhetorical potential as screen emotions proper. For those interested in this debate, see Robert Sharpe, 'Seven Reasons Why Humor is an Emotion', and John Morreall, 'Humor and Emotion', both in John Morreall (ed.), *The Philosophy of Laughter and Humor* (Albany: State University of New York Press, 1987), pp. 208–24.

5 *Film as Film: Understanding and Judging Movies* (Middlesex: Penguin Books, 1972), p. 149.

6 *On Rhetoric*, trans. George A. Kennedy (New York: Oxford University Press, 1991), p. 139.

7 'Prospects for Film Theory: A Personal Assessment', in *Post-Theory*, pp. 37–68.

8 For an account of the assumptions of mainstream cognitive science of the last decade, see Howard Gardner's *The Mind's New Science: A History of the Cognitive Revolution* (New York: Basic Books, 1985), pp. 5–7.

9 A discussion of what he calls the cognitive/evaluative approach to emotion is found in Noël Carroll's *The Philosophy of Horror* (New York: Routledge, 1990), pp. 24–7.

10 Philosophical discussions of the cognitive theory of emotion can be found, for example, in W. Lyons, *Emotion* (Cambridge: Cambridge University Press, 1980); and Robert M. Gordon, *The Structure of Emotions* (Cambridge: Cambridge University Press, 1987).

11 *The Rationality of the Emotions* (Cambridge, Mass.: MIT Press, 1987). Of course, emotion can also lead us astray. The claim is that emotion and reason are not necessarily opposed, not that they are never opposed.

12 Murray Smith, 'Film Spectatorship and the Institution of Fiction', *Journal of Aesthetics and Art Criticism* 53: 2 (Spring 1995): 113–27.

13 'Film Spectatorship and the Institution of Fiction', pp. 118–20.

14 *Engaging Characters: Fiction, Emotion, and the Cinema* (Oxford: Clarendon Press, 1995).

15 *The Philosophy of Horror*.

16 'Brutality and Sentimentality', *Philosophy* 54 (1979): 385.

17 'What is Wrong with Sentimentality?', *Mind* 92 (1983): 524.

18 Quoted from Savile's *The Test of Time* (Oxford: Clarendon Press, 1982) in Marcia Muelder Eaton, 'Laughing at the Death of Little Nell: Sentimental Art and Sentimental People', *American Philosophical Quarterly* 26: 4 (Oct. 1989): 273.

19 Noël Carroll writes of this type of second order response in *The Philosophy of Horror*, as does Murray Smith in 'Film Spectatorship and the Institution of Fiction'.

20 *Gunfighter Nation: The Myth of the Frontier in Twentieth-Century America* (New York: Harper Perennial, 1992) pp. 1–28.

21 See, for example, Hazel Markus and Shinobu Kitayama, *Emotion and Culture* (Washington: American Psychological Association, 1994).

22 'The Image of Women in Film: A Defense of a Paradigm', *Journal of Aesthetics and Art Criticism* 48: 4 (Fall 1990): 357.

16

Engaging Characters

Murray Smith

12 ■ 'Louis Bernard (Daniel Gélin) reveals the details of an assassination plot to Ben McKenna (James Stewart),' from *The Man Who Knew Too Much*.

[. . .] We are now in a position to refine this model, and to address the key question posed in the introduction: what are the various senses of the term 'identification', and how can they be developed into a systematic explanation of emotional response to fictional characters? I argue that we need to break the notion down into a number of more precisely defined concepts: recognition, alignment, and allegiance. These concepts are, however, systematically related, together constituting what I term the *structure of sympathy*. [. . .]

Imagination and Narration

Whatever else it is, engaging with fiction is a species of imaginative activity, not in the traditional and derogatory sense of 'the flight of fancy', but rather in two more complex senses. First, in comprehending, interpreting, and otherwise appreciating fictional narratives, we make inferences, formulate hypotheses, categorize representations, and utilize many other cognitive skills and strategies which go well beyond a mere registration or mirroring of the narrative material. Secondly, fictions prompt and enrich our 'quasi-experience', that is, our efforts to grasp, through mental hypotheses, situations, persons, and values which are alien to us. Our imaginative activity in the context of fiction is, however, both guided and constrained by the fiction's narration: the storytelling force that, in any given narrative film, presents causally linked events occurring in space across time.

[. . .]

I want to propose that fictional narrations elicit three levels of imaginative engagement with characters, distinct types of responses normally conflated under the term 'identification'. Together, these levels of engagement comprise the 'structure of sympathy'. In this system, spectators construct characters (a process I refer to as *recognition*). Spectators are also provided with visual and aural information more or less congruent with that available to characters, and so are placed in a certain structure of *alignment* with characters. In addition, spectators evaluate characters on the basis of the values they embody, and hence form more-or-less sympathetic or more-or-less antipathetic *allegiances* with them. [. . .]

[. . .]

The Structure of Sympathy

We now need to outline the three levels of engagement which comprise the structure of sympathy (recognition, alignment, and allegiance), and the inter-relations among them. These levels and their interactions are then examined in more detail through an analysis of Hitchcock's *The Man Who Knew Too Much* (1956). [. . .]

Recognition

Recognition describes the spectator's construction of character: the perception of a set of textual elements, in film typically cohering around the image of a body, as an individuated and continuous human agent. Recognition does not deny the possibility of development and change, since it is based on the concept of continuity, not unity or identity. [. . .] While understanding that characters are artifices, and are literally no more than collections of inert, textually described traits, we assume that these traits correspond to analogical ones we find in persons in the real world, until this is explicitly contradicted by a description in the text. [. . .] Characters, and fictional worlds in general, rely upon this process in order to be mentally represented at all. [. . .] We perceive and conceive of characters as integral, discrete textual constructs. Just as persons in the real world may be complex or entertain conflicting beliefs, so may characters; but as with persons, such internal contradictions are perceived against the ground of (at least) bodily discreteness and continuity.

Recognition has received less attention than any other level of engagement in studies concerned with character and/or identification, probably because it is regarded as 'obvious'. Certainly, in most films, it is rapid and phenomenologically 'automatic'. The importance of the level becomes apparent in those films which undercut or retard recognition. Films as different as Alexander Dovzhenko's *Arsenal* (1929), Christopher Maclaine's *The End* (1953), Raul Ruiz's *The Suspended Vocation* (1977), and Luis Buñuel's *That Obscure Object of Desire* (1977) all problematize the process of recognition, but to ends rather more diverse than can be captured by a single, gross function. [. . .]

Alignment

The term *alignment* describes the process by which spectators are placed in relation to characters in terms of access to their actions, and to what they know and feel. The concept is akin to the literary notion of 'focalization', Gérard Genette's term for the way in which narratives may feed story information to the reader through the 'lens' of a particular character, though 'identification' is more commonly appealed to: 'The final scene confines itself to what Marlowe, inside a parlor with a killer, could perceive; the film never depicts action outside the house unless he sees it. To a great extent, our "identification" with a film's protagonist is created by exactly this systematic restriction of information.'[1] I propose two interlocking functions, *spatio-temporal attachment* and *subjective access*, cognate with the concepts of narrational range and depth discussed earlier in this chapter, as the most precise means for analysing alignment.[2] Attachment concerns the way in which the narration restricts itself to the actions of a single character, or moves more freely among the spatio-temporal paths of two or more characters. Subjective access pertains to the degree of access we have to the subjectivity of characters, a function which may vary from character to character within a narrative. [. . .] Together these two functions control the apportioning of knowledge among characters and the spectator; the systematic regulation of narrative knowledge results in a *structure of alignment*.
   [. . .]

Allegiance

Allegiance pertains to the moral evaluation of characters by the spectator. Here we are perhaps closest to what is meant by 'identification' in everyday usage, where we talk of 'identifying with' both persons and characters on the basis of a wide range of factors, such as attitudes related to class, nation, age, ethnicity, and gender ('I could really identify with Virgil Tibbs, having experienced that kind of racial hostility myself'). Allegiance depends upon the spectator having what she takes to be reliable access to the character's state of mind, on understanding the context of the character's actions, and having morally evaluated the character on the basis of this knowledge. [. . .] On the basis of such evaluations, spectators construct moral structures, in which characters are organized and ranked in a system of preference. Many factors contribute to the process of moral orientation (the narrational counterpart to moral structure), and hence to allegiance: character action, iconography, and music are particularly salient. [. . .]
   [. . .]

Neither recognition nor alignment nor allegiance entails that the spectator replicate the traits, or experience the thoughts or emotions of a character. Recognition and alignment require only that the spectator understand that these traits and mental states make up the character. With allegiance we go beyond understanding, by evaluating and responding emotionally to the traits and emotions of the character, in the context of the narrative situation. Again, though, we respond emotionally without replicating the emotions of the character. For example, in watching a character perform certain actions, and in seeing the character adopt a certain kind of posture and facial expression, we may infer that the character is in a certain kind of mental state, or possesses certain traits – say, anger as the state, or brutality as the trait. These inferences contribute both to our recognition of the character, and to the pattern of alignment, since we are dealing here partly with a question of subjective access; but such inferences in no way mandate that the spectator be moved to think or feel (let alone behave) in the same way. If we do go on to be moved, by engaging with the character on the level of allegiance, our responses are at a tangent to those of the character: they are [. . .] sympathetic rather than empathic. In order to respond emotionally in this way, the perceiver must first understand the narrative situation, including the interests, traits, and states of the characters. [. . .]

It is in view of these conditions that recognition, alignment, and allegiance comprise a structure of sympathy. [. . .] In understanding 'why the protagonist's response is appropriate or intelligible to the situation',[3] it is only necessary that we have what we take to be, at that moment in the course of the narrative, reliable information about the traits and states of the character, and about the situation in which the character is placed. In sympathizing with the protagonist I do not simulate or mimic her occurrent mental state. Rather, I understand the protagonist and her context, make a more-or-less sympathetic or antipathetic judgement of the character, and respond emotionally in a manner appropriate to both the evaluation and the context of the action.

The Man Who Knew Too Much (Hitchcock, 1956)

Much of the the critical and theoretical comment on the work of Hitchcock has centred on the notion of identification. In particular, critics have observed that his work sometimes elicits a paradoxical identification with villainous, unsympathetic characters. Robin Wood, for example, writes of Hitchcock 'playing identification techniques *against* the natural gravitation of our sympathetic concern';[4] while Raymond Durgnat writes of the '"fishtail" of contradictory identifications and condemnations as we discover the several layers of Norman Bates'.[5] For these reasons, Hitchcock's films provide a particularly good test case for the theory of character engagement. *The Man Who Knew Too Much* will serve to illustrate the concepts of recognition, allegiance, and alignment. [. . .]

The Man Who Knew Too Much may be divided into two, broad movements. Jo and Ben McKenna (Doris Day and James Stewart), an American couple, are vacationing in Morocco with their son Hank (Christopher Olsen). In the course of their travels, they befriend a Frenchman, Louis Bernard (Daniel Gélin), and a retired English couple, the Draytons (Brenda de Banzie and Bernard Miles). Bernard is murdered, but he attempts to pass information regarding a plot to assassinate a French minister on to Ben McKenna with his last words. The Draytons, it emerges, are in some way connected with the murder of Louis Bernard; they kidnap Hank in order to silence Ben McKenna. The Draytons hold Hank in captivity in England; the McKennas pursue them largely without the aid of the police. Hank is located in a London Embassy and is recovered via a ruse in which Jo McKenna, a professional singer, entertains guests at the Embassy with a (loud and lengthy) rendition of 'Que Sera, Sera'. Recognizing the song, Hank whistles it, enabling his father to locate him.

In the first movement, which extends up to the beginning of the McKennas' hunt for Hank in Britain, we recognize the major characters [. . .] and we are aligned exclusively (with a few brief exceptions) with the McKennas. At the same time, this first movement establishes a moral structure which ensures that our allegiance is with the McKennas. In the second movement, the structure of alignment develops so as to disperse our attention over several characters, rather than exclusively attaching us to the McKennas. Moreover, while the McKennas remain the moral centre of the film, the moral structure of the film fragments in the second movement. Let us consider these developments in more detail.

The first movement of the film both attaches us to the McKennas and provides the spectator with access to their subjectivities. That is, the narration follows the spatio-temporal path of the McKennas, only occasionally breaking away to reveal action occurring in a different location; and the McKennas are subjectively transparent, revealing their inner states through actions, expressions, and language. By contrast, when the narration does break momentarily from the McKennas – just prior to the stabbing of Louis Bernard, for example – the characters we witness are largely opaque: we see their actions, but have no access to their subjectivities. (Indeed, the film persistently elicits curiosity by introducing secondary characters – Louis Bernard, the Draytons, the assassin, Ambrose Chappell Jnr. – in this obtuse fashion.) It is this combination of transparency and opacity, couched in a pattern of spatio-temporal attachment which emphasizes the McKennas, which creates the sense that narrative information is being 'filtered' through the McKennas. [. . .]

Up until the murder of Louis Bernard, the McKennas have functioned as an 'alignment unit': that is, the narration has followed them as a couple, much of our access to their thoughts deriving from dialogue between them. The murder results in the splitting of this unit, aligning us more closely with Ben McKenna during the murder and in its immediate aftermath. The murder scene is one of the few occasions within this first movement when the narration attaches us to action other than that involving the McKennas; and yet it ultimately functions to underscore our alignment with Ben McKenna. Since these are, on the face of it, contrary effects, a more detailed examination of the sequence is warranted.

The action takes place in a market-place, where the McKennas are spending a leisurely morning with the Draytons. The narration first aligns us with the McKennas. The Draytons are looking after Hank, and this second group occasionally crosses the path of the McKennas. The narration then breaks with this restriction, in order to follow a scuffle and chase which erupts in the market: Louis Bernard is being pursued (frame 1). Bernard is stabbed (frame 2), staggers towards the group formed by the McKennas and the Draytons, and falls on Ben McKenna. Through a sequence of tighter and tighter shots, and the diminution of background noise, the narration attaches us to Ben McKenna's actions and experience ever more exclusively (frames 3–10). The apex

Frames 1–10 ■ *The Man Who Knew Too Much*: the murder of Louis Bernard

of this movement occurs in the shot represented by frames 9 and 10, in which the camera tracks in towards the characters as Bernard whispers into Ben's ear. [. . .] Over these shots, Bernard communicates some fragmented information regarding the assassination plot; the spectator's alignment with Ben is cemented here, since only the spectator and Ben are party to these revelations. The more omniscient narration during the chase which precedes Bernard's death in fact functions to highlight this exclusive alignment of the spectator with Ben. In this sense, if we take the sequence as whole, the brief 'decentring' of the McKennas only serves to place the subsequent narrational isolation of Ben McKenna in relief.

Following this incident, Ben is interviewed by the police, and then receives a threatening phone call in which he is informed that Hank has been kidnapped. Back at the hotel, he tells Jo about the phone call, and his realization that the Draytons must have been the agents of the kidnapping, thus reforming the earlier 'alignment unit'. This is crucial in reifying a moral structure in the film: from the beginning the McKennas have been presented as a sympathetic couple, but no definitively antipathetic character emerges until this moment. The narration sets up a 'Manichaean' moral structure: a simple opposition of groups representing opposed values. The narration has provided us with our villains – for the moment, at least. The pattern of exclusive attachment to the McKennas is important here, since we later discover that Mrs Drayton is a most half-hearted and guilt-ridden kidnapper. But the Hitchcockian narration does not choose to reveal this to the spectator at this point, thus inviting the Manichaean response. In this way, the alignment structure affects the pattern of moral orientation. Distinguishing alignment from allegiance does not at all deny that the two systems interact. That is why they are defined as operating within a larger system: the structure of sympathy.

The first movement of the film climaxes with the argument between the McKennas in their hotel room in Marrakesh, and their telephone call with Hank, which follows their arrival at Heathrow airport in London. As with the stabbing scene, these scenes function to concentrate our attention more keenly on the characters with whom we are aligned, in this case, both the McKennas. Aside from a brief argument with Buchanan, a British police official, the McKennas are isolated in these scenes. The narration thus dovetails alignment and allegiance: we have been aligned with the McKennas from the beginning of the film, a pattern underlined by their isolation in these scenes; and during the same portion of the film the moral structure clarifies into a dualistic opposition, thus intensifying our sympathy for the McKennas. [. . .] The first movement of the film, then, leads to this convergence of alignment and allegiance, the optimal conditions for an intense and unqualified sympathetic engagement with the McKennas.

The second movement of the film disperses and fragments this convergence, all the time maintaining our sympathetic engagement with the McKennas. Within the structure of alignment, this dispersal occurs as the narration becomes increasingly omniscient; in our terms, the narration attaches us to multiple characters and, again in contrast to the first movement of the film, gives us access to the subjectivities of characters other than the McKennas. The once exclusive pattern of attachment splinters in two ways. Ben and Jo search for Hank separately, effecting a sustained (rather than temporary, as in the first movement of the film) division of the sympathetic characters. Secondly, and more importantly, the narration now periodically aligns us with the Draytons, beginning with the sequence in which the assassin is instructed by Mr Drayton. Up to this point in the film, the narration has only momentarily strayed from aligning us with either Ben or Ben and Jo together.

[. . .]

Parallel with these shifts in the structure of alignment, the narration also complicates the moral structure of the film. In aligning the spectator with the Draytons in the scene in which the assassin receives his instructions, the narration posits a new moral opposition among the kidnappers, between Mrs Drayton, on the one hand, kind and protective towards Hank, and Mr Drayton, the assassin and Hank's guard on the other. The opposition mirrors the larger one that crystallizes at the end of the first movement, between the McKennas and the Draytons. The film thus effects a series of reversals with respect to Mrs Drayton, switching from antipathy to sympathy twice. [. . .] The split between the Draytons performs an even more complex function in the way that it parallels and overshadows a more subtle division that opens up between Ben and Jo McKenna. After the kidnapping, the domineering, controlling traits of Ben McKenna take on a much more troubling and unsympathetic aspect. Up to this point, the difficulties caused in the marriage by Ben's 'benign' patriarchal dominance have been revealed in dialogue – most obviously, in references to Jo's unwillingly abandoned singing career – but largely anaesthetized by the ludic tone of the family scenes. After the kidnapping, however, Ben's control over Jo is cast in a more sinister light, particularly in the scene in which he cajoles her into taking tranquillizers (frame 11). A major thematic concern of the second movement of the film is the (relative) re-empowerment of Jo McKenna within the marriage – she is proven to be at least as capable and insightful in the 'masculine' business of the hunt for the kidnappers – and the consequent renewal of the marriage. However, in moral terms, this division is very minor compared with that between the McKennas and the Draytons, and the new split between Mr and Mrs Drayton. The latter both plays out in more extreme form, and yet diminishes by comparison, the conflict between the McKennas.

Frame 11 ■ *The Man Who Knew Too Much*: Ben McKenna restrains his wife

None of these intricacies undermine our sympathy for the McKennas as a couple, and it is in this sense that they remain the moral centre of the film. The narration manages to introduce moral complexity with respect to the protagonists, without undermining the strong 'melodramatic' opposition set up in the first movement.

[. . .]

The second movement of the film thus complicates the pattern of moral orientation, without displacing the McKennas as the moral centre of the film, and replaces an exclusive alignment with the McKennas with a structure of alignment in which we are alternately aligned with the McKennas and the kidnappers. [. . .]

Two further points regarding the structure of sympathy in general emerge from this analysis of *The Man Who Knew Too Much*. First, [. . .] engagement within the structure of sympathy is conceived as a plural phenomenon. According to the commonplace conception of character identification, [. . .] we watch a film, and find ourselves becoming attached to a particular character on the basis of qualities roughly congruent with those we possess or wish to possess, and experience vicariously the emotional states of this character: we identify with the character. It should now be clear that this scenario conflates many different kinds of response to character, some purely cognitive, some both cognitive and affective, and implies that this articulation of the various kinds of response is the only significant one. Our examination of *The Man Who Knew Too Much* illustrates the way in which spectators may recognize, align, and ally themselves with characters in complex patterns which may preclude or transcend a single, strong engagement with a single character. [. . .] Plural identification – the ramification of character engagement through the variables of level of engagement, number of characters, and time – lies at the heart of the complexity of experience that narrative fiction can offer us.

[. . .]

As a result of the typicality of plural engagement, states such as 'identification' and 'empathy' as traditionally defined, in which we are completely absorbed or 'possessed' by a particular character, are rare (if we grant that such states, strictly defined, are possible at all). Identification or empathy [. . .] would entail, at the very least, that we have recognized a character, have complete access to her knowledge and other mental states, and are sympathetic with the character. It would further require that this engagement is only reinforced by our engagements with other characters: that we are aligned exclusively with this character, and that a firm antipathy is elicited towards all characters whose interests and actions are detrimental to the interests of our 'identification figure'. No complicating sympathy for characters representing other values or goals is possible. We have seen how even in *The Man Who Knew Too Much*, the director so lauded for his skill in eliciting 'identification' varies the patterning of alignment and allegiance far more than this scenario would suggest. Such conditions exist, I submit, only in a very few agitational ('propaganda') films and melodramas.

The second feature of the structure of sympathy that emerges from the analysis of *The Man Who Knew Too Much* is that the three basic levels of engagement which comprise it may interact in various ways. [. . .] But it is important here to recognize that the three basic levels, though they always interact in actual films, are distinct phenomena which should not be conflated. William Lustig's *Maniac* (1982), for example, develops an alignment pattern in which the narration attaches us to a subjectively transparent protagonist whose actions (a series of horrible rapes, murders, and scalpings) are morally repugnant, denying most viewers the necessary conditions for a sympathetic allegiance with the character. Similarly, Steven Spielberg's *Schindler's List* (1994) aligns us in certain sequences with Amos Goeth (Ralph Fiennes) (for example, as he shoots at the Jewish boy who has failed to remove every blemish in Goeth's bathtub); and Hitchcock's *Spellbound* (1945) provides a yet briefer example, in which we are at one point perceptually aligned, through a POV shot, with Dr Murchison (Leo G.

Carroll), the film's chief villain. In all these cases we are, as it were, made to 'identify' informationally with a character from whom we are – simultaneously – emotionally alienated. The distinction between alignment and allegiance attempts to capture this split.

NOTES

1 David Bordwell, *Narration in the Fiction Film* (Madison: University of Wisconsin Press, 1985), p. 65.

2 The notion of spatial attachment is derived from Boris Uspensky, *A Poetics of Composition: The Structure of the Artistic Text and Typology of a Compositional Form*, trans. Valentina Zavarin and Susan Wittig (Berkeley: University of California Press, 1973), p. 58.

3 Noël Carroll, *The Philosophy of Horror: or Paradoxes of the Heart* (New York and London: Routledge, 1990), p. 95.

4 Robin Wood, *Hitchcock's Films Revisited* (New York: Columbia University Press, 1984), p. 223.

5 Raymond Durgnat, *The Strange Case of Alfred Hitchcock; or, the Plain Man's Hitchcock* (London: Faber, 1974), p. 37.

17

The Paradox of Horror

Noël Carroll

In this section, I shall take a look at another apparent paradox that pertains to the genre: what might be called the paradox of horror. This paradox amounts to the question of how people can be attracted by what is repulsive. That is, the imagery of horror fiction seems to be necessarily repulsive and, yet, the genre has no lack of consumers. Moreover, it does not seem plausible to regard these consumers – given the vast number of them – as abnormal or perverse in any way that does not beg the question. Nevertheless, they appear to seek that which, under certain descriptions, it would seem natural for them to avoid. How is this ostensible conundrum to be resolved?

That the works of horror are in some sense both attractive and repulsive is essential to an understanding of the genre. Too often, writing about horror only emphasizes one side of this opposition. Many journalists, reviewing a horror novel or movie, will underscore only the repellent aspects of the work – rejecting it as disgusting, indecent, and foul. Yet this tack fails to offer any account of why people are interested in partaking of such exercises. Indeed, it renders the popularity of the genre inexplicable.

On the other hand, defenders of the horror genre or of a specific example of it will often indulge in allegorical readings that make their subjects appear wholly appealing and that do not acknowledge their repellent aspects. Thus, we are told that the Frankenstein myth is really an existential parable about man thrown-into-the-world, an "isolated sufferer." But where in this allegorical formulation can we find an explanation for the purpose of the unsettling effect of the charnel house imagery? That is, if *Frankenstein* is part *Nausea*, it is also part nauseating.

[. . .]

Works of horror cannot be construed as either completely repelling or completely attractive. Either outlook overlooks something of the quiddity of the form. The apparent paradox cannot simply be ignored by treating the genre as if it were not involved in a curious admixture of attraction and repulsion.

[. . .] The paradox of horror is an instance of a larger problem, viz., that of explaining the way in which the artistic presentation of normally aversive events and objects can give rise to pleasure or can compel our interests.

[. . .]

[. . .] An awareness of the paradox of horror had already dawned on eighteenth-century theorists. The question they asked about tales of terror, as cited, was in fact part of the more general aesthetic question of how it is possible for audiences to derive pleasure from any genre – including not only horror but tragedy as well – whose objects were things that ordinarily cause distress and discomfiture. That is, encountering things such as ghosts or Desdemona's massacre in "real life" would be upsetting rather than entertaining. And, of course, what is disgusting onscreen or on the page is genuinely disgusting. It is something that we would ordinarily seek to avert. So why do we seek it in art and fiction? How does it give us pleasure and/or why does it interest us?

[. . .]

[. . .] It is important to keep in mind that the horror genre, like that of tragedy, most generally takes a narrative form. [. . .] That horror is often narrative suggests that with much horror, the interest we have and the pleasure we take may not primarily be in the object of art-horror as such – i.e., in the monster for its own sake. Rather, the narrative may be the crucial locus of our interest and pleasure. For what is attractive – what holds our interest and yields pleasure – in the horror genre need not be, first and foremost, the simple manifestation of the object of art-horror, but the way that manifestation or disclosure is situated as a functional element in an overall narrative structure.

That is, in order to give an account of what is compelling about the horror genre, it may be wrong to ask only what it is about the monster that gives us pleasure; for the interest and pleasure we take in the monster and its disclosure may rather be a function of the way it figures in a larger narrative structure.

[. . .]

[. . .] I think it is fair to say that in our culture, horror thrives above all as a narrative form. Thus, in order to account for the interest we take in and the pleasure we take from horror, we may hypothesize that, in the main, the locus of our gratification is not the monster as such but the whole narrative structure in which the presentation of the monster is staged. This, of course, is not to say that the monster is in any way irrelevant to the genre, nor that the interest and pleasure in the genre could be satisfied through and/or substituted by any old narrative. For [. . .] the monster is a functional ingredient in the type of narratives found in horror stories, and not all narratives function exactly like horror narratives.

[. . .] Horror narratives [. . .] with great frequency, revolve around proving, disclosing, discovering, and confirming the existence of something that is impossible, something that defies standing conceptual schemes. It is part of such stories – contrary to our everyday beliefs about the nature of things – that such monsters exist. And as a result, audiences' expectations revolve around whether this existence will be confirmed in the story.

Often this is achieved [. . .] by putting off the conclusive information that the monster exists for quite a while. Sometimes this information may be deferred till the very end of the fiction. And even where this information is given to the audience right off the bat, it is still generally the case that the human characters in the tale must undergo a process of discovering that the monster exists, which, in turn, may lead to a further process of confirming that discovery in an ensuing scene or series of scenes. That is, the question of whether or not the monster exists may be transformed into the question of whether and when the human characters in the tale will establish the existence of the monster. Horror stories are often protracted series of discoveries: first the reader learns of the monster's existence, then some characters do, then some more characters do, and so on; the drama of iterated disclosure – albeit to different parties – underwrites much horror fiction.

Even in overreacher plots, there is a question of whether the monsters exist – i.e., of whether they can be summoned, in the case of demons, or of whether they can be created by mad scientists and necromancers. Furthermore, even after the existence of the monster is disclosed, the audience continues to crave further information about its nature, its identity, its origin, its purposes, and its astounding powers and properties, including, ultimately, those of its weaknesses that *may* enable humanity to do it in.

Thus, to a large extent, the horror story is driven explicitly by curiosity. It engages its audience by being involved in processes of disclosure, discovery, proof, explanation, hypothesis, and confirmation. Doubt, skepticism, and the fear that belief in the existence of the monster is a form of insanity are predictable foils to the revelation (to the audience or to the characters or both) of the existence of the monster.

Horror stories, in a significant number of cases, are dramas of proving the existence of the monster and disclosing (most often gradually) the origin, identity, purposes and powers of the monster. Monsters, as well, are obviously a perfect vehicle for engendering this kind of curiosity and for supporting the drama of proof, because monsters are (physically, though generally not logically) impossible beings. They arouse interest and attention through being putatively inexplicable or highly unusual vis-à-vis our standing cultural categories, thereby instilling a desire to learn and to know about them. And since they are also outside of (justifiably) prevailing definitions of what is, they understandably prompt a need for proof (or the fiction of a proof) in the face of skepticism. Monsters are, then, natural subjects for curiosity, and they straightforwardly warrant the ratiocinative energies the plot lavishes upon them.

All narratives might be thought to involve the desire to know – the desire to know at least the outcome of the interaction of the forces made salient in the plot. However, the horror fiction is a special variation on this general narrative motivation, because it has at the center of it something which is given as in principle *unknowable* – something which, *ex hypothesi*, cannot, given the structure of our conceptual scheme, exist and that cannot have the properties it has. This is why, so often, the real drama in a horror story resides in establishing the existence of the monster and in disclosing its horrific properties. Once this is established, the monster, generally, has to be confronted, and the narrative is driven by the question of whether the creature can be destroyed. However, even at this point, the drama of ratiocination can continue as further discoveries – accompanied by arguments, explanations, and hypotheses – reveal features of the monster that will facilitate or impede the destruction of the creature.

To illustrate this briefly, let us consider Colin Wilson's novel *The Mind Parasites*. The story is presented as a compilation of the chronicle of humanity's confrontation with the mind parasites. This chronicle has been drawn from a number of sources. So, from the perspective of the order of the presentation of the fiction, it begins with the presupposition that the mind parasites – called Tsathogguans – exist. But the exposition proceeds by laying end to end successive discoveries of the existence of these creatures, among other things (such as the discovery of the ruins of an ancient city – a red herring, as it turns out). The major character, Gilbert Austin, first discovers his friend's – Karel Weissman's – discovery of the Tsathogguans, which itself comprises a narrative of discovery. Austin then goes through his own process of discovery. In the course of both discoveries the possibility that the discoverer is insane has to be disposed. Austin then proceeds to convince his colleague Reich of the existence of the mind parasites; this is not difficult, but it allows for more ratiocination and the compiling of a little more evidence.

Austin and Reich then impart their discoveries to a select group of other scientists, many of whom are killed by the mind parasites. But enough survive to share their discoveries eventually with the President of the United States. The plot, in other words, proceeds by means of the revelation of the existence of the Tsathogguans to increasingly larger groups of people. But even when Austin has secured sufficient government aid to confront the mind parasites, further discoveries are mandated by the story. Austin says:

> It was maddeningly frustrating. We possessed the great secret; we had warned the world. And yet, in a fundamental sense, we were as ignorant as ever. Who were these creatures? Where did they come from? What was their ultimate aim? Were they really intelligent, or were they as unintelligent as the maggots in a piece of cheese?

Of course, the reader wants to know the answers to these questions as well, and we stay on board to get them till the end of the plot. Moreover, it is not until then that we learn of the properties of the Tsathogguans (and their relations to the Moon) that make possible their final destruction.

[. . .]

Applied to the paradox of horror, these observations suggest that the pleasure derived from the horror fiction and the source of our interest in it resides, first and foremost, in the processes of discovery, proof, and confirmation that horror fictions often employ. The disclosure of the existence of the horrific being and of its properties is the central source of pleasure in the genre; once that process of revelation is consummated, we remain inquisitive about whether such a creature can be successfully confronted, and that narrative question sees us through to the end of the story. Here, the pleasure involved is, broadly speaking, cognitive. Hobbes, interestingly, thought of curiosity as an appetite of the mind; with the horror fiction, that appetite is whetted by the prospect of knowing the putatively unknowable, and then satisfied through a continuous process of revelation, enhanced by imitations of (admittedly simplistic) proofs, hypotheses, counterfeits of causal reasoning, and explanations whose details and movement intrigue the mind in ways analogous to genuine ones.

Moreover, it should be clear that these particular cognitive pleasures, insofar as they are set in motion by the relevant kind of unknowable beings, are especially well served by horrific monsters. Thus, there is a special functional relationship between the beings that mark off the horror genre and the pleasure and interest that many horror fictions sustain. That interest and that pleasure derive from the disclosure of unknown and impossible beings, just the sorts of things that seem to call for proof, discovery, and confirmation. Therefore, the disgust that such beings evince might be seen as part of the price to be paid for the pleasure of their disclosure. That is, the narrative expectations that the horror genre puts in place is that the being whose existence is in question be something that defies standing cultural categories; thus, disgust, so to say, is itself more or less mandated by the kind of curiosity that the horror narrative puts in place. The horror narrative could not deliver a successful, affirmative answer to its presiding question unless the disclosure of the monster indeed elicited disgust, or was of the sort that was a highly probable object of disgust.

That is, there is a strong relation of consilience between the objects of art-horror, on the one hand, and the revelatory plotting on the other. The kind of plots and the subjects of horrific revelation are not merely compatible, but fit together or agree in a way that is highly appropriate. That the audience is naturally inquisitive about that which is unknown meshes with plotting that is concerned to render the unknown known by processes of discovery, explanation, proof, hypothesis, confirmation, and so on.

[. . .]

If what is of primary importance about horrific creatures is that their very impossibility vis-à-vis our conceptual categories is what makes them function so compellingly in dramas of discovery and confirmation, then their disclosure, insofar as they are categorical violations, will be attached to some sense of disturbance, distress, and disgust. Consequently, the role of the horrific creature in such narratives — where their disclosure captures our interest and delivers pleasure — will simultaneously mandate some probable revulsion. That is, in order to reward our interest by the disclosure of the putatively impossible beings of the plot, said beings ought to be disturbing, distressing, and repulsive in the way that theorists like Douglas predict phenomena that ill fit cultural classifications will be.

So, as a first approximation of resolving the paradox of horror, we may conjecture that we are attracted to the majority of horror fictions because of the way that the plots of discovery and the dramas of proof pique our curiosity, and abet our interest, ideally satisfying them in a way that is pleasurable. But if narrative curiosity about impossible beings is to be satisfied through disclosure, that process must require some element of probable disgust since such impossible beings are, *ex hypothesi*, disturbing, distressful, and repulsive.

One way of making the point is to say that the monsters in such tales of disclosure have to be disturbing, distressful, and repulsive, if the process of their discovery is to be rewarding in a pleasurable way. Another way to get at this is to say that the primary pleasure that narratives of disclosure afford – i.e., the interest we take in them, and the source of their attraction – resides in the processes of discovery, the play of proof, and the dramas of ratiocination that comprise them. It is not that we crave disgust, but that disgust is a predictable concomitant of disclosing the unknown, whose disclosure is a desire the narrative instills in the audience and then goes on to gladden. Nor will that desire be satisfied unless the monster defies our conception of nature which demands that it probably engender some measure of repulsion.

In this interpretation of horror narratives, the majority of which would appear to exploit the cognitive attractions of the drama of disclosure, experiencing the emotion of art-horror is not our absolutely primary aim in consuming horror fictions, even though it is a determining feature for identifying membership in the genre. Rather, art-horror is the price we are willing to pay for the revelation of that which is impossible and unknown, of that which violates our conceptual schema. The impossible being does disgust; but that disgust is part of an overall narrative address which is not only pleasurable, but whose potential pleasure depends on the confirmation of the existence of the monster as a being that violates, defies, or problematizes standing cultural classifications. Thus, we are attracted to, and many of us seek out, horror fictions of this sort despite the fact that they provoke disgust, because that disgust is required for the pleasure involved in engaging our curiosity in the unknown and drawing it into the processes of revelation, ratiocination, etc.

[. . .]

Central to my approach has been the idea that the objects of horror are fundamentally linked with cognitive interests, most notably with curiosity. The plotting gambits of disclosure/discovery narratives play with, expand, sustain, and develop this initial cognitive appetite in many directions. And as well, this is the way in which horror fictions usually go.

But it would be a mistake to think that this curiosity is *solely* a function of plotting, even if the plotting of certain types of fictions – namely those concerned with disclosure – brings it to its highest pitch. For the objects of art-horror in and of themselves engender curiosity as well. This is why they can support the kind of disclosure plots referred to above. Consequently, even if it is true that horrific curiosity is best expatiated upon within disclosure plots, and that, in its most frequent and compelling cases, it does mobilize such plots, it is also true that it can be abetted and rewarded without the narrative contextualization of disclosure/discovery plotting. Thus, it can be the case that while horror is most often, and perhaps most powerfully and most primarily, developed within narrative contexts of disclosure, it may also obtain in non-narrative and non-disclosure contexts for the same reason, viz., the power of the objects of art-horror to command curiosity.

Recall again that the objects of art-horror are, by definition, impure. This is to be understood in terms of their being anomalous. Obviously, the anomalous nature of these beings is what makes them disturbing, distressing, and disgusting. They are violations of our ways of classifying things and such frustrations of a world-picture are bound to be disturbing.

However, anomalies are also interesting. The very fact that they are anomalies fascinates us. Their deviation from the paradigms of our classificatory scheme captures our attention immediately. It holds us spellbound. It commands and retains our attention. It is an attracting force; it attracts curiosity, i.e., it makes us curious; it invites inquisitiveness about its surprising properties. One wants to gaze upon the unusual, even when it is simultaneously repelling.

Monsters [. . .] are repelling because they violate standing categories. But for the self-same reason, they are also compelling of our attention. They are attractive, in the sense that they elicit interest, and they are the cause of, for many, irresistible attention, again, just because they violate standing categories. They are curiosities. They can rivet attention and thrill for the self-same reason that they disturb, distress, and disgust.

If these confessedly pedestrian remarks are convincing, three interesting conclusions are suggested. First, the attraction of non-narrative- and non-disclosure-type narration in horror is explicable, as is disclosure-type narrative, fundamentally by virtue of curiosity, a feature of horrific beings that follows from their anomalous status as violations of standing cultural schemes. Second, horrific creatures are able to contribute so well to sustaining interest in disclosure plots to an important degree just because in being anomalous, they can be irresistibly interesting. And lastly, with special reference to the paradox of horror, monsters, the objects of art-horror, are themselves sources of ambivalent responses, for as violations of standing cultural categories, they are disturbing and disgusting, but, at the same time, they are also objects of fascination – again, just because they transgress standing categories of thought. That is, the ambivalence that bespeaks the paradox of horror is already to be found in the very objects of art-horror which are disgusting and fascinating, repelling and attractive due to their anomalous nature.

[. . .]

[. . .] Non-narrative examples of art-horror, such as those found in the fine arts and narrative horror fictions that do not deploy disclosure devices, attract their audiences insofar as the objects of art-horror promote fascination at the same time they distress; indeed, both responses emanate from the same aspects of the horrific beings. The two responses are, as a matter of (contingent) fact, inseparable in horror. Moreover, this fascination can be savored, because the distress in question is not behaviorally pressing; it is a response to the thought of a monster, not to the actual presence of a disgusting or fearsome thing.

If it is true that fascination is the key to our attraction to the art-horror in general, then it is also the case that the curiosity and fascination that is basic to the genre also receive especial amplification in what I have referred to as narratives of disclosure and discovery. There curiosity, fascination, and our cognitive inquisitiveness are engaged, addressed, and sustained in a highly articulated way through what I have called the drama of proof and such processes of continuous revelation as ratiocination, discovery, hypothesis formation, confirmation, and so on.

At this point, then, I am in a position to summarize my approach to the paradox of horror. It is a twofold theory, whose elements I refer to respectively as the universal theory and the general theory. The universal theory of our attraction to art-horror — which covers non-narrative horror, non-disclosure horror narratives, *and* disclosure narratives — is that what leads people to seek out horror is fascination as characterized in the analyses above. This is the basic, generic calling card of the form.

Part V

Must Films Have Narrators?

Introduction

In his *Poetics*, Aristotle distinguishes between narrative and drama. Although both involve the imitation of an event or sequence of events – and hence fall under the concept of *mimesis* – a narrative involves the telling of those events, whereas a drama presents the events directly to an audience.

Is film a dramatic or a narrative medium? On the one hand, when we watch a film we seem to be seeing the events transpiring before our very eyes. Indeed, some of the theorists whose work we read in Part II argued that this was the distinctiveness of film as an artistic medium. On the other hand, films also embody a specific perspective on the events that they depict. A filmmaker's choice of shots and their editing, among other factors, seem to embody something like a visual way of telling a story. Films may therefore be considered narratives, but exactly how they narrate events has been a subject of much theoretical debate.

The term "narration" is ambiguous. On the one hand, it refers to the story itself – that which is narrated. This is the causally structured sequence of events that is the subject of a film. But films often present the events of their stories in a different order than that in which they actually occurred. So, in the famous flashback sequence of Michael Curtiz's *Casablanca* (1942), when Rick remembers his love affair with Ilsa in Paris, the film is sequentially narrating a series of story events that happened at a much earlier time than that during which Rick recalls them. The term "narrative discourse" is often used to refer to this aspect of how the story's events are presented.

David Bordwell attempts to explain the relationship between a film's plot and its story. Because he is influenced by a school of literary criticism known as Russian formalism, Bordwell uses the terms *fabula* and *syuzhet* to refer to story and plot, respectively. He claims that film viewers are much like detectives in that they attempt to construct a film story – what actually happened – on the basis of the clue-like plot of a film. In order to do so, the viewer has to make sense of the narrational strategies that a film embodies.

Bordwell illustrates this distinction using Alfred Hitchcock's great 1954 film, *Rear Window*. There are many events in the story that are kept from viewers as Hitchcock skillfully employs a plot that limits their access to what the main character, Jeff (Jimmy Stewart), sees while looking out his apartment window.

The relationship between film style and plot are somewhat more difficult to grasp. A film's style has to do with its use of available cinematic devices in presenting the plot. So, for example, presenting characters in extended close-ups would be an example of a film's style. Bordwell claims that a film's style works with the plot in presenting the story in a specific way that affects viewers' affective and cognitive attitudes toward the events they see unfolding.

Seymour Chatman's discussion of cinematic narration begins with a puzzle about a film's narrative discourse. If we agree that films involve narratings of their stories, who or what is it that is doing the narrating? Sometimes the answer is quite clear. A film like Billy Wilder's *Double Indemnity* (1944) quickly identifies one of the characters – Walter Neff (Fred MacMurray) – as the narrator of the story, for we hear him in voice-over reciting the contents of a note that we actually see him writing and whose contents are supposed to be presented by the balance of the story. This is a clear-cut case of a film with a *personified narrator*, a character in the story who is depicted as narrating the story. But what about films that do not have such voice-overs, films that do not explicitly adopt a character's or narrator's point of view in depicting their stories' events? Are these films also narrated?

Chatman's answer is an unequivocal yes. He claims that all films have *cinematic narrators* who need not be human beings but who are agents. What these agents are responsible for is the film narrating its story in the precise way that it does. But Chatman does not stop here: using the example of Alfred Hitchcock's *Stage Fright* (1950), he argues that we also have to acknowledge the existence of an *implied author*, for there are times when we have to recognize both the personified and cinematic narrators as subservient to a more controlling presence, namely that of the implied author of a cinematic text. It is for this reason that his reading begins with a short discussion of the idea of an implied author.

Although Chatman is very much influenced by Bordwell, the two disagree about whether narration entails a narrator. Bordwell thinks that we can get along very well without personifying the agency involved in film narration, while Chatman thinks this is a mistake. You will have to decide which author has the more plausible account of film narration.

In his very difficult but carefully argued selection, George Wilson argues against Chatman's claim that films always involve cinematic narrators. Indeed, instead of attacking this claim directly, Wilson chooses to consider an assumption that underlies Chatman's account of both the implied author and the cinematic narrator: that films involve *showings* of their story events. Wilson contends that theorists like Chatman have paid too little attention to the question of the exact sense in which film narratives involve showings of their stories.

One reason why Chatman invoked the idea of a cinematic narrator was to explain how the specific way in which a film depicted its story – its editing and shot choices among other things – amounted to a visual showing of the story events. This was important because, if correct, it would explain how the form that a film uses to present its narration incorporates a specific perspective for viewing its story. Wilson's goal is to provide an accurate account of how fictional films involve *showings*, what he calls "the Fictional Showing Hypothesis."

The version of this hypothesis that he objects to – the Face to Face Version – asserts that, in watching a fiction film, viewers imagine that they are seeing the film's fictional events as if they were in the position of the camera. The problem with this is that it assumes that part of what a viewer imagines when watching a film is what their point of access to the film events is. Wilson claims that this is implausible.

So in place of the Face to Face Version of the Fictional Showing Hypothesis, Wilson proposes a Mediated Version. Here, he relies on a distinction between a motion picture shot and a movie story shot. Any shot in a fiction film is both of these. It is a movie story shot in so far as it tells us something about the fictional characters in its story. But at the same time, the shot also records facts about the actors and sets: it is a motion picture shot. So a shot of the actor Lee Marvin in *The Man Who Shot Liberty Valance* is a motion picture shot of Marvin as a young man, while also being a movie story shot of the film's villain, Valance.

In order to make sense of the idea of a movie as a showing of its story, Wilson thinks we have to countenance the following complex claim: in looking at a fiction film, when we believe that a certain event, registered in a movie story shot, took place – say, the killing of Liberty Valance – then it is also fictionally true for us that the film has presented that event in a motion picture shot. The reason that this bears on the question of whether films involve showings is that Wilson is now in a position to explain what the showing consists in: "the fictional exhibition and sequential arrangement, by means of editing, of *motion picture shots* of the occurrences that constitute the story."

This is a complicated idea to understand. What it asserts is that there is a complex logic to the fictional beliefs that a viewer of a fiction film accepts. Part of the fiction that a viewer accepts is that she is actually seeing shots that record events that actually took place, so that it is as if she were witnessing a documentary of the fictional events. The importance of this account is that, if true, it gives some content to the idea that a fiction film involves a *showing* of the events it narrates that does not involve a viewer imagining seeing those events from the point of view of the camera. As a result, Wilson gives support to the idea that films convey a perspective on the events they depict by means of the formal features of their narratives.

Study Questions

1. Explain the distinction between *fabula* (story) and *syuzhet* (plot). What is the relationship between the two, according to Bordwell?
2. How does Bordwell conceive of the film viewer? What sorts of activity does he posit the viewer as engaged in as he or she watches a film?
3. What role does Bordwell assign to style in filmic narratives? Do you think he pays sufficient attention to it?

4. What is Bordwell's definition of narration? How, if at all, does it reflect the specificity of film as an artistic medium?

5. What does Chatman mean by an *implied author*? What is the difference between an implied author and a real one? Do you agree with his contention that films need to be seen as the product of an implied author?

6. What is the difference between a personified narrator and a cinematic narrator in Chatman's theory? Why does he think that all films involve cinematic narrators? Why does Bordwell reject this contention? Whom do you agree with?

7. Wilson rejects the Face to Face Version of the Fictional Showing Hypothesis. What exactly is it? What reason does he have for rejecting it? Do you agree with him? Why or why not?

8. What is the distinction between a motion picture shot and a movie story shot for Wilson? Is every motion picture shot a movie story shot? Is every movie story shot a motion picture shot? Explain why or why not.

9. What is the Mediated Version of the Fictional Showing Hypothesis? What reasons can you see for accepting it, if any?

18

Principles of Film Narration

David Bordwell

The theory I propose sees narration as a formal activity, a notion comparable to Eisenstein's rhetoric of form. In keeping with a perceptual-cognitive approach to the spectator's work, this theory treats narration as a process which is not in its basic aims specific to any medium. As a dynamic process, narration deploys the materials and procedures of each medium for its ends. Thinking of narration in this way yields considerable scope for investigation while still allowing us to build in the specific possibilities of the film medium. In addition, a form-centered approach sets itself the task of explaining how narration functions in the totality of the film. Narrational patterning is a major part of the process by which we grasp films as more or less coherent wholes.

[There is] a difference between the story that is represented and the actual representation of it, the form in which the perceiver actually encounters it. This crucial distinction may go back to Aristotle, but it was most fully theorized by the Russian Formalists, and it is indispensable to a theory of narration.

Presented with two narrative events, we look for causal or spatial or temporal links. The imaginary construct we create, progressively and retroactively, was termed by Formalists the *fabula* (sometimes translated as "story"). More specifically, the fabula embodies the action as a chronological, cause-and-effect chain of events occurring within a given duration and a spatial field. In *Rear Window*, as in most detective tales, there is an overt process of fabula construction, since the investigation of the crime involves establishing certain connections among events. Putting the fabula together requires us to construct the story of the ongoing inquiry while at the same time framing and testing hypotheses about past events. That is, the story of the investigation is a search for the concealed story of a crime. By the end of the typical detective tale, all story events can be fitted into a single pattern of time, space, and causality.

The fabula is thus a pattern which perceivers of narratives create through assumptions and inferences. It is the developing result of picking up narrative cues, applying schemata, framing and testing hypotheses. Ideally, the fabula can be embodied in a

13 ■ "L. B. Jeffries (James Stewart) spies on his neighbors and becomes convinced one of them has committed murder," from *Rear Window*.

verbal synopsis, as general or as detailed as circumstances require. Yet the fabula, however imaginary, is not a whimsical or arbitrary construct. The viewer builds the fabula on the basis of prototype schemata (identifiable types of persons, actions, locales, etc.), template schemata (principally the "canonic" story), and procedural schemata (a search for appropriate motivations and relations of causality, time, and space). To the extent that these processes are intersubjective, so is the fabula that is created. In principle, viewers of a film will agree about either what the story is or what factors obscure or render ambiguous the adequate construction of the story.

It would be an error to take the fabula, or story, as the profilmic event. A film's fabula is never materially present on the screen or soundtrack. When we see a shot of Jeff looking out his window, his action is a representation which signals us to infer a story event (Jeff looks out his window). The same piece of information might have been conveyed many other ways, many of them requiring no sight or sound of Jeff at all. The staging of the action, as Eisenstein showed, is itself a representational act. This theoretical move lets us avoid that a priori favoring of certain film techniques characteristic of mimetic theories.

The fabula, writes Tynianov, "can only be guessed at, but it is not a given." What is given? What sorts of phenomenally present materials and forms do we encounter? We can analyze the film as consisting of two systems and a remaining body of material, diagrammed in figure 1. The *syuzhet* (usually translated as "plot") is the actual arrangement and presentation of the fabula in the film. It is not the text in toto. It is a more abstract construct, the patterning of the story as a blow-by-blow recounting of the film could render it. The syuzhet is a system because it arranges components – the story events and states of affairs – according to specific principles. [. . .] "Syuzhet" names the architectonics of the film's presentation of the fabula; hence the rightward arrow in the diagram. Logically, syuzhet patterning is independent of the medium; the same syuzhet patterns could be embodied in a novel, a play, or a film.

Style also constitutes a system in that it too mobilizes components – particular instantiations of film techniques – according to principles of organization. There are other uses of the term "style" (e.g., to designate recurrent features of structure or texture in a body of films, such as "neorealist style"), but in this context, "style" simply

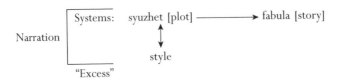

Figure 1 ■ Film as phenomenal process

names the film's systematic use of cinematic devices. Style is thus wholly ingredient to the medium. Style interacts with syuzhet in various ways; hence the two-way arrow in the diagram.

An example may illustrate how syuzhet and style differ. In *Rear Window*, the syuzhet consists of the particular pattern of events (actions, scenes, turning points, plot twists) depicting the tale of Mrs. Thorwald's murder and its investigation and the tale of Lisa and Jeff's romance. When [. . .] I described formal patterns of withheld knowledge or abrupt revelation, I was referring principally to the construction of the syuzhet. The same film, however, can be described as a steady flow of applications of cinematic techniques – mise-en-scène, cinematography, editing, and sound. In one scene, Jeff and Stella are spotted by Thorwald. They step quickly back into Jeff's room (figure movement, setting); they whisper (sound) and douse the lamp (lighting); the camera tracks quickly back to a long shot (cinematography); and all of this occurs after the crucial shot of Thorwald turning to look out his window (editing).

Note that in a narrative film these two systems coexist. They can do this because syuzhet and style each treat different aspects of the phenomenal process. The syuzhet embodies the film as a "dramaturgical" process; style embodies it as a "technical" one. While it would often be arbitrary to separate the two systems in the process of perception, the distinction has precedent in much narrative theory. Indeed, we shall discover one mode of narration that requires us to keep syuzhet and style conceptually separate. Assuming that the distinction is warranted, I want now to spell out the relations between syuzhet and fabula, and syuzhet and style.

[. . .]

[. . .] Three sorts of principles relate the syuzhet to the fabula.

1. *Narrative "logic."* In constructing a fabula, the perceiver defines some phenomena as events while constructing relations among them. These relations are primarily causal ones. An event will be assumed to be a consequence of another event, of a character trait, or of some general law. The syuzhet can facilitate this process by systematically encouraging us to make linear causal inferences. But the syuzhet can also arrange events so as to block or complicate the construction of causal relations. This happens with the false clues in *Rear Window*. Narrative logic also includes a more abstract principle of similarity and difference which I call *parallelism*. Thorwald's murder of his wife has no significant effect on most of his neighbors; one function of the courtyard vignettes is to parallel the romantic relations of Jeff and Lisa with other male/female relations. What counts as an event, a cause, an effect, a similarity, or a difference – all will be determined within the context of the individual film.

2. *Time.* Narrative time has several aspects, well analyzed by Gérard Genette. The syuzhet can cue us to construct fabula events in any sequence (a matter of *order*). The syuzhet can suggest fabula events as occurring in virtually any time span (*duration*). And the syuzhet can signal fabula events as taking place any number of times (*frequency*). These aspects can all assist or block the viewer's construction of fabula time. Again, temporal representation will vary with historical convention and the context of the individual film.

3. *Space*. Fabula events must be represented as occurring in a spatial frame of reference, however vague or abstract. The syuzhet can facilitate construction of fabula space by informing us of the relevant surroundings and the positions and paths assumed by the story's agents. The confinement to Jeff's courtyard in *Rear Window* is an instance of the use of syuzhet devices to advance our construction of fabula space. But the film could also impede our comprehension by suspending, muddling, or undercutting our construction of space.

Depending on how the syuzhet presents the fabula, there will be particular spectatorial effects. Armed with the notion of different narrative principles and the concept of the syuzhet's distortion of fabula information, we can begin to account for the concrete narrational work of any film. It is obvious, for instance, that *Rear Window* depends upon withholding certain fabula information; we can now see that our schematizing and hypothesizing activities are guided by the syuzhet's cues about causality, time, and space. The basic-training aspect of the film's early portions – its tendency to give visual cues, let us draw inferences, and then confirm or disconfirm them by verbal statement – arises from manipulation of causal information. To take a specific scene: while Jeff is asleep, we see a woman leave with Thorwald and wonder if she is his wife; the syuzhet has generated this suspicion that Mrs. Thorwald is still alive by not showing us this woman (who is not Mrs. Thorwald) entering the apartment. The syuzhet of *Rear Window* also blocks our knowledge by limiting space; we can use only narrowly restricted views of the courtyard to construct the fabula. And *Rear Window* is not exceptional in its limitations, concealments, and revelations. For theoretical purposes it may sometimes be convenient to take as an ideal baseline an instance in which the syuzhet is constructed so as to permit maximum access to the fabula. But every syuzhet uses retardation to postpone complete construction of the fabula. At the very least, the end of the story, or the means whereby we arrive there, will be withheld. Thus the syuzhet aims not to let us construct the fabula in some logically pristine state but rather to guide us to construct the fabula in a specific way, by arousing in us particular expectations at this or that point, eliciting our curiosity or suspense, and pulling surprises along the way.

In some cases, the syuzhet will include masses of material that block our construction of the fabula. Such material may encourage us to treat the syuzhet as interpreting or commenting on the fabula. In *October*, both Kerensky and General Kornilov appeal to the slogan "For God and Country." Suddenly we cut to a series of statues of gods from many cultures. These shots do not help us to construct the spatial, temporal, or logical connections among story events; in fabula terms they are a digression. Nonetheless, the sequence constitutes syuzhet manipulation. As a little dissertation on the very idea of God, the passage emphasizes the cultural variability of religion and suggests that an appeal to the holy often veils political opportunism. The inserted material insists in its patterned development that we motivate it transtextually, as a species of rhetorical argument. A novelist's commentary, however digressive, forms an integral part of the syuzhet, and so do Eisenstein's essayistic interpolations.

The syuzhet, then, is the dramaturgy of the fiction film, the organized set of cues prompting us to infer and assemble story information. As [figure 1] on p. 184 suggests, the film's style can interact with the syuzhet in various ways. Film technique is customarily used to perform syuzhet tasks – providing information, cueing hypotheses, and so forth. In the "normal" film, that is, the syuzhet system controls the stylistic system – in Formalist terms, the syuzhet is the "dominant." For example, patterns in the syuzhet's presentation of story information will be matched by stylistic patterns, as when at the close of *Rear Window* a camera movement homologous to that in the opening underlines the changes in the lives of the courtyard's inhabitants.

Still, this is not to say that the systematic employment of film techniques – that is, the film's style – is wholly a vehicle for the syuzhet. When alternative techniques exist for a given syuzhet purpose, it may make a difference which technique is chosen. For instance, the syuzhet may require that two story events be cued as occurring simultaneously. The simultaneity may be denoted by crosscutting from one event to the other, by staging the two actions in depth, by use of split-screen techniques, or by the inclusion of particular objects in the setting (such as a television set broadcasting a "live" event). Whatever stylistic choice is made may have different effects on the spectator's perceptual and cognitive activity. Style is thus a notable factor in its own right, even when it is "only" supporting the syuzhet.

Film style can also take shapes not justified by the syuzhet's manipulation of story information. If in *Rear Window* Hitchcock systematically cut from Jeff's gaze to close-ups of misleading or irrelevant objects which he could not see, then the stylistic procedure itself could vie for prominence with the syuzhet's task of presenting the story. True, we might take this stylistic flourish as a syuzhet maneuver to baffle us about causality or space; but if the device were repeated systematically across the film with no clear link to the developing syuzhet and fabula, then the more economical explanation would be that style has come forward to claim our attention independent of syuzhet/fabula relations. [. . .] For analytical purposes, then, we must grant a potential disparity between the stylistic system and the syuzhet system, even if such a tendency is rare.

It is evident that both syuzhet and style invite the spectator to apply motivational rationales. [. . .] At the syuzhet level, when Jeff and Stella recoil from Thorwald's look, the audience justifies this event as psychologically plausible and compositionally necessary for what follows. At the stylistic level, when Jeff scans the apartment block and the next shot is of Thorwald's windows, we assume the shot to be compositionally relevant, grant it a certain realism (Jeff's point of view), and acquiesce to a generic convention (this could be a suspenseful buildup). In the hypothetical example of patterned cutaways to irrelevant objects, we would try to motivate them compositionally, realistically, or transtextually; but if all were unequal to the task set by the style, we would have a case of "artistic motivation," whereby the materials and forms of the medium constitute the chief object of interest.

It is time for a formal definition. In the fiction film, narration is *the process whereby the film's syuzhet and style interact in the course of cueing and channeling the spectator's construction of the fabula.* Thus it is not only when the syuzhet arranges fabula information that the film narrates. Narration also includes stylistic processes. It would of course be possible to treat narration solely as a matter of syuzhet/fabula relations, but this would leave out the ways in which the filmic texture affects the spectator's activity. We have already seen that the spectator possesses stylistic schemata as well as others, and these invariably affect the overall process of narrative representation. Moreover, by including style within narration, we can analyze stylistic departures from the syuzhet's project. In an earlier example, a cut from Jeff's gaze to irrelevant objects would be a narrational act as much as would a cut to relevant ones. Narration is the dynamic interaction between the syuzhet's transmission of story information and what Tynianov called "the movement, the rise and fall of the stylistic masses."

[. . .]

Throughout my discussion, one particular question may have nagged the reader. I have not referred to the narrator of a film. In what senses can we speak of a narrator as the source of narration?

If a character is presented as recounting story actions in some fashion (telling, recollecting, etc.), as Marlowe does during most of *Murder My Sweet*, the film possesses a character-narrator. Or a person not part of the story world may be identified as the source of parts of the narration. In *Jules and Jim*, a voice-over commentary points up the diegetic world; in *La Ronde*, a *meneur de jeu* appears in flesh and blood to address the audience. Such films contain explicit, noncharacter narrators. But, as Edward Branigan has demonstrated, such personified narrators are invariably swallowed up in the overall narrational process of the film, which they do *not* produce. So the interesting theoretical problem involves an implicit, nonpersonified narrator. Even if no voice or body gets identified as a locus of narration, can we still speak of a narrator as being present in a film? In other words, must we go beyond the process of narration to locate an entity which is its source?

Some theorists believe so. Diegetic theories often identify the narrator as the enunciator, the film's "speaker," but we have already seen that the analogy to speech fails because of the weak correspondences between verbal deixis and the techniques of cinema. Other theorists suggest that the source of narration is akin to Wayne Booth's "implied author." The implied author is the invisible puppeteer, not a speaker or visible presence but the omnipotent artistic figure behind the work. In film, Albert Laffay speaks of *le grand imagier*, the master of images: a fictional and invisible personage who chooses and organizes what we shall perceive. On Laffay's account, at the center of a narrative film stands a ghostly master of ceremonies, invisible twin of the *meneur de jeu* of *La Ronde*.

Since any utterance can be construed with respect to a putative source, literary theory may be justified in looking for a speaking voice or narrator. But in watching films, we are seldom aware of being told something by an entity resembling a human being. Even with the dissective attention of criticism, we cannot construct a narrator for Vidor's film *War and Peace* with the exactitude with which we can assign attributes to the narrator of Tolstoy's original novel. As for the implied author, this construct adds nothing to our understanding of filmic narration. No trait we could assign to an implied author of a film could not more simply be ascribed to the narration itself: it sometimes suppresses information, it often restricts our knowledge, it generates curiosity, it creates a tone, and so on. To give every film a narrator or implied author is to indulge in an anthropomorphic fiction.

There is a fairly important theoretical choice involved here. Literary theories of the implied author, such as Seymour Chatman's, take the process of narration to be grounded in the classic communication diagram: a message is passed from sender to receiver. This has committed theorists to seeking out noncharacter narrators and implied authors, not to mention "narratees" and "implied readers." These entities, especially the latter two, are sometimes very hard to find in a narrative text. I suggest, however, that narration is better understood as the organization of a set of cues for the construction of a story. This presupposes a perceiver, but not any sender, of a message. This scheme allows for the possibility that the *narrational process may sometimes mimic the communication situation more or less fully.* A text's narration may emit cues that suggest a narrator, or a "narratee," or it may not. This explains the range of examples, and the asymmetrical structures, that we often find: some texts do not signal a narrator, or a narratee; others signal one, but not the other. For instance, Robert Bresson's film *Pickpocket* starts with a prologue asserting that the "author" is presenting images and sounds to explain the story. [. . .] This is a way of marking stylistic factors as having an overt, dynamic relation to the syuzhet. Most films, however, do not provide anything like such a definable narrator, and there is no reason to expect they will. On the principle that we ought not to proliferate theoretical entities without need, there is no point in positing communication as the fundamental process of all narration, only to grant that most films "efface" or "conceal" this process. Far better, I think, to give the narrational process the power to signal under certain circumstances that the spectator should construct a narrator. When this occurs, we must recall that this narrator is the product of specific organizational principles, historical factors, and viewers' mental sets. Contrary to what the communication model implies, this sort of narrator does not create the narration; the narration, appealing to historical norms of viewing, creates the narrator. [. . .] We need not build the narrator in on the ground floor of our theory. No purpose is served by assigning every film to a *deus absconditis.*

19

The Cinematic Narrator

Seymour Chatman

The implied author names the convention by which we naturalize the reading experience as a personal encounter with some single, historically identifiable author addressing the public, even if we know nothing about that person's life. But the convention also clearly operates where no such address was intended. Consider, for example, personal diaries, like that of Anne Frank, which were never meant to be seen by anyone other than their authors. We could hardly say that the "real Anne Frank" speaks to the "real us." Clearly, she intended only to speak to herself; still we read the diary as if it addresses us. Narratologically, then, it can only be the implied author of the *Diary* who addresses us.

[. . .]

Turning [. . .] to our modern Babylon, we hear the loud voice of Louis B. Mayer invoking the Holy Book (nothing less) to defend the studio system of film authorship: "If a writer complains about his stuff being changed," commented Arthur Freed, "Mayer always says, 'The Number One book of the ages was written by a committee, and it was called the Bible.'" Though a familiar phenomenon, the collective creations of Hollywood films are likely to be overlooked by narratologists who dwell too exclusively on literary narratives. One well-documented case is *The Red Badge of Courage* (1951), adapted from Stephen Crane's novel and directed by John Huston for MGM. The checkered authorship of this film is particularly interesting, given Huston's usual inclusion in the "pantheon" of *auteurs*.

When *The Red Badge of Courage* opened in New York on August 31, 1951, reviewers treated it as Huston's exclusive achievement. [. . .] Apparently, film critics no less than ordinary readers need to believe in individual and personal, not collective and anonymous, authorship.

That fantasy was dispelled by Lillian Ross's eyewitness account of the making of the film, which appeared in five installments in the *New Yorker* and later as a book titled *Picture*. The facts, as Ross revealed them in pungent detail, were quite otherwise. For one thing, Huston did not have "final cut" or, indeed, any hand in the editing at all. In Hollywood in 1951 it was still customary for directors to give over raw footage to another department of the studio, run by resident editors. This film was edited by Ben Lewis and Margaret Booth, in collaboration with producer Gottfried Reinhardt, after Huston went off to Africa to shoot *The African Queen*. "Editing" in the cinema, it must be remembered, is not merely cutting out excesses but literally assembling the film (as the French say, it is a *montage*). In classical Hollywood production, it is often the editor who decides on such compositional matters as the order of the shots. Imagine a hypothetical literary parallel: one person writes the sentences, and another prunes and arranges them.

Music too was often added to studio films independently of the director's control. Bronislau Kaper, the studio composer who wrote the music for *The Red Badge of Courage*, considered himself not merely a collaborator but a kind of therapist. [. . .] Many others – some less self-impressed about their importance – also contributed to the making of the film, with or without direct instruction from Huston: lighting technicians, set designers, costumers, makeup artists, and the like.

Nor did collaboration end there. To the consternation of MGM, the film inspired negative comments from a sneak-preview audience. Many viewers expressed indifference to the film's antiwar intention, and there was laughter in the wrong places. Fearing a commercial failure, Reinhardt added a voice-over sententiously proclaiming that the film was based on a literary classic, implying that it therefore deserved respect. The voice (that of James Whitmore) was also assigned the task of conveying the protagonist's thoughts, despite Huston's express wish that those thoughts remain implicit in the visuals.

[. . .]

But even voice-over pronouncements of the literary merit of the novel were not enough for Dore Schary, head of production at MGM: he made substantive additional cuts. [. . .] [He] cut the film's original seventy-eight minutes to sixty-nine and rearranged several of its events. As a result, according to Lillian Ross, "the battle sequences added up to an entirely different war from the one that had been fought and photographed at Huston's ranch in the San Fernando Valley." When the audience at the next sneak preview seemed friendlier, however, Schary was confident "that the picture was now a doll. 'Everything is better now, sweetie,' he said to Reinhardt. 'The audience understands this boy now.'"

So, by conservative count, the list of the "real authors" of *The Red Badge of Courage* includes Crane, Huston, Reinhardt, Lewis, Booth, Kaper, and Schary – not to speak of the actors, cinematographer Harold Rosson, designers Cedric Gibbons and Hans Peters, and other production people who made choices about how things should look or sound, with or without Huston's knowledge – plus several hundred Los Angeles moviegoers, to the extent that Dore Schary interpreted their input. These viewers were not some theoretical construct but literal collaborators: their scribbled comments on evaluation cards, collected and nervously interpreted by studio executives, led to a substantial reworking of the film.

Yet despite this motley crew of real authors, the film *The Red Badge of Courage*, for better or worse, gives an impression of unity so strong that reviewers spoke persistently of a single authorial source: it was "Huston's film"; it was Huston who "became discouraged with it," and the like. What they were talking about, of course, was not the real John Huston but the film's implied author.

[. . .]

By its nature, cinema resists traditional language-centered notions of the narrator. Clearly, most films do not "tell" their stories in any usual sense of the word. The counter-intuitiveness of a film's "telling" calls into question "enunciation" theories of cinematic narration. In the 1960s Christian Metz and other film theoreticians, attracted by the success of linguistics, applied linguistic principles to the study of the fiction film. Metz quickly realized, however, that film is not a "language" but another kind of semiotic system with "articulations" of its own. Still, neither he nor other enunciation theorists have succeeded in separating out film's more generally semiotic properties from the linguistic formulas. As David Bordwell has shown, Metz could not, for example, illustrate the utility for film narratology of the linguistic distinction between *histoire* and *discours* drawn by Emile Benveniste.

Among the many critical difficulties of enunciation theory, the most obvious is that verbal activity furnishes no easy analogy with visual activity. Benveniste's theory cannot demonstrate (as Metz suggests) that the camera's "look" constitutes a narration or that the *viewer* somehow becomes the "enunciator."

Bordwell's own theory of film narration is so admirably constructed as to deserve widespread acceptance and extended discussion. My only real criticism is that it goes too far in arguing that film has no agency corresponding to the narrator and that film narrative is best considered as a kind of work wholly performed by the spectator. Bordwell allows for film a "narration" but not a narrator. In a move resembling that of reader-response theorists, he founds his theory squarely on the viewer's activity, seeing in it an act of "construction." From the various cues streaming off the screen and loudspeaker, the audience "constructs" the narrative through intricate hypothesizing, entailing the entire range of mental activity from perception to cognition. Bordwell winnows the literature on visual perception and perspectival systems in art, enriching his findings with sophisticated notions of discourse processing. Bordwell's viewer is not a passive object "positioned" by what happens on the screen but an active participant – indeed, an agent – who virtually creates the film's narration. Utilizing concepts like "schemata" and "templates," Bordwell sketches a persuasive model of what the viewer *does* to turn the flashes and sounds impinging on her attention into a series of perceptible images, which she then interprets as a story.

[. . .]

In my view, it is not that the viewer constructs but that she *reconstructs* the film's narrative (along with other features) from the set of cues encoded in the film. Bordwell admirably describes many of these cues, but he does not explain their mode of existence in the film, only in the viewer. By "mode of existence" I don't mean how some real production team *put* them in the film but how they exist in any projection. The viewer certainly hasn't put them there, so it seems a bit odd to talk about "narration" as if she had.

Bordwell relies on Gérard Genette and Meir Sternberg, but I doubt that either would countenance, for general narratology, a narrative text without a narrator. Though conceding that Sternberg thinks of narrators as "conscious agents," Bordwell believes that film deals only in "processes." He argues that a process can be called, say, "knowledgeable" in the same way that a picture can be called "graceful." There is good reason to agree that a painting or a piece of music or a poem or a film is an "aesthetic object" and that "gracefulness," "cheerfulness," and the like may be said to be among its properties or "aesthetic qualities." But it is one thing to argue that "gracefulness" is a property of an aesthetic object and quite another to make the object, "narration" (rather than the agent, "narrator"), the subject of verbs that *perform* things. Such verbs, by definition, presuppose agency. Objects and processes may have qualities, but only agents can do things. [. . .]

I go into Bordwell's excellent theory in such detail because, except for our differences on the cinematic narrator, it is so close to my own. We both want to argue that film *does* belong in a general narratology; we both want to argue that films are narrated, and not necessarily by a human voice. We differ chiefly in the kind of agency we propose for the narrative transmission. It comes down, as I say, to the difference between "-tion" and "-er."

But there is one other difference, turning on the word "knowledge." In my theory, the narrator communicates all of and only what the implied author provides. How the narrator came to "know" the provided information seems a nonquestion. Without the implied author, it is pointless to talk about "knowledge," even if we substitute "narrator" for "narration." The question is one not of knowing but of how much and what information the cinematic narrator is programmed by the implied author to *present*. Only the implied author can be said to "know," because the implied author has invented it all. For each reading or viewing the implied author invents the narrative, both discourse and story. The cinematic narrator presents what the cinematic implied author requires. Just as it is the implied author who chooses what the adult Pip tells in *Great Expectations*, it is the implied author of *Rear Window* who decides what the "camera" shows "on its own," what it shows as filtered through Jeff's perception, and what it does not show at all. And just as literature has a place for "career-authorship," so does cinema. Indeed, much of *auteurisme* can be better explained as cinematic career-authorship. Part of what Bordwell calls the "transtext" is implicit in the signatures on films: a "Hitchcock" film is likely to entail suspense; an "Antonioni" film is likely to contain *temps mort* holds on bits of the landscape; a "Fellini" film is likely to merge on-screen and commentative music.

Bordwell too readily rejects the need for the concept of cinematic implied authorship, a concept that I find no less vital to cinematic than to general narrative theory. Films, like novels, present phenomena that cannot otherwise be accounted for, such as the discrepancy between what the cinematic narrator presents and what the film as a whole implies. "Unreliable narration," though not frequent, exists in cinema as well as in literature. [. . .] Unreliable narration presents the clearest but not the only case for the implied author. If the sole source of the ostensible story is a narrator, and if we come to believe that the "facts" are not as the narrator presents them, there can only

14 ■ "Jonathan Cooper (Richard Todd) questions his lover, Charlotte Inwood (Marlene Dietrich), concerning the circumstances surrounding her husband's death," from *Stage Fright*.

be some other and overriding source of the story, the source we call the implied author. This possibility exists in the cinema just as much as in literature, though it has not been exercised very often – because, perhaps, the viewing public is not as ready for narrative ironies as is the reading public.

Still there are a few clear-cut examples. The most frequently discussed is Hitchcock's *Stage Fright* (1950). The first half of the film contains a notorious "lying flashback": a false version of a murder is related by Johnny (Richard Todd), an unreliable homodiegetic-narrator. In the first shot we see a frontal view of Johnny and Eve (Jane Wyman) speeding to Eve's father's house. Johnny is saying, "I had to help her [Charlotte Inwood, played by Marlene Dietrich, who has goaded him into murdering her husband]. Anybody would. I was in my kitchen about five o'clock. The door bell rang . . ." Dissolve to what purports to be the "story itself" – Johnny opening the door, then a close-up of Charlotte's bloodstained skirt and Dietrich's voice begging him to help her. Next, Johnny is shown going to Charlotte's home, opening the bedroom door, looking at a poker on the ground near Inwood's corpse, stepping over him, and getting a fresh dress from the closet.

In our first viewing we have no reason to believe that this is not an accurate rendition of events. Only retrospectively, after Johnny admits to Eve his criminal tendency and a previous murder, do we realize that the camera has conspired with Johnny to deceive us, that Johnny's flashback was a lie. Johnny could not have seen Charlotte's husband *already* dead on the floor, because he had killed Inwood himself. Clearly, Johnny *narrates* the first, untrue version of the story, not only in his dialogue with Eve in the car but also *by means of* the ensuing visual sequence. The camera collaborates with, subserves the narrator by misrepresenting, "mis-showing," the facts of the case. Here, seeing is precisely not believing. What we see is literally untrue: it was not the case that Johnny returned for the dress and that he entered the room to see the body already dead. Nor is it the case that "the camera" narrates the false sequence "on its own." Rather, everything that we see and hear follows Johnny's scenario. Thus, even when his voice-over falls silent, he remains the controlling, if unreliable, narrator of the flashback.

So, for this film at least, it does not seem true that "personified narrators are invariably swallowed up in the overall narrational process of the film, which they do *not* produce." At the narrative level, Johnny and Johnny alone "produces" the segment in any narratologically meaningful sense of that word, since every cinematic tool – editing, lighting, commentative music – works to actualize his lie. During these scenes, Johnny prevails over the cinematic narrator. He is "responsible" for the lying images and sounds that we see and hear. Only later does the conventionally reliable cinematic narrator, reappropriating all the cinematic tools, take up the true story. Our judgment that Johnny's version of the story is unreliable depends on our decision that the later version of the story is reliable. And we must acknowledge that this does not happen by chance but is part of a design of communication. Who has invented both the incorrect and the correct versions? Bordwell's theory would have to say "the narration." But which narration, since there are two competing ones? Controlling both narrations there must be a broader textual intent – the implied author. It is the implied author who juxtaposes the two narrations of the story and "allows" us to decide which is true.

In short, in cinema as in literature, the implied author is the agent intrinsic to the story whose responsibility is the overall design – including the decision to communicate it through one or more narrators. Cinematic narrators are transmitting agents of narratives, not their creators. Granted, *Stage Fright* is an unusual movie, but it cannot be ignored in constructing a theory of cinematic narration, for it is precisely the unusual possibility that tests the limits of a theory. A theory of narrative cinema should be able to account not only for the majority of films but also for the narratively odd or problematic ones. Besides, it may well be that unreliable narration will someday become as common in film as it is in the novel.

[. . .]

In short, for films as for novels, we would do well to distinguish between a *presenter* of the story, the narrator (who is a component of the discourse), and the *inventor* of both the story and the discourse (including the narrator): that is, the implied author – not as the original cause, the original biographical person, but rather as the principle within the text to which we assign the inventional tasks.

For if we deny the existence of the implied author and the cinematic narrator, we imply that film narratives are intrinsically different, with respect to a fundamental component, from those actualized in other media. But that implication contradicts the principle that Bordwell himself correctly endorses: namely, that narration is a "process which is not in its basic aims specific to any medium." The substitution of "narration" for "narrator" does not advance Bordwell's desire to find cinema's actualizations of the "more supple principles basic to all narrative representation" (since, presumably, he accepts the existence of "narrators" in literary narratives). It is awkward to a general theory of narrative to say that some texts include the component "narrator" and others do not. As Sarah Kozloff puts it, simply but incisively, "Because narrative films are narrative, someone must be narrating." Or if not necessarily someone, at least something.

Let me recapitulate my conception of the cinematic narrator. Though film theory tends to limit the word "narrator" to the recorded human voice "over" the visual image track, there is a good case to be made for a more general conception of "cinematic narrator." Films, in my view, are always presented – mostly and often exclusively shown, but sometimes partially told – by a narrator or narrators. The overall agent that does the showing I would call the "cinematic narrator." That narrator is not a human being. The *nomina agentis* here refers to "agent," and agents need not be human. It is the cinematic narrator that shows the film, though it may on rare occasions (as in *Stage Fright*) be replaced by one or more "telling" voices on or off the screen.

The cinematic narrator is not to be identified with the voice-over narrator. A voice-over may be one *component* of the total showing, one of the cinematic narrator's devices, but a voice-over narrator's contribution is almost always transitory; rarely does he or she dominate a film the way a literary narrator dominates a novel – that is, by informing every single unit of semiotic representation. The normal state of affairs, and not only in the Hollywood tradition, is for voice-over narrators to speak at the beginning, less frequently at the end, and intermittently (if at all) during the film. Some films do use the technique more extensively. In a few cases the voice-over narrator seems to control the visuals: in *Stage Fright*, *Providence*, and Robert Bresson's *Diary of a Country Priest* (1950), the human narrator's voice dominates, at least in part of the film. In *All About Eve*, Addison De Witt's narration controls the whole introductory set of flashbacks that present the history of Eve's rise in the theater. In the freeze-frame description [. . .] it can reasonably be argued that it is Addison who has frozen the frame, just as he previously tuned out the voice of the old actor presenting the award. In the film's coda, however, after Eve receives the award and goes home, only to find her own little stagestruck groupie waiting to follow in her footsteps, the general cinematic narrator assumes control. At first, then, the image track seems to be the character's construction; that is, the images are at the service of – are an alternative means of communicating – what he says. Later, the general cinematic narrator takes control. But both narrators are the instruments of the implied author.

The cinematic narrator is the composite of a large and complex variety of communicating devices. [. . .]

The different components of the cinematic narrator [. . .] usually work in consort, but sometimes the implied author creates an ironic tension between two of them. It is not uncommon, even in Hollywood films, for the visual track to undercut the story told by a character-narrator's voice-over. In Terence Malick's *Badlands* (1973), for example, the voice of the heroine, Holly, tells a romanticized account of her escapade with the murderer Kit which is totally belied by the sordid action as we see it with our own eyes.

This kind of partial unreliability is unique to two-track media such as the cinema. The disparity is not between what the cinematic narrator says and what the implied author implies but between what is told by one component of the cinematic narrator and shown by another. Whereas in totally unreliable narratives such as *Stage Fright* the conflict must arise through disparities between all the representations of the narrator and what the viewer must infer from the film as a whole, the partially unreliable narration of *Badlands* arises explicitly from a conflict between two mutually contradictory components of the cinematic narrator. Normally, as in *Badlands*, the visual representation is the acceptable one, on the convention that seeing is believing. In theory, at least, the opposite could happen as well – that is, the sound track could be accurate and the visual track unreliable – but in practice, that effect seems very rare; Sarah Kozloff found only one example, in *An American in Paris* (1951). The reason for this imbalance seems fairly obvious. The errant homodiegetic voice-over can easily be understood to have some motive for skewing the events. In *Badlands*, Holly is a naive adolescent, and so we hypothesize that she romanticizes the escapade. After all, she lives in a society so boring that any notoriety, even that of criminals, overrides questions of mere morality. But when the camera is aberrant and the voice-over "straightens it out," the effect is odd and self-conscious. In *An American in Paris*, as each of the three protagonists introduces himself, the camera focuses on the wrong person; the voice-over redirects it. A more usual if weaker case of visual unreliability occurs when the visual track presents a shallow picture of events, which are interpreted with greater profundity by the voice-over narrator; this is the strategy of Bresson's *Diary of a Country Priest* and Stanley Kubrick's *Barry Lyndon* (1975).

There remains a final question about unreliability: does it make any sense to call narrators "unreliable" who are without personality or, as I have called them, "covert"? (This class includes virtually all cinematic narrators and many heterodiegetic narrators of novels and short stories.) It is hard to think of any reason for doing so. Unreliability depends on some clearly discernible discrepancy between the narrator's account and the larger implied meaning of the narrative as a whole. But that discrepancy would seem to depend pretty much on personality: there has to be some *reason* for us to distrust the narrator's account, and the only possible reason would be something in his character. Where there is no character – and hence no motive for giving a questionable account of the story – how can we even recognize that the account is unreliable?

We must remember, finally, that the cinematic apparatus is not always committed to the iconic; sometimes it too employs arbitrary conventions. Obviously, the natural language used in dialogue track, voice-over, or captions is entirely arbitrary. Sometimes a single caption can undercut the hypothesis suggested by all the rest of the film: in Dusan Makaveyev's *Montenegro*, we learn in a caption over the final images that the heroine has just poisoned her whole family. But even the visual track may be noniconic. Say, for example, that the narrator wants to convey the idea that a train trip took a long time. Especially in films of the 1930s, the camera might very well show a montage of overlapping shots of spinning locomotive wheels. From the montage the viewer could infer that the trip took longer than its discourse representation.

20

Narration as Showing

George M. Wilson

In this essay, I will be primarily concerned with the thesis that fiction films presuppose the existence of some narrative-establishing activity of fictional showing. The problems that this claim engenders are surprisingly delicate. Therefore, I will largely leave aside the question that most vexes Chatman and many other writers, i.e., given the assumption that there *is* a presupposed activity of fictional showing, does that imply that there is also a fictional or fictionalized cinematic narrator? I will explore the more restricted topic: is there even a primitive basis for a fictional activity of cinematic narration?

I believe that Chatman does not see how there can be an issue about the existence of fictional showings. He thinks, in effect, that the concept of "a fictional story that is shown" somehow implies the concept of "a fictional showing of the story." Nevertheless, it is doubtful that any such relatively direct connection exists. Grounds for doubt are illustrated by the following rudimentary form of visual representation. Nixon presents, by means of the production of certain hand shadows, a fictional story in which a certain hawk attacks and kills a hapless mole. The hand shadows, occurring in a field of light, depict the hawk, the mole, and their respective actions, and *Nixon* is the agent who actually produces the shadow "text." However, there is no obvious reason to postulate that the hand shadows are themselves the fictional product of some fictional activity of "showing-as-actual" the elements of the depicted tale. Indeed, the very idea that this might be so appears to lack a determinate sense, and, at a minimum, one would want some explanation of and justification for the claim. It is wholly unclear what type of "showing" could be fictionally instanced in such a case. The only showing that appears to be involved in "The Hawk and Mole Story" is the actual showing by Nixon of the pertinent fictional events. In this example at least, the "text" does not instantiate the crucial property of representing and being represented at one and the same time. And yet, it is just this status of the text as both means and object of representation that is basic to the creation of fictional tellings in literary fiction.

The hand shadow example illustrates an important point about the showing of fictional events. If I want to show you what *actually* happened in certain historical circumstances, then I might do so in at least one of two ways. If we are appropriately present at the circumstances in question, I can direct your perceptual attention to the events themselves as they take place. But, alternatively, I might show you the events by displaying to you a picture or series of pictures that visually record, accurately and in enough detail, the historical episode of interest. Similarly, if I want to show you a fictional episode, I can show you a series of fictional events by exhibiting to you a suitable series of pictures in which it is fictional that events of the envisaged kinds take place. My showing you those pictures is sufficient to present the story, and there need not be facts about the pictures, and about the context of their imaginative reception, that make it fictional or make-believe for the viewer that the pictures are the products of some additional "fictional showing." It is for this reason that a special argument needs to be given to justify an inference from "T depicts the fictional incidents in a narrative N" to the conclusion "T involves a fictional showing of the incidents in N."

Similar thoughts apply to the visual presentation of a fictional story in a standard comic strip or comic book, although this case illustrates an additional complication. The story is primarily transmitted by presenting to the reader a sequence of cartoon drawings, each of which depicts a fictional event or situation in the unfolding narrative. Here, as before, it seems that the frames that make up the strip are not imagined to be the upshot of some kind of fictional showing. As in the hand shadow example, it is doubtful that there are any general grounds for positing such a fictional showing and obscure what sort of activity one could be positing. However, we should not state the conclusion too broadly. It is easy to think of possible comic strips in which a fictional showing would be implicated. The frames of the comic strip could be rendered in such a fashion that they are themselves represented as being, say, photographs taken by a witness to the events depicted. Going a step further, one can conceive of ways in which the represented character of the frames and the nature of their selection could convey fictional facts about the personality and sensibility of the "implied" photographer. In this example, there plainly is a fictional activity of showing the story that the viewer is to imagine, i.e., the fictional activity of taking and assembling the photographs. And here there *is* a fictional agent of that activity, i.e., the fictional eyewitness and photographer. Various other more subtle and sophisticated strategies would give rise to analogous fictional results.

The example of comic strips suggests a couple of cautionary morals. First, we should not ask, in the absence of further qualification, whether showings of fictional stories do or do not engender fictional showings or (visual) presentings. The answer is: some do and some do not. Moreover, the same mixed answer generally holds for narrower categories of texts, e.g., the comic strip. Second, when a text that shows its fictional story does involve a fictional showing, it does so in virtue of some relatively clear-cut representational strategy implicit in and appropriate to the imaginative context of the text's reception. Detailed facts about the particular nature of the text and facts about the proper mode of apprehending that text serve to prompt us to imagine about the text that it is the product of an appropriate kind of fictional showing. Naturally, in the case of writing and reading works of literary fiction, the basic components of the implicit representational strategies are highly familiar, ubiquitously deployed, and almost automatically invoked for the reader on the basis of pretty minimal cues. But in other cases – the comic strip is a good example of this – rather special strategies of implicit representation of the text have to be more distinctly set in place.

These conclusions would not be accepted by Chatman, and there is a line of argument against them which is hinted at in some of his discussions. Consider, for example, these remarks: "[W]e must avoid the metaphor that the camera 'sees' *the events and existents in the story world* [my emphasis] at such and such a distance, from such and such an angle. Rather it *presents* them at those distances and angles." Or a bit later: "The convention [in fiction films] is that the particular rectangle of visible material constitutes a 'favored view,' a selection of the implied author which the cinematic narrator is delegated to present." The import of these and related passages is murky, but I believe that we can articulate the basic idea behind them in the following fashion.

First, we are concerned with cases in which a fictional story has been shown by means of a text which either is a single picture or consists of a series of pictures. Let us suppose, in addition, that we are dealing with visual representations that determine an implied vantage point upon the scene. That is, we suppose that these are visual representations each of which determine a position in the implied space of the picture, a position such that the scene depicted is represented as if viewed from that fictional location. This added supposition will cover all of the cases with which we will henceforth be investigating. When we are looking at "perspectival" representations of this sort, viewers normally imagine and are intended to imagine seeing the objects and events depicted in the image, and, moreover, they imagine seeing these contents from a reasonably distinctive visual perspective.

Second, from these suppositions we can construct the relevant argument as follows. In imagining that they actually see the depicted scene, a part of what viewers thereby imagine is that the contents of the scene are being displayed or exhibited to their perception. In the case of fiction film, they imagine the movie shots before them as offering a perspectival view of those contents, and it is the function of the shots to prescribe an imagining of this kind. So, it is in this sense that the shots of a film *present* a view of or perspective on some spatio-temporal slice of the "story world" and *show* us what that view contains. Of course, it is only a fiction that "the events and existents" in that world have been presented and shown in this manner. Both the constituents of the story and the visual exhibition of them are fictional constructions of the work, although the items thus presented belong to the world of the narrative while the "presentings" of them belong to the "world" of the narration. Still, these considerations should be enough to convince us that fiction films *do* incorporate a series of "fictional showings" in their narration, i.e., the fictional presentation of views of characters, actions, and circumstances which are themselves merely fictional. This argument, if correct, would demonstrate that any or almost any showing of a fictional scene or story involves a fictional showing (to the viewer) of the represented elements. Moreover, given the generality of the considerations deployed in the argument, it should work for comic strips as well and would undercut the remarks I made earlier.

[. . .] Let us call this proposal "the Fictional Showing Hypothesis."

[. . .]

After all, if it is fictional for the viewer that she is seeing a scene in the story, then, apparently, it should be correlatively fictional for her that the items in the scene are located, at a viewable distance and a suitable angle, before her gaze. This means, in other words, that it is fictional in her perceptual game of make-believe that she has somehow been situated in the picture's implied space and has had her visual attention directed from that vantage point to the objects and events that it encompasses. On this interpretation, the work of the film narration (in its visual dimension) is to effect a fictional placing of the scene in front of the viewer's receptive and attentive eyes so that she may see it from just that place. Naturally, it is not fictional *in the work* that the viewer occupies such a position and is present as an observer on the scene. It is fictional only in the viewer's imaginative perceptual engagement with the film that this is so. I will call this interpretation "the Face to Face Version" of the Fictional Showing Hypothesis. [. . .]

The Face to Face Version is, however, implausible. It is true that when people actually see a scene from a certain visual perspective, they are, in fact, located in a position which, given the circumstances, offers them that perspective. But it does not follow that if a person *imagines* seeing a scene from a certain perspective, then he thereby also imagines being at a place which offers him that view. Similarly, when, in viewing a perspectival visual representation, a person imagines seeing a scene from the visual perspective established by the pictorial field, he usually does not imagine himself occupying a point in the picture's implied space that would yield this visual per-spective and seeing the scene from that place. As a rule, I think that it is false that we ordinarily imagine ourselves being anywhere in the depicted or implied space of the image. [. . .] In general, when one views a movie, one does not imagine oneself to be present within the depicted and/or off-screen space of the story.

[. . .]

In looking at a picture, the viewer imagines having a veridical visual experience of the items in a certain scene, and those elements, as the viewer imagines seeing them, have what [Gregory] Currie here calls "a perspectival structure." That is, various of the items are presented as foreshortened, as overlapping one another, and as having appropriate relative occlusion sizes. Thus, the viewer imagines seeing the scene from the visual perspective defined by that network of properties and relations. The visual perspective may well be the one a viewer would or might have if he were located at a certain site in relation to that scene, but the identity of a perspectival view is not constituted by its relation to a vantage point from which it could have been secured. Hence, the question is: Can one imagine seeing the scene from a specified perspective without imagining that one is at the vantage point and obtaining his visual perspective from that position? [. . .] The question here is a complex one and deserves more space than I can give it, but the following reflections provide grounds for answering it in the affirmative.

Just as I can imagine romping in the buff on Neptune without imagining anything about how I came to do so or about what makes it possible for me to be dancing on that distant planet, so also I can imagine having a (veridical) visual experience of a scene without imagining anything about how I came to have the experience or about what enables me to have it. In particular, I may imagine nothing about whether I am having that experience *because* I am situated face to face with what I see. These further matters, normally essential either to visiting other planets or to seeing a scene, are simply left *indeterminate* in my imagining.

Perhaps the following thought experiment will help to establish that the concept of "visual experience from an unoccupied perspective" is at least minimally coherent. We seek to conceive of *one* way in which I might imagine seeing a scene from a certain visual perspective without imagining, as part of this, that I am seeing from the implied vantage point. (1) I can imagine in detail the qualitative and perspectival character of the kind of visual experience I would (or might) have if I were to look at a scene S from a "face to face" position P. (2) I can imagine having a visual experience of just that character while imagining that I am *not*, as I have the experience, situated at the vantage point P. Maybe, in the broader context of my imagining, I imagine that a devious neurophysiologist is causing me to have that very visual experience while I am sitting in his laboratory. (3) Finally, I can imagine having this same experience while, nevertheless, imagining of the experience that it constitutes an instance of my *seeing* S. Thus, it may be a part of the broader context of my imagining, that the processes whereby the neurophysiologist induces this visual experience (and others) in me are such that my having the visual experiences he produces count as a kind of "prosthetic" seeing of S and other scenes. Here, then, is a case in which I imagine myself seeing a scene from an unoccupied visual perspective.

I hasten to add that in ordinary cases when we imagine having a visual experience from an unoccupied perspective, my imaginings are *not* contextualized in this manner. First, I do not imagine that I am *not* at P – imaginatively, it is indeterminate where, if anywhere, I am. And, second, I do not imagine anything about the causes and conditions of my having the relevant visual experience – it is imaginatively indeterminate how this came about. Still, the fact that all these important matters are left indeterminate in what I imagine does not preclude me from imagining seeing S from a P-like perspective while I am not at P. The content of such an imagining has the same kind of minimal coherence as the content "running naked on the surface of Neptune," and each content specifies something I can imagine.

Similarly, when looking at a representational picture, we usually imagine having a (veridical) visual experience of the scene depicted, where the qualitative and perspectival character of the experience corresponds in detail to the pictorial field of the picture we are viewing. And we do this without imagining that we are somehow present at the vantage point in the picture. As before, we can imagine this perception from an unoccupied perspective because we imagine nothing about the potential fictional circumstances that would have enabled us to have the visual experience we imagine. Of course, we know a great deal about what it is before our eyes which is actually cueing our experience. The pictorial field prompts and guides our imagining of the visual experience (e.g., determines a certain perspectival structure for it) without establishing much of anything about the causal conditions of the imagined experience. This, I believe, is the standard case when we view perspectival visual representations.

It is the *standard* case, but not the only one possible. For it *is* possible for a perspectival image (a painting, say) to lead the viewer to imagine himself being at the vantage point in the picture and seeing from that place. The artistic strategies that are meant to elicit such an imagining are not frequently deployed, but when they are, they represent an important aspect of how we comprehend the visual significance that the painting offers us. Richard Wollheim, in *Painting as an Art*, describes a class of paintings that involve what he calls "internal spectators," and it partially defines the class that these paintings are visually and dramatically so constituted that they are intended to induce the spectator into imagining himself at the vantage point in the picture. Wollheim carefully delineates the different ways that various classic paintings rely upon the imaginative endeavor in question. For example, he argues that Manet's *Bar aux Folies-Bergère* is a striking instance of the category. A viewer of the painting is encouraged by a panoply of its key features to imagine himself as standing before the bar and as seeing the barmaid with her eyes averted from him. However, one can also conceive of a painting, broadly similar to the Manet both in subject matter and angle of depiction, in which we imagine seeing the barmaid standing behind the bar with her averted eyes, but one for which we have no inclination and are not meant to have any inclination to imagine *ourselves* standing in front of the bar. This example and others like it underscore the point that, in looking at a perspectival representation, imagining seeing a scene from a visual perspective is one kind of imaginative achievement, while imagining seeing from the picture's vantage point is of a different and somewhat more complicated kind. [. . .]

   [. . .]

It is natural, especially for philosophers, to feel discomfort with the position outlined above. Let Q be a possible condition whose realization is obviously essential for it to be the case that P. I have claimed that it is possible for it to be fictional, in a work or game of make-believe, that P, despite the fact that it is not fictional in either the work or game that Q. Worse yet, it can be fictional that P even though, if we were to take the first steps toward imagining how P could have come about, then the supplemented fiction would be paradoxical or otherwise incoherent. Troubling as these claims may be, I think that we will have to learn to live with the discomfort. Kendall Walton has done a lot to support this somewhat severe prescription.

   It is not at all uncommon for it to be fictional for a reader or viewer that she is F-ing and not fictional for her that she is in condition G, even though being in G is obviously required as means to make it possible for her to F. In other words, what she imagines is *merely* minimally coherent. In many "Old Dark House" movies, it is fictional that the ghosts are completely invisible to human eyes, but audience members imagine seeing them as glowing, diaphanous creatures gliding among the furniture. Still, it is no part of the viewers' imaginings that they have special powers that permit them, unlike other human beings, to see ghosts. There are numerous similar examples, but I suspect that the threat of imminent paradox looms as most threatening when the coherence of the foundations of representational and/or narrational practices appear to be at risk – as in the domain of perspectival pictures discussed before. However, the tensions which exist in that case are hardly unique.

When a person reads the text of a work of literary fiction, she imagines herself to be reading the very words (word types) that fictionally were produced by the narrator of the tale. But paradox or incoherence easily impinges in this case also. To illustrate, we begin with what is admittedly a special kind of example, i.e., cases in which the reader imagines herself reading the narrator's own words despite the fact that there are propositions fictional in the work which imply that this should be fictionally impossible for her to do so. Thus, it might be fictional for the reader that she is reading the narrator's diary even though it is clearly indicated, at the end of the work, that this diary must have been consumed in a story-culminating fire. When a reader steps back from the fiction and focuses upon the relevant facts, the situation will strike her as paradoxical. But in the course of reading the work, this same reader is likely to ignore or discount the conflict, and she surely will not stop imagining that what she is reading are the words of the diarist/narrator.

A more common and more subtle conflict of narrational background assumptions is the following. Again, it is usually fictional for the reader that the words she is reading were produced by the narrator, but it is often fictionally indeterminate how those words were initially produced by that narrator. That is, it is indeterminate whether fictionally the narrator originally uttered them out loud or only in his mind or, alternatively, set them down in writing. Moreover, in these same cases, it will also be fictionally indeterminate for the reader how those words came to be *transmitted* to her or to a readership in general. Nothing will fictionally connect an original production by the narrator of the words (whatever mode of production may have been involved) with the appearance "in print" of the text of which the narrator's activity is fictionally the source. The reader will imagine nothing whatsoever about how the words came to be transcribed into a publicly distributed version. Thus, the reader imagines reading a transcription of the narrator's own utterances or inscriptions, but her imagination does not specify anything about what makes it possible for her to do this. Fictionally, it is indeterminate how the reader can be acquainted, as she is, with the product of the narrator's storytelling performance.

Such indeterminacies at the core of the fictions that ground some types of literary narration open up the possibility that a related indeterminacy underlies our fictional perception of narrative events in film and that it does so deeply and extensively. This possibility suggests in turn a serious challenge to the *overall* approach of the Fictional Showing Hypothesis. Chatman holds, and I have agreed with this, that it is fictional for movie viewers that they imagine seeing (on screen) the fictional activities of the characters portrayed. This fundamental fact, they conclude, implies that it is fictional for the viewer that the movie's image track is the product of an "activity" that somehow enables the viewer to see the narrative fictions. I have rejected the Face to Face Version of the Fictional Showing Hypothesis which says that the fictional activity of perceptual enabling is achieved by situating the viewer face to face with the story scenes. But now, our recent discussion demonstrates that it could be altogether fictionally indeterminate for movie viewers what, if anything, permits them to see episodes in cinematic worlds. There needs to be an argument to establish that such a fictional enabling activity is to be recognized as part of the work, an argument to rule out the hypothesis that audiences imagine seeing movie fictions without being expected to imagine a means by which such seeing would be achieved. Chatman supplies the missing argument.

So far, then, we have no plausible reason for supposing that the showing of a fictional film story involves the fictional showing of the events related in the film. However, we have, in this discussion, bypassed an obvious dimension of fiction film which is potentially crucial to the topic. We have concentrated on the fact that cinematic images in fiction films depict fictional characters and situations, but we have ignored the fact that they do this by showing us actors and actresses in real places – cast members who play the characters and places that represent the narrative locales. If we factor in this extra dimension, an alternative conception emerges of what narration in fiction films might be.

Our discourse about movies wavers between reference to shots which are *of* the cast and their performances and reference to shots said to be *of* the characters and the fictional actions they perform. Normally, these vacillating forms of description cause no confusion, but plainly there is an ambiguity in our talk about the "content" of shots in fiction film. Let us signal the rough distinction by saying that a shot is a *motion picture shot* of the actual objects and events before the camera and that the same shot is a *movie story shot* of the fictional characters and their fictional behavior. Naturally, any movie story shot (in a given film) is also a motion picture shot, but not conversely. In fact, let X be a shot in movie M, a shot in which it is fictional that a certain character C performs an action A. Shot X, in M, is also a motion picture shot of the actor who portrays C making the movements that represent the action A. But, if X were edited into a documentary, *The Making of Movie M*, then, in the altered context, it would not be a movie story shot in which C does A. It would merely be a motion picture shot of the actor in the course of playing C. It is not a simple task to give an adequate positive account of the further conditions required for such a motion picture shot to be, in the full sense, a movie story shot, and I will not try to construct one here. Intuitively, a movie story shot is one which has as a primary function, in its filmic context, the role of making it fictional in the movie that P, where its being fictional that P sustains or elaborates the movie's narrative progression.

In any case, we start with the following proposal. If X is a movie story shot in M of a fictional scene S, then *it is fictional for the viewer of M* that X is a motion picture shot of that same scene S. In other words, it is fictionally for the viewer as if the scene S actually took place, there exist motion picture shots of S, and X, as it occurs in M, is one of these. Viewers imagine that the events of the fictional narrative have been registered directly, without dramatic mediation, and that these events are exhibited to us "on screen" in the projection of the film.

There are many potential questions about how exactly this proposal is to be construed, but let us set them aside for now. We have here the basis for an alternative account of the type of narrational activity which movies might implicitly invoke. That is, the fictional showing involved in a fiction film would be the fictional exhibition and sequential arrangement, by means of editing, of *motion picture shots* of the occurrences that constitute the story. On this view, although an image track actually consists, as we well know, of a selection of motion picture shots of actors and actresses acting, we imagine and are intended to imagine that we are shown a selection of motion picture shots of fictional characters and their deeds. If one hears an echo of Metz in all of this, the fact is not surprising. Our new alternative sounds like a description of the business his great image-maker regularly conducts.

If one further aesthetic component were added to the proposal, the result would be, so to speak, a "Mediated Version" of the Fictional Showing Hypothesis. Suppose that we accept the thesis, developed and defended by Kendall Walton, that still photographs and motion picture shots are *transparent*. Walton argues that, in seeing, e.g., a motion picture shot of a real scene S, viewers actually *see* the photographed scene, although, naturally, they see S in a rather special, mediated way; they see S *through* or *by means of* the motion picture photographs. Just as an observer can see a scene by means of mirrors or through a telescope or on live TV, so, in the same natural sense of the word, viewers see photographed objects and events through or by means of photographs. If the transparency of photography is genuine, then our new account of the nature of film narration entails that when a viewer sees a movie story shot of a (fictional) scene S, then it is thereby fictional for her that she is actually seeing S by means of a motion picture shot. Thus, the presentation and ordering of actual motion picture shots in a fiction film have the function of fictionally enabling the viewer to see the progression of the fictional narrative, albeit to see this "photographically."

[. . .]

The Mediated Version of the Fictional Showing Hypothesis offers a novel account of the primitive basis of cinematic narration, and it deserves to be investigated thoroughly. It will be hard to make a serious assessment of the position unless and until it is more fully stated and imbedded in a larger, multifaceted theory of how movies present fictional narratives. As it has been stated above, this version only tells us something about how we imaginatively construe motion picture images in movies. That hardly counts as an explication of the purported activity of visual presentation of film stories.

A more or less random series of events does not constitute a narrative, and a series of movie shots depicting a mélange of unconnected events does not constitute a narration. But the Mediated Version focuses on individual shots and does not address the question of how they come to show an articulated story. The little that has been said in this connection about, for instance, film editing is extremely general and relatively insubstantial. According to the Mediated Version, editing in fiction films is construed by the viewer as a selection and arrangement of motion picture shots of fictional scenes. However, there are several kinds of editing transitions (straight cut, fade, dissolve, etc.), and there are many distinctive structures of editing employed in whole sequences and larger units. It needs to be shown that the Mediated Version allows us to make good sense of how viewers imagine the storytelling patterns that these devices help establish for them. For that matter, something would have to be said about the imaginative effects of camera movement within a single shot. Moreover, even if we assume that the Mediated Version adapts successfully to the presentation of diegetic sound, that adapted account will have to be extended, in some form, to fit soundtrack music and voice-over narration. In fact, the use of intertitles and other written documents in film would need to be considered here as well. A genuine analysis of cinematic narration based on the Mediated Version calls for careful elaboration and defense.

Nevertheless, even the limited proposal we have before us has significant attractions. We have seen that it avoids the implausibilities of the Face to Face Version without denying that movie audiences imagine seeing the fictional action on screen. It does not ask us to believe that we *actually* see the movie fictions (just as we see the actual motion picture shots), through a kind of magical window that opens, from the theater, onto the fictional prospects of the story. Film theorists have been tempted by all these options and by others, but each of them has led pretty directly to conceptual disaster. The Mediated Version promises, at a minimum, to hold the more familiar disasters at bay.

In trying to work out a full-scale theory of cinematic narration, various authors have embraced various theses about how we imagine motion picture shots in fiction films. According to the Face to Face Version, we imagine movie images as objective views of fictional situations perceived from an internal vantage point. Semioticians have tended to treat movie shots as statements which are iconically encoded. Others have favored the idea that the image track implicitly represents the visual experience of a camera observer. And, finally, in recent theory, the shot is often described as if it were a kind of subjectless apparition – a mirage-like visual field – with which the spectator "identifies" in fantasy-driven perception. Compared with any of these, the Mediated Version gives a rather deflationary account. "No," it replies, "we imagine motion picture shots as motion picture shots [or as naturally iconic images], but as motion picture shots for which the fictions they construct are real."

Part VI

Can Films Be Socially Critical?

Introduction

When you go to a Hollywood-produced movie, do you expect to see a film that un-critically endorses the American way of life and value system? If you want to see films that prompt reflection on social issues, do you avoid the cinemaplex and head to the local film "art house" for its latest re-run of the Italian neo-realism classic, *The Bicycle Thief* (*Ladri di biciclette*) (Vittorio De Sica, 1948)? Or do you find yourself critical of the stereotypes regarding gender and race that are sometimes seen in Hollywood films? If so, you have some good philosophical company. This critical view of mainstream narrative cinema was advanced by Frankfurt school philosophers Theodor Adorno and Max Horkheimer, who coined the tern "culture industry" to refer to a vast complex of social institutions, including the film industry, dedicated to the domination of nature in the interest of commercial profit. Many interpret Horkheimer and Adorno to mean that cinema that is produced by the culture industry is mere escapist entertainment that cannot inspire viewers to reflect seriously on social issues.

Horkheimer and Adorno's analysis raises questions. Can films be socially thought-provoking? Is there something about Hollywood-produced film — either related to its context of production or to its filmmaking practices — that positions it to be a purveyor of the dominant social viewpoint? Are the filmmaking strategies favored by Hollywood, Inc. not conducive to prompting reflection on social concerns?

The essays in Part VI address these issues. In their own way each essay departs from the received wisdom that Hollywood movies — due to their narrative and representational strategies and mode of production — cannot prompt viewers to engage in critical reflection on matters of social concern. Horkheimer and Adorno argued that the only kind of art that escapes control by the culture industry is avant-garde art. In contrast, the authors in this section look at the possibility that critical reflection on social matters can be achieved through the study of the filmic practices employed in more conventional Hollywood movies.

Marxist critics Michael Ryan and Douglas Kellner ask: What is it that makes a film politically progressive? Does a progressive film have a certain non-mainstream, formal structure? Some film critics have argued that a film's political message is inherently conservative if the film uses the traditional filmmaking practices, such as emotional engagement with a central protagonist, typical of Hollywood narrative film. Ryan and Kellner respond that this view ignores the importance of a film's form *and* content in challenging the dominant figures of thought, value, and action associated with the political right. Further, they worry that the more austere aesthetics often employed in independently produced films (for example, the films of French director Jean-Luc Godard mentioned in the introduction to Part I) can get in the way of engaging a mass audience in reflections on the problems with a capitalist way of life.

To illustrate these ideas, Ryan and Kellner look at a wide spectrum of film and filmmakers on the political left. An interesting case is the work of director Robert Altman. The filmmaking practices Altman employs require more attention than those utilized in classic Hollywood narrative film; for his films promote engagement with multiple characters and use narrative discontinuities to distance the audience from the depicted characters and events. Yet Ryan and Kellner note that what is missing from Altman's films is a wider progressive vision that shows the viewer the connections between the problems with the lives depicted and the underlying social institutions of American society.

On the other hand, Ryan and Kellner use the example of *Missing* (Costa-Garvas, 1982) to suggest that a film with a more conventional Hollywood narrative can be extremely successful in shaking up established political beliefs and convictions. Radical avant-garde filmmakers would be critical of the film's use of sympathetic engagement with the two central characters to foster a critical awareness of American involvement in the overthrow of the democratically elected, socialist President Allende of Chile in 1973. Yet Ryan and Kellner note that the film was highly successful in getting audiences to reconsider their views on US foreign policy. The authors end with a discussion on the importance of not prejudging which narrative and representational strategies will be useful in prompting critical awareness of social issues in the audience.

In his contribution, Thomas E. Wartenberg takes a look at the popular, but also widely criticized, civil rights era movie, *Guess Who's Coming to Dinner* (Stanley Kramer, 1967). This story of an interracial romance between an African-American doctor, John Prentice, and a young, white woman, Christina Drayton, received a critical response, especially from African-Americans, who objected that the extraordinary character of the African-American male lead undermined the film's endorsement of interracial marriage. Does an African-American male have to be a superstar in order to be an acceptable partner for a white woman, critics asked? While seeing some merit with the film's political ambitions, Wartenberg analyzes the way in which the film's narrative and representations are at odds with its goal of providing a critical examination of the contradictions in the political views of white liberals who sought integration in the 1960s.

First, Wartenberg argues that the film relies on a naive view of racism as an attitude of prejudice based on skin color. This understanding ignores a more complex analysis of racism as a system of social structures that extend privilege and power to members of one racial group over another. Further, the film represents racism as the effect of prejudices that will die out as one generation succeeds another. This misrepresents the need for the social activism of the civil rights movement in order to dismantle racism.

Second, the filmmakers attempt to distinguish the character of John from the racist representations in film of African-American male sexuality, going all the way back to D. W. Griffith's film, *Birth of a Nation* (1915). But in doing so, Wartenberg argues, the film undermines the representation of the young couple as passionately in love with one another, making the couple's reason for wanting to marry in spite of social disapproval unbelievable. Wartenberg's discussion shows the critical potential of a mainstream film like *Guess Who's Coming to Dinner* to examine the issue of race and integration. But his essay also shows how the film's critical potential is contained through a desire to achieve popular success with a white film audience who may not want their beliefs about racism and their role in supporting it critically challenged.

In chapter 23, in an essay written specially for this volume, Angela Curran takes a look at a classic film melodrama, *Stella Dallas* (King Vidor, 1937), to discuss the possibilities that film melodrama offers for critical reflection on the social issues of the day. This film has engaged feminist film critics, who have examined the film's representation of Stella Dallas as a woman who must reconcile her desires for her own life with her role as a good mother. But it is the representation of the ambition of Stella to rise from the working class to the upper class that is the focus of Curran's discussion. Some might argue that the film's depiction of social ascent as a desirable goal seems to be uncritical, leaving little room for reflection on the social transformation of the working class, especially the newly arrived immigrant groups, into the middle and upper classes that was taking place at the time *Stella Dallas* was made. But Curran argues that the film offers the possibility for critical reflection on the social phenomenon of class ascent, in spite of the representation of Stella as a woman who is just not suited to make the transition to the life of the upper class she longs for.

First, Curran discusses how the film alternates between showing that Stella's class ascent is untenable and showing that the upper-class characters who judge her unfit for their social milieu misjudge her character and disposition. In this way, the film sets up a tension between the narrative representation of Stella's class ascent as unsustainable and the emotional engagement with Stella as a sympathetic and morally admirable character. Drawing on Aristotle's *Rhetoric*, Curran argues that the emotional engagement with Stella undercuts the judgment that she is not fit for the class ascent she desires. This leaves a critical space for the viewer to question the treatment of Stella as unworthy of achieving her social ambitions, in spite of the film's representations of Stella to the contrary. Second, Curran examines how the film reflects on the role that the movies play as a "dream factory" in shaping the desires for upward mobility. In one way, *Stella Dallas* is uncritical in that it seems to accept class-ascent as a worthy goal and then shows how movies can facilitate a desire for upward mobility among the working class. On the other hand, the film's ending, with its separation of mother and daughter, also makes clear that class ascent can only be achieved through the rupturing of family ties and connections. Rather than providing an uncritical endorsement of class ascent as an unquestioned good, Curran concludes that the film offers the viewer possibilities for critical reflection on the value of upward mobility and the role that movies play in furthering this social phenomenon.

Study Questions

1. What criticisms have leftists raised regarding Hollywood films? How do left and right view the categories of the individual, society, and history differently?
2. What makes for progressive filmmaking practices, on Ryan and Kellner's view? What are some films they discuss that embody some of these practices?
3. Why is it hard for a filmmaker like Robert Altman to make progressive Hollywood-produced movies, according to Ryan and Kellner? What, on the other hand, do they see as the problems that arise for independently produced films that deny audiences the pleasures of more conventional narrative story telling?
4. How does *Guess Who's Coming to Dinner* understand or represent racism? What are Wartenberg's criticisms of this way of representing racism? Why does he argue that this way of representing racism is at odds with the film's narrative strategy of criticizing the hypocrisies of political liberalism?
5. How does the film represent the process of integration, according to Wartenberg? Why does he argue that this representation is at odds with the historical realities of how the civil right movement achieved integration?
6. Overall, why does Wartenberg fault the film for failing to prompt white viewers to think critically about the source of racism? How does he account for or explain this failure? Do you agree with his assessment?
7. What scenes in *Stella Dallas* represent Stella as unfit for class ascent? Do you agree with Curran that this representation of Stella is in tension with the sympathy that the scenes that follow elicit for Stella?
8. What scenes illustrate the idea that the movies have shaped Stella's desire for class ascent? Do you think that by the end of the film Stella has come to be more critical of her desire to join the upper class?
9. Does emotional engagement with Stella further or inhibit critical reflection on the social phenomena of class ascent the film depicts?

21

The Politics of Representation

Michael Ryan and Douglas Kellner

In this chapter we will consider the work of several filmmakers who have tried to operate from a leftist perspective within Hollywood, and we will compare it with the work of radical independent filmmakers. We will be concerned particularly with the ways in which progressives attempt to recast the dominant representational codes, so that the form of film as well as its content promotes radical alternatives. Form, or means of representation, as much as the content of film, needs to be transformed because the prevailing patterns of thought, perception, and behavior that help sustain capitalism and patriarchy are determined, we would argue, by representations, the dominant forms or modes through which people experience the world. Whether one represents the history of the United States as an epic of realized destiny or as a series of only contiguously related episodes of alternating idealism and brutality makes a difference for how one acts in the world. In addition, socialism would imply a new *form* of life, a new (more democratic and egalitarian) *style* of social organization, which would be inseparable from different modes of representation. If the maintenance of capitalism is dependent on the prevalence of cultural representations that construct a shared social reality, then the development of socialism necessitates different cultural representations, different forms or ways of constructing the world and a sense of one's place in it. If current representations position women as passive objects, blacks as dancers and comics, and poor people as somehow inferior to white male businessmen, then a more egalitarian social arrangement would require different representations.

Form inheres in the very substance of social life. Form not only determines cognition, how one experiences the world; it also determines the shape of social institutions, practices, and values. Morality is a question of ways of being, modes of action, and forms of behavior. And the same can be said of politics, economics, or psychology. The political struggle between Left and Right comes down to a contest over the shape of life, the form it will take. The form of Hollywood film has in recent years come to be characterized as inherently ideological because it tends invariably to reinforce the dominant forms of patriarchal and capitalist life. We differ from the common characterization of this ideological procedure in that we see it not as a matter of cognition, the positioning of spectators as spuriously self-identical, specular subjects who are lured into an imaginary identification that is inherently ideological. Rather, Hollywood forms are in our view ideological because they replicate the figures and narratives that constitute the very substance of those values, practices, and institutions that shape a society of domination.

Spectatorial cognition is merely the end result of a broad process of rhetorical replication whereby those grounding figures of the society (the narrative of individual success, the metaphor of freedom, the synecdochic privileging of efficiency over democracy [. . .] are transcoded into specifically cinematic forms – the male quest narrative, the camera positions of individuated identification, the domestic *mise-en-scène*, [. . .] and so on. Rather than disable the question of form, this reconceptualization of ideology gives it even more force as a required concern of a reconstructive politics. [. . .] Our argument will be that while such work is necessary for a broader project of reshaping the grounding figures of society, it misses the mark by concentrating on the phenomenal consciousness of film viewing. It may be more important to accept the viewing assumptions of narrative realism in order to be better able to change the dominant figures of thought, value, and action that are the substance of society. Instead of only different camera angles, editing techniques, or framing devices which rupture realist narratives, also different character representations, different plot strategies, different moral configurations, different tropes of actions, etc., within the frame of realist narrative. These things are also matters of form, and they go more to the heart of those forms that constitute society as a set of material figures and practices than do the cognitivist forms of the phenomenology of film viewing. We will argue, therefore, that while such modernist formal revisions are essential, they can also get in the way of gaining access to popular audiences in ways that work to reshape the dominant figures and narratives of patriarchal capitalist social life.

1. On the Left Edge of Hollywood

The radical film avant-garde argues that films with leftist content are conservative if they use traditional Hollywood representational forms. Some would push this argument further and argue that only modernist non-Hollywood forms are "progressive." This leaves open the question of what a "progressive text" is. Is a film with conservative content in a modernist form a progressive film? The trouble with this position is that it ignores the role of modernism in cultural history, where it was frequently (as in Eliot and Pound) allied with reactionary politics. Modernist form alone, without a leftist content, is not necessarily progressive. Indeed, [. . .] modernist forms can be welded to quite conservative thematics. A purely formal criterion of progressive politics in film also ignores crucial substantive issues of race and gender. Feminist and non-white progressive texts may operate under a different set of exigencies altogether.

The ideal would seem to be films that are both thematically leftist and formally modernist. But the criterion for judging such matters should be pragmatic, one that measures the progressive character of a text according to how well it accomplishes its task in specific contexts of reception. What counts as progressive varies with time and situation, and what works in one era or context might fail in another. Moreover, the notion of progressive is always differentially or relationally determined. Something is always progressive in relation to something else. Modernist texts tended to be progressive in comparison to the stultifying and ideological bourgeois realism of the late nineteenth and early twentieth centuries (Bennett, Galsworthy, etc.), but as modernism itself became detached from social concerns and became a marketable commodity in the world of art, modernism as such was no longer progressive.

While the idea of the progressive text is variable, it is not entirely indeterminate. Certain uses of certain forms are ideological – camera techniques that suggest natural hierarchies, spectacles that idealize violence as a solution to social problems, voyeuristic objectifications that debase others. The ideal would seem to be forms that provoke critical thought regarding the world, that associate pleasure with egalitarian and empathetic social procedures, that link narrative resolution to ideals of justice purged of militarist and chauvinist themes, etc. – a mix of the best of modernism and classical realism.

Such an ideal is difficult to attain within the Hollywood frame, as we see in the case of Robert Altman. [. . .]

[. . .]

[. . .] The trouble with Altman is that he was so successful that he managed to work his way out of Hollywood altogether. Thus, although he may prove how possible it is to do radical work within the Hollywood representational system, his case may also prove how impossible it is to remain within that system if you become too radical. Altman's work is distinguished by the fact that he operates both on the plane of generic and action conventions and on the plane of image, narrative, and character formatting. His early seventies films (*M*A*S*H*, 1970, *Brewster McCloud*, 1970, and *McCabe and Mrs. Miller*, 1971) subvert the traditional war and western generic conventions and use exorbitant action ploys to satirize conservative values. *M*A*S*H* positions the audience against militarism and authoritarianism by injecting farce into the traditional war format. *Brewster* is based in an absurdist action device – a young man learning to fly – and it concludes with a title sequence that underscores the illusoriness of the Hollywood cinema – the actors appear as clowns engaging in buffoonish acts. And *McCabe* resorts to historical realism to undermine the traditional western conventions. The West is depicted as mean and direct, and the traditional action codes for the western hero (honor, romance, etc.) are left lying in the dirt.

In *Nashville* (1975), scripted by Joan Tewkesbury, Altman intensifies his social criticism at the level of image, narrative, and character construction. The film follows the lives of numerous characters – a BBC reporter, a political campaign worker, a folk group, a housewife, an aspiring country singer, a successful country singer – in a fairly random manner during a weekend in Nashville. All the different narrative strands come together in the end at an outdoor political rally, highlighted by the appearance of a famous country singer, who in the final segment is shot by a neurotic young man. In this and in his next several films, he breaks more radically with Hollywood practices that produce an ideological vision of the world by inviting identification with privileged characters, or through narrations that connote a sense of world order, or through camera strategies that promote a false sense of dramatic intimacy. The narrative of *Nashville* is discontinuous; the characters are multiple (24 in all), with no privileged hero or even privileged object of sympathetic identification, since all are flawed, venal, or manipulative; and the images are constructed in such a way as to distance the audience from the habitual sorts of engagement with the spectacle. On the whole, the multiplicity of points of view and the narrative discontinuities require more attention and thought from the audience than is usual in Hollywood film, and indeed, a theme of the film is that Americans are passive victims of political and culture industry manipulation, so much so that they can sing "You may say that I ain't free, but it don't worry me" when someone has just been shot.

The film is concerned with the distance between image and reality, both on the broader cultural level and in personal relationships, and for this reason its reflexive signaling of its own departure from Hollywood illusionism (by, for example, having Elliot Gould and Julie Christie play themselves) is significant. Thus, what Altman was after was a certain materialism, showing what Hollywood never shows – the sleazy underside of the American Dream of success that is concealed by the stage of cultural spectacle. For this reason it is important that much of the action takes place on or around stages. Private as much as public life is a performance, often deceptive, and what matters is show, spectacle, and platitude, rather than honesty or fidelity. Even the presidential candidate never appears in person; he is only a set of slogans broadcast over a loudspeaker (although his one early slogan sets the theme of the film: "We're all deeply involved in politics whether we know it or not").

Throughout the film the discourses of religion, family, and political democracy are shown to be out of sync with reality, and Altman's editing juxtapositions unfold the contradictions between illusionary ideals and real social practices. Songs about love and family are contrasted with acts of crude manipulation and exploitation in relationships. In one scene the hypocrisy of religious righteousness is underscored by a sequence of shots at different churches depicting characters who have been shown behaving immorally in other contexts feigning piety and demonstrating the class and race differentials that underlie a supposedly Christian society. In the bicentennial world of *Nashville* patriotic sentiments conceal intolerance, public moralistic stances conceal corruption, and the semblance of romance conceals opportunistic exploitation. It is, with other films and film strands we have noted that culminate around 1977, the cinematic highpoint of mid-seventies cynicism.

The film contains few close-ups and few shot-reverse shots that privilege individual points of view and elicit identification with characters. Its style is distinguished by the use of medium and long shots, even for extremely intimate scenes that usually require a different, more personal camera rhetoric. The camera work instantiates a sense of alienation, since no one seems very close to anyone else. This is particularly evident in one scene in which a woman who has just slept with a man gets dressed while he calls another woman he wants to sleep with. His back is to the camera, while all we see of her is her legs. Similarly, the narrative randomness – that the plot shifts have no determinate logic – seems a correlative for the dominant ethos of this world: infidelity. The film is faithful to no story line nor to any character; both the camera and the narrative treat all with equal coolness, as if they were themselves characters in the world – aloof, indifferent, manipulative.

The film departs from individual-based Hollywood narratives by depicting characters as part of social relations and collectivities. This is the point of the intersection of so many different narrative strands during the film, and at the end. It also suggests every-one's complicity in what goes on in society. Indeed, the strategy brings out the theme of failed responsibility. The complex narrative is the objective correlative of social responsibility; it underscores the networking of metonymic social relations between people and the embeddedness of individual subjects in society.

[. . .]

[. . .] Altman's cosmopolitanism seems to feed into an excessively derisive attitude toward American popular culture that risks losing the very audience that probably stands most to benefit from the critiques his film offers. [. . .] Altman's left-liberal political vision is limited; it does not target the underlying institutions of American society, but instead concentrates on fairly epiphenomenal problems like hypocrisy and crassness. He fails to see how those surface disturbances emanate from a social system that by its most fundamental laws promotes opportunism and manipulation. In Altman's vision, those things seem instead to be faults of the very victims of that sys-tem and those laws. His films thus demarcate a major limitation of the antagonistic attitude toward mainstream culture we ascribed to the sixties sensibility. Altman's films evidence all the wry cynicism of that era, laced with some mid-seventies nihilism.

[. . .]

The lesson Altman offers is that what lies beyond ideology is neither realism (as traditional Marxists suggest) nor modernism (as other radicals argue) exclusively. What is missing from Altman is not a sense of experimentation with style or with the tradi-tional conventions and representational forms, nor is it a sense of reality or objectivity. It is rather an ability to represent or conceptualize abstractly what the social system as a system is about, while also empathizing more justly with its victims and seeing the rules of the system in all their impersonality. His failures make all the more acute the question of what the most appropriate and most effective forms for a leftist cinema would be.

2. Within the Hollywood Codes: Political Films

The acceptance of narrative realism as a viable terrain for leftist film work foregrounds the issue of figuration within realism. Rhetoric, the question of which figures will be used to represent and construct the world, shifts to the center of the analysis. Rather than the ideological operations of realist narrative, the crucial issue becomes the rhetorical operations for constructing the social world in a certain way.

The representation of the social world is political and that choice of modes of rep-resentation instantiates differing political positions toward it. Indeed, every camera position, every scene composition, every editing decision, and every narrative choice involves a representational strategy that embeds various interests and desires. No aspect of film merely reveals or depicts "reality." Rather, films construct a phenomenal world and position the audience to experience and live the world in certain ways. We will consider here how differing political interests construct the social world in different ways through representation.

Left and Right vie for a shared terrain, and although each inflects the issues differently, they both deal with the same problems. Three aspects of that social terrain are the individual, history, and society. The Right makes the individual, conceived as an isolated unit, the basis of its political program. We have examined the ramifications of this in regard to the hero. The Left's program also addresses the individual, but as a relational entity and a responsible part of a collective, not as a lone survivalist warrior battling others in the market jungle. Nevertheless, the statist and enforced collectivist biases of the Left have led Left theorists of ideology (Althusser particularly) to condemn the individual (the "subject") as a political category. This position has been picked up by film criticism as the condemnation of all cinematic devices that reinforce an "ideological" sense of "imaginary" ego identity. We disagree with this position, and argue that in general the Left should not dismiss subjectivity as a primary concern, but that the ideology of individualism should be criticized. In film, this means that films that promote individual viewing pleasure or that adhere to representational continuities that reinforce the ego or that use individual heroes are not necessarily ideological. Indeed, psychological research has found that people are more amenable to therapeutic change when an empathetic atmosphere is created in which their fears, desires, and even their most neurotic fantasies are taken seriously and accepted, rather than being sternly dismissed. The same principle no doubt also applies to film.

Just as the Left and the Right represent and use the category of the individual differently, both politically and cinematically, so also they conceive of and use the concepts of history and society differently. For the Right, history is tradition, an authoritative source of truth and power. Usually it is represented as a time of "simpler" (more conservative) social values and institutions (as in the Indiana Jones films or *Star Wars*). For the Left, history is not an authoritative tradition that sanctions the existence of inequality; it is, rather, a domain of struggle between the interests of inequality and those of inequality in which the outcome is undecided. In Left films like *Little Big Man* and *Buffalo Bill and the Indians*, for example, history as myth or as tradition is shown to be a lie, an exercise of representational power in a political struggle.

Similarly, society is conceived and represented differently by Left and Right. [. . .] In fantasy and hero films, for the Right, society is a potentially totalitarian power that threatens the individualist with curtailment of his property, engulfment of his identity, and diminishment of his sexual power. It is a faceless, deindividualized mass. For the Left, society is a source of cooperation and mutual help, as in films like *9 to 5* or *Blade Runner*. It is a network of multiple, interconnected, expanding relations.

Thus, both history and society, like the individual, are terrains of representational struggle shared by Left and Right. How each is represented on the screen helps determine how it will actually be *formed* or constructed in the world. In this section we will concentrate on Left films that deal with political problems and that foreground some of the problems raised by trying to deal with such issues as the individual, history, and society within the traditional Hollywood representational codes without succumbing to the conservative ideologies that frequently inhabit them.

[. . .]

Missing (1982), directed by Costa-Gavras, recounts the story of the disappearance of a young American in Chile after the American-sponsored right-wing coup that overthrew the democratically elected socialist government of Salvador Allende in 1973. The story focuses on the efforts of the father and the son's wife to discover what happened to him. Narrative movement is defined by the transformation of the father, a conservative businessman who is at first skeptical of the wife's story that the United States was involved both in his son's murder and in its cover-up, into a critic both of the coup and of the United States, after he witnesses the brutality of the fascists and uncovers evidence of U.S. involvement.

Missing can be said to use traditionally ideological representational codes to make a counterideological point. But it can also be justly accused of focusing on the personal tragedy of a white North American in a situation in which thousands of Latin Americans were murdered. The personal focus highlights a problem of historical representation in general. The events were the result of an exercise of imperialist power, yet that system of power is impossible to represent in a biographical narrative of this sort. Indeed, it is the prevalence of such narratives and of such ways of understanding life and history that creates the climate that allows structural and historical descriptions of events like those in Chile to be branded "propaganda." If individuals are involved, it's a movie; if classes, it's propaganda. Hollywood narratives tend to frame history as personal events, and while this enlists audience sympathy with broader concerns, it can also reduce those concerns to pathic rather than ethical matters.

Nevertheless, our survey suggests that the film was extraordinarily successful (in a political sense) with audiences: 27% said that it initiated doubts in them regarding U.S. foreign policy. Moreover, 13% said they were shocked and surprised at the events depicted, 23% said they were somewhat surprised, and 55% said that it was "hard to admit we do such things, but we do"; 60% claimed the movie provided them with new information regarding the events in Chile, and 75% said it convinced them that the "American government does wrong things for its own self-interest in foreign countries." On the question of the focus on one American, 80% felt it was "a good way to enlist audience sympathy." Still, as one might expect, the film appealed to a liberal upper-class audience. Only 40% of our sample saw it, and 75% of those earned over $30,000 a year, while the largest percentage of nonviewers earned less than $30,000. And liberals seemed more possessed of information on the events than conservatives or moderates; of the latter, 71% and 67% respectively said it gave them new information, as opposed to 43% of the liberal viewers. Nevertheless, in our interviews with people of various classes and races about the film, the most common words used to describe it were "upsetting," "frightening," "enlightening," and "realistic." A number spoke of being converted by the film to a critical position in regard to American foreign policy, although several people also seemed to indicate that the criticism the film inspired was directed at "the government" in general, rather than at any one specific group's use of the government apparatus to attain its ends. For one, the "realism effect" tended to have a counterideological effect; very few people reported disbelieving what they saw on the screen. In fact, one interviewee remarked that she had not known that the United States "would or had gone that far."

Films in the same leftist vein as *Missing* such as Roger Spottiswoode's *Under Fire* (1983) also demonstrate the possibility of recoding the conventional formulas in ways that transcend some of their ideological limitations. It depicts how foreign journalists in Nicaragua come to sympathize with the Sandinista revolution against the Somoza dictatorship. While a white male hero "saves the day," and the mass-based revolutionary movement is made to seem dependent on one great leader, the film nevertheless uses Hollywood representational forms to gain sympathy for a progressive movement. At one point, audience sympathy is elicited for a young revolutionary who loves North American baseball. This ploy is a familiar motif of war films, but in this case, sentiment is attached to a revolutionary, rather than to the usual patriotic figure when the young man is brutally murdered by an American mercenary.

The crucial (and perhaps unfortunate) importance of identification is clear in a comparison of the public fates of Haskell Wexler's *Latino* (1985) and Oliver Stone's *Salvador* (1986). *Latino* depicts the problematic situation of an American soldier who is Latino, yet who must fight against Central Americans. *Salvador* portrays the worst elements of rightist repression and frankly points to U.S. participation in the atrocities. The importance of using formats which appeal to popular audiences is signaled by the relative success of *Salvador* and the box-office failure of *Latino*. *Salvador* employs a dynamic and comedic representational mode that situates the Right as a narrational nemesis and alternates scenes of violence with fairly traditional scenes of humor or romance. *Latino* is on the whole more didactic, less characterized by concessions to popular conventional representations. But the film is also a lesson in the limits on leftism within Hollywood. Most companies refused to distribute it.

What we are suggesting is that while certain formal devices, such as closure, subjective narration, and personalizing camera work, do serve ideological ends, this does not mean that all closure, all narration, and all personalization are inherently conservative. The Left must begin by reconsidering the values that inform such judgments (the critique of subjectivity, for example, which haunts much leftist thinking). "Personalization" and "subjectivity" can waylay structural understandings of class realities, but they also, as our survey has shown, work to enlist audience sympathies and advance such understandings. While we would argue that certain supposedly ideological representational forms can be recoded and used for counterideological ends, we also suggest that the question of the politics of form should be taken to a different level by emphasizing the way film representation fits into broader rhetorical procedures for constructing the social world. Rhetoric removes the question of politics from the realm of the simple condemnation of subjectivity or realism and brings it closer to the actual processes of political struggle over the construction of the social world in which representation plays a major role. And it makes possible a concept of progressive texts that sees them not simply as departures from identification or realism but as alternative modes for formulating worlds, different constructions of social realities.

3. Beyond Hollywood: The Independent Sector

[. . .]

The independents came of age in the seventies. If one follows the work of film-makers like Chris Choy (of Third World Newsreel) from *Teach Our Children* (1971), about Attica, to *To Love, Honor, and Obey* (1981), about domestic violence, the development from interventionist direct cinema to a more reflective and complex style that mixes representational strategies (from interviews to documentary) and examines the deep context of a social problem is striking. By the late seventies and early eighties a number of independent films had attained national distribution, including *Harlan County* and *The Atomic Cafe*. [. . .] But independent filmmakers themselves were becoming increasingly sophisticated at their craft, to the extent that the mid-eighties witnessed the emergence of a distinct counter-current of semi-mainstream independent filmmakers like John Sayles (*Brother from Another Planet*), Jim Jarmusch (*Stranger than Paradise*), Lizzy Borden (*Working Women*), Spike Lee (*She's Gotta Have It*), Victor Nunez (*Flash of Green*), Eagle Pennell (*Last Night at the Alamo*), and Susan Seidelman (*Desperately Seeking Susan*).

The problem we see facing independents is how to translate superior political vision into a cinematic practice that will attain a sufficient audience to make that vision effective. By definition, avant-garde filmmakers like Yvonne Rainer and James Benning are unconcerned with this problem. In *Journeys from Berlin*, Rainer meditates on the relationship between public and personal politics as she examines the issue of terrorism in the seventies. Her use of discontinuous editing, scene repetition, multiple perspectives, disjunctive juxtapositions, and nonrealist narration is designed to question the sorts of perceptual procedures which accompany mainstream narrative. Benning's *Him and Me* is a series of painterly images that suggest such social themes as industrialization and urban decay; radio voice-overs recall the struggles of the sixties; and ironic subtitles suggest parallels between modern urban life and Vietnam. These and other "deconstructive" films seem unamenable to a popular politics. They are sites of advanced research for the radical intellectual vanguard. Nevertheless, they may well be the testing ground for alternative representational strategies, alternative ways of constructing the social world.

Those independents who are most concerned with political effectiveness are the documentary filmmakers. In such important radical documentaries of this era as *Hearts and Minds*, *Harlan County*, *Union Maids*, *Rosie the Riveter*, *The Wobblies*, *Controlling Interest*, *On Company Business*, and *Seeing Red*, something like a distinct critical documentary aesthetic has made itself evident. While many of these films are fiercely partisan, some adopt a more "objective" style which allows the images to do their own proselytizing. [. . .] Yet concerned as the documentary filmmakers are with reaching audiences in ways that are convincing, the documentary form itself suffers from an essential drawback. Audiences of working people who generally go to films to be entertained may avoid them, even if the filmmakers are fortunate enough to obtain distribution – a much too rare event save for a few films like *The War at Home* and *Harlan County*. A number of people in our survey sample spoke of avoiding certain films because after a long day or week the last thing they want or need is a serious film. Consequently, many of the documentary films may be inherently limited to informed audiences of professional class people. Documentaries can, however, accomplish certain representational tasks which fictional feature films cannot.

The example of Cine Manifest is instructive in this regard. The group made a documentary, *Prairie Fire*, in 1975 about the Non-Partisan League, a grassroots coalition of northwestern farmers who opposed banking, grain, and rail trusts. They followed up that film with a fictional feature about the same topic, *Northern Lights* (1979). *Lights* merges the personal and the political in a narrative about the radicalization of a farmer who becomes a League organizer. The film was quite successful and was widely distributed through a plan whereby the filmmakers would accompany the film to discuss it with audiences. Nevertheless, *Lights* was criticized for permitting the personal story to overwhelm the historical narrative. The historical context of the events, something more easily rendered in the documentary, is left out. But it could be argued as well that it was precisely the personal focus in the film which was more successful as a lure for audiences than the distant and impersonal style that documentary seems to entail.

A growing number of filmmakers are turning to fictional features, and it is in this movement that the most obvious direct possibilities for using film to help transform American cinematic culture are to be found. Two remarkable and controversial films in this genre are Charles Burnett's *Killer of Sheep* and Lizzie Borden's *Born in Flames*. *Killer* is a highly praised film about a black man who works in a slaughterhouse. [. . .]

[. . .]

Several independent filmmakers have attempted to work more within the prevailing Hollywood codes of representation, and easily the most successful of these is John Sayles. His *Brother from Another Planet* (1985) is a science fiction film which uses the metaphor of an escaped black slave from another planet to criticize the exploitation of blacks in America. The mute slave wanders wordlessly through Harlem chased by two white bounty hunters. The ploy forces the audience to observe social conditions from a naive point of view that underscores their brutality. Moreover, the narrative consists of a series of displacements that suggest a network of decentered relations between people. Even the Hollywood-style apotheosis, in which the slave is freed, is due to collective strength, not individualist superiority. Because the primary character is mute, he is experienced through the effects he has on people. This strategy permits the creation of a web of relations between the characters, all of whom come to participate in his characterization.

A rhetorical and deconstructive approach to the problem of political effectivity through film would dictate a more malleable and multiple strategy than now emerges generally from the Left. Discussions of Left uses of film have been handicapped in recent years by a purism regarding form and an absolutism regarding contamination by popular media. Generally more educated and

15 ■ "Joe Morton as the alien 'brother' who crash-lands on earth and lands in New York City," from *Brother From Another Planet*.

culturally sophisticated, Left film activists tend to favor forms more appropriate to their own taste culture – documentary realism and avant-garde modernism. Concentration on these areas of work has resulted in a tremendously rich variety of work. But such concentration leaves the entire terrain of mainstream narrative cinema untouched. When leftists do venture into the Hollywood mainstream, they do so usually to make fictional versions of historical events like *Missing* or *Reds*. Such work is extremely important, as our audience survey has shown. But effective work also needs to be undertaken in other cinematic arenas like fantasy, melodrama, and even comedy. Socialism won't work if it doesn't feel good, and the Left tends to be altogether too dour in regard to "politically correct" cinema, enjoining pleasure while privileging cinematic techniques that punish audiences. What is gained in self-righteousness is lost in effectivity.

Moreover, there are serious political problems with a model of progressive cinema which, like that prevalent in structuralist film theory, excludes pleasure and defines ideology in terms of self-identity or the ego. It should be remembered that Louis Althusser, who stands behind this approach to film, subscribed to the idea that the Party subsumes the will of the masses. Modernist film theory is equally committed to a philosophical program that denies validity to the self and that consequently points toward a political arrangement which would require self-denial and would marginalize self-development. Another, different Marxist theory would make the subjective potentials of the mass of people, their power of "self-valorization," not the Party, into the basis of socialism. And it would promote a different sense of what a progressive cinema is.

Such a cinema would seek to reconstruct the dominant cultural representations which construct social reality. Rather than conceive of the Hollywood representational system as being inherently ideological, it would assume instead that what matters are the *effects* representations have, how they are used in specific historical contexts, and how they affect specific audiences. The notion of effect would not be limited to psychological reaction or opinion. It would also include the way in which representations posit worlds, construct a sense of social reality by orienting perception and feeling in certain ways, so that a common set of psychological dispositions results in a common phenomenal and institutional world. [. . .] Such a cinema would not, however, think of progressive film merely as a set of formal devices or representational practices. It would assume that the meaning and effects of films are always determined and shaped by historical and contextual constraints, by the audiences to whom films are addressed, and by the prevailing social contexts. Such a progressive cinema would be situational and contextual in approach; it would modulate its use of film conventions according to the constraints in existence as well as according to the particular effects or ends that are likely to be generated or gained. It would be a cinema that would, in a certain sense, be noncinematic, in that it would also rely on such things as studies of audiences in order to gauge what representational strategies are likely to be effective. We are clearly assuming that such a cinema would work within the formulae of mainstream cinema, importing to them the advances in representational (and socially constructive) rhetoric developed in the more sophisticated realm of independent filmmaking. It would be a cinema attuned to the desires and the perceptual codes of popular audiences in order to better work with them, reshaping and reinflecting their meanings. Not no narratives, as modernist theorists argue, but more, different narratives, narratives which posit a different world and allow the living of different life stories.

[. . .]

If a socialist alternative is to be developed in the United States as a way out of the impasse of possibilities we have called the American quandary, the Left, we would argue, must overcome its traditional distrust and disdain for popular culture. The Left's dismissal of culture in favor of politics and economics (elections, strikes, party and coalition building, grassroots organizing, etc.) must give way to an understanding of the crucial importance of culture as the seedbed of that support which would allow socialist ideals to be politically acceptable in the United States. [. . .] Culture is the realm in which the psychology of that electorate is formed. [. . .] To a certain extent, culture precedes and determines politics. If this has clear implications for understanding conservative ascendancy in the political realm, it also has implications for formulating a socialist alternative to that power.

[. . .]

[. . .] For socialism to be possible in the United States in a fully democratic manner, it must first become possible in people's minds. To a certain extent, in order for the actuality of socialism to be realized it must simultaneously be represented as something realizable. This is the nature of desire, both personal and political. All such desire is to a certain extent utopian, in the sense that its actual object is always absent from the representation that signifies it. It is for this reason that one could say that Ronald Reagan was actually elected somewhere around the mid-seventies, when cultural imagery first began to summon him forth. The same must be true of an alternative socialist society. To be desired, it must be represented. And it won't be realized if it isn't an object of desire. We will conclude, then, by suggesting that the Left must construct socialism as a possible object of desire in the realms that most attract popular desires – film, but also television and music. The Left must develop an effective politics of cultural representation at the same time that it builds coalitions and formulates economic programs. The latter will make no difference in the world without the former.

22

But Would You Want Your Daughter To Marry One? Politics and Race in *Guess Who's Coming to Dinner*

Thomas E. Wartenberg

Guess Who's Coming to Dinner tells the story of an upper-class, white husband and wife, who at first disapprove of their daughter's intention to marry a black man but later come to embrace the idea. Because the political turmoil of the 1960s – from the civil rights movement to its more radical offspring such as the black power move-ment – had resulted in a heightened awareness of the injustices of America's racialized society, the film can use this story to address the viability of liberalism, with its commitment to integration as a means of undermining racial hierarchy and, thus, achieving equality for blacks. Since the Draytons are "lifelong liberals," their initial hostility to the prospect of a black son-in-law calls liberal integrationism into question. The charge that the film

16 ■ "Dr John Prentice (Sidney Poitier) discusses his desire to marry Joanna Drayton (Katharine Houghton) with Joanna and her father, Matt Drayton (Spencer Tracy)," from *Guess Who's Coming to Dinner*.

investigates is that when the chickens come home to roost, liberals cannot be counted on to honor their ideals.

But the liberals in this film – and this is its point – do not desert the cause of racial justice, despite their initial difficulty in living up to its consequences. By the film's end, both Christina (Katharine Hepburn), the mother, and, more importantly, Matt (Spen-cer Tracy), the father of the young bride-to-be, endorse their daughter's impending marriage. Indeed, the focus of the film is on Matt's arduous struggle to come to accept it. In the end, not only is this father of the bride saved from the charge of hypocrisy, but his embrace of his prospective son-in-law vindicates liberalism as a political philo-sophy and, with it, integration as the solution to the racism of American society.

Guess Who's Coming to Dinner was a popular success when it was released, grossing between seventy and eighty million dollars and winning two of the ten Academy

Awards for which it was nominated (for Best Actress [Katharine Hepburn] and Best Screenplay [William Rose]). From the time of its release, however, critics have been nearly unanimous that the terms in which this film tells its story undermine its ability to make a serious political statement – foremost among their complaints, that the black male lead is so extraordinary and contrived a human being as to be simply unbelievable. [. . .]

These harsh assessments did not go unanswered. [. . .]

Sidney Poitier defended the film's representational strategy, but with a somewhat different emphasis. He contended that the critics failed to recognize Hollywood's complicity in American racism:

> In 1967 it was utterly impossible to do an in-depth interracial love story, to treat the issue in dead earnestness, head on. . . . But Kramer . . . treated the theme with humor, but so delicately, so humanly, so lovingly that he made everyone look at the question for the very first time in film history. *Guess Who's Coming to Dinner* is a totally revolutionary movie. . . . What the critics didn't know and what blinded them to the great merit of the film, was that Hollywood was incapable of anything more drastic in 1967.[1]

According to Poitier, in 1967 the compromised state of the film industry – and by implication, American society generally – required the film to proceed by indirection. Without Kramer's reassuringly tactful handling, this drama of interracial love could not have been produced.

Poitier's characterization of the film as revolutionary reminds us that *Guess Who's Coming to Dinner* did break some long-standing taboos. For example, coming shortly after the repeal of the Hollywood Production Code, it was Hollywood's first film to show a black man romantically kissing a white woman, even if that explosive image was confined to the rearview mirror of a taxicab.

Also, Poitier is right to insist that *Guess Who's Coming to Dinner* be seen as a compromise between the desire to make a politically significant statement about interracial romance – and through it, about liberalism and integration – and a realistic assessment of the obstacles posed to such a project by a racist film industry and society. But his defense of the result ignores the cost to principle of having effected that compromise. As I shall demonstrate in this chapter, *Guess Who's Coming to Dinner* fails to vindicate liberal integrationism in large part because the representational and narrative strategies it adopts to forestall racist responses undercut its antiracist intentions.

Defending Liberalism and Integration

[. . .]

The interracial couple whose romance is at the center of this film comprises Johanna Drayton (Katharine Houghton) – the twenty-three-year-old daughter of Matt, a white, liberal newspaper publisher, and his wife, Christina, the owner of an avant-garde art gallery – and John Wade Prentice – a thirty-seven-year-old African American doctor whom she met while on vacation in Hawaii. He is the son of a retired mail carrier, John Sr. (Roy Glenn Jr.), and his wife, Mary (Beah Richards). The film's action takes place during one afternoon in which the two lovers stop over in San Francisco, the Draytons' home. Johanna thinks that they are there simply to introduce John to her parents, but he has a different purpose in mind.

Johanna has assured her fiancé that his race will not be an issue for her parents, but the older and less naïve John is hardly sanguine about how they will react to the news that their daughter intends to marry a black man, even one as accomplished as he is. Because Johanna is so young and so close to her parents, he has decided to place the couple's future in the hands of the elder Draytons: Unbeknownst to Johanna, he will propose that should either of them express any reservations about the marriage, he will break off the engagement. But John has business to attend to in Geneva – he is on his way to a new, important position at the World Health Organization – so the Draytons will have only a few hours to decide whether they will give the couple their blessing.

[. . .]

Privileging Romantic Love

Faced with the prospect of a black son-in-law, both Christina and Matt squirm with discomfort over where the teaching of their liberal ideals has led their daughter. But Christina has the easier time overcoming her anguish, moved by evidence of how deeply in love her daughter is. [. . .] "Joey has always been a happy person," Christina says:

> But I don't think I've ever seen her so happy as she is now. And I have to be happy for her, Matt, and I am. And proud of the fact that we helped to make her. And whatever happens now, I feel glad that Joey's Joey.

[. . .] Christina is able to give their marriage her blessing because she has changed her way of perceiving the couple; rejecting dominant social norms that would stigmatize the couple as problematic, she comes to see its interracial makeup as exemplary. Her daughter has become the embodiment of the color-blind ideal with which the Draytons had raised her.

Although Matt eventually succumbs, he has a great deal more difficulty doing so. His initial reaction to his wife's about-face – "And I'm thinking only of her own welfare," he insists – is to reproach Christina for not "having her [Joey's] best interest" in mind. [. . .] As Christina tries to make him see, rather than sparing Johanna pain, Matt's opposition will not only prove futile, but will likely also cause her to doubt his integrity.

[. . .]

Interestingly enough, it is Mary Prentice, John's mother, who gets Matt to relent and support the marriage. [. . .]

[. . .] What Mary sees is the passion the two have for one other, and for her this trumps all of Matt's objections. His problem [. . .] is "that men grow old and when sexual things no longer matter to them, they forget it all, forget what passion is." Matt and John Sr. have forgotten the power of sexual passion:

> Now the two of you don't know. And the strange thing for your wife and me is that you don't even remember. If you did, how could you do what you are doing [i.e., stand in the way of the marriage]?

Mary's hope is that Matt will be able to recall his own youthful passion.

And he does: "I admit that I hadn't considered it [i.e., love], hadn't even thought about it," he tells her as he addresses the assembled cast in the film's climactic scene. [. . .] Matt has risen to Mary's challenge, his recollected passion for Christina awakening his sympathy for the young lovers. Endorsing a version of the cliché that love conquers all, he argues:

> And I think that now, no matter what kind of case some bastard could make against your getting married, there would be only one thing worse, and that would be, knowing what you two are, knowing what you two have, and knowing what you two feel, if you didn't get married.

Matt's speech affirms the power of love to transcend whatever obstacles John and Joey will encounter. Indeed, to insist on these obstacles – as Matt had so recently done – one would have to be a bastard.

[. . .]

Matt's transformation not only restores our faith in him, it seals, in its makers' eyes, *Guess Who's Coming to Dinner*'s vindication of liberalism. His opposition to his daughter's marriage to a black man raised doubts about whether liberals could be trusted to act on their principles. Those doubts have been laid to rest. But although the film offers us the satisfactions of narrative closure, this does not mean that the film's vindication of liberalism is successful or even coherent. In fact, there are a number of serious problems with *Guess Who's Coming to Dinner*'s politics – some internal to liberalism, others the product of its makers' narrative and representational strategies – and I now turn to a consideration of some of these.

Representing Racism

A first problem with *Guess Who's Coming to Dinner*, internal to the liberal political orientation it champions, is that it understands racism as an effect of the prejudices of individual social actors. For this reason, the film is unable to acknowledge racism's systematic, structural aspects.

There are two scenes at the very beginning of the film in which our unlikely couple provokes racist reactions. In the first, we see the taxi driver (John Hudkins) who takes the lovers from the airport to the Draytons' home react with distaste when he glimpses their kiss in his rearview mirror and then almost refuse the cab fare that John hands him. In the second of these racist vignettes, Hillary, Christina's employee at her gallery, cannot help showing her surprise and disapproval when she realizes that John and Johanna are involved with one another. The narrative function of these scenes is to build toward the Draytons' encounter with their future son-in-law, but along the way they also exemplify the film's understanding of racism. These minor characters betray their own race prejudice, for they see this relationship as offensive because of the difference in its partners' skin colors.

The same analysis of racism as prejudice underlies the film's representation of Johanna, who embodies its conception of the solution to the problems it addresses. Johanna's color-blindness is, at the level of individual character, the necessary corrective to the moral flaw of prejudice. [. . .] She cannot treat blacks as different from whites because she does not see them as different. Johanna's color-blindness can be presented as the solution to American racism precisely because the film views racism as prejudice based on skin color.

It is this understanding of racism and its antidote that accords with the liberalism that the film sets out to vindicate. Seeing racism as prejudice makes it a problem in the moral character of individual white Americans, a problem that can be solved by pointing out that such attitudes contradict a belief in the essential dignity and equality of all human beings.

[. . .]

As self-evident as *Guess Who's Coming to Dinner*'s understanding of racism as the effect of individual prejudice appeared, it is nonetheless inadequate. For even if Americans were suddenly to decide that skin color has no moral significance, there are structural aspects of racism that would not thereby be eradicated.

For example, consider the Draytons' relationship with their maid, Tillie. The film presents her role in the Drayton family as that of a "mammy," that is, a black woman who has come to identify strongly with the family she selflessly nurtures.[2] Tillie's identification with the Draytons is so strong that she attacks John for attempting to marry Johanna. To the question, "Is there racism in the Draytons' relationship with Tillie?" we might be inclined to respond, "No, for the Draytons treat her as a family member, and without a hint of prejudice." On the other hand, one could argue that the Draytons' attitude – and even the filmmakers' – toward her is, at times, patronizing. But putting this objection aside, it would not at all follow that the situation that links Tillie to the Draytons is free of racism. Black women like Tillie were employed as live-in maids by people in the Draytons' social class as a result of historically conditioned economic factors that limited their life chances. Without access to wider educational and employment opportunities, they were forced in large numbers into low-paying, low-status jobs as domestics, service workers, and so on. So even if none of the Draytons discriminate against Tillie on the basis of her skin color, her role in the household is an invidious, racially determined effect of the structure of American society.

But consistent with the ontological individualism of liberal social theory, *Guess Who's Coming to Dinner* treats Tillie's situation as unproblematic. If the film seeks to vindicate liberal integrationism by contriving a black male paragon, its success implies nothing about the racialized division of labor of which the Drayton household is a microcosm. A conception of racism as a structural phenomenon privileging white Americans just because they are white is simply beyond the film's representational possibilities.

Naturalizing Integration

As the civil rights movement made clear, the racial integration of American society could only be achieved by means of a political struggle. But *Guess Who's Coming to Dinner* naturalizes the process of integration by treating it as the inevitable result of generational succession. In this way, despite its condemnation of American society for its racism, the film adopts narrative and representational strategies that encourage its audience to passively await the arrival of integration rather than actively work for its realization.

This prospect of an immanent generational eclipse of racism partakes of a general sense that *Guess Who's Coming to Dinner* conveys – and that marks the film as a product of the late 1960s – that its present is a time of ferment that is leaving the older generation behind. The film registers its sense of rapid social development by depicting Matt Drayton as bedeviled by the ubiquity of dizzying change.

One example of the way in which time has speeded up is the prominence of air travel, from the title sequence in which we see a large jet land at the San Francisco airport, to John's brief stopover before hurrying on to Geneva. The mere forty minutes that it takes for the Prentices to arrive from Los Angeles is mentioned a number of times.

Other scenes stress instead changes in Matt's social environment – for example, in a discussion between him and John of the racial dilemma in which they find themselves, John assures Matt that things are changing for the better. Matt's response, that nowhere are they changing quite as fast as in his own backyard, indicates his discomfort with the pace of these changes. In a later scene, Matt and his friend Monsignor Mike Ryan (Cecil Kellaway) argue about Matt's opposition to the marriage, Matt protesting that he knows what the couple is up against: "I happen to know they wouldn't have a dog's chance. Not in this country. Not in the whole stinking world." But Mike persists: "They are this country, Matt. They'll change this stinking world."

The change that counts most to the film's narrative, however, is the emergence of a postracist white youth. Whereas, with the exception of Mike Ryan, all the members of the parental generation are infected by bigotry, Johanna's generation is presented as color-blind, free of their elders' prejudices. This is the meaning of the sequence in which a white delivery boy (D'Urville Martin) arrives at the Draytons' bringing steaks for the ever-expanding list of dinner guests. When he agrees to provide a lift for Tillie's assistant, Dorothy (Barbara Randolph), the two exit, boogying to the rock-and-roll blasting from his truck radio. These members of the "new" generation of

Americans seem oblivious to racial difference; they simply enjoy dancing together to *their* music. This idea of an emergent, color-blind youth culture is central to the film's representation of racism as a generational phenomenon, doomed to pass away as naturally as one generation succeeds another.

In a rather more extended scene, in which Matt and Christina go out for ice cream, this naturalization of racism's eclipse is reiterated, albeit with a slightly different emphasis. This time, Matt's belief that American racism justifies his opposition to Johanna's marriage is expressly shown to be old-fashioned, out of step with the times and, in particular, the youth culture of the 1960s. The drive-in to which they go is a hangout for teenagers, who sit around in their hot rods and sports cars listening to loud rock music on their car radios. When the young, gum-chewing carhop (Alexandra Hay) asks for Matt's order, he tells her he cannot remember what he had last time. After she lists a number of flavors, he decides he must have eaten Fresh Oregon Boysenberry, but when she brings him his cone, he takes a first taste and grimaces – this is the wrong flavor. After calling the carhop back, intending to return the ice cream, he takes a second taste and decides that it is not so bad after all. When she finally appears, he lamely informs her that although it was not the flavor he had in mind, he likes it. As he and Christina exit the drive-in, he tells the carhop to remind him of it the next time he comes in.

As the sequence progresses, the carhop's reaction to Matt changes. Initially polite, by the time he leaves, she has come to see him as a trying old man whom she has nevertheless to humor. Still the patriarch in his own household, in the broader social setting Matt no longer seems powerful but instead seems to be slipping into his dotage.

The obvious differences in their tastes in music and cars serve to emphasize the generational gap separating Matt from the teenagers by whom he is surrounded at the drive-in and with whom his daughter is identified. More subtly, Matt is portrayed as unsettled by change – he wants things to remain the same. On the other hand, his reaction to an unfamiliar ice cream flavor suggests that he is not entirely inflexible: Since he finds Fresh Oregon Boysenberry delicious, despite his initial aversion, perhaps Johanna's chocolate boyfriend will be to his liking too once he gets over his initial, and habitual, negative response to novelty.

Guess Who's Coming to Dinner uses this analogy to develop its understanding of racism as an effect of prejudice. [. . .] For whether someone finds a food pleasing is generally assumed to be simply a subjective fact about that person, and a fact that can be changed. In drawing the analogy, the film proposes that a person's response to the race (i.e., skin color) of another is also just a matter of taste – of individual, subjective preference for white skin over black or vice versa – and so as ephemeral as a preference for one or another ice cream flavor. This undergirds the film's optimism that racism can be eliminated. Matt will eventually get used to the color of his daughter's husband, just as he got used to an unfamiliar flavor of ice cream.

Given the importance accorded the themes of change and generational succession, it is surprising that these do not figure as reasons for Matt's change of heart. Although he is repeatedly forced to confess that he is at sea in a world that no longer quite accords with his expectations, he never explicitly acknowledges what this implies about his own opposition to the marriage, namely, that it is based on empirical claims that do not reflect the realities of a rapidly changing society.

[. . .]

But if there is something to be said for the film's optimism, its strategy of representation gives the audience an easy out. For its white members are placed in the comfortable position of identifying themselves as supporters of integration while believing that nothing is required of them to bring it about. If racism will be eliminated through the natural process of generational succession, what need is there for social activism? So, despite their restored faith in Matt at the film's end, viewers can also feel superior to him, for they know that his anguish is unnecessary, much ado about nothing. The film's premature hopes for an inevitable eclipse of racism allow its white viewers to evade the critical self-scrutiny that would be entailed by a serious confrontation with racism; instead, they are permitted to remain as spectators while momentous struggles over the fate of America's Second Reconstruction rage about them.

Conflicting Strategies

The last problem with *Guess Who's Coming to Dinner* that I shall discuss, a conflict between its representational and narrative strategies, arises because of its makers' desire to preempt racist reactions to the on-screen portrayal of a passionate interracial romance. As a result, the film's narrative insistence on the passion rings hollow, for its representational strategy denies the audience convincing visual confirmation. The attempt to defeat racist outrage thus results in the sacrifice of the film's coherence.

We have seen that the makers of *Guess Who's Coming to Dinner* were acutely aware that their story of a love affair between a black man and a blonde woman skirted dangerously close to one of the central racist apparitions in America's psyche, an apparition the movie version of which the film scholar Donald Bogle has called "the brutal black buck" and which he traces back to D. W. Griffith's 1915 classic, *Birth of a Nation*:

> [. . .] Griffith played on the myth of the Negro's high-powered sexuality, then articulated the great white fear that every black man longs for a white woman. [. . .] The black bucks of the film are psychopaths, one [Gus] always panting and salivating, the other [Silas Lynch] forever stiffening his body as if the mere presence of a white woman in the same room could bring him to a sexual climax. Griffith played hard on the bestiality of his black villainous bucks and used it to arouse hatred.

The black male is in effect demonized, represented as in the grip of a sexuality both vicious and, in the presence of white women, uncontrollable. As Bogle points out, this involves the fantasy that white women possess a universal appeal, to which black males are particularly vulnerable.

Even though a half century separates *Birth of a Nation* from *Guess Who's Coming to Dinner*, it was no mistake to fear that many viewers would still, in 1967, identify John Prentice with the demonic sexuality of Griffith's blackface villains. If the film was to achieve its political objectives, it had to tell its story in a way that would not activate this most powerful of all racist tropes; otherwise the audience would not accept John and Johanna as romantic partners.

[. . .]

The film includes a number of specific narrative elements the sole purpose of which is to dissociate John from the stereotype of black male sexuality. For example, early in the film, her mother asks Johanna whether she and John have slept together. Johanna explains that they have not, but adds that it is John – and not she – who is responsible for this. This exchange serves no function other than that of acquitting John of lusting after white flesh. In a similar vein, to emphasize that John's sexual interest is not limited to white women, he is shown appreciatively eyeing Tillie's young assistant, Dorothy.

But by far the most important of these obliquities is *Guess Who's Coming to Dinner*'s determinedly desexualized representation of its central love affair. To prevent John from being seen as sexually voracious, we are offered no visual evidence of his passion for Johanna. For example, in the terrace scene discussed earlier that Christina, Matt, and we witness through a window, the two behave in such adolescent terms that the actors have trouble rendering their lines convincingly.

The importance of these representational choices, understandable though they are, is that what we see on-screen contradicts what we hear in the film's dialogue. Remember that central to its explanation of first Christina's and then Matt's change of heart is the evidence they are given for the unlikely couple's passionate attachment to one another. But it is difficult to credit these claims given the total lack of visible erotic energy between John and Johanna, even allowing for the greater sexual reticence one would expect in a film made in 1967. The film's attempt to make their passion a decisive reason for supporting the relationship finds no direct support in the viewers' experience.

To repeat, my goal in exposing these inconsistencies has not been to establish that *Guess Who's Coming to Dinner* is really a bad film. After all, there seems nearly unanimous agreement among both film scholars and the contemporaneous critics that the film is deeply flawed. But what neither these writers nor the film's makers have acknowledged is the extent to which this is due to the desire to achieve popular success with an audience whose racist attitudes made it difficult to believably portray a grand passion between a black man and a white woman. If *Guess Who's Coming to Dinner* is neutered by the contradiction between its narrative and representational strategies, that is less evidence of inferior filmmaking than of the highly problematic project underlying it. Indeed, in my view, the film warrants more sympathetic treatment than many of its dismissive critics allow, if only because the problematic social context in which and for which the film was made deserves to be factored into an assessment of its merit.

[. . .]

NOTES

1 Donald Spoto, *Stanley Kramer: Film Maker* (New York: G. P. Putnam's Sons, 1978), pp. 276–7.

2 The mammy is one of the central stereotypes discussed by Donald Bogle in *Toms, Coons, Mulattos, Mammies, and Bucks* (New York: Continuum, 1996). For a discussion of the reality behind this stereotype, see Deborah Gray White, *Ain't I a Woman? Female Slaves in the Plantation South* (New York and London: W. W. Norton & Co., 1985), pp. 46–61.

23

Stella at the Movies: Class, Critical Spectatorship, and Melodrama in *Stella Dallas*

Angela Curran

Recent debate has centered on King Vidor's classic melodrama *Stella Dallas* (1937), a remake of a 1925 silent film based on the same name. Feminist film critics have argued whether or not the film develops a critical stance on the viewpoint that mothers are required to sacrifice their own desires for the good of their children.[1] Yet little attention has been given to the film's depiction of class ascent. This is surprising. For starting with the opening scenes showing a young Stella Martin yearning to better herself by leaving her working-class life behind by a marriage to Stephen Dallas, to the closing shots that depict the fulfillment of Stella's desire through her daughter's marriage to a member of the upper class, the film's central focus is on Stella's inability to make the class ascent that she selflessly engineers for her daughter.

Perhaps one reason that not much consideration has been given to the issue of class ascent in *Stella Dallas* is that the film seems to be uncritical in its acceptance of upward mobility as an unquestioned good. Further, the film seems to suggest that social mobility is not possible for a working-class woman such as Stella Dallas, despite her best efforts to transform herself into a woman who fits into the upper class. This seems to be the point made in the notorious scene at the resort where Stella makes a spectacle of herself and unknowingly becomes a laughing stock in the eyes of her daughter's snobby acquaintances. The implication of this scene in the context of the movie seems to be that, although class ascent is a good thing, it is beyond the reach of someone in Stella's pitiful position.

Recently, Stanley Cavell has argued that Stella self-consciously orchestrates her failure to conform to the tastes of the upper class.[2] According to Cavell, it is not simply that the upper-class characters in the film reject her. On Cavell's reading, "Stella learns the futility of appealing to the taste of those who have no taste for her."[3] More specifically, Cavell argues that Stella comes to realize that she no longer wants the approval of her husband Stephen Dallas and, by extension, the upper-class world he inhabits.

Although, for reasons that will become clear, I disagree with Cavell's reading of the film, his essay opens up a line of inquiry related to the film's representation of upward mobility that I will address here: how plausible is it to think that Stella comes to regard the desirability of her class ascent with a critical eye? As I will discuss, by the end of the film – but not before – it is possible to regard Stella as coming to possess a critical attitude toward the value of her earlier ambition to make it into the upper class.

Yet I wish to switch from Cavell's focus on the education of Stella throughout the course of the film, to examine the ways in which the film engenders a critical attitude in the *audience* regarding the desirability of class ascent as a goal. We shall see that *Stella Dallas* is highly interesting in its questioning of the value of upward mobility and the role that melodrama, and the movies in general, play in fostering this ambition in its audience.

This chapter is divided into two main parts. In the first half I argue that the source of Stella's failure at social ascent is not her desire to be something more than a mother; it is her working-class nature and sensibilities, which the film represents as an excessive taste in dress and manner. In the second part I discuss how the film's representation of Stella as unfit for social ascent is in tension with the sympathy the film generates for Stella as the upper class misjudges her. I argue that this tension between image and emotional response provides a means for the audience to question the representation of Stella as unfit for social ascent. In spite of an ending that seems to endorse class ascent as a desire that Stella maintains throughout the film and is achieved through her daughter, I argue that the film presents a critical view of the value of social ascent and the role that movies play in shaping a desire for this.

1.1 Stella's Attempt at Social Ascent

The film version of *Stella Dallas* directed by King Vidor is an adaptation of the novel of the same name by Olive Higgins Prouty (1923). The story is set in the factory town of Millhampton, Massachusetts, and begins in 1919, ten years prior to the Great Depression. It begins with the rapid rise of Stella Martin (Barbara Stanwyck), a young working-class woman with high social ambitions, through her marriage to Stephen Dallas (John Boles), who comes from an upper-class family and is the new manager at the mill where her father and brother work. Stella and Stephen have a daughter, Laurel (Anne Shirley); but when Stephen's job takes him to New York, Stella remains in Millhampton with Laurel to get ahead with the "right" people whom she wants to be like, but of whom Stephen disapproves. Stella abandons the ambitions she had for making it in upper-class life in favor of devoting herself to her daughter's needs. A gulf begins to develop between Stella and Laurel when the latter starts to move in her father's social circles. Stella comes to realize that her lack of refinement is getting in the way of her daughter's successful marriage into the upper class. Pretending to have a desire to have a life on her own, apart from Laurel, Stella stages a trick to alienate herself from her daughter so that Laurel will go and live with Stephen and his new upper-class wife, Helen Morrison (Barbara O'Neill). In the final scene of the film,

Stella stands alone in the pouring rain, crying tears of joy as she peers in through the window of the mansion in which her daughter is being married to her upper-class beau. The film ends with Stella walking toward the camera, looking victorious.

At the start of the film Stella's marriage to Stephen seems like a means to a better life. Although Stephen was left penniless after his father committed suicide over financial debts, his upper-class pedigree and job as manager of the mill places him in a different social and economic class from the working-class "mill hands" Stella has grown up with. From her father's reaction to hearing that Stella did not return home after a date in the evening with Stephen, we see that Stella's father is a gruff patriarch who dominates not only Stella but also her brother and her mother, whose drab appearance and downtrodden demeanor contrast with Stella's drive and sparkle.

In this light Stella's determination to use her looks and charm to win Stephen seems like her best hope to get out of an abusive family situation and achieve her ambition for a better life.[4] In spite of the desirability of social ascent, the film proceeds to show that Stella's desire to make a better life as part of the upper class is untenable. What I now wish to show is that there is a tension in how the film represents the source of Stella's failed class ascent.

On the one hand, the film locates the source of the failure in Stella herself: in some scenes the film suggests that Stella simply does not have what it takes to move up into the upper class. Here the film represents Stella's working-class nature in visual terms as an excessive display in behavior and dress. This excess marks Stella as possessing a fundamentally different nature from the elegant refinement of a "real" upper-class woman like Helen Morrison, who eventually replaces Stella as Stephen's wife and becomes Laurel's stepmother. On the other hand, as I shall discuss, the pathos the film generates for Stella as her character and intentions are misinterpreted forms the basis for the audience to question the view that Stella is not good enough for the upper class, as well as begin to question the value of class ascent itself.

1.2 Class as Excess

Stella's increasingly crude appearance and behavior in social functions attended by the upper class has been examined in feminist film criticism of the movie. As Linda Williams notes, as the film progresses Stella displays "an exaggeratedly feminine presence that the offended community prefers not to see."[5] This excessive behavior and dress is best illustrated in the scene at the resort mentioned earlier. Dressing up to impress the mother of Laurel's upper-class boyfriend, Stella dons extreme high heels, a flowery dress with ruffles and black lace, and a white fur wrap with the full animal head and legs intact. Her manner is over the top as well: she ostentatiously flaunts her presence when she tips a hotel bellhop inappropriately and sashays her way through the hotel. Feminist film critics have read Stella's excessive dress and manner in this scene as a visual marker for womanly desire.[6] Read along these lines, the film centers upon the conflict between this sexual desire – the desire to be "something else besides a mother" that Stella feigns near the end of the movie in order to separate herself from

Laurel – and Stella's desire to be a good mother. Even though Stella has, long prior to the scene at the resort, resolved this conflict in favor of being a good mother, Williams argues that her *image* projects womanly desire: the upper-class community in the film proceeds to ostracize her for the suggestion that a woman could somehow accommodate both desires.

While Williams is correct in noting the sexual connotations of Stella's image in the scene at the hotel, this criticism of the gender stereotypes in the film overlooks the way in which the real source of Stella's inadequacy as a mother to Laurel lies not in inappropriate womanly desires but in her lower-class standing.[7] For while a longing to be something besides a mother is a desire Stella expressed right after the birth of Laurel, she gives up this desire soon after she is left alone to raise Laurel while Stephen works in New York. The main and only source of fulfillment in her life becomes her role as Laurel's devoted mother. The source of her failure to make it with the upper class is thus not her womanly desire but her lower-class nature and sensibilities, which the film suggests that she cannot – or will not – fundamentally change despite her marriage to Stephen.[8]

Stella's nature as a working-class woman is marked by an excessive presence that she displays from her first encounter with Stephen. She waits in her yard overly dressed up in a skirt and shirt with ruffles to catch Stephen's eye as he leaves the Mill at the end of the day. But he pays Stella no more attention than he does the women at the mill who also, her brother tells Stella, are trying to attract Stephen's interest. Stella puts on an excessively flowery, if also feminine, dress and hat and takes her brother his lunch at work as a pretense to meet Stephen. Her dress is overdone in both instances, even if it is contrasted with the crude kind of feminine excess that she displays later on at the resort. In the scene where Stella first meets Stephen, she is dressed in ruffles and feminine frills to deliberately compensate for her lack of cultural capital – the social graces, money, and education – that she should have if she is to attract an upper-class man like Stephen. But within the visual economy of the film the ruffles and frills – as well as the excess of fur, lace, and make-up in the scene at the resort – serve as a reminder or marker of Stella's inadequacy with respect to the social graces that come naturally to a woman like Helen Morrison.

In the scene at the River Club, Stella evokes Stephen's disapproval (and the attention of others in attendance) with her flashy costume jewelry and the exuberant manner with which she flies around the dance floor with Ed Munn (Alan Hale). In the quarrel that follows as they return home, Stephen objects to Stella's cheap costume diamond necklace and earrings. Though Stephen says that the costume jewelry is not important "in itself" – but, "what is to become of us is important," he says – he reminds Stella that prior to their marriage, she professed her desire to have Stephen teach her how to dress and act like all the refined and "well-bred" people they were watching on the movie screen. At the time Stephen responded that it was not "well bred" for Stella to speak and act like something she is not and he told Stella she was fine as she was. Yet the scene following the dance at the River Club shows that Stephen's attitude has changed.

Believing now that Stella's taste in clothes is an expression of a class difference that threatens their marriage, Stephen wants Stella to assimilate to his social sensibilities. Stella's reply to Stephen also reverses her earlier position: she refuses to have him instruct her on "the one thing she knows more about" than Stephen – i.e., how to dress. Here it is clear that Stella's excessive taste in clothes is a measure of a fundamental difference in social class between the two of them: although her style appeals to the (presumably) nouveau riche crowd at the River Club, Stella will not be able to fit in with Stephen and his old money sensibilities so long as she is unwilling or unable to follow his recommendations.

17 ■ "Stella (Barbara Stanwyck) embarrasses her daughter, Laurel (Anne Shirley)," from *Stella Dallas*.

The scene that most vividly represents Stella's failure to transform herself into a member of the upper class is the much-discussed scene at the resort, previously mentioned, where Stella dresses up, in the words of one resort resident, like "a Christmas tree." This scene is not the first time Stella has drawn disapproval from the upper-class community her daughter socializes with. In an earlier scene on the train, Stella unknowingly draws the unfavorable attention of Laurel's teacher and the mother of Laurel's schoolmate when she laughs uproariously at Ed Munn's practical joke with the itch powder. This causes the women to think that Stella is having an extra-marital affair, while in reality she has just turned down Ed's proposal that Stella get rid of Stephen and take up with him. But what differentiates the incident on the train from the one at the resort is that in the latter, but not the former, case, Stella was, by every indication, trying to gain the approval of the upper class. Not only is her attempt a failure, but also the scene renders her attempt to transform herself as a "debasement" of Stella, through the representation of her body and dress as an excessive presence that she cannot overcome, despite her best efforts.[9]

1.3 Unwilling or Unable?

At this point let me address Cavell's argument that Stella's display at the resort is something she contrives in order to remove herself from the company of Stephen and the upper-class crowd that disapproves of her. Perhaps the strongest objection to this reading comes from a consideration of the scenes that lead up to Stella's making a spectacle of herself at the resort.

As noted before, early on in the film Stella gives up her ambitions of getting in with the "right people" in favor of devoting herself to taking care of her daughter. As Laurel grows up, she is increasingly exposed to the upper-class life through her father and in particular through her stays at the home of Mrs Morrison. After these visits, Laurel comes home wanting some of the things she experienced there. For example, in one scene Laurel asks her mother if it would be possible for them to live in a house of their own, not an apartment, even if it is not "a great big house" like that of Mrs Morrison. In the next scene we see a meeting between Stella and Stephen's lawyer, who informs her of Stephen's desire for a divorce. Rather than granting him one, Stella accuses Stephen of trying to turn Laurel against him by giving his daughter things and taking her to places that Stella cannot. She then says that she is going to give Laurel some of the things she has been wanting while Stephen pays the bills for this.

In the next sequence we see Stella going to beauty salons and buying clothes to achieve a more glamorous image. This is then followed by the visit by Laurel and Stella to the resort, where Stella disgraces herself and Laurel through her dress and manner. I think that the spectacle that Stella makes of herself at the resort needs to be read alongside this previous sequence. These scenes show Stella attempting to become more attractive in order to compete for the favor of her daughter, whose desires are becoming more orientated to the upscale lifestyle of Mrs Morrison and her father. Here Stella is attempting to challenge the perception of herself as somehow inadequate in the eyes of her husband and possibly even Laurel. The scenes that lead up to the episode at the resort therefore suggest that Stella is out to show Stephen that she too can give Laurel the kind of life that Stephen has been giving her. Her dressing up at the hotel should be read as part of this attempt to impress Laurel.

It is true that in an earlier scene, when Stephen drops by unexpectedly at Christmas, Stella is shown altering her dress by removing some lace to make it more in line with Stephen's taste. This could be taken to show that Stella is aware that a more refined look is what is called for when she associates with the upper class. This raises the issue of whether Stella is unable to adapt herself to the upper-class taste or simply unwilling.

In a sense this scene suggests that Stella is able to dress in accordance with Stephen's buttoned-down taste, if she were willing to take his sensibility in clothes as a guide for herself. But we see from the quarrel Stella and Stephen have after the dance at the River Club that this is something that Stella is not willing to do. On the other hand, Stella has every reason to think that Stephen is simply stuffy and that her dress at the resort will meet with the same approval that she received from Spencer Chandler and Ed Munn at the River Club. Stella is unable to see that the excess of furs and lace she wears at the Resort Hotel will only serve to make her look ridiculous in the eyes of the upper-class crowd there, who share Stephen's understated sense in dress and behavior.

2.1 Resources for Critical Spectatorship

Given the spectacle that Stella becomes when she tries to fit in with the upper class, one might draw the conclusion that the viewpoint of the film is the affirmation of a modified class ascent: although desirable, social ascent is not possible for Stella, even though it is possible for Stella's daughter. This is because there are basic differences between the working and the upper classes and these differences cannot be overcome in spite of the working classes' ambitions to the contrary. This depiction of Stella's situation could relate not only to the working-class people who formed part of the audience for melodramas like *Stella Dallas*, but also to the thousands of immigrants who were coming to the United States at the time the film was made. The message would be that assimilation and social ascent are not possible for immigrants, but are available only to their children, who are more easily able to assimilate and adopt the manners and customs of the new country.

But this reading of the film, which locates the failure of Stella's social ascent in her own nature as a working-class woman, is at odds with another central narrative thread: that the upper-class characters in the film fail to recognize Stella's true worth and intentions. The film shows that social ascent is not possible for Stella, and it also seems to go to an extreme in representing her attempt at social ascent as a crude failure. Yet the movie also evokes intense sympathy for her based on the privileged access that the audience is given to her true nature and intentions. This sympathy, evoked as Stella learns of how the crowd at the resort has reacted to her, provides the means for the audience to question the film's representation of Stella as unfit for the upper class.

To help us understand how this is so, we can bring in some ideas from Aristotle's discussion of the emotions in his *Rhetoric*. This book presents Aristotle's insights on how an orator goes about influencing the audience to accept certain beliefs and take certain actions. As Aristotle recognizes, inducing certain emotions in the audience is a key strategy for motivating belief and action. For, Aristotle explains, emotions are "those feelings that so change men as to affect their judgments" (1378a20).[10] There are several ways to interpret what Aristotle means in saying this. But one interpretation that is relevant for our purposes points to what we can call an evaluative account of the emotions. Emotions constitute the expression of our recognition of the value that people and things have. Anger, for example, occurs in connection with the voluntary slight or damage of something that is valued or important (1379a10 ff.). Love or friendly feeling (*philia*) is a way of recognizing and responding to the value that we perceive in another person. And pity occurs when we feel pain at the thought that an evil has befallen someone who does not deserve to suffer (II, 8). Because emotions are important ways in which we register and respond to the value that things have, they are capable of altering our previous judgments on the worth of things; for our emotional responses to people and things embody a viewpoint on who and what it is we consider important.

We can relate Aristotle's views on emotions as evaluations to the role that sympathy for Stella plays in challenging the representation that she is not good enough for the upper class. On Aristotle's understanding of pity, the pathos the film generates for Stella does not render her pathetic or lower in value than the upper-class characters who ostracize her. On the contrary, in feeling pity for Stella, the audience responds to and recognizes the real worth of her character and her intentions. The emotional response to her situation, therefore, embodies a viewpoint on the inherent worth of her character and person that conflicts with the image of her as too vulgar and unworthy of upper-class life.

I believe that the tension the film develops between the images that Stella projects – to the upper-class characters in the film as well as to the audience of *Stella Dallas* – and the reality of Stella's character and worth is not simply a contradiction in its representation of Stella and the source of her failure at social ascent. For the film shows repeatedly — with Stephen's visit to Stella at Christmas; on the train where Stella's behavior draws the disapproval of Laurel's teacher; and at the resort where Stella tries to be glamorous and fails — that the images that Stella projects to the upper class do not represent her true nature or worth. This tension between image and inner worth is part of the film's more general concern with examining the conflict between the reality of a person's life and the illusion constructed through the images a viewer sees portrayed on the screen. In engaging with the role that the movies play in shaping as well as distorting the audience's sense of an individual's life possibilities, the film goes beyond the domain of sympathy for a misunderstood heroine and uses this emotional response to develop a critical perspective on the value of class ascent and the role movies play in shaping a desire for this. I now turn to a discussion of this issue.

2.2 Stella at the Movies

Early in the movie we see that the ideas of Stella as a consumer of film images and of the movies as a dream factory for shaping our desires are explicitly presented. Stella and Stephen go out for a date at the local movie house. Stella is absorbed in the story, which shows couples dancing at an elegant establishment followed by a happy ending and a couple's embrace. Stella cries at the ending, and as she and Stephen walk home, she tells him of her desire to act like him and the other upper-class people in the movie. This scene, and another that shows Stella reading about the lives of the rich and famous in a photo-play magazine, points to the power of mass media images in general, and movies in particular, in shaping a viewer's sense of her life possibilities. Here the position of Stella in the world of the film parallels the situation of the viewer of the film *Stella Dallas*, with the cinema spectator of the 1930s increasingly subject to images of wealth and consumption projected up onto the screen.

The film closes with a much-discussed scene that is generally recognized to refer to the earlier depiction of Stella at the movies. Having succeeded at alienating herself from Laurel, Stella stands outside the home of Stephen and Helen, hanging on the bars of a gate as she peers through a brightly lit rectangular window that opens up on the scene of Laurel being married to her upper-class beau, Richard Grosvenor. The lit window can be taken as a figure for the film screen that Stella looked up at all those years ago when she was at the movies with Stephen. Stella cries with joy as she watches the marriage vows. She looks down, as if someone was looking at her, in a pose that is reminiscent of the look she had when Stephen smiled at her crying at the end of the movie. She turns and walks away from the window, going down the street with a look of joy. The film ends as Stella walks straight toward the audience and the melodramatic theme song for the movie plays in the background.

This scene raises three questions: First, what is the reaction of the audience to Laurel's marriage and Stella's witnessing of it? Second, what is Stella's reaction to Laurel's successful marriage, and how does this relate to her earlier desire to be like the people in the movies? Third, what do the earlier and final scenes suggest that the movie is saying about the role that movies play in shaping social ambitions?

In answering the first question, we need to consider the ways in which the film deviates from a typical plot structure for melodrama. As a film genre, melodrama features a protagonist who is pitted against forces beyond her control, yet is in the end vindicated, in part because she displays admirable qualities that evoke the audience's sympathy and admiration. Sometimes the forces the protagonist battles are forces of nature, but often the forces the central character battles are social prejudice. But the key point is that in typical melodrama the initial failure to recognize the protagonist's real motives and worth is often eventually clarified through the public recognition by a character or characters in the film of her goodness and true intentions.

In *Stella Dallas*, on the other hand, there is no public recognition within the terms of the film of the nature of Stella's real value. Arguably, Mrs Morrison is the only character who understands the enormous sacrifice that Stella has made for Laurel. For this reason, the film ends without emotional closure for the audience. For any joy the viewer feels at the sight of Laurel's happiness is curbed by an intense sympathy for Stella, which, as previously argued, is based on a recognition of Stella's inherent worth and the evident unfairness of her situation. It is left to the audience, who is given privileged access to all the characters' points of view, to question the social necessity of Stella's situation as well as the value and social costs of the class ascent itself, especially since it has led to the disruption of family life. Through its lack of emotional closure, the film provides the means for the audience to question the value of social ascent as an uncontested good.

What about Stella? Is she still the naive viewer from her earlier days at the cinema? Or, like the audience, has she learned to question the value of social ascent? She is certainly joyful as she watches Laurel's marriage and also sad, presumably because it has been achieved through the separation of mother and daughter. She also looks triumphant as she walks away down the street. But is she happy because she has helped Laurel achieve what she still desires for herself?

I think it is possible to think that Stella has changed her mind on the value of class ascent, for herself at least, if not for Laurel. It is important to remember that Stella's belief that Laurel wanted the lifestyle of the upper class brought her to make a spectacle of herself at the resort. For she was trying to fit in with the glamorous lifestyle that she believed Laurel wanted. The evidence from the film suggests that Stella had long ago given up on her ambition to be part of the upper class in favor of the life of a devoted mother. Moreover, Stella realized that she could participate in the upper-class life that Stephen offered her only if she was willing to conform to his image of what she should be like. When she makes an appearance at the resort, dressed to impress, she is in a significant sense reprising a role and a goal that she had long ago abandoned.

Stella's appearance at the end of the movie, without any frills or adornments, attests to her lack of ambition to impress others with her dress. It might be argued that this is simply evidence that she has been beaten down by life's circumstances, but is not proof of any second thoughts she has regarding the value of the social ascent she failed to achieve. But it is just as reasonable to think that Stella no longer desires to impress others through her dress or try to present a façade of something that she is not. Cavell's observation that "Stella learns the futility of appealing to the taste of those who have no taste for her" rings true; except that I would argue that Stella's recognition that social ascent is not what she wants for herself occurs much later in the film.

Further, what should we make of Stella's walking toward the audience as the film ends? In the first scene we see Stella as a spectator enthralled with the images of wealth and refinement that she sees on the screen. In the final scene, there is another reference to Stella as a spectator as she watches the wedding through the lit window. But is Stella still a naive or uncritical spectator of what she sees? By walking toward the audience, she is symbolically expressing her identification with the film viewer, who has been brought, I have argued, to a critical reflection on the value of social ascent. By representing Stella as symbolically joining the audience, the film points to the idea that, like the viewer, Stella has been changed by what she has witnessed and is no longer the naive viewer of film images she once was.

Finally, let us briefly consider the earlier scene at the movies and the closing scene in relation to the issue of the movie's role as a dream factory for creating social ambition. *Stella Dallas* is highly unusual in evoking the figure of the film screen as a medium who gives birth to class ascent and social ambitions. Insofar as the film moves the viewer to regard class ascent in a more critical light, it also enables the audience to regard the movie's role in promoting a desire for social ascent in the same way. By prompting the audience to question the film's own depictions of Stella as an excessive, working-class woman, *Stella Dallas* can even be understood to be making a subtle comment on how the images in such a film can distort the lives of the working class.

This leads me to one last comment on the film's representation of class ascent and its relation to the gender stereotypes that have been much discussed in the film. I have argued that the central source of Stella's failure to make it in the upper class is not her desire to be "something other than a mother," as previous feminist film commentators have argued. Rather, it is Stella's class difference that offends the sensibilities of the upper class. Even though this is clearly what the film is concerned to show, it also disguises the issue of class by defining Stella's unworthiness in the eyes of the upper class in sexual terms: Stella is thought of as a "good time" girl whose enjoyment of a fun time has sexual overtones (e.g. the scene on the train with Ed Munn, and Stella's flaunting of her body as she walks around the resort looking for Laurel). So it is not surprising that discussion of the film has centered on the gender stereotypes of Stella as either independent woman with desires of her own or self-sacrificing mother. Class may be the final stop for socially critical cinema: it was the case at the time *Stella Dallas* was made, and, arguably, it remains the case today.[11]

NOTES

1 See Ann Kaplan, "The Case of the Missing Mother," and Linda Williams, "Something Else Besides a Mother," in Patricia Erens, ed., *Issues in Feminist Film Criticism* (Bloomington and Indianapolis: Indiana University Press, 1990).

2 See Stanley Cavell, *Contesting Tears: The Hollywood Melodrama of the Unknown Woman* (Chicago and London: Chicago University Press, 1996), ch. 5.

3 Ibid., p. 202.

4 With this depiction of Stella's family situation, the film evokes a stereotype of working-class people, especially working-class men, as rough and hard-bitten in relating to members of their family.

5 Williams, "Something Else Besides a Mother," p. 149.

6 See Kaplan, "The Case of the Missing Mother," and Linda Williams, "Something Else Besides a Mother."

7 Linda Williams seems to acknowledge this point when she says that the representation of an excessive feminine presence, which she analogizes to a fetish, "functions" as a blatantly pathetic disavowal of much more pressing social lacks – of money, education, and power. The spectacle Stella stages for Laurel's eyes thus displaces the real social and economic causes of her presumed inadequacy as a mother onto a pretended desire for fulfillment as a woman – to be "something else besides a mother" ("Something Else Besides a Mother," p. 151). Yet Williams continues to focus on Stella's claim to desire to be "something else besides a mother" as the central source of the conflict in the movie. Yet her own analysis in the paragraph quoted points to Stella's lack of social capital as the real source of Stella's failure to achieve social ascent.

8 In this next section I will address Cavell's claim that Stella is able but unwilling to adapt herself to the tastes of the upper class.

9 See Lea Jacobs, *The Wages of Sin: Censorship and The Fallen Woman Film, 1928–1942* (University of California Press, 1995), p. 137.

10 Aristotle, *Rhetoric*, trans. Jonathan Barnes, in *The Complete Works of Aristotle: The Revised Oxford Translation* (Princeton: Princeton University Press, 1984).

11 I thank the members of the Faculty Film Seminar at Mount Holyoke College for their many helpful and insightful comments at a presentation of an earlier version of this paper.

Part VII

What Can We Learn From Films?

Introduction

When you think of the activity of doing philosophy, what images come to mind? Perhaps you think of some serious looking men and women – some with unkempt hair and faded elbow patches on their corduroy blazers – sitting around a table and debating issues such as the existence of God, the possibility of human freedom, or whether or not an action is morally right if it promotes the greatest happiness for all. An image of your philosophy professor attending a Saturday matinee of Tom Cruise's *Vanilla Sky* (Cameron Crowe, 2001) probably does not occur to you.

Yet starting with the publication of Stanley Cavell's work, *Pursuits of Happiness: The Hollywood Comedy of Remarriage*, almost 20 years ago, philosophers have recognized that films can embody a form of philosophical reflection. It is not hard to see why. Anyone who has seen the classic film *Rashomon* (Akira Kurosawa, 1950), which depicts four different viewpoints of a heinous crime, cannot fail to reflect on the nature of truth and whether it is relative to the perceiver. More recently, the thriller *Memento* (Christopher Nolan, 2000) examines fascinating questions regarding the connection between personal identity and memory. And the new German film, *Run, Lola, Run* (*Lola rennt*) (Tom Tykwer, 1998) uses the plot-device of screening three different follow-ups to the same event to prompt viewers to consider the role of fate and chance in affecting how our lives unfold. But how is it that film, an inherently visual medium, can raise philosophical questions? What is it that we can learn as philosophers reflecting on film?

Each selection in Part VII interprets an individual film or a film genre as offering philosophical insight. In his essay, philosopher Stanley Cavell analyzes the barriers that exist to Peter Warne and Ellie Andrews, the central characters in *It Happened One Night* (Frank Capra, 1934), becoming a romantic couple. Cavell's discussion focuses on the infamous blanket Peter puts up to shield Ellie from him during their night in a motel room while on the run from Ellie's father. On one level the blanket symbolizes the social obstacles in the way of Ellie and Peter's union: Peter is a working-class journalist who has just lost his job; Ellie is from a high-society family. She is also newly married to King Wesley, an aviator whom she wed to get out from under her father's control.

Cavell takes Kant's metaphor of there being a limit or barrier, as in the blanket, to our knowledge and applies it to our relationships with each other. Since each human being has a private realm, one known only to him or herself, how are we able to transgress that barrier and achieve relationships of genuine intimacy? Cavell thinks that *It Happened One Night* provides an answer to this question, one that accords with his own philosophical insights: it is a matter of acknowledging the other as an equal partner. In doing so, we obtain knowledge of ourselves and the other person.

When we attain the latter sort of knowledge, we enter into what Kant calls a "realm of ends" in which we acknowledge other rational, finite beings as our partners in an ideal human community. That this is a difficult achievement for human beings is part of what the film illustrates.

Cynthia A. Freeland examines a sub-genre of the horror film that is gaining in popularity, what she calls "realist horror." These films feature ordinary, albeit horrific, human beings in the role of the monster figure, e.g. Hannibal Lecter from *Silence of the Lambs* (Jonathan Demme, 1991) or the title character from *Henry: Portrait of a Serial Killer* (John McNaughton, 1986). Freeland argues that realist horror is a sub-genre that poses problems for a major account of horror films presented by the philosopher Noël Carroll (see chapter 17 for a reading from Carroll's book on the philosophy of horror).

Noël Carroll argues that intellectual fascination with the monster is central to our interest in horror movies. Monsters are revolting, Carroll acknowledges, yet they are also fascinating for they are impure creatures that violate our conceptual categories, e.g. the character of the Wolf Man in the Lon Chaney films, who is part human and part wolf. The plot of the horror movie piques the viewers' interest in the monster for it shows the protagonist tracking, discovering, and confirming the existence of the monster. On Carroll's theory, then, it is this intellectual interest with the dramatic representation of the monster that is the source of the viewers' pleasure from horror films.

Freeland argues that Carroll's account of horror cannot explain viewers' attraction to realist horror. First, the monsters in realist horror films are repugnant and terrifying, yet they do not violate our conceptual or scientific categories – these monsters are often based on real-life people. Second, because of this fact, realist horror films blur the line between art or film and reality. This raises the question how it is that viewers can have a distanced emotional response to realist horror narratives – something that Carroll calls the emotion of "art-horror" – when they know that the films represent real-life people and violence. Freeland concludes that viewers' interest in these movies may be morally problematic, though she also suggests realist horror films such as *Henry* or *Silence of the Lambs* can prompt viewers to call into question their fascination with the serial killers these movies portray.

Can films "screen" philosophical arguments and claims? This is the subject of Thomas E. Wartenberg's essay on the blockbuster science-fiction film, *The Matrix* (Wachowski, 1999). Wartenberg examines one author's view that philosophy is a form of critical reflection. If we accept that this is true, how is it that film, which is an essentially visual medium, can embody a form of critical reflection, one that often takes a discursive or written form?

One central philosophical technique for prompting critical understanding is the "thought experiment." Here a philosopher constructs a possible situation for a reader to consider as part of a philosophical argument that may challenge the reader's beliefs and patterns of action. René Descartes advances a famous thought experiment challenging our claims to knowledge in the first of his six *Meditations on First Philosophy*. There Descartes imagines that he may have been created by an evil genius who brings it about that Descartes is deceived even about those beliefs he thinks are the most certain. If this is possible – and Descartes sees no reason to think that it is not – then all of Descartes's beliefs up to that point are less than certain.

Wartenberg argues that *The Matrix* advances ideas that are an analog to the central ideas in Descartes's thought experiment about the evil genius. First, the audience sees a world in which the denizens of the Matrix – a perceptual illusion created and maintained by computers that have taken over the world – are deceived into believing in a world that does not exist. In the fictional world of the film, then, the evil genius hypothesis is true, at least for some of the film's characters. Second, the beginning of the film aligns the viewer's viewpoint with that of the central protagonist, Neo (Keanu Reeves), who takes the red pill offered by Morpheus (Laurence Fishburne) and comes to realize that he was deceived about the nature of the world he inhabits. Through this revelation, the film suggests to the audience that they, too, were mistaken in their beliefs about the reality of things in the fictional world of the film. In this way *The Matrix* illustrates the skeptical hypothesis that Descartes describes in his evil genius argument and may generate the same kind of perplexity in the audience regarding the certainty of their beliefs that Descartes does in his readers.

In his essay on the popular hit comedy *Groundhog Day* (Harold Ramis, 1993), Joseph H. Kupfer draws on philosophers as diverse as Friedrich Nietzsche and Aristotle to show how the film instructs its audience on fundamental issues in moral philosophy. *Groundhog Day* is the story of a cynical television weatherman, Phil Connors (Bill Murray), who unenthusiastically goes to Punxsutawney, Pennsylvania to cover the town's annual celebration of February 2, Groundhog Day. Through some cosmic tinkering, a horrified Phil finds himself caught in a seemingly endless repetition of Groundhog Day, with Phil being the only person who has knowledge and a memory of each of the previous day's repetitions. Kupfer evokes an idea of the nineteenth-century German philosopher, Nietzsche, to frame Phil's predicament in philosophical terms. Nietzsche challenges his reader to imagine that her life, exactly as it has been lived, would repeat itself again and again, indefinitely. How would you greet this news, Nietzsche asks? Nietzsche thought that by considering the possibility of the eternal return, we can look at our lives differently and henceforth act in such a way that we can embrace the possibility of the eternal return of our actions.

Phil's situation is not an exact illustration of Nietzsche's theory, for under the eternal return hypothesis we are to imagine that our lives will remain exactly the same and repeat themselves again and again. Phil, on the other hand, is able to retain the knowledge and memories he gained from his previous repetitions of Groundhog Day and apply them to the new repetition of February 2. His situation is nonetheless a variation of the eternal return hypothesis, for through the repetition of the same day he is able to see the lack of meaning in the way he is living his life.

Kupfer draws on ideas from Aristotle in his *Nicomachean Ethics*, who argues that in order to live well and flourish a human being must exercise his natural capacity for virtue or moral excellence. This capacity is exercised as well as further developed through the repetition of actions that cultivate a virtuous character. Once Phil realizes the lack of meaning in the way he is living his life, he seeks to make the changes in his desires and actions that will enable him to greet the repetition of each day with joy, rather than dread. Through repeatedly performing actions that are motivated by Phil's newfound desire to care for the concerns of those around him, he develops and exercises his capacity for living a good life. He also develops a sense of beauty through creative activities such as playing the piano and ice sculpting. On Kupfer's reading, then, the film depicts Phil's transformation from a self-centered individual into an aesthetically refined and morally exemplary individual through the repetition of actions that foster a virtuous character and a sense of aesthetic appreciation.

In arguing that films can offer a certain kind of philosophical insight – on our relations with others, our fascination with the monstrous, or the nature of knowledge – these authors show why it is valuable for philosophers to study film. It is not simply a matter of showing how the theories philosophers have offered can apply to films; these essays show that the ideas that some films advance or examine embody a sort of reflection on philosophical issues. This means that films do not simply support or confirm a philosophical system: examining the philosophical ideas inherent in some films can give rise to interesting challenges and questions for the theories philosophers have offered, as well as open up new ways of posing philosophical questions.

Study Questions

1. Cavell makes use of Kant's philosophy to explain the idea that our lives are shaped by intellectual and social barriers. What keeps us from entering into a community with others?
2. What are the social obstacles that Peter and Ellie must overcome in order to become a married couple? Do you agree with Cavell that the film illustrates some difficulties of entering into "the realm of ends" with others? What scenes support Cavell's reading?
3. Cavell argues that the film does not present either Peter or Ellie as the dominant partner, but represents both as equally active. Do you agree? What are some scenes that might challenge Cavell's view?
4. What is realist horror, according to Freeland? What are the two key features of this genre that Freeland illustrates with reference to *Henry: Portrait of a Serial Killer*?
5. What is Noël Carroll's analysis of the response of "art horror" to the representations in horror films? Why does Freeland argue that realist horror poses a problem for Noël Carroll's account of the appeal of the horror movie?

6. What are the two kinds of morally problematic messages found in realist horror films? Do you agree with Freeland that films like *Henry: Portrait of a Serial Killer* or *Silence of the Lambs* can prompt audiences to look critically at their fascination with the monster?

7. What differences does Wartenberg note between philosophy and film as intellectual practices? Why do these differences make it hard to see how film can illustrate philosophical ideas or claims?

8. What is a philosophical "thought experiment"? What is the thought experiment Descartes entertains regarding the deception hypothesis? How does the film *The Matrix* "screen" or illustrate Descartes's deception hypothesis, according to Wartenberg?

9. Does *The Matrix* depict a fictional world in which Descartes's deception hypothesis is true? Or does the film suggest an answer to Descartes's worry that there are no criteria for determining whether or not an evil demon is deceiving him?

10. What is Nietzsche's idea of the eternal return? What is the question Nietzsche wants us to consider when we imagine our lives returning again and again? Why does Kupfer suggest that *Groundhog Day* illustrates Nietzsche's idea?

11. What is egoistic hedonism and how does *Groundhog Day* represent Phil as an egoistic hedonist at the start of the film? What changes does Phil go through as he reacts to the realization that February 2 is repeating itself?

12. What is Aristotle's account of virtue? Why does Kupfer argue that Phil illustrates Aristotle's view of how people realize their human potential? Do you agree that *Groundhog Day* shows Phil's transformation into a virtuous person?

13. Do you agree with the readings in this section that films can assert or advance philosophical ideas?

24

Knowledge as Transgression:
It Happened One Night

Stanley Cavell

Not knowing whether human knowledge and human community require the recognizing or the dismantling of limits; not knowing what it means that these limits are sometimes picturable as a barrier and sometimes not; not knowing whether we are more afraid of being isolated or of being absorbed by our knowledge and by society – these lines of ignorance are the background against which I wish to consider Frank Capra's *It Happened One Night* (1934). And most urgently, as may be guessed, I wish to ponder its central figure of the barrier-screen, I daresay the most famous blanket in the history of drama. [. . .]

The blanket dividing the space, and falling between the beds, is the man's idea as the principal pair, for the first of three times we will know about, prepare to share a cabin in an auto camp. The woman is understandably skeptical: "That, I suppose, makes everything all right." He replies that he likes privacy when he retires, that prying eyes annoy him, and goes on at once to situate the blanket allegorically: "Behold the Walls of Jericho. Maybe not as thick as the ones Joshua blew down with his trumpet, but a lot safer. You see, I have no trumpet." Wise in the ways of Hollywood symbolism, as generally obvious as the raising and lowering of a flag, we could already predict that the action of the film will close with the walls tumbling down. But then let us be

18 ■ "Ellie (Claudette Colbert) and Peter (Clark Gable) on either side of the blanket, a.k.a. 'The Wall of Jericho', in the motel room," from *It Happened One Night*.

wise enough, if we care about this film, to care about the rigors of this symbolism. The question the narrative must ask itself is how to get them to tumble. That this is a question, and the kind of question it is, is declared late in the film when the second blanket is shown unceremoniously pulled down by the suspicious owners of this second auto camp. Of course it is easy to pull it down if you do not know what it is, or care. So an early requirement for its correct tumbling is that the pair come to share a fantasy of what is holding it up.

An immediate complication is insinuated concerning who must use the trumpet. As the man, the wall in place, their spaces ready for the night, prepares to undress, he says: "Do you mind joining the Israelites?" – that is, get over to your side of the blanket. Now anyone who knows enough to refer to the Walls of Jericho – say a Hollywood script writer – knows that the Israelites are the attacking force and that it is they who have the relevant trumpets. Thus the man is repeating his claim that he has no trumpet and is adding that whether the walls come down will depend on whether the right sounds issue from her side of the wall. You may think this is pushing popular biblical study too far, but while it may be most common for audiences to interpret the allegory so that Clark Gable is Joshua and at the end blows the trumpet, it should be considered that we do not *see* this and that, for all we are apprised of, we are free to imagine that it is the woman who is still invited to make the move and who gallantly accepts the invitation. (So why don't we exercise that freedom?) If the trumpet is the man's, then presumably the blanket-wall represents the woman's virginity, or perhaps her resistance, even conceivably her reserve. I shall not deny that these symbolisms are in train here, but I wish to leave it open to the film to provide us with some instruction about what, a third of the way through our century and for a couple of persons not exceedingly young, virginity and resistance and reserve consist in, what the problem is about them.

I guess I would not place such emphasis on the possible ambiguity concerning who blows the trumpet apart from my taking this film as one defining the genre of the comedy of remarriage; for it is an essential feature of that genre, as I conceive it, to leave ambiguous the question whether the man or the woman is the active or the passive partner, whether indeed active and passive are apt characterizations of the difference between male and female, or whether indeed we know satisfactorily how to think about the difference between male and female. This is why I said that this genre of film rather refuses the distinction between Old Comedy and New Comedy, in the former of which the woman is dominant, in the latter the man. This is also a reason I have also called the genre the comedy of equality. [. . .]

[. . .]

Now we must start asking specifically what there is between just these two people that just this mode of censoring or elaboration is constructed between them. And for this a further elaboration of certain features of the genre of remarriage comedies will help. [. . .] The father's dominating presence is handled most wittily in *The Lady Eve* and most oratorically in *The Philadelphia Story*; but it is given its most pervasive handling in *It Happened One Night*. The entire narrative can be seen as summarized in the first of the newspaper headlines that punctuate it: Ellie Andrews Escapes Father. And throughout her escapades with Clark Gable, Claudette Colbert is treated by him as a child, as his child, whose money he confiscates and then doles back on allowance, whom he mostly calls "Brat," and to whom he is forever delivering lectures on the proper way to do things, like piggyback or hitchhike. After his first lecture, on the proper method of dunking doughnuts, she even says, "Thanks, Professor," a title more memorably harped on in *The Philadelphia Story*. In the genre of remarriage the man's lecturing indicates that an essential goal of the narrative is the education of the woman, where her education turns out to mean her acknowledgment of her desire, and this in turn will be conceived of as her creation, her emergence, at any rate, as an autonomous human being. ("Somebody that's real," the man will say, half out of a dream-state, at the climax of the film, "somebody that's alive. They don't come that way any more.")

But perhaps I should justify including this film under the genre of remarriage at all, since while it is true that a late newspaper headline satisfyingly declares Ellen Andrews Remarries Today, what the film – or the newspaper – thinks it means is not that she is to marry the real object of her desire again. [. . .] I might, again, say that the matter of remarriage is only one of an open set of features shared by this genre of comedy and that the absence of even that feature may in a given instance be compensated for by the presence of other features. Most pointedly, here, a film that opens (virtually) with the following exchange between a daughter and her father –

> ELLIE: Can't you get it through your head that King Wesley and I are married? Definitely, legally, actually married. It's over. It's finished. There's not a thing you can do about it. I'm over twenty-one, and so is he.
> ANDREWS: Would it interest you to know that while you've been on board, I've been making arrangements to have your marriage annulled?

– by that fact alone has a claim in my book to be called a comedy of remarriage, because a central claim of mine about the genre is that it shifts emphasis away from the normal question of comedy, whether a young pair will get married, onto the question whether the pair will get and stay divorced, thus prompting philosophical discussions of the nature of marriage. We might accordingly say here that the issue of remarriage is present but displaced. [. . .]

The idea of displacement seems to me right as far as it goes, but it does not explain how the issue gets displaced onto just this pair, what it is about them that invites it. It feels at the end as if they are marrying again, and not merely because of the plain fact, significant as it is, that the wedding night is shown to be set in yet another auto camp – which thus repeats two of the three nights they have already spent together – but specifically because what we have been shown in the previous auto camps is something like their marriage. We know of course that they have not been legally, actually married, but we also know that those things do not always constitute marriage, and we may freely wonder what does. Our genre is meant to have us wonder. [. . .]

[. . .]

A major thematic development is under way, based on food. Here are the opening words of the film, preceding the initial interview quoted earlier between father and daughter.

ANDREWS: On a hunger strike, eh? How long has this been going on?

CAPTAIN: She hasn't had anything yesterday or today.

ANDREWS: Send her meals up to her regularly?

CAPTAIN: Yes, sir.

ANDREWS: Well, why don't you jam it down her throat?

CAPTAIN: Well, it's not as simple as all that, Mr. Andrews.

ANDREWS: Ah, I'll talk to her myself. Have some food brought up to her.

CAPTAIN: Yes, sir.

And then the father's object during the ensuing interview is to get his daughter to accept food from him; he even tries to feed her, but she responds as though he is trying to jam something down her throat; and when she deliberately knocks to the floor the tray of food he has had sent up, he slaps her, upon which she runs from the cabin and dives from the yacht to escape him. The angry refusal of food is thus directly established as an angry, intimate refusal of love, of parental protection; the appreciative acceptance of food in the auto camp cabin asserts itself as the acceptance of that intimacy. This relation has also been prepared earlier by the man's having denied food to her on the bus. It occurs just after he has moved out the flirt by claiming to be her husband. Colbert orders a box of chocolates from a vendor on the bus and Gable sends the boy away. He explains this husbandly act by saying that she can't afford chocolates and telling her that from now on she's on a budget; but the implication is clear enough that he is instructing her not merely in what is worth spending but in what is worth eating, say in what is worth consummation. (And in what manner what is worth consuming is worth consuming – recall the lecture on doughnut dunking.)

The next night, in the field, she complains of hunger, and when later the man, after disappearing, returns with a bunch of carrots, she refuses them, saying she's too scared to be hungry. The next morning he offers them again:

ELLIE: What are you eating?

PETER: Carrots.

ELLIE: Raw?

PETER: Uh-huh. Want one?

ELLIE: No! Why didn't you get me something nicer to eat?

PETER: That's right, I forgot. The idea of offering a raw carrot to an Andrews. Say you don't think I'm going around panhandling for you, do you? Better have one of these. Best thing in the world for you, carrots.

ELLIE: I hate the horrid things.

He is exasperated by the irrationality of her refusal of good food, perhaps by the return of her past over her recent show of genuine feeling, and perhaps he would like to jam the good food down her pretty throat.

Ellie's refusal here aligns Peter even more directly with the opening position of her father, and it sets up a repetition of the earlier pair of actions toward food: again Peter denies her something to eat, again for a moral reason, and as a result she soon accepts food that he has provided for her. The man giving them a lift has stopped in front of a lunchroom:

DRIVER: How about a bit to eat?
ELLIE: Oh, that would be love –
PETER: No thanks. We're not hungry.
DRIVER: Oh, I see. Young people in love are never hungry.
PETER: No.

. . .

PETER: What were you going to do? Gold-dig that guy for a meal?
ELLIE: Sure I was. No fooling, I'm hungry.
PETER: If you do, I'll break your neck.

When they get out of the car to walk around and stretch their legs, the driver hurries out of the lunchroom and takes off with their belongings. Peter runs after the car. After a dissolve, Ellie is waiting beside the road and Peter shows up in the car alone. As they drive off Peter asks Ellie to take the things out of the pocket of his coat, which she is holding, to see what they might exchange for gasoline. One thing she finds in the pocket is a carrot, which, after a hesitation, overcoming something, she begins slowly to nibble, hunching down inside herself. Seeing her eating this food of humility, Peter is won to her. He had liked the taste she showed in people (except for the man she got married to, but then as her father had said, she only did that because he told her not to), but he had despised her sense of exemption from the human condition, a sense he calls her money. Eating the carrot is the expression of her acceptance of her humanity, of true need – call it the creation of herself as a human being. No doubt he is also won because eating the carrot is an acceptance of him, being an acceptance of food from him. It is also an acceptance of equality with him, since he has been living on that food. [. . .]

  [. . .]

Then we have again to ask why he withdraws from her when she is drawn past the barrier to his side of things; moreover, when her being drawn seems to remove the remaining impediment to the marriage of their minds. In the previous sequence she accepted her relation to common humanity, and in crossing the barrier she accepts the role of Israelite; the initiating sound has come from her side of things. What is the matter? Why, after all, is he surprised by her? Why can he not allow the woman of his dreams to enter his dream? But just that must be the answer. What surprises him is her reality. To acknowledge her as this woman would be to acknowledge that she is "somebody that's real, somebody that's alive," flesh and blood, someone separate from his dream who therefore has, if she is to be in it, to enter it; and this feels to him to be a threat to the dream, and hence a threat to him. To walk in the direction of one's dream is necessarily to risk the dream. We can view his problem as one of having to put together his perception of the woman with his imagination of her. This would be precisely the right tumbling of the Walls of Jericho. It is a way to frame a solution to the so-called problem of the existence of other minds. The genre of remarriage invites us to speak of putting together imagination and perception in terms of putting together night and day – say dreams and responsibilities. Each of its instances has its own realization of this project. But the sublimest realization of it in film is Chaplin's *City Lights*.

Surely, it will be said, a simpler explanation for Peter's rejection of Ellie's advances is that legally she has a husband. But, first of all, Peter could have said that; and second, that seems not to bother him a few moments later when Ellie is back on the other side of the barrier. And how would this explanation accord with Peter's leaving to get a thousand dollars in order to tear down the Walls of Jericho, and by selling their story? It is a very mysterious nest of actions.

Whatever the actions mean, the fundamental fact about them is that he leaves, he continues his withdrawal from her, he panics. It is that fact that any explanation must explain. [. . .]

[. . .]

It is no wonder that Peter is confused by Ellie's appearance to him, and he is not to be blamed for an act of rupture, or abandonment, that he cannot heal. We might understand his leaving her asleep as his intuition that they require, and his going in search of, a divorce; and understand his failure to accomplish this as his discovery that it cannot be accomplished alone. His task reverses, or reinterprets, the story of Sleeping Beauty: the prince wishes for the maiden to stay asleep until he finds his way to the authority to kiss her, but a witch has put a curse on her to awaken, after a hundred years, a moment too soon.

[. . .]

We have available a reading of the allegorical confusion Peter suffers in leaving Ellie while he goes to sell their story. The telling of the story is to have the effect of authorizing their marriage, of divorcing them from their pasts, she from her father and her legal husband, he from his private fantasy; of making something public. He calls it "the biggest scoop of the year." But what is the scoop, what is *their* story? He tells the editor he needs the thousand to tear down the Walls of Jericho and that her marriage is going to be annulled so that she can marry someone else, namely him. But that is *not* news, because his abandoning her means precisely that he does not know, or have it on good authority, that they can marry. He is behaving as though announcing the event in the newspaper will not only make it public but make it happen. And maybe this could work, for some story other than his own. When the editor acquires conviction in the story, from the authority of the story itself, in the face of clear evidence against it, what he says to Peter in consolation is that, with a great yarn, something always comes along and messes up the finish. This would presumably be reality. It is not Peter who has messed up the finish of the yarn; on the contrary, the only yarn is the one he has written for the editor, and the editor accepts the finish. He accepts what we have accepted. Their story has already happened; it cannot be *made* public if *this* is not public. What has made it public is a film, and in that sense a yarn. A newspaper story, coming after the fact, has no further fact to come after here. That the yarn that has happened has no assured finish in the future happiness of the pair, and is in that sense messed up, is part of the logic of the human work of construction, of art, of its transience and its permanence, as John Keats and Wallace Stevens best say; and part of the logic of the human emotion of love, what Freud calls its biphasic character; not something that this man is singularly to be blamed for.

It is notable that Peter never does transgress the barrier. When Ellie does not respond to his belated question about whether she really means what she has so passionately declared, he looks over its top, and, when he is dressed to leave, blows a kiss over it. As a man he is merely playing out the string of his confusion. Seen as a surrogate for the film's director, he is playing out the condition of film and its subjects, that their maker has to kiss them goodbye, that he or she is outside, that when the play is done his work is absolutely over, unlike the case of theater. He has become the work's audience, the viewer of creation, its first audience, but with no greater power over it therefore than any later one. He puts himself in the hands of higher powers, not unlike the duty of a romantic hero. He has accomplished his remarkable feat. His reward must be *conferred*.

I said earlier that in working like a movie screen the barrier represents both an outer and inner censoring, and more recently that the man's problem in connecting the woman's body and soul, that is in putting together his perception and his imagination, his and her day and night (so that his capacity for imagination becomes his ability to imagine *her*), is a framing of the problem of other minds. Putting these notions together in turn, I would read the instruction of the barrier along these lines. What it censors is the man's knowledge of the existence of the human being "on the other side." The picture is that the existence of others is something of which we are unconscious, a piece of knowledge we repress, about which we draw a blank. This does violence to others, it separates their bodies from their souls, makes monsters of them; and presumably we do it because we feel that others are doing this violence to us. The release from this circle of vengeance is something I call acknowledgment. The form the man attempts to give acknowledgment is to tell their story. The film can be said to describe the failure of this attempt as a last attempt to substitute knowledge for acknowledgment, privacy for community, to transcend the barrier without transgressing it. Only of an infinite being is the world created with the word. As finite, you cannot achieve reciprocity with the one in view by telling your story to the whole rest of the world. You have to act in order to make things happen, night and day; and to act from within the world, within your connection with others, forgoing the wish for a place outside from which to view and to direct your fate. These are at best merely further fates. There is no place to go in order to acquire the authority of connection. The little community of love is not based on the appeal of the law nor on the approach of feeling. It is an emblem of the promise that human society contains room for both, that the game is worth the candle. You cannot wait for the perfected community to be presented. And yet, in matters of the heart, to make things happen, you must let them happen.

25

Realist Horror

Cynthia A. Freeland

A Chicago man steals corpses and skins them to make himself a suit. A drifter from Texas confesses to 600 murders. A Milwaukee man cannibalizes and has sex with the corpses of numerous boys he has killed.

These sketches illustrate realist horror narratives.[1] They begin in the newspapers but move swiftly to Hollywood contracts and major motion pictures. It is no news that art imitates life: Mary Shelley's monster was born out of Galvani's experiments on the publicly displayed bodies of executed criminals, and nineteenth-century newspapers inspired the more chilling episodes in Dickens, Poe, and Dostoyevsky. But the ties between fact and fiction have become increasingly intricate and ramified. The fiction of *The Silence of the Lambs*, based partly on facts about real corpse-stealer Ed Gein, permeated media coverage of the arrest of cannibalistic serial killer Jeffrey Dahmer, and publicity over Dahmer's arrest in its turn threatened the box-office take and opening date of the horror film *Body Parts*.

What is it to engage in a philosophical examination of realist horror? An important precedent in the western tradition is the ancient Greek debate about tragedy. Plato faulted tragedy because it (like horror) appeals to the audience's baser instincts, obscuring truth and showcasing scenes of overwhelming terror and violence. Aristotle defended tragedies as worthy *representations* with a distinct cognitive status, and he described a positive aspect, *katharsis*, of our emotional reactions of pity and terror to such representations.

I am not the first to observe a parallel between tragedy and horror. Noël Carroll's recent *The Philosophy of Horror* brings horror into the western aesthetic tradition by supplying a framework that recalls Aristotle's defense of tragedy in the *Poetics*.[2] In this paper I want to show that such a classical approach will not work for realist horror. I argue this by illustrating how little it can say about a key example, *Henry: Portrait of a Serial Killer*. Realist horror requires us to think in new ways about the moral assessment of films precisely because of its realism – or rather, because of what we may call its postmodern reweaving of the relation between reality and art. Later, I focus further on this reweaving and propose my own alternative to the classical approach, to ground a more fruitful and subtle discussion of moral issues raised by realist horror.

The Classical Approach

Plato attacked tragic poetry for confusing people who took it to be more vivid than reality itself. It was crucial for Aristotle to show that we recognize and evaluate tragedies as imitations (*mimeseis*), in which plot *represents* action and characters *represent* people. Carroll's *The Philosophy of Horror*, like Aristotle's *Poetics*, examines a genre that seems to rely upon our direct, problematic interest in fearful violence. Again like Aristotle, Carroll argues that this genre evokes a distinct aesthetic response built upon a somewhat distanced intellectual interest in plot. We enjoy tracking the suspenseful narrative, and so we put up with the revulsion that Carroll calls "art-horror."[3] Art-horror is a distanced emotional response to a representation: though monsters in horror are repellent and scary, they do not threaten us directly, and we are protected by knowing they are in fact impossible. They fascinate us because they violate our conceptual categories, arousing in us a strong desire to know something unknowable.

This theoretical defense of horror fails to work for the entire subgenre of realist horror because it depends crucially upon the fictitious nature of the monsters at the center of horror. Carroll defines a monster as "any being not believed to exist according to contemporary science." This requirement is essential to keeping the emphasis on narrative or plot and to preserving the particular aesthetic response Carroll approves, art-horror. He seems to see in the psychotic killer a sort of falling away from an essence of horrific monstrousness. So he is forced to discount a film like *Psycho* as horror, for example, because the monster in it is naturalized: "He is a schizophrenic, a type of being that science countenances." (38)

Yet realist horror is a prevalent and important subgenre of horror that deserves consideration. *Psycho* and *Peeping Tom*, both released in 1960, initiated a significant shift in the horror genre. They chillingly depicted "ordinary" men who were unable to connect with the reality around them. Due to traumas of childhood and sexual repression, so the story went, they become mad slashers. This scenario has become formulaic in numerous subsequent variations; and the subgenre became the dominant form of horror in the 1980s.

To see the limitations of Carroll's Aristotelian or classical approach to horror, I want to look in some detail at one example, *Henry: Portrait of a Serial Killer* (1990, prod. 1986, John McNaughton), a movie loosely based on the story of real serial murderer Henry Lee Lucas. *Henry* is exceptionally interesting – and also disturbing – for its realism of style and amoral viewpoint. It violates the usual rules of both the horror genre in general and the slasher in particular. It offers no audience identification figure, nor does its plot depict any righting of wrongs. As a horror movie, though, this film succeeds by creating terror and unease, both promising and withholding the spectacle of violence.

[. . .]

The plot of *Henry* seems flat and random. Certain events occur when Becky, the sister of Henry's roommate Otis, moves into their small Chicago apartment and disrupts their somewhat repressed homosexual partnership. Victimized by incest, Becky has sought refuge with her brother who also proves abusive. A parole violator and drug pusher, he repeatedly kisses Becky and demands to see her breasts, as her father had. Becky tries to normalize the household by getting a regular job and fixing meals, but her efforts fail. (At one point the film cuts from the corpse of the woman Henry has exterminated to a shot of a fish Becky is vigorously cleaning in the kitchen sink.)

[. . .]

The most graphic and bloody of the murders in *Henry* is Henry's murder of Otis, whom he has caught raping Becky. Henry blinds Otis and then stabs him while lying atop his body in an orgiastic, sexualized attack. Henry chops up Otis's body and loads it into large garbage bags which he packs into suitcases and dumps in the river. He leaves town with Becky, who looks at him and says "I love you Henry." "I guess I love you too," he says. The car radio plays the song, "Loving you was my mistake." They stop for the night at a motel room and get ready for bed. Becky looks up trustingly at Henry who says it's time to turn in. The next morning we see Henry shaving with a straight razor, getting dressed and leaving the motel room – alone. He piles suitcases into the car, and later stops along the road to set a suitcase along the berm. In close-up we see blood seeping through the soft-sided case. That's it, she's dead. Inevitable. Henry drives on in his beat-up old brown Chevy. The movie ends.

Henry is an example of realist horror: based on a real serial murderer, it features a possible, realistic monster. But the classical account of horror modeled on Aristotle's defense of tragedy will not work for this movie. Carroll makes these central claims about the subject matter and construction of horror films. First, horror concerns monsters. Though they may seem possible, they are not real. Our central interest in horror is cognitive, learning about the monster who violates our conceptual categories. And so, second, horror films can be described and assessed mainly in terms of their plots. Our reaction to such narratives is the aesthetic response of art-horror, a revulsion contained by our knowledge that the monster is fictitious, rather than a direct interest in realistic spectacles of violence. But Carroll's central claims are violated by realist horror, where monsters and plots function differently from the way they do in classical horror. Let me comment further by reexamining these two key features, monster and plot, in *Henry*.

First, in realist horror like *Henry*, the monster is a true-to-life rather than supernatural being. Henry *is* a monster. Like many movie monsters, he seems all-powerful, unpredictable, and a source of hideous violence. His approach to his fellow humans is loathsome. He is nevertheless a possible being; he is based upon a real Death Row killer, Henry Lee Lucas. Of course, we do not believe in watching the movie that this monster threatens us, and yet monsters like him do threaten us – there are men who kill others randomly on the streets, in stores, and in their homes. What is monstrous about both versions of Henry is not simply the deeds done but the attitudes, the flatness: "It all seemed fun to start with." [. . .]

Other instances of realist horror also feature a realistic or possible monster. It is common for us to regard contemporary serial killers and other "heroes" of realist horror films as monsters. Jeffrey Dahmer or Ed Gein, as much as "Buffalo Bill" or Hannibal Lecter, are horrific, loathsome, disgusting creatures that skin, eat, or have sex with corpses, and kill without remorse. Our interest in killers like Henry Lucas or Dahmer, the basis on which they quickly achieve a certain celebrity status, seems to amount simply to a basic fascination with the sheer fact of their monstrousness. This fascination may even acquire an erotic edge; films like *Henry* or *The Silence of the Lambs* work to generate such an allure. The brilliant and charming Hannibal Lecter engages in an intensely intimate relationship with young FBI agent Clarice Starling in *The Silence of the Lambs*. Henry is chivalrous to Becky, and she responds by eroticizing him. The film conspires in this, as the camera lingers on the good-looking young actor, Michael Rooker, who plays Henry. He is treated iconographically as a Marlon Brando/James Dean angry young rebel, complete with pout, mumbles, short curly hair, square jaw, and white T-shirt. What is most striking is that Becky begins to eroticize Henry just when she learns he's a killer; but isn't this the source of our fascination, too? [. . .] The case of Ted Bundy being played by Mark Harmon in the TV movie *A Deliberate Stranger* is another example of this phenomenon; Jeffrey Dahmer and the Menendez brothers acquired groupies during their trials.

[. . .]

From the allure of the real-life monster, I move to explore the second key feature of *Henry*, its displacement of interest from plot onto spectacle. *Henry* is not a narrative of discovery; rather, it moves the viewer through a gradually intensified spectacle into climax and denouement. *Henry* shocks and announces its gory nature by its opening graphic sequence of nude corpses. But it reveals spectacle slowly, and the scenes that depict killings play with the viewer's emotions in non-standard ways. When Henry and Otis kill the man in the TV pawn shop, while the murder is vicious and gruesome, it is rather comically cross-cut with one of Becky washing the hair of a large Chicago matron spouting racist slogans. After this murder the spectacles begin to crescendo through the murder of the family to climax in the particularly intense, brutal and sexualized murder of Otis. Finally as a diminuendo or anticlimax, restoring symmetry with the opening sequences, *Henry* ends after implying the off-screen murder of Becky.

Realist horror, whether fictive or factual, like *Henry*, typically showcases the spectacular nature of monstrous violence. Realist horror is like other film genres that rely chiefly upon spectacle (for example the musical or hard-core pornography film); in these genres, plot serves to bridge together the "real thing" the film promises to deliver. Although *The Silence of the Lambs* offers many conventional plot elements, it too allows spectacle a major role. The movie highlights the skinned bodies of Buffalo Bill's victims and the bizarreness of his underground den and moth fetish. In the outer story, Lecter is an even greater master of spectacle, operating with a Nietzschean aesthetic all his own. We witness one of his grotesque aesthetic acts (almost a piece of performance art itself) when he orchestrates the murder of his two guards as part of a seamless whole that includes his drawings of Clarice with a lamb, a dinner of rare lamb chops, and Bach's *Goldberg Variations*. The murder is not simply bloody (it is that) but it is artistically arranged, with one body stretched on high as a disemboweled angel and another man's face skinned off to provide Lecter's own disguise. [. . .]

An emphasis on the spectacle of random violence rather than plot in realist horror would lead philosophers from Plato and Aristotle to Noël Carroll to downgrade this genre. Plato categorized our drive toward violent spectacle as lowest among his rank-ordering of human desires, and in the *Poetics* Aristotle argued that spectacle is the "least artistic" of tragedy's six parts. Carroll follows Aristotle in emphasizing plot, which again, like Aristotle, he sees as the focus of our cognitive interests in horror – hence as having greater legitimacy than a "mere" interest in spectacle. In other words, in this tradition, realist horror has little merit aesthetically and would no doubt have to be condemned as morally perverse.

Against this classical approach I have several things to say. First, I think realist horror is a subgenre of horror. But such films rely crucially upon the realism of their horror, the possibility of their monsters, the showcasing of gruesome spectacle, and (at least in the case of *Henry*) the flat randomness of their structure. And second, realist horror films *can* be good movies. That is, they can be well-made constructions or representations that effectively carry out their aims of evoking suspense and horror. I would cite *Henry* or *The Texas Chain Saw Massacre* as examples; *The Silence of the Lambs* won many Oscars, including Best Motion Picture. Realist horror forces us to attend to the very problem of moral perverseness that Carroll wants to avoid: that we are somehow attracted to monsters and to the horrific spectacle itself. The orchestrated representation of violence evokes an ambivalent thrill as we react to realistic depictions of horrific events we know to be possible. I find standard critiques of our direct interest in such monsters and spectacles both simplistic and naive. We need room for a subtler sort of moral assessment. The intricacy of interconnections between the news and film plots necessitates more reflection upon the representational character of violence in realist horror, and it also calls for the use of a different strategy than the classical approach.

An Alternative Strategy

I have described two key features of realist horror, the fascination of the realistic monster and the foregrounding of gruesome spectacle over plot, that prevent this genre from neatly fitting within a classical theory like Carroll's. As I use the term, a classical theory, like Aristotle's in the *Poetics*, has three elements. We first understand there is a clear relation between art and reality: artworks imitate or represent reality. Second, we describe the construction of such imitations, focusing on plot and narrative. Aristotle discerned key patterns that involve a hero, an action, a mistake or *hamartia*, a downfall, and a denouement or unwinding. Carroll similarly describes variations in horror plot patterns. And third, in a classical theory we describe the aesthetic/emotional reactions that such representations aim at producing or evoking. Both Aristotle and Carroll argue that such reactions are unproblematic or unperverse.

Now, I contend that realist horror problematizes the classical approach by thwarting the initial assumption that we can draw a clear distinction between artistic imitations and reality. Realist horror must be understood as a particularly postmodern phenomenon. I mean by this several things. In the immediacy of transmission of the news and in the growing world of infotainment, realistic elements from news stories are easily, commonly, and quickly integrated into new feature film plots. Conversely, fictitious characters (like Hannibal Lecter) are alluded to in presenting or describing real ones (like Jeffrey Dahmer). In addition, realist horror can present violent spectacles with an uncanny immediacy right before our eyes, with the immediacy that the camera also allows on our nightly news. Let me say more about the postmodern aspects of realist horror in relation to each of the three key elements I just identified for classical theories.

First, most significantly, there is an increasingly intricate interweaving between fiction and reality about monsters. Numerous film characters (like Henry) are based on real killers, and there are also docudrama films about real killers (like Ted Bundy), and re-created "reality TV" shows enacting deeds of real killers (like George Hennard). In addition, real killers in the news (like Jeffrey Dahmer) may be described in terms of fictional killers (Hannibal Lecter), or they may have been inspired by fictional killers. John Hinckley, Jr. committed his crime after obsessively identifying with film character Travis Bickle in *Taxi Driver*. Bickle's character was modeled on real attempted assassin Arthur Bremer, who was himself inspired by the film character Alex in *A Clockwork Orange*. Hinckley corresponded with serial killer Ted Bundy (before his execution) — subject of his own TV movie, *Deliberate Stranger* (1986) where he was played by *People* magazine's "Sexiest Man Alive," Mark Harmon. Other real killers or slashers in the news (the Menendez brothers, Lorena Bobbitt) become celebrities in trials that construct them in the media as alternative types of fictional characters (abused victims or vengeful villains).

Second, as news and reality interweave, there is a diminishing role for the constructedness of plot. Plots in realist horror, like stories on the nightly news, are dominated by the three r's: random, reductive, repetitive. Both are about gruesome acts, spectacle, and aftermath, more than about action, downfall, motives, mistakes, and justice. And so, third, it is inappropriate to speak here of any specifically aesthetic or distanced reaction of art-horror. Instead, like the news, realist horror evokes real, albeit paradoxical, reactions: at the same time it is both emotionally flattening (familiar, formulaic, and predictable in showcasing violence), and disturbing (immediate, real, gruesome, random).

I want to move away from talk about the aesthetico-emotional responses of *katharsis*, or art-horror, to seek a subtler and more nuanced moral assessment of realist horror films. I propose a method of *ideological critique*. I am interested in asking these sorts of questions: how do realist horror narratives operate as a discourse that creates knowledge and power? Whose interests do they serve? Ideological critique interprets film texts by identifying how they represent existing power relations so as to naturalize them. Such readings can register contradictions between surface and deeper messages, so can offer more complexity than the moral psychological condemnation of realist horror as perverse. I mean that a good ideological reading can enable the critic to question and resist what she sees as problematic moral messages of films.

This strategy has pitfalls, because the critic may seem to assume a superior stance by identifying encoded relations of dominance that standard audiences are unable to discern (and of course, the critic is prey to her own ideological biases). So a potential limitation of this kind of reading is that it seems to downplay the audience's ability to construct readings against the grain of the film. I want to be careful in my position, then, as a critic diagnosing ideologies, because I recognize that audiences may resist or even subvert ideological messages of realist horror. Horror is an innovative film genre where new directors get their start and new film techniques are developed. Horror movie audiences can be surprisingly sophisticated and critical, exhibiting loud and oddball reactions to scenes in movies — including reactions that deconstruct apparently intended messages or highlight horror's peculiar forms of humor.

There is no particular map for ideological critique; it is more like a possible guide to use in studying a film genre. As I use it, it reflects my own concern with issues that are especially likely to be raised in realist horror. These typically concern gender, since so much of realist horror involves male violence against women, but there also may be issues about violence in general as it relates to social class, race, urban alienation, etc. Focusing on the examples I have mentioned so far, I can identify two particular sorts of morally problematic messages typically conveyed in realist horror, related to what I have called the key features of this genre, the monster and the spectacle.

Monsters in Realist Horror

Some argue that the only way to deconstruct or undo the damaging myths of fascination of monstrous killers is to argue, persuasively and rationally, that they are not extraordinary or monstrous, and deserve no particular attention. My response here is somewhat Baudrillardian or cynical: it seems simply too late or impossible to undo the kinds of mechanisms that currently exist for making such figures famous, for portraying Bundy for instance by the "sexiest man alive," as *People* magazine once dubbed Mark Harmon, or for instant hysterical recreations of disasters at Waco or Killeen. So if rational resistance has become impossible in the society of spectacle, then the alternative is to understand that we/the masses are enjoying spectacle as hyperbolic charade. We have begun to take the spectacle to extreme forms that make it deconstruct itself when we make the repulsive one-eyed short and dumpy Henry Lucas into the handsome Brandoesque Michael Rooker, or the cannibal Lecter into the fascinating genius-villain played by Anthony Hopkins in an Oscar-winning performance.
[. . .]
  [. . .]
In realist horror, male sexuality is a ticking time bomb, a natural force that must be released and will seek its outlet in violence if it is frustrated or repressed. Since women, and usually the monster's mother (as in *Henry*, *Psycho*, *Silent Madness*, or real-life accounts of criminals like John Hinckley), are scapegoated as sources of this repression, they are shown somehow to deserve the violence they evoke. The net effect is

that we simply accept as a natural and inevitable reality that there will be vast amounts of male violence against women.

Nevertheless, I believe that the formulaic depictions of violent male sexuality in realist horror can come to be seen *as* just that, formulas. Many prominent examples of contemporary horror employ self-parody and bizarre humor, recognizing and poking fun at the audience's participation in the formulas of the genre (including gender stereotypes). Consider changes that occurred in the sequel to *The Texas Chain Saw Massacre*. Both Part I and its successor are framed by a grim announcement that "this film is based on a true story"; but the realism of *Chain Saw I* has vanished by version II to be replaced by hyperbolic violence, violence as excess. Key scenes in this film play with the sex/ slash formula in hilarious ways. The unforgettably frightening Leatherface from the first *Chain Saw* has here become a rather pitiful younger sibling who gets a crush on the heroine and is teased about it by his brother. When Leatherface first moves to attack Stretch he becomes mesmerized by her long naked legs in a scene that blatantly parodies the notion of buzzsaw as phallic substitute. The point is driven home (as if it needed to be) when the patriarch of the cannibalistic family tells his son sternly "Sex or the saw, son, you have to choose."

Films like *Henry* or *The Silence of the Lambs* may actually lead audience members to question their own fascination with the monstrousness of the serial killer and to query associated icons of male heroism. This is a tricky point to demonstrate. Realist horror films may undercut the standard *Psycho* explanation that scapegoats women, particularly mothers, for male violence. I have suggested that something like this occurs in *Henry*, a film that relies upon but simultaneously empties out the formula "he did it because of his mother." Similarly, *The Silence of the Lambs* contrasts one stereotyped psycho killer whom the FBI can explain ("Buffalo Bill") with another whom they cannot begin to fathom. Although many news accounts struggled to attribute to Luby's mass-murderer George Hennard a motive stemming from his rejection by local women, others looked beyond this to discuss the man's work history, war record, and access to guns.

Spectacle in Realist Horror

As I argued above, realist horror highlights spectacle over plot, and this means that one ideological effect of such narratives is to perpetuate a climate of fear and random violence where anyone is a potential victim. Paradoxically these films send out the comforting message that we are safe because the violence is, at the moment, striking someone else. The emphasis on pessimism and powerlessness in realist horror also obscures the truth about factors that produce a climate of violence: racism; inequities in education, health care, social and economic status, and political power; urban blight and flight; drug use; and gun laws. So instead of the horror prompting action and resistance, it works to produce passivity and legitimize current social arrangements. Realist horror even furthers a conservative agenda pushing for increased police patrolling, stricter jail sentences, more use of the death penalty, etc. Realist horror narratives may showcase the frightening spectacle precisely in order to invoke images of safety by offering structures of explanation and power that champion traditional forces of law, criminal justice, and medicine (especially psychiatry). This is the route typically pursued by so-called "reality television" shows, most of which revel in the horrific spectacle for some minutes before offering up a happy resolution: the man who put a nail into his heart with a nailgun is saved by the hospital team; the Hawaiian radio broadcaster during the hurricane gets married over the air to provide everyone a reason to celebrate after the disaster; the "Top Cops" arrest the cop-killing drug-dealers (delivering a few gratuitous punches in a shockingly racist sequence in reenactment), etc. In other words, in the face of domestic violence, marriage is redeemed as salvational; in the face of health care inequities the emergency teams are celebrated; in the face of racist Los Angeles cops we see that the black offenders (in reenactment) really are scary and violent scum, etc.

But there is more to be said about this specularization of gruesome violence. Again, what is going on involves a blurring, even inversion, of the classical relation between *mimesis* and reality – simulations of violence can precede and come to define reality (this is Baudrillard's notion of the hyperreal[4]). [. . .]

Of course, it is tempting to stop after pronouncing a negative verdict about this increasing dominance of the spectacle, or making the critical points I made just above. This supposes that audiences are seduced and perhaps controlled or victimized by the increasing spectacles of violence offered by the modern entertainment industry, with as the result an obscene sort of flattening that equates all experiences and produces indifference, as even horrific disasters like Chernobyl or the Challenger explosion become, in Baudrillard's terms, "mere holograms or simulacra." Nevertheless, I again want to insist that as members of the masses, we bear some responsibility for our participation in the specularization of violence. I think that realist horror, by its very hyperbolic excess, may actively encourage the audience in its critical awareness of its own interest in spectacle. Recall that *Henry*, for example, is a particularly self-reflexive movie that forces viewers into the viewpoint of the murderers themselves as we become spectators, alongside Henry and Otis, watching their video-recorded home movies of murders. This naturally prompts audience unrest and questions, so I do not think it is sufficient to analyze it as an exercise in ideological control. Much the same is true, I would argue, of *The Silence of the Lambs*, which problematically encourages the audience to sympathize with brilliant serial killer Hannibal Lecter. Other realist horror films allude to the use of surveillance devices in our culture to problematize the spectacle of violence. For example, in *Menace II Society* the character O-Dog is criticized for repeatedly watching and screening a videotape that recorded his murder of a Korean store owner.

19 ■ "Murder as Style? Another victim of sociopath Hannibal Lecter (Anthony Hopkins)," from *Silence of the Lambs*.

[. . .]

Conclusion

Realist horror is like ancient tragedy in that it presents horrific events and features an element of problematic spectacle; these are in each case set within a broader context of somewhat regimented representational devices. The similarity is strong enough to have tempted philosophers to build upon it in fashioning a theory of horror that may work as a defense of the genre. But I have argued that a classical approach to realist horror does not work, for various reasons. Realist horror showcases spectacle, downplays plot, and plays upon serious confusions between representations of fiction and of reality. I do not believe that my task as a philosopher of film is to defend the genre of realist horror. Instead I want to describe it and comment upon its appeal. My own strategy of reading this genre involves me, admittedly, in a sort of tension: ideological critique focuses on problematic ways in which realist horror films create discourses of knowledge and power, serving conservative and patriarchal interests, and it is likely to produce a critical view of realist horror. But I have also tried to foreground the horror and mass media audience's ability to produce subversive interpretations, acknowledging that viewers do indeed have a significant power and interpretive role in reading, and resisting, realist horror films.

NOTES

1 I am grateful to Noël Carroll, Anne Jaap Jacobson, Doug Kellner, Justin Leiber, and Tom Wartenberg for comments on earlier versions, and to Doug Ischar, Lynn Randolph, and Bill Simon for watching and discussing *Henry* with me.
2 Noël Carroll, *The Philosophy of Horror, or Paradoxes of the Heart* (New York and London: Routledge, 1990).
3 "Art horror" is a complex aesthetic and emotional response; see Carroll, *Philosophy of Horror*, 179–82.
4 Jean Baudrillard, "The Precession of Simulacra," in Baudrillard, *Simulations*, trans. Paul Foss and Paul Patton (New York: Semiotext(e), 1983).

26

Philosophy Screened:
Experiencing *The Matrix*

Thomas E. Wartenberg

One aspect of the development of the philosophy of film in recent years has been the proliferation of philosophical interpretations of films.[1] This growth can be measured in a variety of ways. Here, let me just call attention to a number of recent books that focus on film as a source for philosophical enlightenment, such as Peter French's *Cowboy Metaphysics: Ethics and Death in the Western*,[2] Joseph Kupfer's *Visions of Virtue in Popular Film*,[3] and my own, *Unlikely Couples: Movie Romance as Social Criticism*.[4] These three books – and there are others that I could have chosen as equally significant – show that philosophers are turning with increasing frequency to film as a way of doing philosophy and that they see film as a resource for enriching philosophic discussions of a range of ethical, social, and even metaphysical questions.

Despite this trend, there have been very few discussions of the question of what legitimates this procedure, of how films can have philosophic content. Although philosophers such as Stanley Cavell and Ian Jarvie discussed this as early as 1971, it is not an issue that has attracted the sustained attention from philosophers that a variety of other questions have that fall, broadly speaking, within the realm of traditional aesthetics.[5] I think this is unfortunate because, as the number of books and articles that link film and philosophy grows, it is important that we have a better understanding of what relationships there can be between these two areas of intellectual production.[6]

Clearly, this is a large topic and I cannot hope to discuss it thoroughly in the space of a single paper. For that reason, I have chosen to focus initially on what seems the least problematic and most straightforward way in which film and philosophy can intersect: when a film illustrates a philosophic claim or theory. I say that this is the most obvious candidate for a relation between film and philosophy for a number of reasons. First, it takes philosophical practice as a given, something that we are all supposed to understand. It then assigns a completely unambiguous role to film, that of illustrating the philosophic idea that is presupposed as the philosophic target of the film. In addition, it assigns a clear role to the philosopher of film who is writing about the film in question: Her task is leading the reader to acknowledge that the film illustrates the philosophic idea she claims to see in the film.

This is the approach taken, for example, by Christopher Falzon, in his recent introductory text, *Philosophy Goes to the Movies*.[7] In it, he canvasses a range of philosophic problems from an array of philosophic sub-disciplines. In discussing each of them – such as the metaphysical question, "What is a human being?" or the ethical question, "Is there a right way to act?" – Falzon always turns to specific films to illustrate the philosophic position that he wishes to subject to critical examination. To take one example, let's consider Falzon's discussion of dualism – a metaphysical theory about the nature of human beings adopted by, among others, René Descartes in his *Meditations on First Philosophy*.[8] As is well known, a dualist holds that human beings are composed of two distinct substances, mind and body, that – despite their differences – are united together and somehow interact with each other in the human being. In order to illustrate this theory, Falzon invokes a variety of different films – including some cartoons – that involve a mind existing outside of its normal body. Among the films he considers are Carl Reiner's *All of Me* (1984), which he characterizes as the first "in the string of 'mind swap' movies"; Jerry Zucker's *Ghost* (1990), a film in which a protagonist returns to earth as a ghost; and Brad Silberling's *Casper* (1995), a film based on the comic book character, Casper, the friendly ghost. Falzon's procedure is to argue that these films presuppose a metaphysics of dualism, for only on the assumption that the mind and body are separate substances, he claims, can the narratives of these films make sense:

> As I have mentioned, the dualist view of human beings means that it is possible for the mind to exist separately from its body. The dualist view is thus presupposed in a number of fantasy films where someone's mind becomes separated from their body in some way.[9]

This is all we get as general justification of his use of dualism to interpret a range of different films that involve what we might call "roving minds," minds that become separated from the bodies to which they belong.

Having established, he believes, that Cartesian dualism is the metaphysics behind these films, Falzon goes on to canvas a range of objections to this theory of the human being and then show that the films are incoherent because of their dependence on this metaphysics. For example, he rehearses a problem with dualism that goes all the way back to the *Objections* to Descartes' *Meditations*: How can a mind, conceived of as something of a totally different nature than the body and, hence, non-physical, affect the physical world of real things? He argues, following Daniel Dennett, that there is something paradoxical in the way in which Casper the friendly ghost and other similar cartoon and film ghosts are represented. For if the ghost can pass through doors and such at will – and thus be immune from physical laws – how is it that they can move physical things, a capacity that presupposes being subject to physical laws? Films like *Casper* and *Ghost* demonstrate the incoherence of Cartesian dualism as a metaphysical theory, according to Falzon, because they show us a world that is paradoxical.

It is important to recognize that Falzon's text – and others like it – is intended to introduce students to philosophy. I have no quarrel with the idea of using film in this way. Indeed, the appearance of a number of books with similar methodologies to

Falzon's suggests that film is a good way to make philosophical issues real to today's students. To cite one example in a slightly different genre, *The Matrix and Philosophy* contains twenty essays by philosophers who use the film as a vehicle to discuss issues in epistemology, metaphysics, ethics, and aesthetics.[10] Clearly, the idea that popular culture in general – and film more particularly – is a vehicle for introducing philosophy to a broad public is becoming increasingly popular. My concern is that there is a tendency in such attempts to make the transition between these two areas too quickly and unproblematically. There are a number of important issues that Falzon and others ignore but that need to be thought about by philosophers employing this methodology.

First, to return to the specifics of Falzon's claims, there is a question of whether it makes sense to see all films and cartoons that use roving minds as presupposing the same metaphysical account of the human being. Many more films than Falzon cites have had recourse to ghosts – think, for example, of the famous *Topper* series from the 1930s. Does Falzon really think that *all* films and cartoons that have ghosts or other forms of roving minds in them equally well illustrate Cartesian dualism? This does seem to be his view, for he does not ever use a specific feature of one of these films or comics to justify his claim that it illustrates dualism. Indeed, it seems that he relies on the ubiquity of this mode of representation to justify the significance of his critique of their metaphysics. But why should this vast variety of representations all presuppose an identical metaphysics? I'm afraid that I just don't see how Falzon justifies this assertion.

There is also the question of whether he is right to claim that the films presuppose Cartesian dualism or even to see the films as dualist in any sense. What is it about *Cartesian* dualism that makes it the most appropriate metaphysics for roving mind films? For example, philosophers and, indeed, people in general believed in ghosts well before the seventeenth century, and they did so on the basis of different ontologies than Descartes'. As Falzon himself recognizes, Plato was not a Cartesian dualist, but he certainly thought that our souls could separate from the bodies in which they normally were entrapped. But if this is so, why not use these films and cartoons to illustrate Plato's distinction between the worlds of becoming – in which we are embodied – and being – in which we exist as disembodied forms? Falzon has not provided a convincing explanation of why it is this precise form of dualism that these films illustrate, nor even why the films need to have a dualist ontology at all, since a ghost could be conceived of as a quasi-material type of being that obeyed peculiar physical laws. Indeed, the use of shadows as a means for their representation suggests just such a metaphysics.

The questions I have raised so far have to do with the specifics of Falzon's use of roving mind films and cartoons to illustrate and critique Descartes' metaphysics of personhood. But there are a variety of more general questions about this use of film that Falzon also fails to acknowledge and to which I think philosophers interested in film need to pay careful attention.[11]

To begin with and not surprisingly, all of Falzon's examples of philosophical claims are taken from written texts, virtually all within the Western tradition of philosophy.[12] This means that he is operating with a taken for granted but not explicitly acknowledged understanding of philosophy as embodied in written texts. What makes these texts philosophic, he tells us, is their employing "a form of reflection in which we try to think about, clarify, and critically evaluate the most basic terms within which we think and act."[13] Philosophy is therefore a second-order discipline for Falzon, one that looks at that which is often taken for granted and seeks to provide it with a critical rationale. It thus involves a discourse about that which it subjects to philosophical criticism, a discourse that reflects upon that way of thinking or acting.

Let me quickly acknowledge that I am fully aware that philosophy also takes place through verbal discussion. Falzon would presumably say that there is nothing about the critical reflection that is philosophy that requires it to be written rather than spoken. But the question of whether this is so is not one that concerns him, although it has been the focus of heated discussion in recent years. For my purposes here, I will simply follow him in treating philosophy as primarily written, in order to focus on the issue of whether films can equally well embody this form of reflection.

But what assures us that films share this capacity for critical reflection with philosophy? After all, they are a very different type of medium, one that includes verbal discourse only as a part. To be sure, most sound tracks include language as well as music, so that our understanding of a film depends on our grasp of what is said in it. And even silent films used intertitles and thus included a discursive element. Nonetheless, it is the visual dimension of film that most theorists recognize as at least equally central to its character as an art form. Because the visual aspects of films are crucial to our experience of them, we need to think about how an essentially but not exclusively visual medium can embody the form of critical reflection associated with certain written texts.

Recognizing this disparity between philosophy and film as intellectual practices and products brings with it a host of questions about the relation of an essentially discursive medium to an essentially visual one that are completely passed over by Falzon. Indeed, the very idea that a visual medium can illustrate a *claim* made discursively is one that requires some thought and reflective discussion and is itself a subject for philosophic discussion. Is it obvious that films naturally function as illustrations of philosophic ideas, claims, or theories, as Falzon and others seem to assume? If it is, what gives film this natural role? What about film as an artistic medium allows it to be made use of by philosophers in this way?

In order to address this and similar issues, I want to ask a slightly different question, one that I think highlights what is at stake here: Can philosophy be screened? This way of putting the issue highlights the distinctive character of film that makes its suitability for philosophizing something that needs to be put in question. In raising this issue, I am explicitly asking a question about both philosophy and film, and their supposed mutual suitability to one another. I want to know what it is about philosophy that allows it to be screened, if it can be; and I am asking what about film makes it capable of screening an issue initially put forward in a written discursive text.

If this question does not seem pressing, let me relate it to two other, rather similar ones. One concerns the question of metaphors and paraphrase. Philosophers and literary theorists have worried about the question of whether a metaphor is paraphraseable or whether something gets lost in the attempt to specify its meaning. "Juliet is the sun" is a metaphor that the love-struck Romeo utters in Shakespeare's famous play. It is possible to paraphrase the metaphor and thereby to explain its meaning. For example, we could say that Romeo makes an analogy between Juliet and the sun, so that just as the sun is the center of the solar system, Juliet is the center of Romeo's life. Or, just as the sun is necessary for life, so is Juliet for Romeo. But even as we try to paraphrase Romeo's metaphor, we see that the paraphrase differs from the original in a variety of ways. For one thing, to understand the metaphor, we need to think about the parallel between the two entities that are identified and to arrive at a suitable interpretation. With the paraphrases, that work has already been done for us. But this results in specific interpretations of which likeness Romeo is thinking about, the very thing that the metaphor had left unstated. For this reason, it makes a difference whether one reads the metaphor or its paraphrase. The meanings of the two are not identical.

I want to ask whether there might not be an analogous problem in screening a philosophic issue. Is there something unique to a philosophic text that keeps the attempt to screen it from retaining its meaning? Or, to turn the tables, is there something distinctive about the screen version of a philosophic claim that makes it unique and different from the text version? Or, perhaps, are film and written philosophy simply two different ways in which critical reflection can be embodied, as Falzon must assume?

The second issue concerns translation. Since the publication of W. V. O. Quine's *Word and Object*, philosophers have generally been worried about the possibility of a translation maintaining meaning across languages.[14] Quine argued that our attempt to translate a language always involves the imposition of our assumptions about the world onto the other language. In his famous example, *gavagai* – a term from a mythical language encountered by an English-speaking linguist – can be translated as either rabbit or undetached rabbit part, depending on which ontology we prefer. There is no way to tell what the word actually *means*, which ontology the "natives" actually believe in.

The relevance of this to our concern is that it suggests that meaning is tied to its medium of expression, so that a film transparently *illustrating* a philosophic claim or theory becomes a problematic notion. If we accept Quine's argument, an idea cannot be illustrated, if we mean by that term "put into a different form with no alteration of meaning."

These worries can also be supported by a more general worry that many philosophers have about the possibility of philosophy actually being done on screen.[15] While they may feel comfortable with the notion that a philosophic idea such as mind-body dualism could be illustrated on film, they would be very uncomfortable with making much of this or with claiming that this meant that film was a medium in which philosophy could actually be done.

One reason for such reticence about the philosophic capacity of film is a conception of philosophy according to which argument is the central method of philosophic discourse. As Monty Python tells us in the famous sketch, "The Argument Clinic," an argument is "a series of statements intended to establish a proposition. . . . It is not simply contradiction." As a philosophic method, argumentation attempts to establish a thesis by deriving it from a set of more basic claims through agreed upon principles of reasoning. The *locus classicus* for this tradition is Spinoza's *Ethics* that is structured like a geometry textbook with definitions, axioms, and postulates from which are derived the essential claims of Spinoza's philosophy. While few contemporary philosophers emulate Spinoza's rigor, many still accept logical argumentation as the sole method for philosophic thinking.

There are many who believe that such a conception of the nature of philosophic methodology is unduly limited. Both within Continental and analytic philosophy, there are examples of important philosophers whose work can be assimilated to deductive arguments only at great cost. They would maintain that the reduction of philosophy to explicit argumentation is a serious mistake.

Now if we accept Falzon's characterization of philosophy as a form of critical reflection, we can say that it aims at unsettling our established habits of belief and action in order to reestablish them on a firmer, more critically aware foundation, but that this does not mean that there is only one method for so doing. In fact, various different discursive techniques have a place in this project besides that of a simple deductive argument. Here, I want to focus on one: the "thought experiment." In a thought experiment, the reader is instructed to consider a certain possibility that she might not have considered before, a possibility that often is at odds with her established patterns of belief and action. Once this possibility is entertained as a real possibility, then the reader is confronted with the question of what justifies her customary belief rather than the possibility put forward in the thought experiment.

We have already looked at one thought experiment: that invoked by Quine in an attempt to convince his readers of the indeterminacy of translation. He asked us to consider the situation of a hypothetical linguist confronting a foreign tribe. It is by invoking this imaginary scenario that Quine establishes his argument.

It is this element of philosophical argumentation that I think film is capable of embodying, albeit in a distinctive manner. For this reason, I will endorse the idea that film is capable of philosophizing in at least this one way.

To prepare the way for this argument, I want to look in some detail at one of the most famous thought experiments in the history of Western philosophy, Descartes' invocation of the evil genius hypothesis in the first *Meditation*. Later, I will show how a film presents an analogous thought experiment and so, in my view, needs to be thought of as actually philosophizing.

So let us focus on the commonly accepted belief that our sense experience is a reliable guide that gives us an accurate picture of the way the world is. Descartes, as is well known, didn't think this was so. Indeed, his skeptical project in the first *Meditation* is to "withhold my assent no less carefully from things which are not plainly certain and indubitable than I would to what is patently false" (*Meditations* 18). He presents this as a necessary part of his overall project "to establish anything firm and lasting in the sciences" (*Meditations* 17). What he finds, however, is that his established way of thinking makes it impossible for him to maintain his skeptical attitude, for the sway of habit makes it hard to withhold assent from those perceptions that "keep coming back again and again, almost against my will," for, as he tells us, they "seize upon my credulity" (*Meditations* 22). Given this fact – the tenacity of the habitual – how can Descartes succeed at his task of dislodging the hold of received ways of thinking?

At precisely this point, Descartes introduces his famous thought experiment involving an evil genius:

Thus I will suppose not a supremely good God, the source of truth, but rather an evil genius, as clever and deceitful as he is powerful, who has directed his entire effort to misleading me. I will regard the heavens, the air, the earth, colors, shapes, sounds, and all external things as nothing but the deceptive games of my dreams, with which he lays snares for my credulity. (*Meditations* 22)

Descartes' supposition of the evil genius provides him with a means of realizing his project of doubting every belief for which he lacks certainty. It does so because it provides him with an imaginary account of how this possibility – one in which nothing that he formerly believed was true – might have come to pass. Without it, he cannot fully entertain the possibility as one that could be true. This thought experiment is thus a crucial step to his philosophic argument.

You'll recall that we are interested in the question of whether philosophy can be screened and I said that we would look at the thought experiment as a possible philosophic form that film could embody. So we now have to ask: Is it possible for a film to screen a thought experiment that is, in some sense to be specified, the same or analogous to a written one? Does it communicate as well, as certainly? Is there anything about a visual thought experiment that distinguishes it from a written one and that makes it especially convincing?

In order to approach this question, I want to consider the Wachowski Brothers' 1999 film, *The Matrix*.[16] This film, I shall argue, screens Descartes' skeptical claim that, for all we know, we could be having exactly the sense experience that we are now having in the absence of there being the external world in whose reality we now believe on the basis of those perceptions. Call this *the deception hypothesis*. *The Matrix* shows us a fictional world in which the deception hypothesis is true. It accomplishes this by means of a narrative that updates Descartes' evil genius thought experiment with one featuring a vast array of malevolent computers. After establishing this claim, I will return to a more general consideration of film as screening philosophical thought experiments.[17]

The conceit of *The Matrix* is that what the characters experience as reality – and their reality is pretty much the world that its audience would have inhabited in 1999, the year of the film's release, although the film supposedly takes place some 200 years later – is actually a huge, interactive perceptual illusion – the Matrix – that is created and maintained by the computers that have taken over the world.[18] According to the film, this situation is the result of the computers' victory over human beings in a devastating war. The triumphant computers now "farm" human beings in a manner analogous to how we humans have farmed animals for food. The wrinkle is that electricity is the product that such farming aims to harvest. According to the film, the human body actually produces more energy than it consumes, so it is for surplus energy that the computers breed humans and keep their bodies alive in a huge skyscraper-like complex. Although the film never explains it fully, we are left to presume that the reason for the existence of the Matrix is that humans need to have their minds distracted while their bodies produce the required electrical energy.

With this scenario, *The Matrix* presents what I have called a *screening* of the deception hypothesis. That is, upon viewing *The Matrix*, a viewer must confront the question of whether it might not be the case that all of her perceptual experience could be what it now is without there being a world that resembles those perceptions.

Now my claim about *The Matrix* raises a number of questions. How does the film raise this question? Does its doing so amount to a real screening of a philosophical claim? Does the screened version of Descartes' claim carry the same conviction as the written one? What, if anything, does this tell us about the nature of film?

In order to answer these questions, we need to look more closely at certain aspects of the film's narrative. The film's protagonist is Neo (Keanu Reeves). The film begins with his being contacted by Trinity (Carrie Anne Moss) who, we later learn, is part of an underground war against the dominance of the computers. Throughout the early scenes of the film, although he is clearly bothered by something about his world and trying to get to the bottom of his worries, Neo is not convinced that the world that he believes to be real is anything but that. Only as the result of the intervention of Trinity and her cohorts does he come to realize that the world that he had taken to be real is in fact an illusion, merely apparent.[19]

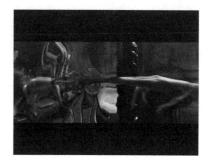

20 ■ "Neo (Keanu Reeves) realizes the illusion of the Matrix with the help of Morpheus (Laurence Fishburne)," from *The Matrix*.

Neo's revelation occurs after he swallows a pill offered to him by Morpheus (Laurence Fishburne), the leader of the rebels.[20] He has been given a choice between two pills, with the assurance that one – the blue one – will allow him to return to his former life as if nothing had happened, while the other – the red one – will let him see the reality of his situation and learn what the Matrix really is. After taking the red pill, Neo is led by Morpheus into a large room filled with computer and video equipment operated by a number of people all clad, like Morpheus and Trinity, in black leather. He is placed in a chair and electrodes are taped to his chest and inserted into his ear. Morpheus explains that the pill Neo has taken is part of a trace program that will help him and his associates find Neo's location. Although neither Neo nor we know enough to understand Morpheus' explanation at the time, it turns out that Neo's body is actually located within the complex in which the computers have housed people's bodies. (Later in the sequence, Neo and we get to see this.) The rebels have the equipment to pierce through the apparent world of the Matrix and determine where Neo really is. Once they have done so, they will be able to rescue him by unplugging him from the computer network and then bringing him aboard their ship.

After a quip by Cypher (Joe Pantoliano) comparing Neo's impending journey to Dorothy's in *The Wizard of Oz*,[21] Neo sees his own image in a mirror. Suddenly, the image fractures, lights appear in it, and it seems to move like a liquid. Neo reaches out to touch the mirror and his finger goes into it, as if it were a liquid metal, like mercury. When he withdraws his finger, the liquid mirror is pulled with it, eventually falling back into its own space. As this is going on, Morpheus asks Neo if he has ever had a dream that he was sure was real. He then invokes a quasi-Cartesian puzzle: Once you awoke, how would you know the difference between the dream world and the real world? As the mirror-like substance begins to move up his arm and onto the rest of his body, Neo begins to fibrillate and go into cardiac arrest. At just this moment, the rebels locate his body and the screen momentarily goes black.

Although the scene continues, I want to pause to consider what has happened to this point. I believe that the film actually provides its viewers with a visual experience that is analogous to Neo's, an experience in which the world that was taken to be real – and I'm talking about the imaginary world that the film projects – begins to exhibit irregularities that suggest perceptual experience is not an accurate guide to the nature of reality. After all, as we have been looking at the screen, we have been assuming that the images that we have seen are an accurate guide to the nature of the fictional world of the film. That is, all along we have been assuming that the images that we see are images of objects and persons that are real in that fictional world. But as Neo begins to see irregularities in his experience, the filmmakers disrupt our experience of that world as well, providing us with an actual experience (albeit of a fictional world) of the possibility that our experience is not an accurate guide to the nature of reality itself.

In so doing, the film transforms our awareness of the screen as opening up a world to us into an awareness of the screen as containing representations for which there might not be any corresponding objects in its fictional world. This realization is an exact parallel of the one that Neo has, although his realization has to do with a world that is real for him. The film can accomplish this by making us aware that it has similarities to the giant computer simulation of the Matrix, for it also presents a world that is not real.

Before Neo awakens to find himself on the rebel ship, Nebuchadnezzar, he actually sees the gigantic structure in which all of the world's humans are hooked up into the mega-network, the Matrix. The scene we have been discussing continues and what we see – including the naked body of a man – turns out to be Neo in reality, outside of the Matrix. He surfaces in a large, womb-like tank in which his body has been kept submerged. Neo's body is coated with a thick (amniotic) fluid and has electrical umbilical cords attached to the arms, chest, and the back of the head. As he looks around, seeing reality for the first time, he sees many similar tanks connected into huge skyscraper-like structures that emit lightning frequently. This is the reality lying behind the Matrix, the human body farm that produces the electricity that keeps the computers in power. A bug-like creature descends on him and disconnects one of the cords. All the other cords pop off of Neo's body and he goes down a long water-slide into a pool of water. He sees a light and door in the ceiling of this building from which a large claw descends, captures him, and pulls him through the door into the light. Neo finds himself aboard ship among the crew, but with much less glitzy surroundings. To end the scene, Morpheus intones, "Welcome to the real world."

What the film has here depicted is a situation that is an analogue of Descartes' evil genius thought experiment, only it is treated as real within the film's narrative while Descartes was only contemplating a possibility that he later denies could be real. That is, the film reveals that what all of the characters had taken to be real – and what we viewers had accepted as the film's imaginary reality – was no more than an interactive computer program.

All of this goes by very quickly in the film. Later scenes establish the validity of the deception hypothesis – at least for those creatures who have not cracked the Matrix – by including scenes in which the characters are "trapped" within the Matrix intercut with scenes of the reality behind this orchestrated illusion. One example has Neo fighting with Morpheus.

As Morpheus repeatedly instructs Neo to reject his belief that the world of his experience is the real world, the film cuts to the other members of the ship's crew who are watching Neo and Morpheus on television monitors. This juxtaposition of illusion with the reality that lies behind it not only ensures that the film's viewers understand how the Matrix is supposed to work but they also see in the Nebuchadnezzar's crew a group of viewers analogous to themselves who are able to see the illusion of the Matrix while recognizing it for what it is.

In these scenes and others like them, *The Matrix* is able to do something with film that had never been done before, at least to my knowledge. Beginning with our sense of film as a medium that reveals a (fictional) world to us, the film shows us that the world that we were taking to be (fictionally) real was merely a projection. Of course, there is a history of self-reflexive films that ask us to think about the nature of film itself, a history that goes back, at least, to Buster Keaton's 1924 masterpiece, *Sherlock Junior*. In that film, the Keaton character actually enters the projected world of a film, allowing Keaton to play with questions about the relationship between the film world and the real world. The difference is that *Sherlock Junior*'s audience is always itself aware of the difference between the real and film worlds as depicted within Keaton's film. But as we experience *The Matrix*, we initially believe in the (fictional) reality of the world that is depicted by the film. As Neo comes to see that the world he had believed to be real was only a computer simulation, *so do we*. That is, we share his experience of coming to see that the "real world" of the film is only a computer projection and, hence, merely apparent, and that there is an underlying (fictional) reality that differs in marked ways from this illusory one.

As a result of its ability to portray the possibility that the deception hypothesis is true, albeit only of a fictional world, the film is able to lead its audience to see that something analogous could be true of our world. Once we accept the possibility of the Matrix doing what it does, we must wonder whether we are not in the situation of the inhabitants of the Matrix. Indeed, this is why the film invokes the rather bizarre claim that, although the actual present of the film is somewhere around 2200, the computers have chosen to recreate an illusory world whose present is 1999, the year of the film's making. Because Neo and the members of his world are experiencing a world whose structure resembles that which the audience members at the time of the film's creation actually inhabited, it presents the audience with the question of how they know that the situation of the human inhabitants of the Matrix is not identical with their own.

So what I am claiming is that *The Matrix* has screened an analogue to Descartes' evil genius hypothesis. Both the film and Descartes' thought experiment are attempts to render the deception hypothesis compelling. We still need to consider whether they are equally so.

Before moving in that direction, I want to examine how the film screens another feature of Descartes' text. Earlier in the first *Meditation*, Descartes had invoked the possibility that he could now be dreaming as a first step in problematizing our faith in the reality of the external world. When we are dreaming, we often take the beings and events about which we are dreaming to be real, indeed so real that we may even have trouble telling whether something that occurred in a dream was real when we later remember it. Descartes asks us to consider whether what we think of as our real life might just be an extended dream, so that the people and objects that we think of as real are just figments of our overwrought imaginations.

In the film, we witness a sequence in which Neo is arrested and interrogated by the computer forces known as agents. It is a scary experience for him, one that ends with the agents injecting a bug-like creature into him through his belly button. As this rather horrifying event ends, Neo is shown to be awakening from a nightmare and we – along with him – assume that he had just had a bad dream. Here, the film has relied on a technical possibility that has been exploited by films for some time: They are able to frame a sequence in such a way that what the audience took to be part of the screened world was really just a subjective experience of one of that world's characters.

However, the film reveals that Neo was not just dreaming shortly thereafter, when he is literally debugged by Trinity prior to his being taken to Morpheus aboard the Nebuchadnezzar. When we see the very bug that had been injected through his belly button being sucked out, we experience a revelation that reverses our already reversed understanding of what we have seen: Neo's arrest was not the dream we had taken it to be, but the real event in the screen world that we had first taken it to be.

In this sequence, *The Matrix* has already toyed with our understanding of the reality of what we are seeing on the screen, albeit in ways that are not revolutionary. In so doing, however, the filmmakers play on the analogy between film and the Matrix. For our belief in the "reality" of the (fictional) world that we see on the screen is created and controlled by the filmmakers in an analogous manner to how the experience of the inhabitants of the Matrix is determined by the computers. Our understanding of reality as of a completely different order than dreams is undermined by these reversals.

With this understanding of these central sequences from *The Matrix*, we can return to the question of whether a film can illustrate a philosophic position. As you will recall, I was critical of too quick an assimilation of films to the philosophic position that they were supposed to illustrate. In what way does my argument amount to something other than an assertion that *The Matrix* illustrates Descartes' claim that our sense experience might be exactly what it is now but there might be no external world corresponding to it, i.e., the deception hypothesis?

To see why the film is something more than an illustration of the deception hypothesis, consider a film – let's call it *The Matron* – identical to *The Matrix* except that viewers are always aware that Neo and his ilk are deceived about reality, say by our sharing the epistemic perspective of the crew of the Nebuchadnezzar who watch the Matrix world on their TV screens. *The Matron* would illustrate the deception hypothesis by showing viewers a world in which it is true. The difference is that in *The Matrix*, because we share Neo's epistemic limitations, we actually are taken in by the deceptive world of the Matrix as fully as he – only we are deceived about the nature of a fictional world while he is about his real world. We thus participate not only in the deception but also its subsequent removal.

It is the experience that viewers of *The Matrix* have watching the film that makes it more than an illustration of a philosophic text, that qualifies it as actually philosophizing. It does so by placing the film's viewers in an epistemic position where they are faced with the question of what justifies their belief that they are not in an analogous situation to that of the Matrix's inhabitants.[22] It does this, as I have said, by actually deceiving them about the fictional world they are watching. So they have to admit that, in that fictional world, the deception hypothesis is true. At the same time, within the fiction, Morpheus has repeatedly asked Neo questions like, "How would you tell the difference between the dream world and the real world?" that pose skeptical doubts akin to those of the first *Meditation* and that viewers puzzle over as they watch the film. They are thus left with a skeptical doubt about their own experience: How do I know that I am not trapped in a Matrix-like situation?

Placing a person in an epistemic situation where they are made to wonder whether a certain belief or action is justified is, of course, a mark of the philosophical. What better way to characterize the practice of Socrates in the early dialogues of Plato than to say that he made his interlocutors puzzled about certain key concepts or beliefs that structured their world? If *The Matrix* is able to engender a similar perplexity in its audience, doesn't it make sense to see it as actually philosophizing?

Two comments are immediately called for. First, not all of *The Matrix* is philosophy in my view. Once Neo has understood his situation, the film becomes a rather routine adventure film that pits a band of human rebels against the renegade computers. While this plot is, no doubt, intended as a comment on the role that technology has assumed in our lives, it is not philosophy itself. Further, because Neo has had his skeptical doubts resolved, this part of the film distracts viewers from their own skeptical doubts through their concern for the fate of the rebels in the face of overwhelming odds.

Second, even if you grant my argument that *The Matrix* is philosophy, it is important to realize that the film does not make a major contribution to the discipline. Cartesian skepticism has been perhaps the central focus of modern Western philosophy. Attempt after attempt has been made to free us of its hold in one way or another. It may even be something of a commonplace to see the history of this tradition not as a series of footnotes to Plato, as Whitehead once claimed, but as a succession of ever-broader rejections of Cartesianism. From this point of view, *The Matrix* is a reactionary philosophic film in so far as it implants in our minds with renewed vigor the haunting specter of complete deception. But having a reactionary agenda does not disqualify a work from counting as philosophy.

My claim, then, is that *The Matrix*, because of its complex narrative structure, is a film that genuinely philosophizes. Its use by Falzon and others as a means of introducing people to the pull of skepticism succeeds because the film itself engenders skeptical doubts in its viewers. Because the film actually philosophizes in this way, it makes sense to place it in the context of philosophic texts that raise similar issues.

That a film can actually make a contribution to philosophy is, no doubt, a surprising conclusion for many. As I indicated earlier, *The Matrix* provides an example of only one type of philosophic contribution possible from film. Discussion of others will have to wait for other occasions. In the meantime, however, I hope that my argument will help philosophers see that film is a philosophic medium, but one whose contributions to philosophy need to be carefully articulated.

NOTES

1 The Leverhulme Foundation has supported my work on this paper. The paper has benefited from comments made by audiences at the University of Kent-Canterbury and the University of Southampton where it was first presented.
2 (Lanham, MD: Rowman and Littlefield, 1997).
3 (Boulder, CO: Westview, 1999).
4 (Boulder, CO: Westview, 1999).
5 Stanley Cavell, *The World Viewed* (New York: Viking Press, 1971) and Ian Jarvie, *The Philosophy of the Film* (New York: Routledge & Kegan Paul, 1987).
6 While there is a growing body of literature on the relationship between philosophy and literature, discussion of film has remained mostly untouched by it. I am thinking here of Martha Nussbaum and others who argue that literature can make a substantial contribution to ethics.
7 Christopher Falzon, *Philosophy Goes to the Movies: An Introduction to Philosophy* (London: Routledge, 2002).
8 René Descartes, *"Discourse on Method"* and *"Meditations on First Philosophy,"* translated by Donald A. Cress (Indianapolis: Hackett Publishing Co., 1980). Future references to this text will be given parenthetically as *Meditations*.
9 Falzon, *Philosophy Goes to the Movies*, p. 62.
10 *The Matrix and Philosophy*, edited by William Irwin (Chicago and LaSalle: Open Court, 2002). Irwin has edited an entire series of such books about popular culture and philosophy.
11 In the Introduction to his book, Falzon does raise some issues about his use of film to illustrate philosophical issues. His trading on an ambiguity in the term *image*, however, vitiates his discussion. While images in the sense of metaphor and other non-literal uses of language undoubtedly play a role in philosophical texts, this cannot establish a relationship between those texts and works like films that employ *visual* images, as Falzon argues: "My interest in images is not so much in the role of the image in philosophy as the philosophy we can discuss in the image" (*Philosophy Goes to the Movies*, p. 5).
12 I shall use the term *discursive* to include both aural and written texts.
13 Falzon, *Philosophy Goes to the Movies*, p. 9.
14 W. V. O. Quine, *Word and Object* (Cambridge, MA: MIT Press, 1960).
15 Of course, we could make a film of a philosopher actually making a philosophic argument, but this is not what is meant.
16 Falzon himself does discuss *The Matrix* as an "updating of the evil genius argument" (*Philosophy Goes to the Movies*, p. 29). But even though he recognizes that the film puts viewers in an analogous situation to the characters in the film, he does not draw any philosophical conclusions from this, merely comparing the film to others that employ similar narrative strategies. But the films he cites – such as *The Usual Suspects* (1995) – do not give us deceptive visual experiences, but only engender false interpretations of what we see.

17 A number of the essays in *The Matrix and Philosophy* point out that the film also presents an analogue of Plato's myth of the cave from *The Republic*. However, in the film's version of reality the world of appearances is not so much a distinctive realm of being but an intersubjective illusion generated by the computers that make up the Matrix.

18 I think that the term "The Matrix" as used by the film refers both to the apparent world that most of the world's inhabitants believe to be real – "It is the world that is pulled over your eyes that blinds you to the truth" – and to the vast ensemble of computers, human beings, and structures that lies behind this reality. I think this ambiguity is not harmful to understanding my claims.

19 As has been frequently noted, Neo's journey resembles that taken by one of the prisoners in Plato's Allegory of the Cave who learns that what he had taken to be reality was only a shadow in comparison with the full-blooded reality he encounters on his journey.

20 Throughout the film, there are references to *Alice in Wonderland* suggesting that Neo's trip and Alice's have much in common. Here, he is offered two pills, one red and one blue. The red pill will show him reality, while the blue one will allow him to return to the Matrix without remembering what he had learned.

21 Cypher compares Neo's journey to Dorothy's trip from Kansas to Oz. This is an inversion of what happens, for Neo, unlike Dorothy, moves from illusion to reality.

22 Alex Neill asked how I would distinguish the situation of viewers of this film from that of a hypothetical group of students who could be made to embrace skepticism by a precisely placed blow to the head. My response is that viewers, but not students, can give reasons for their being in the state, because their experience of the film's fictional world grounds their skepticism about their own perceptual experience.

27

Virtue and Happiness in *Groundhog Day*

Joseph H. Kupfer

How, if some day or night a demon were to sneak after you into your loneliest loneliness and say to you, "This life as you now live it and have lived it, you will have to live once more and innumerable times more; and there will be nothing new in it, but every pain and every joy and every thought and sigh and everything immeasurably small or great in your life must return to you. . . ." If this thought were to gain possession of you, it would change you, as you are, or perhaps crush you. . . . How well disposed would you have to become to yourself and to life to crave nothing more fervently than this ultimate eternal confirmation and seal?

Friedrich Nietzsche, *The Gay Science*, Aphorism 341

Virtuous Living Versus Egoistic Hedonism

In the passage quoted above, Nietzsche's thought experiment entertains the idea of the eternal return of our way of life to prompt us to reflect on whether we are living the good life.[1] The question of the good life recurs throughout history, receiving a variety of responses. The ancient Greek philosophers Plato and Aristotle argued that living virtuously is the good life. Although virtuous action cannot guarantee well-being or happiness (eudaimonia), acting virtuously is central to it and is the only thing within our power to secure our happiness. Both philosophers take great pains to distinguish goodness from pleasure, partly because they see the life of self-centered pleasure seeking (egoistic hedonism) as the perennial rival to the moral life they champion. Harold Ramis's film *Groundhog Day* (1993) interprets and adapts the philosophy that living virtuously is the good life. The film dramatizes its philosophical adaptation, moreover, by means of a humorous version of Nietzsche's idea of the eternal return.

[. . .]

Groundhog Day tries to show why a life of egoistic hedonism is necessarily self-defeating and filled with ironies. Egoistic hedonists look at actions merely as the means to pleasure, their own pleasure in particular. The goal in life is to maximize pleasure – itself a passive state, not an activity. As a consequence, hedonists miss out on the enjoyment of activities that are done for their own sake. They are thereby also deprived of the delight found in realizing their moral, intellectual, and artistic potential in those activities. The irony is that a life of hedonism is actually much less pleasant than a virtuous one.

In the Platonic dialogue *Gorgias*, Callicles says that the point of life is to have great desires and then to be able to satisfy them. Indeed, power is the ability to dominate other people so as to better gratify one's appetites. Socrates' rejoinder is that a life of egoistic hedonism is like filling a leaky vessel. No sooner are an individual's desires satisfied than they require replenishment. Selfish pleasure seekers cannot make progress because their current appetites increase in strength and new appetites indefinitely multiply. The hedonists' flurry of activity to quench their desires in effect leaves them standing still, or worse off, because they are always left wanting more.

[. . .]

[. . .] Unless we rationally reflect on how we live, we cannot disabuse ourselves of false beliefs that undermine our happiness, such as mistaken opinions about pleasure and power. Examining ourselves enables us to recognize the general lineaments of human nature and, with that, the human good. In *Groundhog Day*, self-knowledge includes knowing ourselves, and what is good for us, in our individuality. When Phil Connors is thoughtful of others and acts for their welfare, he exemplifies the universally valuable virtue of kindness. However, when Phil perfects his talent for playing the piano and his receptivity to poetry, he is achieving a good born of his individuality.

[. . .]

Our characters and minds are most permanent because they are most independent of life's vicissitudes. Aristotle notes that "no function of man possesses as much stability as do activities in conformity with virtue." Without these inner resources of character and intellect, hedonists are at the mercy of external conditions to provide them with either more of what they already want or the means to satisfy new appetites. The desirability of hedonism is revealed as illusory once individuals are deprived of novelty of situation or circumstance. The sweetest things in their novelty must become tedious when indefinitely repeated.

Of course, the good life is not lived alone; it also includes friends. According to Aristotle, friendships based on utility and pleasure are inferior types of friendship. The only genuine friends are those who love each other's virtuous character. True friends take pleasure in doing virtuous things for and with each other, and they value one another for their own sakes. Because moral character is long-lasting, these friendships are the most enduring and also the most beneficial.

[. . .]

The lesson taught by Plato, Aristotle, and *Groundhog Day* is that egoistic hedonism must fail because individuals cannot successfully pursue their happiness directly. Happiness comes about only as the indirect result of realizing our human potential in activity that is intrinsically valuable – primarily, virtuous activity. The implication is that happiness is achieved only when we forget about ourselves. Having examined our lives and thought through the importance of virtue and self-development to the good life, we must put aside concern for ourselves. [. . .]

No philosophical argument can demonstrate once and for all that a virtuous life is better than its hedonistic counterpart. For this reason, Plato and Aristotle offer narrative support for their view with fables, myths, and stories of famous people. In *The Republic*, Plato cites the tale of Gyges whose magic ring makes him invisible. The invisible Gyges is able to please himself at the expense of others, with apparent impunity.

Groundhog Day constructs its fable around the Nietzschean conceit of the eternal return. It is similar to the story of Gyges, however, in that Phil Connors alone remembers what has transpired from one recurring day to the next. Phil is rendered figuratively invisible in that other people cannot "see" what he has done the day before. Phil is able to satisfy his desires without seeming to pay the price, just as Gyges appears to escape retribution. However, even as Phil and Gyges cannot be seen by other people, so do they not see the harm they inflict on their moral character by their self-indulgent way of life. We turn now to the film to see how it illustrates and develops the view that the good life is a virtuous one.

All the Pleasures of Punxsutawney

Groundhog Day extends Nietzsche's idea of imagining our actual lives as recurring eternally by giving Phil Connors (Bill Murray) the chance to relive any way of life he can imagine over and over. Of any pattern of living he thinks is ideal, Phil will have to ask whether he would choose it if he had to live it always. The result of imaginatively enlarging Nietzsche's question is also to put our own actual lives in perspective, just as Nietzsche originally intended. Envisioning our actual or idealized pattern of living as recurring forever can liberate us from the cramped, selfish habits into which we have fallen willy-nilly, with neither thought nor care. Imagining ourselves locked into a particular way of life can vivify for us, as perhaps nothing else can, the meaningfulness or meaninglessness of that life.

The theme of repetition is figured from the beginning of the story when television weatherman Phil Connors and his crew return to Punxsutawney, Pennsylvania, to film the town's annual celebration of Groundhog Day. Just as the town reenacts the festivities that commemorate the anticipation of seasonal change, Phil must repeat his coverage of the event for the fourth consecutive year. He yearns for a big-time network job and hates the small-town hoopla of the celebration. Phil is unaware of how small his own life and outlook are. Phil will learn just how much his life can expand and he can grow by having to relive the same Groundhog Day until he sees the light and begins living virtuously.

Before that happens, however, the film has great sport with Phil's egoistic hedonism. Once Phil realizes that he is the only person who knows the same day is repeating and has memory of all of them, he goes to work grabbing for all the pleasurable experiences he can cram into the ever-present Groundhog Day. *Groundhog Day* telescopes what we surmise is an extended period of Phil's life into a series of hilarious vignettes in which he eats what he wants, steals money, watches movies, plays with people like a puppeteer, and seduces women. All but Rita (Andie MacDowell), who is impervious to Phil's wily ways.

Eventually, Phil tires of his life of pleasure and, bored beyond endurance, tries to kill himself. In rapid, giddy succession, we watch as Phil tries every way at his disposal to dispose of himself – all to no avail. With the dawn, a new Groundhog Day awaits Phil, in which he despairs once again at his meaningless existence. Only when Phil shows concern for other people and starts developing his own talents does he begin to enjoy life. Only when he stops looking at Rita as a sexual conquest does he come to appreciate her as a potential lifetime companion. Virtuous living and genuine regard for other people and himself free Phil from his despair and, as providence would have it, from the eternal return of Groundhog Day.

[. . .]

The film depicts several changes in Phil's response to reliving Groundhog Day. He moves from fear and confusion at repeating the same day, to delight at the opportunity to indulge himself, and then to despair over his deadening life of hedonism. Only when Phil is committed to improving himself and the lives of other people can he affirm a way of life he chooses. Overshadowed by Phil's glaring error in weather prognostication is his long-standing, mistaken forecast about what would bring him lasting happiness. He had thought that a life of pleasure, generated by money and fame in television, would satisfy him, and he disparaged Rita, saying that she was "not [his] kind of fun." By story's end, Phil will have changed his mind about the nature of the good life and Rita's role in it.

On what should be the day after Groundhog Day, Phil awakens to the same rock song that awakened him on Groundhog Day, "I Got You Babe," and the same disc jockey chatter. He is unnerved by the duplication, fearing for his sanity. When he arrives at the site of the Groundhog Day ceremony, he asks Rita to slap his face, as if to bring him to his senses or wake him from a nightmare. In Rita's hands, the slap will become a comic trope. We will watch her slapping Phil over and over as she figures out, again and again, that his behavior is not that of genuine friendship but only calculated to seduce her.

The repeated, unrequested slapping will bring Phil to his senses part of the way – he will realize that he cannot succeed in fooling Rita. But it will not fully awaken him to his deepest moral failure. The film intimates that we cannot be brought fully to our senses by something someone else does to or for us, such as a literal or figurative slap in the face. Understanding the right way to live necessarily requires a self-revelation, as we are struck by what is wrong with how we live.

The endless repetition of Groundhog Day dictates that no one can initiate new behavior because no one can remember what has happened on the previous, identical day – except Phil. For everyone but him, each Groundhog Day is experienced anew. Once he realizes the fantastic conceit on which his subsequent life rests and that he alone remembers what has occurred during the previously repeated Groundhog Days, Phil adapts to his situation with aplomb. Recalling what has transpired and acting without physically suffering the consequences the next day, Phil benefits at the expense of other people.

Day after repeated day, Phil ferrets out and stores information about his unsuspecting victims. Chronicling the lives of attractive women, for example, he uses the information to romance them. Attuned to the inattentiveness of the drivers of the armored car, he steals money in their keeping. The behavior is a logical extension of Phil's selfish pleasure seeking.

[. . .]

Even in its playful references to other films and actors, *Groundhog Day* takes sensitive stock of Phil's moral nature. Standing with his latest girlfriend in front of a movie theater showing "Heidi II," Phil is dressed as the character played repeatedly by Clint Eastwood in the famous "Spaghetti Westerns" directed by Sergio Leone – such as *A Fistful of Dollars*. As Phil imitates Eastwood's speech and wields a facsimile of his familiar little stogie, we hear the signature Spanish guitar and whistle from Leone's western movies. The irony of Phil seeing a Heidi film "over a hundred times" is that the Heidi story is about love, family, and friendship, whereas the Eastwood character Phil impersonates is a rugged loner.

Despite the comic incongruity between Heidi and Eastwood's solitary gunslinger, *Groundhog Day* aligns its Heidi movie with the much-sequeled westerns by inserting the "II" after the Heidi title. Just as Eastwood repeated his role as the no-name drifter in several Leone films, Phil repeats his self-scripted role of seducer and play-actor. Moreover, Phil's behavior is portrayed as an imitation, or shadow, of an actor playing a movie character. He even asks his girlfriend of the moment to call him Bronco. Phil is so lost in layers of disguise from himself that the thought of self-reflection cannot even cross his mind. The character Eastwood plays is a friendless stranger who always leaves town at the movie fiction's conclusion. Phil is also without friends, and he is a stranger to himself who would like nothing more than to leave Punxsutawney.

Futile Pursuit

The only real challenge for Phil is Rita, the producer of Phil's weather program. She represents all that Phil is not: gentle, unassuming, caring, and considerate of the needs of other people. Whereas Phil is sarcastic and wisecracking, Rita is genuine, open, and sincere. She relishes life's ordinary joys and ordinary people, including Punxsutawney's corny celebration of Groundhog Day. Even though Phil has months of repeated Groundhog Days to perfect his seductive ploys, he gets nowhere with Rita.

Rita seems impervious to Phil's charming chicanery. No matter how much he emulates her tastes in literature, social causes, or family life, he cannot get to her. The suggestion is that Rita's moral character unwittingly protects her from Phil's veneer of goodness. It is as if she sees through his charade, her virtue providing a touchstone for its likeness in others. Rita illustrates Aristotle's observation that virtuous individuals find their greatest pleasure in the good character of other people. She cannot be fooled because her true mettle responds only to the sterling character of other individuals and not its imitation.

Groundhog Day conveys the futility of Phil's conniving with cinematic repetitions. Phil repeatedly meets Rita at the hotel bar, reviewing her taste in drinks and toasts until he has them down pat. In swift succession, we see the recurring scenes of Phil talking about and reciting nineteenth-century French poetry with Rita and playing in the snow with her. And, of course, we also see the rapid-fire sequence of goodnight slaps Rita administers to Phil's face.

[. . .]

As Rita and Phil lie quietly in the snow, panting and laughing from their exertions, the romantic mood is underscored, and commented on by the lyrics of the song "You Don't Know Me" on the soundtrack. Rita does not (yet) know what Phil is up to, but Phil also does not (yet) know himself or the value for him of the Nietzschean recurrence. The song includes the phrase "You give your hand to me," which echoes the lyric "So put your little hand in mine," from the morning wake-up song "I Got You Babe." Rita will not give her hand to Phil, he will not "get" her, until Rita trusts him. She will not trust him until he is genuinely good.

Phil must understand himself well enough to see what is wrong with his self-centered pleasure seeking. Once he sees this, he will be able to forget himself by immersing himself in artistic, intellectual, and virtuous activity. Until he sees, and then ignores himself, the you of "I Got You Babe" refers ironically to Phil himself. He has only himself, and in his present condition that is not nearly enough to make his life meaningful.

[. . .]

The film connects the themes of knowledge and love in the conversation Phil has with Rita about what she wants from life. After their last snow scene, and the playing of "You Don't Know Me," Phil takes Rita back to his apartment. When Phil tells Rita that he loves her, she becomes annoyed and replies, "You don't even know me." Rita tells him that what he feels is not love and demands that Phil stop saying he loves her. Of course, Phil knows Rita better than she can realize, but I interpret the film as raising the question of what knowing someone well enough to love truly involves. The exchange indicates that Phil is mistaken in thinking that such knowledge is equivalent to accumulating information about the person, just as he is mistaken in thinking that happiness is found in accumulating pleasures. We are left to speculate that perhaps knowing another person well enough to love involves working together and sharing the joys and tragedies that mark the stages of life.

Rita persists, saying that she could never love anyone like Phil because he loves only himself. Phil insightfully responds, "That's not true. I don't even like myself." Phil's heedless grabbing for pleasures is not genuine self-love. Self-love involves seeking what is truly good for ourselves, and we cannot do that unless we meet the Platonic challenge to know ourselves. The story implies that if we seek our good based on that self-knowledge, we will work for our moral improvement. Moreover, self-improvement requires extending ourselves on behalf of other people. We cannot simply or directly improve our moral character the way we can simply and directly perfect our golf swing or our facility in French.

[. . .] Only by grace of the repeated Groundhog Day can Phil exhaust the allure of his hedonism and begin to acquire the self-knowledge necessary for self-love. By linking Phil's doubtful claim to love Rita with his confessed lack of self-love, *Groundhog Day* also suggests that we cannot love another person until we truly love ourselves. Therefore, the self-knowledge that is needed to love ourselves may also be a prerequisite for loving another person.

Having experienced what will be his last slap of the film, Phil walks away from Rita's hotel, past ice sculptures. "You Don't Know Me" is repeated for the last time, played by a somber, solo saxophone. The movie metaphor of coldness is insinuated here with frozen imagery. It signifies not only the freezing of time for Phil but that Phil is frozen as a person. He is frozen inside an uncaring, cold heart, and his capacities for moral, artistic, and intellectual growth are immobilized.

However, the icy image also points positively to the reformed person Phil is to become. When Phil turns over a new leaf, his talent development includes teaching himself to sculpt ice! The film will therefore repeat the ice sculpture symbol, but with inverted meaning, especially as Phil will use the sculpture to express Rita's beauty and his genuine affection for her.

From Despair to Virtue

The morning after Rita's last slap, a close-up of Phil's digital clock shows the numbers flipping to the accompaniment of a loud, ominous, industrial turning sound. We hear and feel the oppressiveness of the daily repetition for Phil before we see him express it. When the disc jockeys repeat the phrase, "It's cold out there, today," we sense just how chilling Phil's existence has become for him. Phil corroborates the diagnosis in his daily television coverage of Groundhog Day, saying: "It's gonna be cold. It's gonna be grey. And it's gonna last you for the rest of your life." His despair is overt. He is ground down, as if by big industrial-strength gears, by the endless repetition of the life he first thought so delicious in its promise of limitless pleasure.

[. . .]

Phil has no genuine friends, although his relationship with Rita might be described charitably as an incipient friendship of pleasure and virtue. She is the only one whose company Phil enjoys and whose character stirs a vague sense of decency or admiration in him. Phil's lack of true friends contributes to the torpor of his life. He has no one with whom to share his aspirations and fears, his ideas and talents. His loneliness compounds his despair. A virtuous friendship can help us through bleak periods and point us to the moral activity in which our happiness lies.

As a consequence of his lack of meaningful activity and friendship, Phil finds his life of self-centered pleasures unendurable. His only recourse is to end it – by death or change. When he discovers he cannot kill himself, Phil undertakes virtuous activity as a practical necessity. He is driven to a morally salutary life by the natural human desire to live well.

As a model of a good person, Rita is a catalyst for Phil's change. He sees what he could be and that he would have to be virtuous, as Rita is, in order to be worthy of her friendship. Rita provides Phil with a moral alternative to the tedium of unsatisfying pleasure seeking and an incentive to the moral life. Phil eventually convinces Rita of the recursive loop of Groundhog Days by telling her about everyone in the diner and then predicting exactly what is about to happen. He does not show off his knowledge, as we would expect him to on the basis of his previous, cocky weather forecasting, but instead describes everything in a matter-of-fact way. He is totally honest about the daily repetition, and Rita replies: "Maybe it's not a curse. It depends on how you look at it." Nietzsche's point, exactly.

Back in his room that evening, Phil is relaxed and natural with Rita as he shows her how to pitch cards into a hat. We soon realize that perfecting this routine presages Phil's disciplined pursuits of piano playing and ice sculpting. The desultory pastime will be replaced by serious, but playful, artistic development. The quiet evening ends with Rita falling asleep in Phil's bed after they cuddle tenderly. When Phil wakes up from his honest, unmanipulative night with Rita, he begins to change. He gives the old derelict money, instead of giving him the usual brush off. At the Groundhog Day festival, Phil brings Rita and Larry refreshments, helps with the equipment, and treats them with professional respect.

The piano music Phil hears while reading in the diner continues on the soundtrack as Phil goes to take his first piano lessons. Instead of mocking Phil, as the earlier tunes did, the piano music becomes a motif of his growth. With the melody playing on, Phil takes the derelict to the hospital, calling him "Father," where the old man dies. He will die over and over, whether Phil feeds him extra bowls of soup or applies mouth to mouth resuscitation – urging him, as "Dad" and "Pop," to breathe.

In trying to rescue the aged tramp, and calling him by paternal names, Phil appears to be adopting the old man. The behavior is radically different from Phil's former pretense of wanting to adopt the children with whom he and Rita repeatedly have snowball fights. Failing to save the derelict humbles Phil by teaching him his limitations, even within his privileged knowledge of the recurring Groundhog Days. Some things even he cannot change, and this contrasts with the opportunity the relived Groundhog Day gives Phil to change the morally decaying course his life had been taking. The irreversibility of the old man's sickened condition suggests that Phil was lucky to have caught his life's downward spiral at the moment he did. Later, it might have been too late for Phil to change.

[. . .]

Phil's behavior illustrates how the nonmoral virtue of humorousness or wit can be incorporated into such moral virtues as considerateness and kindness. When the wife of the mayor (Brian Doyle-Murray) tells a group of people at the evening party how Phil saved the mayor's life by expelling a chunk of beef from his throat, Phil suggests that next time the mayor not try to swallow the whole cow. Instead of feeling foolish and beholden, the mayor can laugh along with Phil and the other partyers. Phil also uses humor to deflect praise from himself, a

21 ■ "A changed Phil Connors (Bill Murray) buys a homeless man (Les Podewell) a meal," from *Groundhog Day.*

way to foster humility without calling other people's attention, or even his own, to it. For example, Phil is thanked by a woman for straightening out her husband's back and told that the husband can now help her around the house. Phil replies to the husband, "Sorry to hear that, Felix," as if Phil had done the husband more harm than good!

The film even changes the import of its humorously repeated, comic signature of quick-paced repetitions. Recall the succession of slaps from Rita, information gatherings by Phil, and suicide attempts by him. The compressed repetition in those cases conveyed Phil's futility. The new Phil is presented performing a batch of good deeds in short order: catching a boy falling from a tree, helping ladies with a flat tire, saving the mayor from choking. Now the suggestion is of fertility rather than futility. The repetitions imply still more virtuous actions to come for as long as Phil relives Groundhog Day.

Practice Makes Perfect

The reformed Phil undertakes long-term, arduous projects that require discipline and fortitude. Phil enjoys life because he grows through the efforts he expends. He grows artistically, as a pianist and ice sculptor, intellectually, as a lover of literature, and morally, as a performer of good deeds. Only by committing himself to far-reaching goals is Phil required to exert himself in the activities that develop his human capacities. Although Phil embarks on his self-improvement in order to win Rita's love, he comes to enjoy the activities for their own sake. The result is a life made meaningful by activity that is intrinsically valued. Piano playing, poetry reading, lifesaving – all are undertaken by Phil as ends in themselves. At the same time, Phil comes to value people for their own sakes, not for what they can provide him.

[. . .]

The consequence of not worrying about what he is getting out of the disciplined artistic or moral endeavors is that Phil is enriched. His interior life, in all its emotional, intellectual, and moral complexity, is enhanced in ways impossible for his self-centered behavior to achieve. Absorbed in himself, Phil missed out on what the world of art, thought, and other people had to offer. In the cultivation of his artistic talents and in his moral habituation, Phil exemplifies an Aristotelian view of how people realize their human potential.

Groundhog Day illustrates that artistic and moral activities are causally connected and also resemble one another. For example, developing his artistic talents requires that Phil exhibit discipline, a moral virtue. Until his disciplined behavior becomes habitual, moreover, Phil needs self-control to give up the easy pleasures he enjoyed before his change of heart. Before he can take pleasure in doing virtuous or artistic things, Phil must be able to withstand the tugs of appetite or the shoves of emotion. As with morality, the arts have an objective structure and standard. Playing the piano is not a matter of private desire or approval, like finding some clothing attractive or some foods tasty. To make good music, individuals must learn the structure of sounds and fit their senses and motor skills to it. Phil's love of music and devotion to it represent a recognition of a value that does not depend on him or his appetites. Instead of valuing something because he wants it, Phil now wants something because he appreciates its value.

[. . .]

Just as Phil's humor is incorporated into morally virtuous action, so his artistic abilities are put to generous use. Phil makes beautiful music and ice sculptures for other people to enjoy instead of using his talent to further his own interests. In the scene in which he sculpts Rita as a gift to her, *Groundhog Day* again infuses warmth into cold. The beauty of Rita's face, which Phil depicts in ice, not only captures her good heart but also reveals his own. Giving through our artistic creations is giving of ourselves, not only in the sense of sharing our talents and energies but also in giving our sensibility and feelings.

Love and Virtue

Where Phil used to see other people as opportunities for his personal advantage, he now views himself as a resource for the benefit of others. Rather than demean people, Phil goes out of his way to spare people's feelings, including sparing them the embarrassment of being grateful to him. He works to improve the lives of his neighbors at his own expense instead of exploiting them for his own ends. Phil no longer amuses himself by slighting Punxsutawney. His arrogance is replaced by humility – a subtle effect of respecting the value things possess without reference to himself.

Rita's moral goodness is the first thing Phil understands and values for its own sake, apart from his self-interest. Rita's virtue is the impetus for his moral transformation, and by movie's end, Phil has begun a friendship of virtue with Rita. Phil is more motivated by furthering Rita's happiness than by how happy she can make him. As Aristotle remarks of the highest form of friendship: "Those who wish for their friends' good for their friends' sake are friends in the truest sense." Over months of Groundhog Days, Phil's character has matured to a level comparable to Rita's, so that they are "alike in excellence" and therefore capable of a friendship of virtue.

[. . .]

Phil has been blessed by a benign Nietzschean demon, who bestows on him the gift of experiencing his usual life in distilled, exaggerated form. He is thereby spared a failed life. Phil's egoistic hedonism becomes intolerable as it might not otherwise have become, because in ordinary life, selfish pleasures can themselves conceal what is wrong with devoting oneself to their pursuit. *Groundhog Day* shows Phil freed by the eternal return to experience and understand his self-absorbed life for what it is, and change before it is too late.

Just as Phil finally gains the love of the woman he wants by relenting in his seductive enterprise and becoming more virtuous, so too does his endless repetition of Groundhog Day end when he finds meaning, and therefore joy, in living each repeated day. When he enthusiastically embraces the people of Punxsutawney, Phil's moral character evolves and he finds life fulfilling. The town Phil Connors began by reviling has become the place in which he wants to settle down with Rita, although they will "just rent" at first. The creature Phil Connors once found so cloyingly stupid, the groundhog named Punxsutawney Phil, has become his namesake. By film's end, Phil Connors is truly Punxsutawney Phil – the town's most caring, civic-minded citizen.

NOTE

1 The view that Nietzsche's notion of eternal recurrence is practical rather than cosmological or metaphysical is supported by several recent interpretations. For example, Maudemarie Clark writes, "We can avoid thus making Nietzsche's doctrine [of eternal recurrence] dependent on cosmological support if we interpret his doctrine of recurrence as the [practical] ideal of affirming eternal recurrence," *Nietzsche on Truth and Philosophy* (Cambridge: Cambridge University Press, 1990), p. 252; see also pp. 245–86.

Suggestions for Further Reading

General Introduction

The following books contain useful essays, addressed to professionals in the field, that discuss a range of issues in the philosophy of film:

Richard Allen and Murray Smith, eds., *Film Theory and Philosophy* (Oxford: Clarendon Press, 1997).

David Bordwell and Noël Carroll, eds., *Post-Theory: Reconstructing Film Studies* (Madison: University of Wisconsin Press, 1996).

Cynthia Freeland and Thomas Wartenberg, eds., *Philosophy and Film* (New York: Routledge, 1995).

I Do We Need Film Theory?

Claire Colebrook, *Gilles Deleuze* (New York and London: Routledge, 2002), esp. ch. 2, "Cinema: Perception, Time, and Becoming," which gives a lucid explanation of the key ideas of Deleuze's theory of cinema.

Robert Stam, *Film Theory: An Introduction* (London: Blackwell, 1999). An introduction to central topics in film theory, including realism, narration, style, cognitivism, and semiotics.

II What Is the Nature of Film?

Noël Carroll, *Theorizing the Moving Image* (Cambridge: Cambridge University Press, 1996). Contains a range of essays about the nature of film.

Stanley Cavell, *The World Viewed: Reflections on the Ontology of Film* (Cambridge: Harvard University Press, 1979). A groundbreaking study of film in the context of modern art.

Gregory Currie, *Image and Mind: Film, Philosophy, and Cognitive Science* (Cambridge: Cambridge University Press, 1995). Presents a sustained argument from a cognitive perspective.

Carl R. Plantinga, *Rhetoric and Representation in Non-fiction Film* (Cambridge: Cambridge University Press, 1997). A look at the modes of persuasion and representation in a variety of non-fiction films.

III Do Films Have Authors?

There are many studies of individual directors that proceed on the basis of the *auteur* theory. One good one is Robin Wood, *Hitchcock's Films Revisited* (New York: Columbia University Press, 1989).

Berys Gaut, "Film Authorship and Collaboration," in Richard Allen and Murray Smith, eds., *Film Theory and Philosophy* (Oxford: Clarendon Press, 1997), pp. 149–72. A careful, analytic exploration of issues surrounding the attribution of authorship in film.

Andrew Sarris, *The American Cinema: Directors and Directions, 1929–1968* (Chicago: University of Chicago Press, 1985). Applies the author's theory of authorship to American cinema.

IV How Do Films Engage Our Emotions?

Bertolt Brecht, "The Modern Theater is the Epic Theater," in John Willett, ed., *Brecht on Theatre* (London: Methuen and Co., 1964). The famous German playwright contrasts the key differences between his "epic" theater and Aristotelian "dramatic" theater as to how theater should engage the emotions.

G. M. Grube and C. D. C. Reeve, *Plato's Republic*, Books II and X (Hackett Publishing Company, 1992). Contains Plato's classic critique that ancient Greek poetry "waters" the emotions and is an invitation to irrationality.

Carl Plantinga and Greg Smith, eds., *Passionate Views: Film, Cognition, and Emotion* (Baltimore: Johns Hopkins University Press, 1999). Contains essays written from the perspective of cognitive film theory on how cognition and emotions work together in our response to film.

Murray Smith, *Engaging Characters: Fiction, Emotion, and the Cinema* (Oxford: Clarendon Press, 1995). A groundbreaking study on spectator response to characters in fiction film.

V Must Films Have Narrators?

David Bordwell, *Narration in the Fiction Film* (Madison: University of Wisconsin Press, 1985). The first exploration of the role of narrative in fiction films.

Seymour Chatman, *Coming to Terms: The Rhetoric of Narrative in Fiction and Films* (Ithaca: Cornell University Press, 1990). Explores the nature of narrative through a comparison of fiction and film.

Jerrold Levinson, "Film Music and Narrative Agency," in David Bordwell and Noel Carroll, eds., *Post-Theory: Reconstructing Film Studies* (Madison: University of Wisconsin Press, 1996), pp. 248–82. An examination of the difficulty in assigning narrative agency to music that originates from outside the fictional world of the film, and a proposal for a solution to this problem.

George Wilson, *Narration in Light* (Baltimore: Johns Hopkins University Press, 1979). A unique combination of theoretical essays and interpretations of specific films that focus on those issues.

VI Can Films Be Socially Critical?

Theodor Adorno and Max Horkheimer, "The Culture Industry: Enlightenment as Mass Deception," in J. Curran et al., eds., *Mass Communication and Society* (London: Edward Arnold, 1977). Contains the authors' critique of the movie industry and its role in promoting a distorted viewpoint of social reality.

Daniel Bernardi, ed., *Classic Whiteness: Race and the Studio System* (Minneapolis: University of Minnesota Press, 2001). This volume contains a variety of essays on the topic of race and classical Hollywood film and also includes an excellent bibliography.

Patricia Erens, ed., *Issues in Feminist Film Criticism* (Bloomington and Indianapolis: Indiana University Press, 1990). A collection of essays of feminist film criticism, including essays on methodology and re-reading Hollywood films, as well as essays on films by women directors.

Sue Thornham, ed., *Feminist Film Theory: A Reader* (New York: New York University Press, 1999). A recent anthology of essays by feminist film critics, including essays on race, gender, and class in mainstream cinema.

Thomas E. Wartenberg, *Unlikely Couples: Movie Romance and Social Criticism* (Boulder: Westview Press, 1999). A critical examination of films that present romantic unions between those partners who are "unlikely" in terms of their race, class, or sexual orientation.

VII What Can We Learn From Films?

Aristotle, *Poetics*, ed. and trans. Stephen Halliwell (Cambridge, MA, and London: Harvard University Press, 1995), ch. 9. Presents Aristotle's view that the generalizations contained in ancient Greek tragedies resemble the generalizations on character and action studied by philosophers.

Noël Carroll, *The Philosophy of Horror, or Paradoxes of the Heart* (New York and London: Routledge, 1990). Drawing on themes from Aristotle's *Poetics*, the author gives a philosophical account of the appeal of horror films.

Peter A. French, *Cowboy Metaphysics: Ethics and Death in Westerns* (Lanham, MD: Rowman and Littlefield, 1997). Looks at ethical issues raised in some classic film westerns.

Stephen Mulhall, *On Film* (London and New York: Routledge, 2002). Examines the *Aliens* trilogy as an example of how films reflect on philosophical issues.

Index

Note: French film titles beginning *L', La, Le, Les,* and English titles beginning *The,* are filed under the following word. Page references in italics indicate illustrations and their captions.